Popular
Movements
and Political Change
in Mexico

Published in association with
The Center for U.S.–Mexican Studies,
University of California, San Diego

Popular Movements and Political Change in Mexico

edited by
Joe Foweraker & Ann L. Craig

Lynne Rienner Publishers • Boulder and London

Published in the United States of America in 1990 by
Lynne Rienner Publishers, Inc.
1800 30th Street, Boulder, Colorado 80301

and in the United Kingdom by
Lynne Rienner Publishers, Inc.
3 Henrietta Street, Covent Garden, London WC2E 8LU

Library of Congress Cataloging-in-Publication Data
Popular movements and political change in Mexico / edited by Joe
  Foweraker and Ann L. Craig.
      p. cm.
  Includes bibliographical references.
  ISBN 1-55587-211-5 (alk. paper)
  ISBN   1-55587-219-0 (pbk. : alk. paper)
    1. Political participation—Mexico—History—20th century.
  2. Government, Resistance to—Mexico—History—20th century.
  3. Social movements—Mexico—History—20th century. 4. Mexico—
  Politics and government—1970- I. Foweraker, Joe. II. Craig, Ann
  L.
  JL1281.P67 1990
  323.3'0972—dc20   90-34593
                                                                    CIP

British Cataloguing in Publication Data
A Cataloguing in Publication record for this book
is available from the British Library.

Printed and bound in the United States of America

The paper used in this publication meets the requirements
of the American National Standard for Permanence of
Paper for Printed Library Materials Z39.48-1984.

*For
Craig
and
Jack and Max*

Contents

Preface

During the past twenty years, popular movements have changed the relationships between state and civil society in Mexico, as groups of peasants, students, women, teachers, and city dwellers have crowded into the political arena to pose new challenges to old mechanisms of political control and co-optation. This effervescence of political activity in civil society has attracted a good deal of academic attention, but there has been no corresponding attempt to assess its impact on processes of institutional change. This is the main focus of the essays in this book, all of which address the interactions between popular movements and the Mexican political system.

It was three years ago that we first conceived this project, and from the beginning we had two main academic concerns. First, it seemed important not to rehearse old arguments but to explore new lines of analysis. Hence, the authors in this volume have been encouraged to draw on their extensive case materials to analyze the multiple ways in which popular movements engage with regional and national politics. Second, we wanted to combine a common attention to questions of organization, strategy, and legal and institutional constraints with an eclectic search for new analytical tools. In other words, we welcomed a degree of conceptual audacity. We therefore hope that the essays in our collection break new ground in the study of popular movements and offer a different perspective on the political changes presently occurring in Mexico.

These essays were commissioned either for the research workshop we held in March 1989 at the Center for U.S.-Mexican Studies at the University of California, San Diego, or for the panel that followed at the 1989 meeting of the Latin American Studies Association. Many colleagues and friends contributed to these conversations, and among them we especially want to thank Judith Adler Hellman, Ignacio Marván, Enrique Semo, and David Torres. We are also especially grateful to two of the contributing authors, Neil Harvey and Gerardo Munck, who helped us throughout. Neil Harvey worked hard as workshop rapporteur, and Gerardo Munck and Miguel Centeno translated two of the essays.

Many individuals and organizations have provided us with financial support, including the British Academy, the Nuffield Foundation, Michael Rothschild (dean of Social Sciences at the University of California, San Diego), and UC MEXUS in the person of Eric Van Young. We are grateful to these supporters. But above all we wish to acknowledge the essential financial and logistical support of Wayne Cornelius, director of the Center for U.S.-Mexican Studies at UCSD, who encouraged us to write up the project, met most costs of the main meeting from a Ford Foundation grant to his center, and subsequently provided additional support for translating and editing from a Tinker Foundation grant.

Like so many other books, essays, and articles published on Mexico, this book would never have been either conceived or completed were it not for Wayne Cornelius's role in promoting Mexico-related research. For the past ten years, scholars from all over the world with a passion for Mexico have found an intellectual home in his center as visiting research fellows and as participants in workshops and conferences. Together they have produced an impressive body of research and writing, of which this collection is just a very small part. All of us who have benefited from the center are indebted to Wayne Cornelius for a decade of selfless dedication to the study of Mexico.

The staff of the center has helped with our work in more ways than we can mention. Our very warm thanks to Graciela Platero, Patricia Rosas, Sandra del Castillo, and Carol Christopher for their commitment and good humor.

We both have young boys, namely Craig in San Diego and Jack and Max in England. Neither of us supposes that our respective offspring really understand what has kept us busy all this time. But in recognition that our boys are very forgiving people, we dedicate this book to them.

J. F.
A. L. C.

FTDF   Federación de Trabajadores del Distrito Federal/Federation of
              Workers of the Federal District
IMSS   Instituto Mexicano del Seguro Social/Mexican Social Security
              Institute
INFONAVIT   Instituto del Fondo Nacional para la Vivienda de los Trabajadores/
              National Fund for Workers' Housing
INMECAFE   Instituto Mexicano del Café/Mexican Coffee Institute
ISSSTE   Instituto de Seguridad y Servicios Sociales de los Trabajadores
              del Estado/Institute of Social Security and Services for State
              Employees
JLCA   Junta Local de Conciliación y Arbitraje/Labor Conciliation and
              Arbitration Board
LNC   Liga Nacional Campesina/National Peasant League
LNDR   Liga Nacional de Defensa Religiosa/National League for Religious
              Defense
LP   Línea Proletaria/Proletarian Tendency
MAP   Movimiento de Acción Popular/Popular Action Movement
MAS   Movimiento al Socialismo/Movement toward Socialism
MAS   Mujeres en Acción Sindical/Women in Union Action
MLN   Movimiento de Liberación Nacional/National Liberation
              Movement
MRM   Movimiento Revolucionario del Magisterio/Revolutionary
              Teachers Movement
MRP   Movimiento Revolucionario del Pueblo/Revolutionary
              Movement of the People
OCEZ   Organización Campesina Emiliano Zapata/Emiliano Zapata
              Peasant Organization
OIR-LM   Organización de Izquierda Revolucionaria–Línea de Masas/
              Organization of the Revolutionary Left–Mass Tendency
PAN   Partido Acción Nacional/National Action Party
PCM   Partido Comunista de México/Mexican Communist Party
PEMEX   Petróleos Mexicanos
PMS   Partido Mexicano Socialista/Mexican Socialist Party
PMT   Partido Mexicano de los Trabajadores/Mexican Workers Party
PNR   Partido Nacional Revolucionario/National Revolutionary Party
PPR   Partido Patriótico Revolucionario/Patriotic Revolutionary Party
PPS   Partido Popular Socialista/Popular Socialist Party
PRD   Partido de la Revolución Democrática/Party of the Democratic
              Revolution
PRI   Partido Revolucionario Institucional/Institutional Revolutionary
              Party
PRM   Partido de la Revolución Mexicana/Party of the Mexican
              Revolution
PRS   Partido de la Revolución Socialista/Party of the Socialist
              Revolution
PRT   Partido Revolucionario de los Trabajadores/Revolutionary Workers
              Party
PSUM   Partido Socialista Unificado de México/Unified Socialist Party of
              Mexico

SAM	Sistema Mexicano Alimentario/Mexican Food System
SEP	Secretaría de Educación Pública/Ministry of Education
SNOA	Sindicato Nacional de Obreros Agrícolas/National Union of Agricultural Workers
SNTE	Sindicato Nacional de Trabajadores de la Educación/National Union of Workers in Education
SRA	Secretaría de Reforma Agraria/Ministry of Agrarian Reform
STERM	Sindicato de Trabajadores Electricistas de la Revolución Mexicana/ Union of Electrical Workers of the Mexican Revolution
STUNAM	Sindicato de Trabajadores de la UNAM/Union of Workers at the UNAM
SUTERM	Sindicato Unico de Trabajadores Electricistas de la República Mexicana/Sole Union of Electrical Workers of the Mexican Republic
TABAMEX	Tabacos Mexicanos/Mexican Tobacco Institute
TELMEX	Teléfonos de México/Mexican Telephone Company
UCEZ	Unión de Comuneros Emiliano Zapata/Emiliano Zapata Union of Communal Landowners
UGOCM	Unión General de Obreros y Campesinos de México/General Union of Workers and Peasants of Mexico
UNAM	Universidad Nacional Autónoma de México/National University
UNORCA	Unión Nacional de Organizaciones Regionales Campesinas/ National Union of Regional Peasant Organizations
UOI	Unión Obrera Independiente/Independent Workers Union
UPN	Universidad Nacional Pedagógica/National Education University
USED	Unidad de Servicios Educativos a Descentralizar/Educational Services Units to be Decentralized

ORGANIZATIONS

Asamblea de Barrios/Neighborhood Assembly
Comité de Defensa Popular, Chihuahua/Committee for Popular Defense, Chihuahua
Comité de Defensa Popular, Durango/Committee for Popular Defense, Durango
Corriente de los Trabajadores del Arte, la Ciencia y la Cultura/Current of Workers in Art, Science, and Culture
Corriente Democrática/Democratic Current
Frente Patriótico Nacional/National Patriotic Front
Frente Popular "Tierra y Libertad"/"Land and Liberty" Popular Front
Mesa de Concertación Sindical/Forum for Union Cooperation
Movimiento Sindical Ferrocarrilero/Railroad Union Movement
Organización Revolucionaria Punto Crítico/Revolutionary Organization Punto Crítico
Partido dos Trabalhadores/Workers Party

1

Introduction

1

Popular Movements and Political Change in Mexico

JOE FOWERAKER

Few observers of Mexican politics doubt any longer the importance of popular movements for the political changes and political challenges that the country faces. It is now widely recognized that the proliferation of popular movements is one of the most significant political developments of the past twenty years. Moreover, the breadth and impetus of these movements have come to present a strong challenge to the existing system of political representation and control; recent events (and especially the elections of July 1988) have suggested that popular movements might be the wedge that will force an authentically democratic opening within the political system overall.

But if popular movements are seen to be important, and if this importance has been recognized academically by a spate of studies of individual movements, there has been no corresponding effort to assess the political significance of the movements, and, in particular, their impact on the political system itself. Therefore, this collection of essays addresses the interaction of popular movements and the political system, and especially its forms of political mediation and control at local, regional, and national levels. In doing so the essays maintain throughout a dual emphasis: on the one hand they analyze the political organization and strategic initiatives of the movements; on the other they synthesize the range of institutional responses to popular initiatives and seek to characterize the system's margins of political maneuver.

In this regard these essays represent a new departure not only in the study of Mexican politics but also in the literature on popular movements as it has developed to date. This literature has been dogged by problems of definition and has failed to achieve any consensus on how to conceptualize popular political practices. These failings were flagged by Boschi, who found a literature that consistently overlooked the links between popular movements and the state structure, which "is ignored both in its repressive potential and in its ability to endure and adapt to changes," let alone in its importance for "the movements' emergence and their raison d'être" (Boschi 1984:13). More generally, Boschi criticized widely held assumptions about the noninstitutional nature of popular movements and argued convincingly that the "tendency of movements to acquire an institutional component is

3

perhaps inherent to the logic of collective action and, by extension, that an organizational imperative emerges at some point in the process of mobilization" (Boschi 1984:2).

The problems Boschi found to be so widespread in the literature on popular movements are simply not present in these essays. Each author in this collection has eschewed tired assumptions and preconceived ideas about popular movements in order to address a new set of questions on the basis of new, and nearly always extensive, empirical research. In other words, the essays break new ground in the study both of Mexican politics in particular and of popular movements in general. Together they contribute to the creation of a new perspective on the political changes presently occurring in Mexico, and of a different language for talking about them. And it is in this connection that they part ways with Boschi, who painted a "disappointing picture" of popular movements' capacity for achieving institutional change. Here it is agreed that the popular impact on the political system has already been both far-reaching and profound, even if the changes do not necessarily favor the popular movements themselves.

What follows, by way of introduction, is a review of the principal areas of analytical advance achieved in these essays. This is not to suggest that the essays do not refer to real and substantive developments in the Mexican politics of the past twenty years. They do. But all the authors have been encouraged to draw on their research into real political process in order to establish relationships and argue for causalities. Hence, the organizing principle in each essay is analytical, not expository. Nor is it to suggest that the collection expresses a full analytical consensus in explaining the political impact of popular movements. On the contrary, it includes some sharp analytical debates. But even if some differences of opinion are temporarily obscured, it does seem prudent to stake out the main areas of analytical inquiry. My aim is not so much to provide answers as to raise questions, and so provoke a more critical reading of the essays themselves.

In my own view, a reading of these essays reveals several key analytical issues that tend to occur and recur in all the arguments in this collection. These issues should not be understood as disconnected topics but rather as interrelated elements of an analytical inquiry that focuses on the definition of popular movements and the senses in which they are or are not "new"; on their organization and on their place in the political organization of Mexican civil society overall; on their strategies and the ways those strategies emerge; on the legal and institutional terrain where popular struggle is waged; on the political practices of the movements, and especially their challenge to clientelism and *caciquismo*; and last, but by no means least, on their impact on political and institutional change within the Mexican political system. These introductory remarks will address these issues in turn, but some degree of overlap is inevitable in a commentary seeking to integrate these issues into a more comprehensive approach to popular movements in Mexico.

THE DEFINITION OF POPULAR MOVEMENTS

What are popular movements? And how do they differ from class struggle, urban protest, or peasant jacquerie? The short answer is that they are defined not so much by their social composition as by their political practices, both toward state institutions and toward other actors in civil society, especially political parties. Although this provisional definition clearly begs the further question, What are their political practices? it marks a decisive shift from economic and social definitions of popular movements and places them squarely in the political sphere. Moreover, these practices are open to investigation and analysis, and remain relatively independent of competing characterizations of the movements in the Mexican context. Whether they are the bearers of enduring revolutionary aspirations, or simply a trade-union type of organization with limited and concrete goals, their practices remain the same. In this sense, there is growing agreement with Touraine (1987), who has argued that there is no adequate definition of such social actors in Latin America that does not include "the form of their participation in the political system."

This clearly cannot mean that popular movements have no social base. On the contrary, a distinguished tradition of social historians (Barrington Moore, E. P. Thompson, James Scott) has demonstrated the importance of the moral outrage created by unequal economic and social conditions, and popular movements can be seen in part as the organized political expression of such outrage. By extension, class and class struggle continue to be far more important than many want to admit, and there is broad agreement that Laclau and Mouffe's arguments on Europe, for example (Laclau and Mouffe 1985), do not apply in Mexico. This residual element of the definition is important in Mexico because it excludes entrepreneurial organization from the realm of popular movements, even though such organization has become increasingly important in Mexican civil society in recent years.

But although it is impossible to deny the insertion of the movements in historically specific social structures, they are primarily *popular* and not social—mainly because they comprise a struggle to constitute the "people" as political actors. In other words, popular movements are defined not by the interests they represent (such interests living a sort of "prepolitical life" in the economy or society) but by the demands they make, and the demands emerge through the process of popular organization and strategic choice. At the same time, these demands are determined to a degree by the laws and institutions and state policies that bear on popular organization. Popular movements, then, do not express the "birth of civil society" so much as the creation of political subjects in civil society; and so-called social movements cannot exist in a separate social sphere that allows only "external" relations with the political system.

It is true, however, that the demands that popular movements in Mexico have come to make are of a trade-union or "welfarist" kind, concerning wages, security, and services of all kinds, including housing, education, and health provision. In short, they are immediate, pragmatic, and concrete; and in this sense the movements in Mexico play an analogous role to that of trade unions at an early moment in liberal state welfarism in Western Europe (and again may therefore reflect class as much as popular struggles). Castells (1983) was possibly the first to note that the viability of such movements depends closely on their success in solving the immediate and practical problems of the group or community, which in Latin America usually requires negotiation of some sort with the state; and there is some consensus that popular movements in Mexico must seek above all to acquire this *capacidad de gestión*—the ability to get their demands met.

Popular movements are thus defined in some degree by the demands they make, and therefore by their practices toward the state. They are also, however, often defined by their practices toward political parties. Comparatively, the material demands of Mexico's movements are seen as very different from the "post-material" demands of contemporary movements in Western Europe. But in both Mexico and Europe equally the movements tend to be characterized by their autonomy of political parties, especially those of the left. But, as Gerry Munck suggests, such "autonomy" may merely reflect specific theoretical views that offer no alternative to the unstructured spontaneity of popular movements precisely because any collaboration with political parties threatens absorption by the system they reject. In fact, as this collection demonstrates, the contacts between movements and parties have always existed in Mexico, and today every movement contains its political "currents" and party organizations. This does not deny "antiparty" sentiments within the movements, which served a precise political objective in preserving unity despite state attempts at disarticulation. But even these sentiments, Tamayo argues, have been progressively overcome through the local and municipal struggles of the 1980s, which found fullest expression in the National Revolutionary Coordinating Committee in 1985. In other words, electoral coalitions between movements and parties were widespread long before the emergence of the National Democratic Front (FDN) and did much to reverse the decline of the movements in the early 1980s. Possibly popular movements never rejected parties per se so much as manipulation by these parties—which can be understood as one part of their more general challenge to clientelism.

If popular movements in Mexico are still distrustful of the organized "left" in this particular sense, the left has always taken a keen political interest in the movements; and, according to Boschi (1984), throughout the continent, left parties expect more from the movements than the movements do from the parties. But this no longer exhausts the movement-party question in Mexico, which has taken on new significance with the rise of *neocardenismo*. And here there is no consensus whether *neocardenismo* is itself a popular movement that entered the electoral arena as the last and greatest of the national coordinating committees; whether, more modestly, it expresses the convergence of different popular movements in a single electoral moment; or whether, most skeptically, Cárdenas drew only a small part of his support from the popular movements. Furthermore, the lack of agreement on matters of fact leads to opposing interpretations of the phenomenon either as old-style populism, incorporating inchoate movements into the personal following of a charismatic leader, or as new popular organization pursuing alliance strategies that broaden the struggle for political change. These questions recur in different analytical contexts, and any "answer" must include consideration of popular political organization and strategy.

THE PERIODIZATION OF POPULAR MOVEMENTS

Deciding whether popular movements are a "new" political phenomenon is not merely a matter of weighing the historical evidence. The periodization of the movements is also an element of their definition. Thus, if the movements emerging after 1968 are new, then there has been some form of political rupture and things political are changing; if, on the other hand, they continue the popular political organization and practices of yesteryear, then politics itself is as usual.

Although nearly every contemporary movement has historical forerunners, it is argued that the very accumulation of movements after 1968 works a qualitative change in the relationship between popular movements and the political system. Moreover, this accumulation is given continuity through a new popular leadership, which begins with the generation of 1968 (the struggle in Juchitán may have had long historical roots, as Jeffrey Rubin demonstrates, but its contemporary organization required the students), and achieves a national expression, first in the syndical arena of the 1970s, and then in the electoral arena of the 1980s. This sea change in popular politics finds a striking metaphor in the explosive occupation of the Zócalo (the historic central square of Mexico City), which begins in 1968 and recurs as popular mobilizations increase, providing a measure of the (re)appropriation of public and political space by the "people."

One specific indication of the novelty of the phenomenon is the important role played by women in the post-1968 popular movements, especially in the urban and teachers' movements. The mass base of the urban movements is female (even if their leadership is still mainly male), and women clearly play the key part in the organization of low-income neighborhoods. Even where women are not directly involved in strictly political organization (as they clearly are in Teresa Carrillo's case study of a women's union-based movement among the garment workers of the capital), they may yet be active, as Kathleen Logan argues, in organizing civil society and pressing political demands. Among these actors, at least, the old boundaries between public and private may be breaking down, as domestic issues such as male violence against women are assumed by popular struggle. So although class contradictions are never entirely absent, the specifically popular dimension of contemporary struggles is seen in female mobilization.

Not everyone is convinced by these arguments, and historians especially are reluctant to cut off the political mobilizations of earlier in the century from modern times. They note that the period of political tranquility they refer to ironically as the *paz priísta* was relatively short, possibly only fifteen to twenty years, and then only partial. Moreover, there are clear historical precedents for female political mobilization in the Catholic movements of the first forty years of the century: the National League for Religious Defense of 1926–1929 was present in dozens of cities and represents one of the biggest popular movements in twentieth-century Mexico. The historical record of female political practices in general is still very incomplete, and social scientists may anyway make too little of what evidence is already available. In short, arguments that allege that popular movements are now more numerous, or that they mobilize new political actors, may not be sufficient to demonstrate their novelty.

No one can deny that there are important traditions of popular struggle in Mexico, but this assertion cannot automatically deny a specific political content to the contemporary movements. And although patterns of accommodation and conflict between popular movements and the political regime may be discernible from the 1930s, and not just the 1970s, the novelty of the contemporary movements may be seen in their links with, and insertion into, the political system. As Ann Craig argues, the question of the legal and institutional terrain where popular struggle must be waged remains constant, but the laws and institutions change: The 1930s were a period of corporatist construction, with popular movements collaborating in and even encouraging the spread of clientelistic and patrimonial lines of control; in recent years, by contrast, the neoliberal project of the PRI government appears committed to dismantling the corporatist centerpiece of the terrain, and popular movements throughout the country are challenging the traditional forms of clientelistic control.

In this connection, the accumulation of contemporary movements is again important because it contributes to a change in the balance of social forces that makes the challenge to clientelism, and even presidentialism, more open now than in the past. It is not necessarily the case that this challenge is now more successful: The dissolution of such deeply rooted forms of political control as *caciquismo* may take a long time. And whereas there is evidence that this is occurring, there is no proof that the movements have arrived at a historical turning point. But the challenge is now one of principle, and the principle is expressed in the demand that "rights"—land rights, labor rights, human rights—be respected. In other words, the novelty is not merely in the accumulation of movements, or even in a changing balance of social forces, but rather in a changing political culture, where popular movements no longer make petitions or ask for benefits but make demands and insist on basic rights. This is tantamount to challenging the prerogative of the PRI government to rule arbitrarily: the application of the law, an *estado de derecho*, and accountable government; a return to the republic, and the constitution made real.

Whatever the conclusion of the debate over the post-1968 "novelty" of the popular movements, it cannot conclude the discussion of their periodization. Even if the years after 1968 are seen as a new era in popular politics, this cannot mean that there have been no political changes during this time. Possibly a distinction must be made between the longer-term "structural crisis" of the import-substitution industrialization model, on the one hand, and, on the other, the "real" crisis that struck in 1982: During the 1970s organized labor and the middle classes defended themselves quite successfully, and the "union uprising" sought independent, if parallel, organizations, whereas in the 1980s living standards dropped drastically and big industry and the big unions associated with it lost force rapidly. And beyond the onslaught of the "real" crisis, more complex periodizations are possible, which highlight new forms of popular organization and alliance, new state policies like the "political reform," and new projects of the capitalist class. The periodization of popular movements, like their definition, must finally refer not so much to changing economic conditions as to changes in the legal and institutional terrain, and to changes in the political practices of the movements themselves.

POPULAR ORGANIZATION
VERSUS THE DISORGANIZATION OF CIVIL SOCIETY

If 1968 is a historical watershed, then the subsequent popular movements can be seen as a rising tide of popular organization, with the thousands of leaders of the generation of 1968 providing the principle of continuity between tens of apparently separate movements (the leaders going from movement to movement and even galvanizing Indian and municipal struggles). This is the strong image projected by Carlos Monsiváis of "a society getting organized" (Monsiváis 1987*a*) and used to good effect by Francisco Pérez Arce in this book. But Pérez Arce himself doubts that the movements have ever achieved an "organic consolidation," and others question the real degree of political continuity between the different movements. Indeed, Sergio Zermeño replies with the provocative and apocalyptic vision of a civil society in radical disarray. The social disruption caused by the modernizing thrust of Mexican society is thrown into a "double disorder" as this same society careens unchecked into the deep and unforgiving crisis of the 1980s. The rapid destruction of emerging "intermediate identities" pulverizes civil society, breaking it into a thousand unconnected pieces. Tens of millions of children and teenagers without jobs, homes, or prospects drift like flotsam and jetsam in a sea of exclusion. Directly contrary to Monsiváis's image, Zermeño's is one of "a society disintegrating."

The Zermeño thesis raises serious doubts about the importance of popular movements in Mexican civil society. After all, the great majority of the population is not organized in popular movements (and may not even vote); and popular movements themselves may therefore just be a tiny organized part of a civil society crumbling under the impact of the economic crisis. Even electoral support for *neocardenismo* may come more from disaffected but disorganized middle classes than from popular organizations. On the other hand, the radical anomie of urban youth should not be taken as a paradigm for an atomized civil society writ large; and it must be remembered that in most popular struggles at most moments in modern history only a small minority of any population associates civically, and only a handful organizes politically. In the social disarray so graphically described by Zermeño, militancy in a popular movement becomes a heroic act.

There is no denying the magnitude of the economic crisis, but it does not lead ineluctably to civil disorganization. Equally, there can be no assumption that if the economic crisis is resolved, then Mexico's political problems will automatically disappear. Despite the crisis, Mexican civil society is still seeking forms of popular organization (both political and economic); and if the crisis does indeed destroy some of the popular movements, others survive and even flourish. In particular, were it not for the crisis, many women would not be participating in popular movements in the way they are, as breadwinners, mothers, or both. In short, popular movements have a variable and conjunctural capacity for survival. Zermeño replies that if there are organized sectors, they are likely to be limited to the "integrated" part of civil society, like the students and middle classes more generally (their "integration" being achieved through participation in the university, the parliament, the assembly); and that if there is still a process of popular mobilization, it is outrun after 1980 by the rapid destruction of all operational and incipient organizations.

The outcome of this debate is germane to an understanding of *neocardenismo*. If Zermeño is right, then Cuauhtémoc Cárdenas is a populist leader with direct links to the unmediated masses—the candidate of the "disorganized society." But populism does not necessarily imply a lack of popular organization; and in Latin America at large populist projects have often been underpinned by those mass sectors that are the most organized— as Murmis and Portantiero's critique (1971) of Germani's notion of the "disposable masses" (Germani 1962) made clear in Argentina. But Zermeño's argument is buttressed by an idea of the "bureaupolitics" of the PRI government, which absorbs and atomizes popular organization, denying civil society the space to develop and defend its own "identities"; and this interpretation bears not only on the character of *neocardenismo* but also on the secular possibilities of political democracy in Mexico. As Pizzorno (1985:69) has argued in one of the most theoretically audacious essays of the past decade, "there is a value that democracy alone realizes: it isn't the freedom of political choice but freedom of political identification. That is, the right these identifications have to exist, their right not to be nullified or even determined solely by the authority of the national State."

THE POLITICAL STRATEGIES OF POPULAR MOVEMENTS

Popular movements in Western Europe are said to seek a noninstitutional style of politics because of the growing perception that the conflicts and contradictions of advanced capitalism can no longer be solved by "*étatisme,*" increasing political regulation and a lengthening bureaucratic agenda (Offe 1985). Quite the opposite is true in Mexico, however, where all these things are still seen as necessary and inevitable for demands to be met and needs satisfied. In other words, popular movements in Mexico seek institutional recognition in order to get material improvement; and, despite a sometimes radical or revolutionary rhetoric, they pursue these ends through political exchanges and gradualist strategies. The political outcome is a range of particular and differentiated forms of linkage between popular movements and the political system, which the movements will then seek to fix and validate in law. This "institutionalism" (as I call it in my own essay) is the hallmark of popular political practice, and the only alternative to this quest for a *capacidad de gestión* is violence and political sterility.

The notion of "institutionalism" should not be taken to imply an absence of political conflict. Such conflict can occur both inside and outside the (corporative) institutions of the state, as Maria Cook's and Neil Harvey's contributions demonstrate in some detail. Moreover, as Jeffrey Rubin suggests, some popular movements at some moments have been antistate, anticapitalist, militant, and violent. Contemporarily, the struggles "inside" the state have proved most successful strategically. But even here institutionalism has not dissolved the conflict and the killing: Eight years of conflict between the "democratic teachers" and the Revolutionary Vanguard in Oaxaca left a tally of seventy teachers assassinated. Nonetheless, the movements (including the teachers' movements) have continued to strive for institutional insertion and so are "properly characterized by a pattern of negotiation with the State, which corresponds to saying that they are institutionally framed phenomena" (Boschi 1984).

The "institutionalism" of the movements indicates a constant search for the political links that will achieve effective representation, but widespread conflict shows there is no popular conformity to institutional criteria or to traditional ways of doing politics in Mexico. It is true that increasing political exclusion has spurred some popular movements to adopt more sophisticated and less confrontational strategies, including new forms of organization and new political alliances, but they still struggle to get representation on their own terms. Thus, popular movements challenge the exclusionary policies of the PRI government in particular, and (as I discuss below) they challenge the clientelistic patterns of political control in general. They are both "institutionalist" *and* nonconformist.

Just as institutionalist practices can be conflictual, so the popular struggle for legality is often pursued by illegal means. The struggle against *charrismo* in the SNTE (the National Union of Workers in Education), as Pérez Arce argues, has often had recourse to illegal methods in order to restore legality and to see the statutes respected, whereas the very origin of many an urban popular movement is an illegal act of land invasion, for which the movement nonetheless seeks legal sanction and state support. But if every popular movement makes a clear strategic distinction between legal and extralegal initiatives, the legal situation itself is often highly ambivalent, with the PRI government insisting on the rule of law while using this same law to stop the movements and repress political dissidence. Hence, popular support for the law can never be unconditional, even though every popular movement always appeals to the law and struggles to have it upheld.

In this connection it is useful to recall the traditional British distinction between common law, which reflects social reality as it is lived, and constitutional law, which does not so much reflect the reality as envision its transformation. What Gramsci called the "civilizing capacity" of the latter kind of law found such a comprehensive expression in the Mexican Constitution of 1917 that popular demands for the simple application of the law can still support a radical struggle over the form of political regime. This is not to suggest that such a struggle will in fact occur. It is not a prescriptive statement about Mexico's political future but an analytical statement about the nature of the links between popular movements and the political system. The consequences are twofold. On the one hand, shifts from uncompromising militancy to legalism and negotiation, or vice versa, will be less likely to indicate the changing nature of popular organization than moments of strategic and often conjunctural choice; on the other, although popular movements will always meet particular institutional obstacles in each locality and region of the country, in principle the law is universal and may increasingly encourage national organizations and struggles of national scope. In recent years this distinction between local and national struggles has come to express a strategic division between different arenas or "fronts" of struggle: on the one hand, the community, the union, and the respect for "rights"; on the other, elections and the policies and legitimacy of the PRI government. To a large extent the government itself had encouraged entry into the electoral arena through the political reform of 1977 and after, but all politics is local politics, and it took constant mobilization and a recurrent search for intersectoral alliances before sectoral demands could be generalized at the national level. The candidacy of Cuauhtémoc Cárdenas encouraged the popular movements to resolve their differences by shifting the focus of their political activity into a different arena, condensing their demands into a broad electoral coalition against the PRI. Although it is clear that the National Democratic Front vote of July 1988 was more than the sum of the popular movements, there is no doubt about the diverse and massive presence of these movements in the coalition.

The front's rapid rise to electoral prominence appears to indicate a dramatic advance, which has disseminated popular demands and legitimated popular leaders. But, equally, electoral defeats can erode this legitimacy, whereas *neocardenismo* may still lack a more permanent and positive principle of unity beyond a radical rejection of the austerity policies of the

PRI government, or, as Zermeño would have it, beyond the *caudillismo* of Cuauhtémoc Cárdenas. And despite *neocardenismo's* appeals to nationalism, a "national-popular will" (Gramsci 1971) to replace the historical project of the PRI will be difficult to forge in such a heterogeneous nation as Mexico. For these reasons it is open to debate whether the entry into the electoral arena expresses a substantive shift to electoral politics and a demand for liberal democracy *tout court*; or whether it reflects a strategic choice to forge new alliances within this arena and extend the scope of the struggle, while continuing to build sectoral organizations and press immediate and concrete demands. A further, closely related debate concerns the changes in the popular movements themselves that made the shift possible: Did the increasing institutionalization of the movements allow effective electoral activity? Or did the mass base of the movements respond to the populist appeal and push their leaders to participate?

On one reading, the political struggle within the national electoral arena for "effective suffrage" and citizens' rights is an extension of traditional popular struggles for legality and for the application of the law. In other words, whether the shift is substantive or strategic, the principle of continuity from sectoral to electoral struggle is provided by the common goal of an *estado de derecho*, and Mexican civil society discovered in the National Democratic Front at least a temporary vehicle for a national response to illegal manipulation by the PRI government. This does not resolve the strategic ambivalence of popular movements that organize to negotiate collective demands but participate in electoral and postelectoral campaigns for citizens' rights, but it does serve to emphasize two fundamental aspects of the popular movements' political practice. First, whether on the sectoral or the electoral fronts, popular movements have come to challenge clientelism and *caciquismo* as expressions of individual, and therefore nonnormative, alegal, and often corrupt forms of political control (a point I elaborate upon below); and, second, the strategic choices of popular movements may be conditioned by their demands, their internal organization, and the correlation of social forces that confront them, but primary among these elements of explanation will always be the legal-institutional terrain linking civil society to the state, and the strategic opportunities it provides.

THE LEGAL-INSTITUTIONAL
TERRAIN OF POPULAR STRUGGLE

Every political struggle in modern societies, including popular movements, takes place on a specific legal and institutional terrain that shapes and conditions the development of the social forces in struggle. The theorists are in no doubt on this point. "Short of their evolving as revolutionary parties," asks Boschi (1984), "what impact could movements have other than through creating spaces of interaction within existing structures?" Touraine is adamant that popular movements respond first and foremost to state intervention, rather than to the initiatives of other social actors in civil society (Touraine 1987:130). This is the terrain where Gramsci sees social forces waging their "war of position" (Gramsci 1971), and, as such, its configuration will reflect the balance of social forces in society at large over the longer term; but its specific contours are created by government policies and priorities, some of them designed to favor some forces more than others.

This approach does not ignore the importance of economic and social conditions for every social struggle but simply insists that the web of laws and institutions facing social actors contain the spaces for political action. Thus, forms of popular organization in the Laguna, as Ann Craig demonstrates, were clearly a dynamic result of the interaction between government policy, on the one hand, and, on the other, local leadership and local strategic calculation. In particular, the existence and even wording of the law could indicate what demands the "authorities" might be prepared to accept or support, and both Craig and Juan Manuel Ramírez agree that demands come to be put in a language legitimated by the legislative process. In this way, laws and institutions not only shape popular organization, as Maria Cook argues for the "union uprising" of the 1970s, but they also generate discourse, which may change the terms of political argument and even the content of political demands.

Uniquely in Latin America, the popular masses in revolutionary Mexico played a key role in the construction of the corporatist state and in the formulation of public law (labor law, agrarian law, electoral law). But Jaime Tamayo argues forcefully that the use of this law has become entirely discretional, so that even plainly illegal government initiatives may be legalized ex post facto. Juan Manuel Ramírez illustrates this use of law in the urban context, where the PRI government controls land not according to prescribed legal norms but in arbitrary and usually clientelistic fashion, and clearly for purposes of political control. Thus, Mexican law is at the disposition of the political authority, and so always has a casuistic content, being applied only if and when the government ordains it. In fact, the predominant patterns of political control in the forms of clientelism and *caciquismo* deny the very possibility of juridical authority because they are vested in an individual and nonnormative exercise of power. In place of an *estado de derecho*, the "institutional charisma" (in Weber's evocative language) of the PRI government means that popular movements cannot count on a nonarbitrary rule of law; and contemporarily this has provoked them to challenge the institutional boundaries of the regime, especially in the electoral arena. Until very recently, PRI government control of the electoral commissions meant that virtually any result was possible—and "legal."

But the boundaries of the regime are not always clear, partly because of the geopolitics of the legal-institutional terrain, and especially the relationship between the federal state, on the one hand, and, on the other, state governments and local *cacicazgos*, or clientelistic systems of power holding. This question is thrown into high relief by the essays from Jeffrey Rubin, Maria Cook, and Neil Harvey, all of which explore popular movements in the particular context of the southeast of the country. In this region the revolution was bitterly resisted by the caciques of the landed class, whereas the Cárdenas reforms of the 1930s were diluted or reversed; contemporarily the federal state often appears as a mediating force, which acts to contain conflict and violence. A comparison with Guatemala makes the compelling argument that, in this context at least, the Mexican state should not always be understood as the perverse agent of the social drama (Kowarick 1985). More importantly, a regional perspective (and Neil Harvey's essay in particular) reveals the crisis in local forms of corporatist representation and their displacement by federal state agencies. As the legal and institutional terrain becomes saturated with these bureaucratic agencies, tensions grow between federal and state governments, and even among federal agencies.

A regional perspective also questions the integrating and unifying capacity of the state's corporatist strategies, which no longer appear to compose a stable pattern of political organization and representation through the decades. Despite a minimum national corporatist consistency achieved through the syndical corporations of the PRI, in the regions corporatism has always remained a skeletal frame for complex processes of negotiation between state apparatchiks and local caciques. Nonetheless, the "corporatist state" is still an important part of the twentieth-century story and central to the legal and institutional terrain, and the contemporary attack on this centerpiece has led to the most radical change in the nature of this terrain since the 1930s.

Popular movements express a general process of the strengthening of Mexican civil society in recent years, but the most coherent political project to emerge from this society comes from the entrepreneurial groups that have pressed for a more restricted and "neoliberal" state. Indeed, it has been argued (Marván Laborde 1988) that the entrepreneurial mobilization and organization that has succeeded in shifting the terrain in this way is unprecedented in Mexican politics, and that the shift itself is even more significant than the "political reform" of the late 1970s (which itself altered essential elements of the regime, such as the monopoly of political representation by the PRI). Moreover, whereas in some countries of Western Europe a similar neoliberal or neoconservative project to restrict the political arena has coincided with the "new social movements'" aspirations to autonomy and "noninstitutional" politics, in Mexico the popular movements have taken the field to combat this project and defend the corporatist state— or, more accurately, to defend the social pact inscribed within it. And in this regard, it appears possible that in Mexico the project is leading not only to less economic protection but also to less political "protection" and, in particular, to a far less effective corporative control of the electoral arena. Thus, the contingent outcome of this project of political exclusion is to open up new political spaces for the strategic initiatives of popular organizations.

But is there not some contradiction in talking of popular movements that defend the corporatist state, with its institutional charisma and discretional use of law, while struggling simultaneously for an *estado de derecho*? There is contradiction, but not so much in the strategic trajectory of the popular movements as in the very nature of the authoritarian state itself, which, it will be remembered, Linz first characterized an "a strange combination of Reichsstaat and arbitrary power" (Linz 1964). The popular movements clearly defend corporatism for the social pact it enshrines, and not for the clientelistic lines of control it contains and organizes. In short, they struggle for the Reichsstaat, but against the arbitrary power of *charrismo* and *caciquismo*. Whatever the short-term shifts in the legal-institutional terrain, this is the longer-term significance of the political practices of popular movements in Mexico today.

POPULAR MOVEMENTS
AND THE CHALLENGE TO CLIENTELISM

It has already been suggested that although "autonomy" may have political value for popular movements, it does not describe their practices, which, on the contrary, consistently seek linkage with the political system in order to solve immediate problems and satisfy concrete demands. "Autonomy" cannot therefore be constructed abstractly as "separateness" from the political system and as the polar opposite of political representation, but is in fact a concrete condition of such representation. At the same time, clientelism and *caciquismo* act to deny linkage and prevent effective representation, and so popular movements automatically mount a challenge to these traditional mechanisms of political control. Juan Manuel Ramírez's essay, in particular, shows how urban popular movements have resisted the clientelistic and patrimonial controls of the PRI government, rejecting the political culture of petitions and concessions in favor of popular projects and political confrontation.

It would be mistaken to believe, however, that *caciquismo* has gone completely unchallenged in the past. Both Rubin and Knight talk of Cárdenas's corporatist state as a "Swiss cheese state" shot full of holes occupied by regional *cacicazgos*; and in subsequent decades movements arise recurrently to challenge the caciques and take control of the party. And Jeffrey Rubin, arguing from his case study of Juchitán, agrees that the one constant throughout the complexities of its political history is the opposition to *caciquismo*. But only in the present decade has this corporatist state entered into general crisis, which is simultaneously a crisis of the social pact (undermined by economic decline and fiscal pressure) and a crisis of the *caciquismo* that was always its political sinew. This is because the strategic initiatives of the popular movements, and especially their search for political alliances built around horizontal networks of leadership and solidarity, have rendered increasingly ineffective the use of clientelistic forms of control. If in the past *caciquismo* may often have had a popular base, this is now far less likely to be the case, and corporatist structures are increasingly under attack insofar as they simply camouflage the operation of *caciquismo* and clientelism more generally.

This comprehensive challenge to the clientelism that has traditionally informed the main ways of doing politics in Mexico has inevitably had repercussions on the configuration of the legal and institutional terrain. One dramatic illustration was given by the earthquake in Mexico City, where the PRI government was obliged to abandon its own renewal projects in the face of popular mobilization and organization and recognize alternative projects proposed by popular movements in the technical and legal language of the state. This was a convincing demonstration of a popular potential for policy initiatives that countered the clientelistic assumptions of the government, and this successful challenge carried over into the formation of neighborhood committees, the election of representatives to the assembly, the dissemination of the demand for an authentically elective government of the Federal District, and a clear electoral triumph for the opposition throughout the capital in July 1988.

Finally, if the challenge to clientelism and *caciquismo* is different now than in the past, it is also because the federal state itself has launched an attack on regional and local *cacicazgos* in favor of a more centralized and neoliberal state. On more than one occasion in the past, the PRI government has seen its reforming policy initiatives stopped by the resistance of caciques, which explains the failure of the Madrazo reforms of 1965 and the de la Madrid reforms of 1983–1985. On both those occasions the failures sparked popular protest, but today popular protest coincides with the rapid construction of more centralized and concerted forms of political mediation (Foweraker 1989*a*). Several of the essays that follow refer to this process, and to the conflicts it engenders between the federal executive and state governments that shield caciques, or state corporations that provide their institutional base. But even then the direction of political change is not entirely clear. Popular movements are challenging clientelism and so creating the possibilities for a normative application of the law and an *estado de derecho*, but does a neoliberal authoritarian government offer any guarantee of this? The challenge to clientelism and to the manipulation by the PRI government, whether in corporative or electoral spheres, may serve as an operational definition of democratic process in Mexico, but do the emerging forms of political mediation hold out some hope for a more democratic system? In sum, what kind of political change is taking place in Mexico?

POPULAR MOVEMENTS AND POLITICAL TRANSFORMATION

It appears undeniable that important political changes have occurred in Mexican civil society. There are the new political objectives condensed in the idea of citizenship, the new forms of organization and association, the new strategies implicit in a wide range of political alliances. But there is no guarantee, in theory or history, that changes in civil society will automatically be translated into changes within the political system. The government may be discredited, but it seems that the state still has ample margin for reaction and recuperation. Indeed, Zermeño's argument, the "system" itself is characterized by a capacity for constant and rapid reaction to political struggle in civil society; by absorbing or destroying the social identities generated through the struggle it maintains itself intact. But many believe that this capacity has been constricted by the reduced margin of maneuver available to state institutions and, moreover, that the revolutionary project of the PRI government is no longer secure. The future is no longer inevitably defined by an endless succession of PRI administrations.

The impact of popular movements on the political system is not signaled by spectacular effects (although the elections of July 1988 may be the exception to prove the rule). For the most part, popular movements contribute to political change through their continuous attempts to achieve linkage with the political system, which tend to change the institutional configuration of the system itself. In particular, the challenge to clientelism and *caciquismo* forces changes in the legal and institutional relations of the state, within a process of change that is specific, differentiated, and gradual. In this context Marván Laborde (1988) points to divisions in the state apparatus and the decomposition of traditional forms of political control, whereas others point to the fractures within the one-party system and the damage wrought to presidentialism. But above all, Marván Laborde asserts, the qualitative change in the system is condensed in a new pluralism in the relations between civil society and the state. One of the keys to this development is the institutionalization of the popular movements and their links with new political parties, both of which have had to be recognized by the state. The loosening of the ties that bind state institutions together is leading ineluctably to a slow dissolution of the isomorphism state–PRI government, which is the principal axis of political domination.

Within this general process, the July 6, 1988, election seems to mark a sea change in the political culture of the country, above all because this change was expressed electorally. And there is no doubt that the electoral result came as a surprise, even though many believe that it was the cumulative result of twenty years of popular mobilization (from July 26, 1968, to July 6, 1988, to be precise). In effect, the PRI candidate, running on a ticket of "modernity," had to rely on votes from the most backward regions of the country in order to scrape home, and history seemed to be leaving the PRI behind. But the months of mobilization that followed indicated that political culture cannot be changed overnight, with neither the PRI nor the National Democratic Front embracing a new political pluralism, and the subsequent elections returned to the traditional pattern. Moreover, it is evident to everyone that political repression is at least constant, and probably increasing, that political violence against popular movements is unremitting, and that public assassination is now common. The push for pluralism is met by narrower limits of political tolerance and increasing exclusion of political dissidence. Whether democracy has entered the historical agenda is open to question. What is sure is that political confrontation is increasingly defined by competition between different and exclusive democratic projects (including that of the PRI itself). In the meantime no political actor in Mexican civil society is ready to assert that the emperor has no clothes.

What is most immediately in doubt is the political outcome of the neoliberal or "modernizing" project of the present administration, which appears to require the dismantling of the corporatist mechanisms that have served the PRI so well. In other words, it is an exclusionary project that can only deepen the divide between the people and the grand institutions of government. When there is sudden conflagration in civil society the government will send out the fire brigade, but the PRI itself will not "leave the palace to be near the people" (as Zermeño put it). The PRI's project seeks to convince the people of their citizenship in a democratic state when the PRI itself is not convinced, and then persuade them to vote for the PRI and its unpopular policies.

Against this Juan Manuel Ramírez and others argue that the system is not and cannot become less corporatist, and that the PRI project seeks to refurbish and rationalize corporatism and not dismantle it. Indeed, the system may be more corporatist than ever, with new forms of consultation and *concertación*, but with government targeting opposition groups rather than its own loyal corporate constituencies. In this view, the whole system finally rests not on individual representation and citizenship but on collective representation and economic-corporate identities. And if the neoliberal project undermines traditional forms of political mediation, then the newly "liberal" authoritarian state will develop new forms of collective control and representation (as well as continuing to develop its repressive capacity). But even if this is true, it is once again an open question whether a more flexible and streamlined corporatism will work, or whether the PRI itself has the clarity of purpose and political will to make it work. Just as the *neocardenista* Party of the Democratic Revolution (PRD) is not clear whether it is a party of citizens or a party of popular movements, so the PRI is no longer clear if it is a government of citizens or of corporations.

The consensus of opinion indicates that the regime will continue, and so will the opposition. Repression will continue, and so will the fluctuating rhythm of popular mobilization. The PRI government seems to have little to offer those it wishes to "reincorporate," but the opposition has no alternative economic project. Yet something happened in July and the latter months of 1988 that is bound to leave an important historical residue, and this was the historic political encounter between the middle classes and the popular movements of Mexican civil society. In 1988, as in 1968, the students of Mexico City played a key role in the mobilization. In 1968, however, the contacts between the student movement and the organizations of civil society were minimal; in 1988 the popular movements of this society burst onto the historical stage with extraordinary force. In 1968 the PRI government crushed the student movement without compunction, but in 1988 its frenetic rather than decisive attempts to separate the "integrated" from the "excluded" have met with variable success.

The differences between the two historical moments are clear. In 1988, unlike 1968, the PRI government was laboring under a chronic economic crisis for which there appears to be no solution. In 1988, unlike 1968, the PRI government faced an increasingly organized civil society with an unprecedented capacity of mobilization and protest. In 1988, unlike 1968, the PRI government had lost charisma and conviction because of a series of broken revolutionary pledges. Madero's promise of liberal democracy had never been fulfilled, but widespread protest at electoral fraud made the present PRI government responsible. Lázaro Cárdenas's vision of social justice had finally disintegrated under the impact of unending austerity measures. And even Alemán's program of constant economic growth had collapsed. The response of the PRI government is a neoliberal project of economic and political reform that nevertheless strikes at the heart of the most enduring of all revolutionary pledges—that of national sovereignty. It is for this reason that *neocardenismo* was able to unite middle classes and popular masses, if only temporarily, on the common ground of nationalism. And it is for this reason that 1988, like 1968, may signal a historical turning point.

2

Linkages Between
Popular Movements and
the Political System

2

Identity and Ambiguity in Democratic Struggles

GERARDO L. MUNCK

*We must be realists in order to become visionaries and
we can be visionaries without being millenarians.*

The process of expanding the civil, political, and social rights of citizenship,
a true "politics of democracy," has been linked conceptually, in both the
classic European phase and more recent times, with the notion of social
movements. The latter have been seen as sources of change, as carriers of a
new form of politics, as they challenge established forms of representing
interests, the legitimacy of various state roles, and conceptions of human
rights—and redefine nontransferable rights. Current changes in Latin
America, likewise, can be fruitfully explored in terms of the link between
social movements and the broader politics of democracy.

This essay reviews the multiple problems faced by analysts of Mexican
and other Latin American social movements. It considers the ideas that
emerge at the point of intersection of several theoretical perspectives and
research traditions, and then contrasts the views more commonly found in
the U.S. literature (which are too narrow and ultimately flawed) with the
broader European perspective. Even though the latter draws upon the fairly
amorphous notions of identity and autonomy, it does provide an extremely
useful framework for considering the relationship between a group and an
environment populated by other social movements, political parties, and the
state.

The specificity of Latin American social movements is cast primarily in
terms of the pattern of regime change, with the Mexican case situated within
this contextual frame. The conditions for (successful) collective action are
considered, as a prelude to the elaboration of a general hypothesis regarding
the interaction between social movements and national politics in Brazil,
Argentina, and Mexico. The essay concludes by considering some of the
permanent dilemmas rooted in the tension between social movements and
their environment, particularly as they concern the analyst of these social
movements. The underlying premise is that only by seeing the distinctiveness
or autonomy of the social sphere—the arena par excellence of social
movements—and the political sphere can we adequately explore the key

issue of linkages between top-down and bottom-up practices.

APPROACHING SOCIAL MOVEMENTS: WHAT'S "IN" THEM?

In the wake of the political and social agitation of the 1960s and early 1970s, analysts in both Western Europe and the United States gave much attention to a series of new social actors: the social movements centered on the environment, gender issues, nuclear weapons and the prospects of peace, regional autonomy, students, gays and lesbians, blacks and civil rights. These social movements rejected conventional forms of doing politics, thus providing a vehicle to pursue politics by other means. They also posed serious problems for similarly conventional forms of analyzing politics.

As a result of their effort to understand these social phenomena, an important part of the Western European intellectual left was forced to depart from until then faithfully defended Marxist tenets. The theorizing that ensued grew from a consideration of broad changes perceived in society, most commonly conceptualized in terms of a shift from modernism to postmodernism. The "new" social movements, in a more restricted sense, were seen as the actors that most clearly personified the change or shift in "the structure of feeling" within the larger societal context. Reacting against a sense of egalitarianism found in some lowest common denominator, the validity and dignity of "the other" was asserted. The need to acknowledge "the multiple forms of otherness as they emerge from differences in subjectivity, gender and sexuality, race and class, temporal (configurations of sensibility) and spatial geographic locations and dislocations" (Huyssen 1984:50), furthermore, was seen as central to postmodernist thought's pluralistic stance, and its anti-avant-gardism.[1]

In the United States the interest in social movements did not develop as clearly against a theoretical background of class theory and Marxism. Here the study of social movements derived much of its distinctiveness from the influence of rational-choice writings on collective action (Klandermans and Tarrow 1988:4–7; Tarrow 1989; Cohen 1985:674–690; Birnbaum 1988:17–36). The influence of Mancur Olson's (1965) conceptualization of strategic calculation as the implacable calculus of self-interested rational actors, leading to the ominous free-rider problem, was pervasive. Even though most authors working within the "resource mobilization" approach posited solidarist groups with collective interests (thus stressing collective incentives), in place of Olson's individualistic calculus (which was only to be swayed by selective incentives), collective action was still understood as a form of strategic action based on a cost-benefit analysis. Olson was criticized in particular by showing how the costs of participation could be lowered, but the critique did not escape the limits of the Olsonian problematic.

The main problem with rational-choice, individualistic, and intentionalist theories of collective action is that they lack an explanation of the ends—the projected goals of collective action—and how some form of consensus about them is arrived at (in a collective manner). In other words, to postulate strategymaking in terms of a means-ends rationality necessarily entails some discussion of the nature of these ends; this issue, however, was never adequately addressed. Indeed, rational-choice theory was unprepared to explore this terrain.

Continental European studies of social movements, with their different style of analysis (in comparison to their U.S. counterparts), conceptualized the problem of ends or the substantive content of rationality in terms of the notion of *identity*. The processes whereby identities are formed, whether class-based, gender-based, or whatever, rather than being bracketed out of consideration are seen as central questions. Issues of strategy are not devalued in the process. Rather, attention to the process of formation of collective identities is seen as a crucial step prior to explanations in terms of strategic choice, the reason being that "in order to evaluate interests—that is, to calculate costs and benefits—the calculating subject has to be assured of an *identifying collectivity*" (Pizzorno 1985:57; my emphasis).

In approaching social movements, the first task the analyst faces is one common to all sociocultural studies. The general problem of analyzing cultural or social phenomena is that they "*cannot . . .* support a clear demarcation between what is 'in' and what 'out' of the relevant entities or phenomena" (Margolis 1986:26). It cannot be simply assumed that "the empirical unity of the [collective] phenomenon . . . really exists" (Melucci 1988:330–331, 339–342; Touraine 1988b:11; Mainwaring 1987); rather, actors must be seen as undergoing a process of identity construction. For a sense of unity is something that must be forged and maintained, and not taken as a given, as in rational choice theories.

In sum, the very existence of a relatively unified actor, rather than something to be taken for granted, is one of the main things that needs to be explained. Only on the basis of a constructed identity does it make sense to talk of strategies. The importance of a focus on identity, furthermore, is confirmed in that collective action cannot be reduced to instrumental rationality, because "collective action is never based solely on cost-benefit calculation and a collective identity is never entirely negotiable" (Melucci 1988:343). Thus, although the "resource mobilization" approach points to the importance of understanding the leaders of social movements, seen as strategizing actors having certain resources at their disposal, only by drawing upon the European "new social movements" approach, in particular through its elaboration of the more amorphous notion of identity, can we hope to explain how strategic calculations are made, i.e., how they are framed within the minds of leaders. If rational-choice theory, drawing upon the arsenal of game theory, has provided a fairly elegant way of explaining action in terms of a tight means-ends rationality, there is necessarily more to collective action than getting from here to there. Moreover, rational-choice theorists never seriously deal with the "there" and with the question of why certain actors may want to get there. These issues can only be addressed by linking micro- and macrolevels of analysis, and not by adopting the microreductionist view rational choice favors.[2]

NEW SOCIAL MOVEMENTS AND THEIR ENVIRONMENT

If defining how a group develops a sense of "in-ness" is a first step in the analysis of social movements, it is only by considering the connection between inward-and outward-looking aspects of social groups that we can arrive at a full understanding of social movements. Indeed, a definition of social movements must be advanced in terms of the relation between a social group and its environment. This is so because a distinguishing characteristic that sets social movements apart from other social groups is that the former try to bring about change in their social context. In a sense, a social movement's very ability to survive as such depends on its capacity for collective action and its public recognition as a social force. This amounts to defining social movements as agents of contestation of the boundaries of the dominant order: they do not quibble about the means but are engaged in a struggle over the ends.[3] The presence of nonnegotiable elements may annul the possibility of purely instrumental action, but it does not signify that social movements do not engage in strategic action (Touraine 1988*b*:68; Offe 1985).[4] In other words, identity and strategy, or expressive action and strategic action, although connected through a tense and ambiguous relation, are not incompatible.[5]

Social movements are first of all concerned with their own *autonomy*. The argument for autonomy hinges on the demand that the members of social movements have a right to determine (in a democratic and open manner) their sense of community or collective identity. This is a first step, entailing activity of a symbolic and ritual type, a process Hobsbawm calls the "invention of tradition," after which issues of strategy arise (Johnson 1988:230–235). The turn to *strategic action* is only partially a question of choice. Social movements necessarily have to engage in strategic action, both to challenge an established order and to gain recognition. Their choice regarding entry into the strategic arena is confined to a question of timing, that is, to when but not if. At the same time, the concern with autonomy cannot be abandoned.

On entering the stage of strategic actions, a whole new set of problems arise. Thereafter, the thorny issue of means and ends, in particular, presents a constant challenge to the integrity of social movements. If a group is to live up to its promise of engaging in a new form of doing politics, of transforming the contexts it faces, and thus become a social movement as defined above, it is inevitable that the means be consistent with the ends. Questions of the style of practice are not secondary, which is to say that the way things are done is just as important as what is done. Strategic action, in short, puts social movements face to face with "the demonic problem of politics: the tendency of means to create their own ends, or the difficulty of realizing our chosen ends except through means that bring about results we do not want" (Unger 1987:396, 411).

In sum, social movements are marked by two tensions. One is the never fully resolved tension between the need for autonomy and the just as pressing need to engage with the environment. A second one derives from a situation in which social movements are never totally immune to being dominated by strategy at the expense of vision, in which the means-ends logic is reversed. The importance of these tensions is given in that either a turn inward to a defensive identity or a reversal of the means-ends logic spells the demise of the social movement.

Starting from the interior of a group, therefore, we inevitably have to move to a consideration of its relationship to the environment (Melucci 1988:333, 342; McAdam, McCarthy, and Zald 1988:699–704, 718–723; Castells 1982). The tendency for social movements to relate to their environment in an ambiguous fashion is clearly illustrated by the fairly common defensive attitude displayed toward political parties and the state, based on a fear of being absorbed or co-opted.

Political parties have been the primary tool for conquering governmental power, at least in the Western democracies. The differences between parties and social movements, particularly in the phases of emergence of social movements, are vast and important. Social movements, understandably, do not want to be "used" by parties, reduced to a number of voters in the polling booths or added to the head count in demonstrations. But, as underlined above, a group solely concerned with preserving its identity intact, to defend its autonomy, forgoes opportunities to change its environment and thus become a full-fledged social movement. Thus, parties must be seen also as potential allies in a program of societal transformation. The relationship is clearly bound to be a tense one, because social movements and political parties can be seen as having partially complementary but also competing agendas. Differences can be worked out so as to bring about more effective action; but tension should always characterize the relationship. Otherwise, most likely the social movement will have been absorbed by the party.

The state, no doubt, is one of the chief actors in the environment of social movements, and it is important in many respects. To adopt a common terminology, we can see the state both as a dependent and independent variable. As an independent variable, the state enters explanations in terms of how it affects the opportunities and obstacles faced by groups within civil society, through the multitude of ways in which the state reproduces society. In short, the emergence of social movements and their likelihood of maintenance are partly explained by state action (Birnbaum 1988:8, 32, 50–54; Tarrow 1988:429–430). As a dependent variable, the state is a primary target of the actions of social movements. In one sense, protest movements of the poor are often aimed at very specific parts of the state apparatus that relate to their daily experience. But in a broader way, the state is a dependent variable in the analysis of social movements inasmuch as social movements envision the takeover of governmental power, not simply the affecting of governmental policy.

LATIN AMERICAN REALITIES

Having considered the main theoretical notions needed to understand social movements, I turn now to the realities of Latin America. In the North, social movements emerged outflanking a well-established political party system unable to represent the constituencies of social movements. The linkage with parties, still uncertain in the Latin American cases, transforms the nature of the social movement–party linkage problem. The specificity of Latin American social movements resides, above all, in that they emerge in a context of regime transformation. In Latin America, social movements emerge within a political system in flux, in which the transition to a democratic regime and its consolidation are the broad agenda of society. Social movements must be seen, therefore, as one part of this larger process.

As a survey of the studies on Latin American social movements shows, regime form appears both as an independent and dependent variable.[6] In the initial stages of the social movements, the emphasis is on how the particular characteristics of the regime impact upon their formative process. The usual story goes that oppressive regimes disarticulated former identities, in particular those based in relations of production, and gave rise to new ones. The most common movements thus formed included the feminist movement; neighborhood associations and other territorially defined communities concerned with questions of access to land, housing, and essential services; human rights groups; environmentally oriented groups; labor and rural groups; church associations linked to ecclesiastical base communities and liberation theology; and youth movements. This trend toward new forms of participation and organization was explained in part by the forced "privatization" imposed from above by repressive regimes, which closed off channels of politics used until then. As the cost of acting in more conventional ways became too high, people were forced to focus more energy on "the private," to seek new channels for action. This "birthmark" was crucial in defining the specificity of Latin American social movements.

Thereafter, with the transition to democracy in the 1980s, social movements had to face different issues. After a period of "freezing," political parties resuscitated and showed themselves to be capable of mobilizing vast sectors of the population.[7] All of a sudden social movements had to reconcile themselves with the fact that they were not the only game in town. The dynamic of social movements was then very much affected by the electoral process and the game of party competition. Later, once new democratic governments were set up and the consolidation phase proper began, social movements continued to face similar problems: because of the focus on formal institutions, their role was continually deemphasized (Boschi 1987:205; R. Munck 1989).

The Mexican case does not fit easily within this synoptic overview, which draws more on cases in South America, like Brazil, Argentina, and Chile, which have undergone long periods of military rule. But there is some overlap. Mexico's political system did begin to change in 1968. Because of a series of long-term factors—among them the stronger state left as a legacy of the revolution, the three decades of steady and satisfactory economic growth since 1940, a subordinate military, and the closeness of the United States—and some short-term, unpredictable factors such as Echeverría's statesmanship and the 1970s oil boom, Mexico's government did not take the bureaucratic-authoritarian turn. Yet it did face similar pressures. The ruling coalition thus set out on a reformist course within a favorable context in 1977. But time ran out on them with the end of the oil boom and the beginning of the debt crisis in 1981/82. Thereafter, the dynamics of Mexican political change has been closer to the rest of Latin America.

Within this context, the role of social movements has clear democratic connotations. The constituents of social movements in Mexico, as in Latin America in general, are mainly disaffected groups that, unlike most sectors of organized labor, clearly do not have a stake in the current system. Not having formal occupational status, these people do not have a strong organizational base and no economic clout. In short, they have nothing to cash in as part of an exchange with the government. They are not an available mass the state would want to co-opt and buy off with a share of the redistributed wealth, as in past populist experiences. One of their major resources is, thus, their numbers. But even in politics this resource cannot be cashed in unless translated into votes. Thus, in an age of economic stabilization plans and no wealth to redistribute, one of the main demands of this group has to be for equality, for the right to participate on the basis of "one person, one vote." Hierarchical patterns of representation of a corporatist form only exclude them. The demands of social movements, therefore, necessarily spill over into the political arena, because access to power, or at least influence on power, given economic conditions, is needed to satisfy their demand for tangible benefits—or the more negative demand of spreading the misery more equally. From here springs the great potential that the actions of social movements can form a part of a wider democratic project.

If this is the structure of the choices faced by Mexican social movements, what are the conditions for (successful) collective action? The problem must be approached by jointly considering top-down and bottom-up practices. The specificity of the linkages between these forms of practice within the Latin American context highlights, in particular, the full importance of an autonomous social sphere. Some old insights from comparative politics are useful to make the point. Alexander Gerschenkron, Barrington Moore, Albert Hirschman, and Philippe Schmitter have maintained, via a timing-of-industrialization line of argument, that late developers modernize on the basis of a state-led process. At least, in comparison with earlier developers, the state takes on more important roles than those of actors situated unambiguously in civil society. Furthermore, as the Latin American literature underlines, along with a stronger state, there has been a recurrent tendency for mobilization to be channeled through populist forms of participation, which in the long run can be, and usually are, used to demobilize previously "incorporated" groups.

The stronger state and populist forms of mobilization underline the need to see the democratization of the state as premised on a highly mobilized civil society. This, in turn, can only be attained when civil society provides an autonomous sphere in which to base mobilization of a truly bottom-up nature. But such a form of action has only rarely occurred in the Latin American historical record, as groups emerging as social movements get crushed or co-opted before they can fully blossom. Furthermore, in Latin America the difficulties of the task faced by social movements, the dilemmas they face, are accentuated because part of their demands entail petitioning scarce subsistence goods from the state.

Although we should avoid a characterization of social movements based on their pursuit of material or nonmaterial goods, it is true that Latin American social movements are affected by the pressures of economic scarcity in a way that differentiates them from their counterparts in Western Europe.[8] The importance of this distinction is given by its impact on the crucial issue of timing, namely, how much time social movements have to emerge and mature before having to confront the state. If, in Latin America, to turn away from the state, à la "self help," is a ridiculous utopian notion, the practical imperative of having to confront the state on extremely short notice presents grassroots groups with a cruel dilemma. Not only does the statist tradition of the Latin American region make the maintenance of autonomy a more central issue than in Western Europe, the conditions under which this autonomy is to be defended and strengthened are also much more adverse. We could say that in Latin America the window of opportunity for potential social movements is both smaller and remains open for less time than in Western Europe. This grim picture of the central dilemmas social movements face, instead of giving way to flights of optimism, prepares the ground for a crucial question: How can social movements fulfill a role in current democratic processes?

The value of small-scale experiments for projects of larger change is undeniable. The tendency for them to remain isolated and insignificant is just as apparent. The role of social movements, therefore, must be conceived in a way that sees the task of democratization of the state as ultimately depending on the joint action of social movements, seeking "autonomy and voice without isolation," and political parties.[9] Because social movements tend to adopt a "self-limiting character," focusing their activities within civil society, political parties must assume an important role in globalizing the democratic project in which social movements engage. Within a system of representative democracy that retains an important role and is not devalued from the perspective of the democratic project,[10] it is crucial for social movements that their linkages to parties become closer as their contribution is explicitly recognized, but that the political sphere does not swallow up the social sphere, that is, that the autonomy of the social is respected.

Yet, the respect of the social sphere always remains in jeopardy. As Viola and Mainwaring write, "the recent trend has focused too much on formal democratic institutions. Democracy, which had been devalued [in the 1960s and early 1970s], has virtually become the only value in some discussions about the transition, while questions about repression against popular sectors, agrarian reform, popular participation, and regional equity have been neglected" (Viola and Mainwaring 1985:213). Thus, it should be emphasized that without denying the role of a revamped party system, it is crucial to acknowledge that in transitions from authoritarian regimes, the formula of social organization based on the political party, which pressures the state, ceases to be *the only* way of redefining the terrain of politics (Garretón 1986:24–29). In other words, realism about the impact of big politics on other processes can never justify losing sight of the equally important dangers of top-down politics. This is where social movements have great contributions to make, in challenging authoritarian practices by asserting their own democratic practices.

Without arguing the institutional specifics of alternative proposals, it is important to insist that something more than political parties is needed to keep democracy alive. For whereas political democracy is not a sham, it is clearly not enough. The role of social movements hinges very much on this "something more" Latin American democracies seem to need. But just as a democratic government can be said to need social movements as agents of mobilization and vehicles for unrepresented groups in society, so can the phrase be turned around to emphasize that social movements need democracy as soon as possible. More specifically, they need a popular yet not populist form of government, one that, although not antiparliamentarian, does not encroach upon their demands for autonomy. The practical force of the dilemmas faced by social movements can therefore be seen to overlap with those of the maintenance of a democratic system, even though this overlap is not complete; that is, there are shared problems, but these do not exhaust the particular issues that arise in each sphere.[11]

The processes under consideration, given the close ties between social movements and national politics, are vast and complex. Drawing on recent developments in Brazil, Argentina, and Mexico, however, a general hypothesis regarding this interaction can be ventured. The independent variables to be considered are: (1) the strength of the regime, measured in terms of the degree to which the state intervened actively in reshaping civil society and state-society relations and the levels of repression,[12] and (2) the characteristics of the transition process, considered in terms of the form of the transition (whether or not it was a process controlled from above), and the duration of the transition phase (whether it was a long or short process). These two variables have a joint impact on the dependent variable, the window of opportunity allowed for the emergence and consolidation of social movements, which, in turn, will affect the nature of the government. Within this framework, it appears that longer and smoother—i.e., more controlled—transitions from more constructively interventionist and less repressive regimes are more conducive to the consolidation of the new practices of social movements at the level of civil society, though it still remains unclear whether the greater authoritarian legacy at the level of the state outweighs these novel developments.[13]

Comparisons of the recent transitions in Argentina and Brazil (Viola and Mainwaring 1985) show that Argentina's 1982–1983 transition signified both a clear break with the military regime inaugurated in 1976 and a return to politics as practiced before the military coup. The trade-off in this case was that, whereas this form of transition did do away with the authoritarianism within the state in a more definite fashion, it also made it harder for organizations that emerged during the military period to adapt to the new context. The story of the Mothers of the Plaza de Mayo epitomizes the many disillusions of social movements in Argentina's new democracy. In contrast to Argentina, Brazil's 1974–1985 transition was a long process, carefully guided and controlled from above.[14] The trade-off here was that state authoritarianism was not as drastically affected as in Argentina, yet emergent forms of organizing in civil society had a more suitable terrain on which to move. The novelty represented by the formation of the Partido dos Trabalhadores (Workers party) illustrates the possibilities of this path.

The level of repression of authoritarian regimes seems to enter as an important variable, though its impact is ambiguous. On the one hand, we can clearly distinguish the impact of repression in terms of the disarticulation of previous identities, a process that opens up the possibility of the constitution of new identities. Yet repression always provides an obstacle to the organization of any movement, making a push for democracy a strategic interest of social movement. The degree of constructive intervention by the government and the duration and form of the transition also deserve attention. Thus, Argentina's military government (1976–1983) was more repressive than Brazil's (1964–1985), but it remained isolated from civil society and collapsed in a way that led to a more radical swing to democracy. Under these circumstances, old actors had a greater chance of surviving the "return to normalcy," and social movements, unless extremely adept at shifting gears (a skill determined in part by the sort of issues on which they focused their activity), tended to be displaced. In Brazil, a lower level of repression was combined with a lengthy transition, controlled or led by a regime that actively sought to reformulate state-society relations. A return to the pre-1964 situation was much more unlikely.[15]

The Mexican case is closer to that of Brazil than to that of Argentina (Cammack 1988). The level of repression in Mexico has been comparatively low; a shake-up likely to spark the emergence of new identities can be seen to come from the consequences of the economic crisis, however. The transition process starting in 1977 has been characterized as a gradual and controlled process (Middlebrook 1986; Levy 1989; Cornelius, Gentleman, and Smith 1989), which allows for a bottom-up strategy of accumulation of forces, conducive to the formation of cohesive and autonomous identities. Also, because the Mexican government has actively intervened within society, it is unlikely that the situation will undergo an Argentine-like swing, thus making it improbable that emergent groups will be swept away before having a chance to gain in organizational strength.

The window of opportunity, therefore, appears to be fairly favorable within a Latin American context, even though the danger still looming large in the Mexican case is that *neocardenismo* could end up being no more than another populist trap—a new version of the PRI-run corporatist system that social movements are currently fighting. Here, social movements will be able to confront a historically strong state only by establishing linkages with political parties that respect their autonomy and voice. Therein lies their potential to contribute to the advance of democracy as a double-sided process, entailing not only the democratization of civil society but also the democratization of the state.

AN ASIDE ON PRACTICAL/ANALYTICAL DILEMMAS

The importance of the role of the state in the present analysis makes it crucial to work at the intersection of the political sociology literature and that on social movements and collective action (Birnbaum 1988:54). This task is made easier thanks to the advances in the literature on theories of the state in the last two decades. Yet students of social movements in both the North and the South justly criticize the excessive abstraction of this theorizing. Ruth Cardoso (1983:218), for example, criticizes the lack of any specific analysis of the functions of the state, which are relegated to blanket statements about its disciplinary and authoritarian character. Similarly, Renato Boschi (1987:184) points out that differences in the local, discrete performance of the state can lead to different forms of collective action with various types of impact. In sum, "theories of the state carry the risk of surveying the terrain of collective action from so high an altitude that crucial processes and internal variations cannot be seen" (Tarrow 1988:436).

Although these criticisms are amply justified, it is only fair to point out that the extensive debates on the state did at least demystify some of the worst aspects of the demonology of the state. Crucially, most theorists acknowledged that the state is not a monolithic entity. Whether they stated, like Poulantzas, that there is class struggle within the state, or simply that divisions within the state can be exploited by social movements, theorists made the point that the state is not an impervious enemy (McAdam, McCarthy, and Zald 1988:721; Unger 1987:410-411). Furthermore, they set forth convincing arguments, as more than simply an analytical issue, that the autonomy of the state makes it an actor in itself. Thus, for analysts of social movements sympathetic to bottom-up forms of practice—which constitute part of the definition and attractiveness of their objects of study—

it remains an unavoidable reality that the state matters. A top-down form of analysis cannot be abandoned, not only because it is a target of action but also because it conditions and sets the rules for the actions of social movements.

Even though we can distinguish between bottom-up (or basist) and top-down (or statist) approaches, it remains true that analysts will generally find the power of the state much more impressive than that of grassroots movements. It is necessary to avoid falling prey to this likely bias, this seduction by the "effects of power." Changes that originate at the grassroots level have other characteristics from those that originate from above. They creep up on us, take us by surprise; they have an element of spontaneity, especially in the period of their emergence. Also, although elite politics is not easy to study given the smaller number of elite agents, the problems entailed in such research are different. Grassroots politics is not as overtly strategic as elite politics. Issues of identity and the dialogical constitution of interests are more important. We are dealing, I think it is fair to say, with a different kind of actor than in elite politics, which is apparent when we realize that in explaining social movements amorphous notions such as "the people" (*el pueblo*) do lead to important insights. Eventually, as the resource mobilization school has stressed, organization becomes crucial to social movements. In the case of successful social movements, we witness the creation of formal social movement organizations (SMOs) (McAdam, McCarthy, and Zald 1988:716ff). In the process, social movements become more conventional, though still district from political parties. Then it is easier to detect the significance or potential of the movement.

These comments are especially crucial for the studies done on Latin American social movements, which are incipient at best. If this work is going to survive as a research program, the standards of productiveness and neatness used to judge studies of elite politics cannot and should not be applied. This is not to sanction sloppy research or a lack of analytical focus, but rather to recognize that our model for dealing with different fields of practice and experience "could hardly be convincing unless it rested on arguments regarding *the properties of the domain in question*" (Margolis 1986:24; my emphasis). If standards from one field are imposed on another, in the fashion of intellectual colonialism, we run the danger of losing sight of emerging actors that could be carriers of great democratic potential. This is where the normative and the empirical overlap: intellectuals have a role in helping shape, form, and define the identity and role of social movements. If social scientists dismiss them as unimportant, then it will be so much easier for political parties and the state to play them down. At this point there may be nothing to be very objective about, so the distance between analyst and object of analysis is hardly perceptible.

The closeness or partial overlap of practical and analytical concerns raises the stakes of the task of defining the particularity of the forms of action practiced by social movements. Analytical confusions are costly in more than an academic way. What makes the issue so confusing is that at the heart of the debate between top-down and bottom-up approaches to social practices is the contested notion of politics and alternative definitions of democracy. If statists primarily talk about politics as having to do with little more than issues of government, basists ("rank-and-file-ists") retort that politics is about power. From the latter perspective, civil society, just as much as the state, is an arena for public debate and decision. The problem becomes, then, how to think of representative forms of government, an issue on which basists usually must concede ground to more statist views.

Yet all this does not mean that the two views are mutually exclusive or contradictory. What is at stake, rather, is the adequacy of conceptualizations of the *linkage* between the two counterposed views. A clarification of this matter can proceed by way of constructing two scenarios, derived from statist and basist assumptions, to illustrate the way in which they are misconstrued options. Though certain authors display an affinity for one or the other way of seeing social movements, it is important to see the two scenarios not as positions held by any one particular author. Rather, the exercise tries to exemplify the tendencies present in any attempt to analyze social movements and to situate them within a larger social and political context.

I call the two scenarios the "incorporated but dependent" and the "autonomous but isolated" scenarios. In the "incorporated but dependent" scenario, top-down action is emphasized, primarily through the attention given to the strategic choices of elites. The danger—from the perspective of social movements, or, more accurately, nascent organizations with the potential to become social movements—is that they will be absorbed, co-opted, or corrupted. Rather than changing the world, they are changed. Their potential is lost or never realized, and a new form of politics never fully corporatized. They are accepted or incorporated because they have been made dependent and normalized, made to fit standard rules and ways they do not contest. Because the issue of power is seen as a prime concern of these actors, political strategizing is seen as essential to the future of social movements. Yet to be taken seriously, social movements have to abandon radical notions of difference and emphasize universality and exclusion: We are all the same, but we have been left out. The raison d'être of social movements, therefore, is to do the job political parties have left unattended, that is, to represent the excluded. Thus, whereas the issue of social movements' linkages with political parties and the state emerges clearly in this way of thinking (along with the possibilities of social movements transforming into parties), because the autonomy of social movements is only tenuously asserted and defended, there is a hidden tendency for this autonomy to be the first casualty of political strategizing, and for populist forms of organization and action to gain the upper hand.[16]

In the "autonomous but isolated" scenario, bottom-up action is emphasized, especially in the form of grassroots mobilization. Yet this form of action is mostly of a defensive type, that is, aimed at the protection of a group's identity as against the intrusion of outsiders. This form of enclave communalism represents, in short, the obverse side of right-wing individualism. In this scenario, groups run the risk of being so irrelevant that they will be forgotten and come to naught. They are ineffectual because the principled defense of autonomy means that the moment of strategy never arrives. This is so because the problem of how an emphasis on different identities is to be accepted in wider circles is not adequately addressed. Given a radical critique of notions of representation, interests are not easily conceptualized, and, more pragmatically, nothing is said about the question of how and by what criterion social movements are supposed to establish links with political parties. The state, or power from above, tends to take on a monolithic dimension, leading to a pessimistic view of the very possibility of thinking about global projects that do not reproduce oppression. Thus, with the problems of direct democracy and questions of scale haunting this perspective, the hidden danger is that the search for Rousseau unwittingly leads to Hobbes.[17]

The dilemma for the analyst concerns how to assess the role of social movements within each alternative scenario. If we define success as full acceptance, meaning that the social movement organization is recognized as a central political actor (a "valid interlocutor" in Latin American parlance), the likely result in the first scenario is that the process of incorporation from above makes it meaningless to talk of a social movement as an actor (Boschi 1987:182, 185; Klandermans and Tarrow 1988:3; Touraine 1988b:69). In the second scenario, on the other hand, no actor ever really emerges on the political scene. In both scenarios, thus, we see failed social movements. Put a different way, to change the small picture, the big picture has to be changed too. Seen in these terms, in the first scenario, because we have the reversal of the means-ends logic, any transformative capability is lost, and with it the possibility to effect changes. In the second, because a purely defensive behavior never challenges the broader roots of the problem, the locally circumscribed grassroots action is bound to peter out. It is clear that both scenarios lead to flawed courses of action, and ultimately to a defraudation of expectation, the nonfulfillment of promises.

What is lost in these two scenarios is the sense of ambiguity characteristic of the practices of social movements. This must be recognized and assessed on a social terrain seen as distinct from the political sphere and the state. Thus, the above form of judging success should be complemented with a second form of assessment, which emphasizes the centrality of the notion of the autonomy of civil society. Given that social movements are at home primarily in this social arena, a purely political standard of assessment is likely to overlook Tilman Evers's "hidden reverse side" or Manuel Garretón's "invisible transition," and fail to see that a self-limiting behavior can follow from a very clear strategic assessment of the possibilities faced by a group in a particularly unfavorable context (Evers 1985:52–54; Garretón 1987:chap. 4). Seen only as an initial stage, the conceptualization of social movements as "self-limiting" can therefore be affirmed, together with the necessity for a "political moment" (Garretón 1987:184-185; Touraine 1988b:81; Unger

1987:405).

This vision is consonant with an understanding of democracy as a double-sided process, consisting of the democratization of civil society and the state. Because these two tasks have different "moments," the eminently strategic question of when they are to overlap depends on many contingencies of timing, which cannot be resolved outside of these contingencies. Clarifying the conceptual distinctiveness of the moment of identity and the ambiguous advance toward political action as key characteristics of the politics of democracy, however, allows us to recognize the working of concrete social movements.

In sum, the issue of assessment of the efficiency of groups aspiring to become social movements, with a transformative capacity, must be addressed. Most commonly, social movements are assessed in terms of their ability to "translate" their practices and mobilizational potential into political action. Indeed, the impact of social movements on the political system has to be the ultimate test of their promises. However, an all-or-nothing evaluation may not be the most adequate in studying ongoing processes. The social phenomena under consideration are, in many cases, of very recent origin. Some are only starting to undergo tests regarding their ability to survive as organizations. Thus, some sense of the different stages through which a social movement evolves is essential. It is just as necessary to focus on the ultimate test. In the rapidly fluctuating context of Latin American politics, this test usually arrives sooner than expected. The cost of failure, of lost opportunities, is hard to estimate. On the other hand, the obstacles to establishing an autonomous social sphere that will enable success, given the statist tradition of the region, are hard to overemphasize.

CONCLUSION: EXPANDING POSSIBILITIES FOR DEMOCRATIC INTERVENTION

This essay attempts to create a space for thinking about grassroots action in relation to a democratic project, without being naive about the realities of the state. Attention to the differentiated realities of the state is crucial: the state should not be seen as a savior nor as the devil, though it always is a powerful actor on the local scene. Concretely, it is in the interest of social movements to have a popular form of government, and not a populist government that co-opts and demobilizes them, ultimately seeking the identification of social groups with the state. The task of democratizing the state thus corresponds to the centrality of the state in modern times. In this, the maintenance of autonomy must be seen as a precondition for effective action by social groups. This democratic project is distinct from the vanguardism of the 1960s. Fundamentally, it is based on a radical critique of the logic that sees it possible to achieve democracy through nondemocratic means. The new identities embodying this project are thus not only fairly restricted in scope but also marked by great ethical cohesion.

The contribution of social movements to democratization in Mexico in the last two decades has not received the attention it deserves. Yet to avoid misinterpreting the movements' possible roles, we must beware of trying to judge them according to the fairly standard interpretations of the process of extension of citizenship rights based on the classic model of working-class action. The difference in the current processes is not that the struggle for citizenship is over, but that "the different aspects of the social conflicts have increasingly become separated" (Melucci 1988:330). When we consider the linkage among democracy, citizenship, and social movements, we necessarily have to do so in a different way. What is called for, thus, is not a linear extension of the notion of citizenship, but a reformulation of the concept. In general, we can talk of a new politics of democracy, based on an increasingly more mobilized civil society emphasizing long-ignored, bottom-up forms of action, which forces us to reconceptualize the notion of citizenship so as to accommodate for particularity (Connolly 1987:10).

The problem of democracy, broadly conceived as the empowerment of people to decide on issues crucial to their well-being and happiness, is therefore shifted, at least initially, from a distant state to a more narrowly defined and closely felt "us." The shift entails a redefinition of identities, of what "we" are and what "our" problems are. It also involves a change in approach to problem solving: a top-down view, with its grand strategizing, is temporarily replaced by a bottom-up view, building on small perceptions and insights, on the actions by small groups of people. Initially, the insights of a more statist perspective are lost, or at least devalued. But this need not be the case in the long run. Indeed, the latest elaborations by theorists of social movements have moved precisely in the direction of combining top-down and bottom-up views, stressing the linkages among the state and political parties *and* social movements. These developments have enriched our political analysis by providing a more balanced and complex conceptualization of state-society relations. They have also expanded the possibilities for democratic intervention.

NOTES

I would like to thank Ann Craig and Joe Foweraker for their encouragement and support throughout the writing of this paper.
    The epigraph at the beginning of this chapter is taken from Unger, 1987: 365.
    1. The notion of class remains important to several analysts of social movements and to those who have shifted to more cultural analyses. Touraine, for example, writes that "cultural orientations are the stakes in relations of domination"; yet whereas he stresses that the central conflicts are currently over culture, he also maintains that "the notion of social movement is inseparable from that of class" (Touraine 1988b:55, 58, 41–42, 68–69). A brief survey of the "modernity versus postmodernity" debate can be found in Poster 1989:12–33. For the more recent Latin American debate, see the contributions to the September 1987 issue of *David y Goliath. Revista del CLACSO* (Buenos Aires) XVII, 52.
    2. Because of the reductionist approach of rational-choice theory, contextual

factors are not easily conceptualized within its framework. Yet, "the behavior [of actors] cannot be explained by the consciousness of the actors themselves. . . . The [social] relations and not the actors should be studied. . . . Sociology, thus, should never underestimate the study of interaction [which takes actors as its point of departure], but it must not divorce it from the recognition of the field of relations" (Touraine 1988b:49; see also Margolis 1986:26–27, 131, 154). Without rehearsing the by now well known need to resolve the structure/agency problem without falling into false dichotomies of atomistic individualism and undifferentiated collectivism, one can still underline the need to acknowledge the reality of society, understood as social relations. Without the concept of social structure, or something like it, we cannot make sense of persons and what they do. Even if society does not exist apart from the practices of individuals and cannot be studied except through its effects, the existence of society is a necessary condition for any intentional act. Thus, in rejecting an "intentionalist" perspective, we need not deny that human action is characterized by intentionality and purposefulness. The social sciences must have a nonreductionist basis to account for collective action, in which the status of human agency is preserved yet the myth of creation done away with. This type of enterprise has been a central concern of Continental European thinking in the last years. Though known for its structuralist propensities in the 1960s, "from the 1970s there has been, in both countries [France and Germany], an effort to reconstruct a theory of the subject as agent of change" (Poster 1989:61). Touraine's concern with the "return of the actor" is only one example. Liberal or individualistic approaches, in other words, do not have a hegemony over conceptualizations of agency.

3. Though I define social movements in this way, I still employ the term in its looser usage, to denote the actions of a particular social group or organization with merely the potential of becoming a social movement. The definition can be seen as an ideal type against which particular cases can be measured. Thus, a continuum can be drawn between one pole, representing total acceptance of things as they are, and another pole, representing a group's full contestation of the rigidities of the social order and total control over its actions. Obviously, concrete cases are always mixtures, but they can be usefully classified according to the degree to which they embody a challenge to the systemiclike qualities of their context. Touraine, for example, argues that the concept of social movement should "not be used to designate any type of force for change or for collective action, [but] must be reserved for truly central conflicts, those that call into question the social control of historicity, of the models for the elaboration of the relations between a concrete social ensemble (which we can continue to call 'society' for simplicity's sake) and its environment" (Touraine 1988b:26). This kind of definition, which is closely tied to the notion of the group's capacity to bring about social change, is crucial to any effort to approach concrete social movements from a clear theoretical stance that avoids the problems of empiricist forms of analysis.

4. This is not to say that strategic choice alone can adequately explain business as usual, or routine matters either. The macrohistorical frame cannot be bracketed out, for the analysis of history does not admit of the freezing operation neoclassical economists claim to perform through their standard invocation of the *ceteris paribus* formula. In short, talk of strategic choice without context or structure is a sure sign of positivist social science and naive historiography. Contextual factors are always there in a very real way; they are not present simply as passive constraints, marking an outer border or limit to action as a parameter would do, but actively discouraging certain courses of action while just as actively facilitating others.

5. Unger writes that "strategic calculation alone never suffices to tilt the scales

in favor of an unmistakably risky course of action." Thus, there is a need for a "visionary impulse," for the "formulating of a visionary language" (Unger 1987:430). Przeworski (1985) has shown very convincingly that socialism is not in the rational interest of workers; that is, that strategic calculations alone cannot be an adequate framework to deal with basic changes, regardless of whether our interest is programmatic or explanatory.

6. The most extensive project so far was sponsored by CLACSO. Together with the general volume, edited by Calderón G. (1986*b*), the project produced volumes on individual countries. There is the research, influenced by Laclau and sponsored in part by the Center for Documentation on Latin America, based in Amsterdam (Slater 1985*b*; Laclau 1985; Evers 1985), and the special issue on new social movements of the *Boletín de Estudios Latinoamericanos y del Caribe* 41 (December 1986). General efforts at conceptualizing social movements in the recent historical context include Boschi 1984; Evers 1985; Calderón G. 1986*a*, Eckstein 1989; and Touraine 1987. The latter is an ambitious attempt to conceptualize the linkages between social movements and the political system. See also Mainwaring 1987, and Boschi 1987. Only a few comparative studies on social movements within Latin America have been completed. See Castells 1982; Mainwaring and Viola 1984; R. Munck 1984.

7. This scenario, of course, fits some countries better than others. The "freezing" metaphor, quite useful in the case of Chile or Argentina, does not apply very well to Brazil (see Cavarozzi and Garretón 1989).

8. Fernando H. Cardoso writes, "It has caught my attention that the enormous revival of social strength in the last years . . . has moved, not to claim [*reivindicar*] the disintegration of the state, but rather to ask the state for . . . some action, at the local level, capable of offering to those that have nothing and desire a lot, something concrete" (F. Cardoso 1984*a*:29, my translation). A case can be made that part of the specificity of social movements in the Latin American context relates to the centrality of the state as a target of action. Rarely is business seen as the culprit, except in the case of foreign-owned businesses; instead the state is seen as responsible for just about everything that happens to popular groups. The state appears to be more visible, more tangible and present in Latin America than in Europe and especially the United States.

9. Cardoso has written some of the most stimulating passages on social movements, and their relationship to political parties and the state (F. Cardoso 1984*b*:50, 53–56). Cardoso is also one of the few well-known scholars critical of O'Donnell, Schmitter, and Whitehead's analysis of transitions from authoritarian rule, criticizing in particular their focus on divisions within authoritarian regimes as the primordial explanation of regime transformation. Not surprisingly, his writings stress the value of the autonomy of social movements, whereas O'Donnell, Schmitter, and Whitehead consider the push of social movements merely as instrumental for other processes of interest (F. Cardoso 1984*b*:51). Boschi has also indicated that "the role played by social forces from below in this process [of transition to democracy] is usually overlooked by those who emphasize instead the peaceful, gradual transition from the top down" (Boschi 1987:205).

10. Touraine, likewise, is blunt in stating that "democracy must be identified with the notion of representativity, above all." He thus accepts that there are "representable social actors, that is actors who are defined, organized, and capable of action *before* they have any channel of political representation" (Touraine 1988*b*:151, my emphasis). Laclau's understanding of the notion of interests is very different. Interests do not stand in a relationship of exteriority to anything and do not have the fixity postulated in conventional notions of representativity. For him, "political practice constructs the interests it represents" (Laclau and Mouffe 1985:20–21, 83–

84, 118–121). In other words, just as there is no representational theory of knowledge and language, interests are forged in and through the political process. He would have to disagree with Touraine's schema, which would be criticized on the same grounds as the Marxist theory of the vanguard party. It seems difficult, within Laclau's language, to conceptualize the linkage between political parties and social movements, except in a negative way conducive to a basist position that accentuates the risks of isolation of social movements.

11. See O'Donnell's discussion of the interaction between political and social conditions for the construction of political democracy in Brazil (O'Donnell 1988b:84).

12. These correspond to Mann's (1988:5–9) distinction between the state's infrastructural and despotic power, respectively.

13. Argentina and Brazil exemplify two of the main forms of transition from authoritarian rule, each divergent in terms of the strength of the authoritarian regime.

| | Regime Strength | | Transition | |
	Constructive Intervention	Repression	Form	Duration
Argentina	Low	High	Collapse	Short
Brazil	High	Moderate	Controlled	Long

The paradoxical assessment of the interaction between social movements and national politics, which is distinct for Argentina and for Brazil, is supported by O'Donnell. He emphasizes that in Argentina a greater degree of democratization of the state still leaves the recent democratic government vulnerable to an authoritarian regression by the "vía rápida" of a coup. In the case of Brazil, the greater authoritarian legacies at the level of the state make the new democracy more likely to suffer a "slow death," provoked by the progressive restriction of civil power (O'Donnell 1988a:49–52, 56–62).

This general hypothesis is intended to provoke ideas (where to look, what variables to consider, what dilemmas to stress). It points in the direction of a testable hypothesis, but refinement of the variables and further specification of the causal links are needed before that stage. These serve as markers to guide us through a complex theoretical and empirical terrain. The development of our knowledge on social movements and their interaction with national politics depends on an endeavor that goes back and forth between international comparison (as attempted here) and case studies on a regional basis, comparisons between different historical periods within a single nation (as in the rest of this book).

14. The transition really ends with the popular election of the president in November 1989.

15. The post-1973 Chilean military regime is an intermediate case. It is characterized by a high level of repression (as in Argentina), combined with a fairly controlled transition (closer to the case in Brazil than to that in Argentina), but on the basis of a failed experience to reformulate state-society relations on a positive ground to any important extent. Alongside the reemergence of old political parties in 1983, there are important signs of change in their behavior and their linkages with groups in civil society.

16. Guillermo O'Donnell, Philippe Schmitter, and Laurence Whitehead introduce social movements within the context of the "resurrection of civil society," following the dark night of military dictatorships and other forms of authoritarian rule, only to have them fit into an elegant game of elite pacts as bargaining chips in the hands of

political party leaders. In this scheme, for a successful transition to political democracy to occur, the first thing the all-important political parties must do is become "not so much agents of mobilization as instruments of social and political control," the reason being that popular demobilization is a precondition for the parties to enter into a series of elite-negotiated pacts to ensure a smooth and secure transition (O'Donnell, Schmitter, and Whitehead 1986:48–59). Strangely, whereas political democracy is held up as a newly discovered end in itself, social movements and grassroots organizations do not receive equal treatment. A practically exclusive focus on the nation-state, on politics at the national level, betrays the politicist bias. It is an extremely difficult task to disentangle biases in conceptual elaborations from the hard realities being described. It remains of utmost importance, however, to steer clear of "posing (because of certain fundamental assumptions) a fundamental state/society split." Boschi warns that this form of analysis has led to the problem, in the Brazilian literature on social movements, that "either it is assumed that a highly mobilized society exists from the bottom up, or that the society is manipulated by the state from the top down" (Boschi 1987:201).

17. Przeworski is eloquent in writing that "unfortunately authoritarian regimes often produce as a counterreaction the romanticization of a limited model of democracy. Struggle for political power is necessary. Yet what we need, and do not have, is a more comprehensive, integral, ideological project of antiauthoritarianism that would encompass the totality of life" (Przeworski 1986:63). Foucault's difficulty in articulating a political vision that goes beyond the level of microdespotisms is illustrative of some of the dilemmas confronted within this scenario (Connolly 1987:93–94; Poster 1989:30–33, 48–50, 61, 64–65). Manuel Castells explicitly addresses the issue of political strategy as faced by grassroots social movements. One of the limitations of the social movements he studied was their isolation, in geographic, social, and political terms. He warns us of the dangers of a communal utopia, which must be overcome by relating their activities of the overall process of political change (Castells 1982). Boschi (1987:183–184), likewise, provides a biting critique of the romantic ideal of "autonomous collectivism."

3

Popular Organization and Institutional Change

JOE FOWERAKER

DEFINING LINKAGE: AUTONOMY VERSUS REPRESENTATION

The linkages between popular organization and processes of institutional change are central to the interpretation of Mexican politics today. Yet there is no systematic study of these linkages in the literature. Research has tended to focus on the two poles of the relationship between popular struggle and the political system rather than on the relationship itself. This is owing to the conceptual problems posed by popular movements that aspire simultaneously to more autonomy and more representation. In my view this contradiction of terms is more apparent than real, and its resolution can reveal key aspects of the process of "linkage politics."[1]

Inquiries into popular autonomy often conflate suspicion of political parties with strategic caution toward state co-optation. Although it is true that the internal democratic procedures of popular movements will affect the degree of organizational independence of both parties and state,[2] a lateral autonomy of political parties is different from a vertical autonomy of the state; and although one has been the general rule, the other has not. Moreover, it is suggested that anything less than a complete autonomy of the state leads to the "constant destruction of democratic channels and spaces," which entails a defense of the strategic viability of popular movements "with restricted identity" (Zermeño 1987). Implicit here and elsewhere is a notion that popular struggles for material provision can be divorced from the realm of politics per se.[3] This mistaken impression finds fullest expression in Evers's (1985) Arcadian vision of popular experiments in social life as a "small-scale counterculture" uncontaminated by relations of political power.[4]

The reality is less comfortable. The political exclusion of popular organization may be increasing,[5] and where it is effective it will leave popular movements "condemned to sterility," especially where the movements have failed to secure affiliation to larger regional or national organizations (Marion S. 1987). For the same reasons attempts at independent syndicalism have prospered less than democratic currents within state syndical corporations. Hence an insistence on total popular autonomy suggests a "Jacobinism" (Laclau 1977) that seems unrealistic in the political conditions created by the historical success of state transformism (Foweraker 1988), which has consistently deepened and complicated the institutional penetration and control of Mexican civil society. In these conditions popular movements depend for their survival and success on the effective representation they can achieve, and on the ways their organization and strategy condition their insertion into the political system overall. The absolute quality of the concept of autonomy therefore prevents a more relative, more concrete, and more contingent approach to linkage politics.

Here I intend to develop just such an approach by combining conceptual inquiry with specific reference to the case of the teachers' movements within the SNTE (National Union of Workers in Education) during the decade of the 1980s. There are good reasons for focusing on this case in particular. First, teachers have traditionally acted as one of the principal "transmission belts" of the system overall and in their community roles are the living links that have allowed the PRI government to reproduce the kinds of consensus and consent that have been called "hegemonic." Second, the SNTE is one of the key corporate pieces of what I shall call the legal-institutional terrain, and its ubiquitous presence gives it a political projection not directly dependent on the federal bureaucracy. Third, and perhaps most important, the SNTE is strategically central to what Aziz Nassif (1987) has termed Mexico's "corporatist democracy" insofar as SNTE machinery and SNTE cadres have run electoral campaigns, mobilized the vote of the dominant PRI party, and controlled the voting booths. In other words, the SNTE (and the democratically organized teachers) link the two principal operational fields of the terrain, namely the corporative and the electoral, at a historical moment when their mutual influence and mutual incursions are becoming increasingly important to linkage politics.

Through the combination of conceptual inquiry with these empirical references I shall proceed to demonstrate that although popular movements may aspire to autonomy, they must seek to survive in the real world of institutional politics. Hence, every aspect of popular identity, organization, and mobilization will be influenced by institutional constraints and opportunities; equally, popular politics can only occur at all in intimate interrelation with state laws and institutions. These are the premises of *any* argument that aims to explore the impact of popular movements on processes of political change. Thus, however intense the theoretical debates about the nature or degrees of autonomy, it must be recognized that the real resolution of such debates only occurs in popular political practice, where popular actors face the continual political choices implicit in the construction of popular movements. In other words, if popular actors appear to have less difficulty than social scientists in understanding the problems of autonomy and linkage politics, it is because they face them as practical and everyday problems of survival and advance.

This becomes strikingly clear from a glance at the case materials. The teachers organizing within the teachers' movements have known how to avoid direct confrontation with the state when the balance of forces could not justify it and they have even been content to seek conjunctural alliances "with the apparatus."[6] In the early moments of the teachers' movement in Chiapas, demands for autonomy followed the denial of effective participation; but these demands were dropped once mass mobilization had impelled such participation. In this way, "autonomy" is intrinsic to the strategic and conjunctural variations implicit in popular struggle (Marván Laborde 1988) but never an absolute end in itself.

Equal care must be taken with the concept of representation, which can imply that interests are defined a priori in economic and social life and then "represented" at another level of society called the political (Laclau 1985), rather than being defined in the process of struggle itself. The clue here is given by Castells (1983), who suggests that popular movements are defined not by their social location but by the demands they generate (which unite the social actors within them). Thus, rather than focusing on the prepolitical life of interests, what matters are the demands that emerge from processes of popular organization and strategic invention. In this perspective, popular representation means pressing for demands that themselves relate increasingly to the nature and forms of linkage to the political system. Social and economic demands become political, and syndical struggles automatically take on political objectives. And not only because the state moves against the popular movements, but because the popular movements seek linkage with the political system (and struggle to get it on their own terms).

Once again, this is something the protagonists of popular struggle have clear. There must be an institutional insertion, a *capacidad de gestión*, which promotes a response to demands and a solution to problems. The alternative is the sterility of exclusion and an organizational decline following loss of confidence in popular leadership. But the negative terms of this equation include the charges of betrayal leveled against collaborationist strategies— and even against democratically elected popular leaders[7]—and the "institutional repression" and vertical control of popular organization, exercised most notoriously by the Revolutionary Vanguard[8] against the democratic teachers. On occasions, poorly calculated linkage politics leads to the division and disarticulation of the movement, as occurred with the teachers' movements in Chihuahua in the 1970s (Luna Jurado 1977) and in Morelos in the early 1980s.

In the syndical arena the phenomenon of *charrismo* condenses the contradictions of linkage politics. The corrupt clientelism created a network of syndical fiefdoms throughout the SNTE that exercised close control of principals, supervisors, and directors, as well as ensuring the political loyalty of the union's sectional executive committees. This complex and extensive *cacicazgo* seemed to present an insuperable obstacle to the teachers' movements precisely because it refused to take up their demands. But, equally, the movements gathered impetus whenever and wherever it became apparent that the official "representatives" had failed to represent these demands, and nearly every movement struggled to dismiss its sectional committee and elect a new and "democratic" one.[9] In other words, *charrismo* denies linkage, and popular struggle aims to establish or restore it (the first step for the teachers being the capture of the sectional committee). In analogous fashion, the mass mobilizations, marches, and sit-ins in Mexico City (by the National Coordinating Committee of Workers in Education, the CNTE, and by similar committees in other sectors) can be understood as popular struggle "leapfrogging" the institutional obstacles in order to claim direct linkage at the doors of the SNTE, the SEP (the Ministry of Education), or the Ministry of the Interior. Geography is merely the metaphor.

The teachers' movements advanced their struggles through the parallel organizations of the Central Struggle Committees, and insofar as they succeeded in wresting some control from the Vanguard and getting their problems solved in negotiation with the regional delegations of the SEP, then they had achieved "legality in practice." But a discussion document for the National Assembly of the CNTE in January 1982 (Salinas and Imaz Gispert 1984) recognized that this was not enough, and the objective at every moment had to be to "legalize the results of the struggle carried on for the democratization of the SNTE." This lesson had been learned in costly fashion in Morelos in March of the previous year, when the movement was cheated of its "democratic" congress. Only legal forms and statutory procedures could cement new measures of representation: legalizing political advances was the only way to achieve more effective linkages. The teachers' movement had recognized the inevitable institutionalism of popular-democratic struggle.

INSTITUTIONALISM AND THE LEGAL-INSTITUTIONAL TERRAIN

If autonomy is strategically unviable and politically unrealistic, the notion of "institutionalism" appears to return the debate to the political "participation" of the modernization paradigm. Where the teachers' movements failed to capture sectional committees, they nonetheless insisted on the institutional means for the broadest possible participation, including the participation of independent unions in the Labor Congress (Congreso de Trabajo). But when Manuel Hernández suggested smilingly from Cerro Hueco prison that the leaders of the movement in Chiapas "had been radicals," he clearly did not mean that they had come to accept the system, but rather that they had achieved a more modulated vision, firm in strategy but flexible in tactics. The movements now worked to democratize the legal apparatus of the SNTE, with the conquest of sectional committees as a prime objective. Thus, institutionalism does not reflect passive participation so much as the projection of grassroots change into the political system, where it can find more permanent expression. In other words, institutionalism reflects conscious choice and strategic action. Moreover, as grassroots change will not automatically entail broader political changes (Mainwaring 1987), such action must require changes in the legal and institutional relationships of the political system itself.

Educational decentralization came about in response to popular struggle, and by rupturing lines of vertical control, and so prizing the mass of teachers from the grip of their traditional syndical leaders, the project also came to catalyze this struggle (Street 1984). In short, at the same time that the SEP was tightening the bureaucratic links between its federal apparatus and regional delegations, the Revolutionary Vanguard encountered increasing difficulties of centralized control, so unsettling the delicate balance of force between the SEP and the SNTE at state level. Both this temporary effect and the more permanent reform clearly demonstrate the capacity of the popular movement not merely to influence the federal conjuncture, but also to condition the institutional configuration of the system.

These optimistic claims do not deny the contrary case that popular movements are equally shaped, and sometimes co-opted, by the system In my view, this is just as inevitable as the institutionalism of the movements themselves. If it is true that "popular-democratic struggle is first of all a struggle to form the 'people,' before it is a struggle between the 'people' and 'officialdom' (Jessop 1980), then the state will often lead this process of formation. Whether this is a good or bad thing is not a question of principle but of conjuncture and strategy. In illustration it is clear that the first democratic councils of the teachers' movements, designed to cement the alliance between teachers and parents, were formed through the municipal education committees of the SEP, which sought to extend its lines of vertical control. In this connection it must be stressed that, in this as in every democratic struggle, institutional *form* is as important as institutional content, if not more so (Foweraker 1989*b*).

Sadly for some, there is little in this perspective to encourage either "satanization" of the state or glorification of the popular movements. Kowarick (1985) has noticed how the state comes to be seen as "the perverse agent of the social drama," whereas popular movements are seen to engage in struggles of "increasingly superior quality." In fact, just as popular movements promise no utopian future (and certainly not a socialist one), so Mexico's *democracia bárbara* compares favorably with most other political regimes across the continent over the past thirty years. So it is important to suspend political judgment and recognize that popular struggles are limited in their aims and constrained in their political scope. This is simply to assert that popular movements struggle in conditions which are not of their own choosing, and have to struggle in order to modify those conditions, defined in the first place by the legal and institutional terrain that links civil society and the state.

The notion of legal-institutional terrain is broader than that of Stepan's "political society" (Stepan 1988), as well as less constitutionally oriented and more sensitive to the balance of forces in society at large.[10] Popular struggle has to take place here if only because there is nowhere else. But this does not mean, as Zermeño (1987) seems to suggest, that all popular initiatives must meet an equal fate in the procrustean bed of state laws and institutions. On the contrary, this is above all a strategic terrain continuously shifting under the impact of both popular organization and state initiatives. On the one hand, the state is a nonmonolithic institutional ensemble constantly engaged in internal organization and reorganization; and these internal relations (between executive and syndical corporations, for instance) are often pseudolegal, nonconstitutional, and nonnormative.[11] On the other, popular movements mobilize to create and exploit those opportunities for strategic advance that have often been called "political spaces."

Laclau (1985) talks of popular movements articulating a plurality of concrete demands, and so promoting a proliferation of political spaces. But the effect is unlikely to be this direct because political spaces require new institutional relationships. It is true that the teachers' movements were occasionally recognized as "valid interlocutors" by the SEP in a way that would have been inconceivable in the 1950s; but such recognition depended not only on the movements' capacity for mobilization and intrinsic success in weakening *charrismo*, but also on the breaches that had opened up between SEP and SNTE at the state level as a result of educational decentralization. Moreover, the disputes between administrative (SEP) and syndical (SNTE) personnel, and the bureaucratic disruption that was both cause and consequence of them, actually provoked popular organization and struggle in several instances. Thus political spaces reflect institutional shifts and changing government priorities and hence are inherently unstable: Echeverría's attempt to ally with the alternative leadership of the electricians ended with military intervention; Reyes Heroles's encouragement of the teachers' movements ended with SEP and SNTE combining to tighten legal and institutional control throughout the national territory. Even acquiring a degree of legal recognition, or success in "negotiating the institutionalization of opposition" (Salinas and Imaz Gispert 1984), provides no political guarantees, as was clear when the National Executive Committee of the SNTE dismissed "democratic" sectional committees by the simple expedient of refusing to convoke a congress and so revoking their mandate.

What finally configures the legal and institutional terrain, therefore, is the "war of position" (Gramsci 1971) in all its organizational and strategic variations; the linkages between popular organization and the political system are only as stable and predictable as the results of the war itself. But rather than leave the question there, I want to proceed to a more differentiated analysis of the terrain and focus on the moments (organizational, strategic, conjunctural, and geopolitical) that most affect the political and strategic choices taken by popular movements. I shall continue the inquiry with reference to the SNTE and the teachers' movements, not least because they will be seen to have a special relevance to the subsequent discussion of the relationship between popular movements and *neocardenismo*.

LEGAL-INSTITUTIONAL TERRAIN AND WAR OF POSITION

Each PRI government administration of the past twenty years has taken major initiatives to shape the legal-institutional terrain to its own advantage. Echeverría's political opening aimed to revitalize the role of the PRI's syndical corporations, whereas López Portillo's political reform and de la Madrid's moral renovation switched the strategic emphasis to the electoral arena. Over the short term these initiatives seemed successful. Despite Echevería's reverses, the syndical policies of the 1970s bound many independent unions to the corporate bias of government through the incentives and sanctions contained within the Labor Congress (where even recalcitrant syndical tendencies found a margin of political maneuver);[12] and if the political reform did not finally divide the electoral left, it did considerable damage to the cohesion of at least some popular movements.[13] But the central change, the strategic displacement of the priority channels of "representation" from the corporative to the electoral arena, was to prove counterproductive.

In the meantime the struggle over the terms of political representation was unremitting. Wherever the teachers' movements advanced, the SNTE/SEP attempted to reduce authentic majority representation to the status of a dissident minority. This well-tried tactic had turned the tables in Guerrero, Hidalgo, and the Valle de México by the end of February 1981, where the SNTE retained its sectional committees despite their rejection by the majority of teachers (the few committee posts conceded in each case not offending the purposes of the political reform). Such tactics were effective insofar as they were supported by constant institutional intimidation, not to mention more informal campaigns of verbal and physical abuse. Institutional responses included inaction, disinformation, and broken pledges, as in the extraordinary episode in Morelos where the secretary general of the SNTE falsified his own signature to an agreement, and later denied he had been present for the signing. But these nonnormative and pseudolegal demarches were combined with major administrative initiatives[14] in order to contain popular insurgency while maintaining institutional cohesion.

The tactics designed to disarticulate and disperse popular organization range from the brutal to the refined and compose a complex and traditionally effective *juego de desgaste*.[15] But if the game is well known, it has usually been characterized as zero-sum (a question of elimination or survival), whereas I see it as a question of advance or retreat. In other words PRI government tactics are condensed in a strategy of the "institutionalization" of popular struggle, which is inscribed in the inevitable institutionalism of this struggle. Kowarick is right to suggest that "state bureaucracies give rise to conflicts and demands which are structured in such a way as to dilute and segment . . . multiple groups in their actions to conquer wider socioeconomic and political space" (Kowarick 1985); but every state initiative which increases the legal and institutional density of the legal-institutional terrain not only extends the political constraints on popular movements but also multiplies their strategic opportunities for achieving more advantageous forms of linkage.

POPULAR MOVEMENTS AND WAR OF POSITION

Popular struggle (recalling Przeworski 1977) is first of all a struggle to constitute the "people" within its own organizations,[16] and the eventual form of these organizations contributes to condition the nature of the linkages between popular movements and the political system. Very often the principles of organization are directly democratic to ensure an accountable leadership that cannot be co-opted, and decentralized to promote close enough contact between base and leadership to prevent division. In the case of the teachers' movements, such organizational forms were both pragmatic (seeking to resolve syndical questions close to their point of origin) and political, with the vigilance committees designed to prevent the insidious separation between grassroots and leadership as existed in the SNTE itself. On the evidence, active engagement of an organized base was more effective in stopping quick decapitation of the movements than in preventing internal divisions, which were often exacerbated by assembly-led democratic mechanisms.[17]

Popular movements are not the political expression of some pristine democratic demiurge and are permeated by ideological disputes and political confrontations that reflect internal power struggles. Such internal struggles provide much of the energy and impetus of the movements and so, at the very least, are a necessary evil; but insofar as different factions compete for the loyalty of the base there is a clear potential for division and decline, with the movement at the mercy of the machinations of government. This tendency was dramatically demonstrated in the fate of the teachers' movement in Chihuahua (Luna Jurado 1977), and has afflicted every teachers' movement in greater or lesser degree, as different factions fight for the negotiating space (*capacidad de gestión*) that may give them hegemony within the movement. Indeed, leadership disputes often turned on the question of institutionalism, with basist and ultrademocratic leaders seeing any contact with the state as betrayal, and moderate and "verticalist" leaders seeing negotiation as necessary to the resolution of demands. The debate both within and outside the teachers' movements on the relative efficacy of the two leadership styles still continues,[18] but what is beyond doubt is the crucial influence this factional infighting has had on the definition of political strategies.

Two key choices define the strategic thrust of the popular movements: first, the decision to work within the syndical corporations of the state, or with its administrative agencies (institutionalism and the promotion of linkage); second, the search for strategic alliances (combating state transformism or assuaging the effects of linkage). The teachers' movements adopted both strategies simultaneously, knowing the necessity for a *capacidad de gestión* and seeking to broaden resistance to institutional repression. In previous analysis of these strategies (Foweraker 1988), I may have confused formal possibilities with real achievements, and it is important to emphasize that alliances of national scope were always politically precarious and lacking organizational capacity. The teachers' movements in the CNTE were important to the rise of these national coordinating committees over the years of intense formation from 1976 to 1982,[19] but were finally left quite isolated from other popular struggles (partly because their alliance strategy was never well defined). At the same time, it must be recognized that the alliances never sought organization so much as mobilization, which was the essential complement to the institutionalism of the movements and graphically described by the Proletarian Tendency as "negotiations in Paris, war in Vietnam."[20] In other words, even where legal linkage is the final goal, the political advances must be impelled by the pressure of mobilization. But as mobilization mainly occurs around particular issues and demands, the rhythm of this part of popular struggle tends to be conjunctural.

This conjunctural trajectory of the teachers' movements is notorious, and corresponds not only to the evolution of their own demands and strategies but also to shifts in the internal relationships of the state itself. Thus, the rise of the movements reflects the dissatisfaction in sectors of the federal bureaucracy with the prepotent position of Jonguitud, the "leader-for-life" of the Revolutionary Vanguard, and (after June 1980) the confrontation between SEP and SNTE, especially at the regional level, over educational decentralization (see above). These conflicts were overdetermined in the states where the movements were strongest (Chiapas and Oaxaca) by state governments with little commitment to the SNTE and still less to the Revolutionary Vanguard.[21] The implicit support given to the movements also coincided with a moment when the state was still pursuing a strategy of co-optation, or one that could turn the movements to its own ends (including educational decentralization); the movements took advantage to achieve their first democratic sectional committee. Furthermore, the rise of the movement in Oaxaca sees the first intervention by the Ministry of the Interior, in implicit recognition that the SNTE is failing to fulfill its traditional task of mediation (once the disputes between SEP and SNTE become public). As the teachers' movements become national in scope, and the conflicts intensify in Morelos, Hidalgo, and the Valle de México, this ministry intervenes more comprehensively in their negotiations with the SEP and the SNTE. Its concern is to clear the streets, but the result is to complicate the question of institutional cohesion and, by extension, the calculation of strategic choices.

In large measure this favorable conjuncture was the creation of Reyes

Heroles's reform project, which sought to combine administrative modernization with an attack on syndical *caciquismo*.[22] In the case of the SNTE, Heroles's plan was to wrest power from Jonguitud by creating many new "decentralized" cadres that would owe him no loyalty and no favors. But the conjuncture changed rapidly with the death of Heroles and the electoral rebellion in the north, and the new minister, González Avelar, sought a rapid realignment with the SNTE in order to reassert electoral control in Chihuahua, Sonora, and Sinaloa (and to protect his own presidential ambitions). At the same time, the movements lost the benign state governments that gave them succor in their chief regional bases of social support (Chiapas and Oaxaca) and, with the "institutionalist" strategy deadlocked, focused again on economic demands in the face of a PRI government now fully committed to its austerity program. Institutional realignment within the state had changed the conjuncture and so restricted the movements' possibilities for political advance. But both favorable and unfavorable conjunctures were conditioned in some degree by popular mobilization, first in the South, and then in the North.

The teachers' movements themselves were never a single movement, but many movements with different trajectories and different forms of struggle rooted in the specific conditions of different regional contexts. On the one hand, this heterogeneity was an effect of the legal-institutional terrain, which was itself not uniform. The SNTE was inserted differentially into specific systems of local and regional power (*cacicazgos*), through different types of political alliance, so that, under the pressure of popular mobilization, some of its forms of mediation entered into crisis but others hardly at all. In particular, with the educational decentralization, there are growing frictions between the Revolutionary Vanguard and several bureaucratic cliques over municipal presidencies and state deputyships, especially in openly hostile states where governors rejected the permanent presence of another governor (Jonguitud, who was governor of San Luis Potosí at the time) in their territory. On the other, a certain localism and regionalism was inscribed in the movements' intrinsic principles of organization, which defended the local base against the "center"—the Revolutionary Vanguard—while the PRI government did all it could to keep the movements regionally separate (and repress regionally while staying silent nationally). The result was that the CNTE could achieve no national strategy except a minimum agreement to win its economic demands and retrieve the SNTE for the grassroots, and had to proceed tactically on the basis of regional autonomy. This unequal development of the movements was not a fatal weakness, no more than the inability to construct a permanent national leadership; but there is no doubt that it led to a certain lack of political initiative, and, in particular, to a poor appreciation of the strategic advantage of the interbureaucratic wrangles within the state. And this is probably true a fortiori of other popular movements with aspirations to national coordination.

INSTITUTIONALISM AND INSTITUTIONAL CHANGE

Despite the teachers movements' sometimes extraordinary political mobilizations, it is evident that the PRI government had succeeded in imposing agreements that had effectively institutionalized the struggle. This is just one instance of a general process, which has created new forms of linkage with the state. But just as popular movements have become institutionalized, so they, in turn, "have had a decisive impact on the forms and margins of maneuver of state institutions" (Marván Laborde 1988). By way of example, Marván Laborde cites the impact of the syndical "insurgency" of the 1970s on the renovation of official syndicalism at the end of that decade. But although general accounts of popular movements have nearly always emphasized the importance of their capacity to affect the state and have insisted that "state reorganization is an essential element in popular democratic struggles" (Jessop 1980), they give no clear indication of how this must occur. Indeed, they often admit that there is no necessary connection between changes in social relations at the grassroots and institutional change within the state (Mainwaring 1987). Here the emphasis has been on institutionalism, meaning the incremental negotiation and renegotiation of the links between popular movements and the dominant institutions of national life, and the way this process is conditioned by organization, strategy, conjuncture, and geopolitics. In other words, it is in seeking and shaping their linkage with the political system that popular movements have contributed to change its institutional configuration, and this process begins at the grassroots.[23] In this perspective, it is redundant to ask whether the Mexican political system can change because it has been changing for at least fifteen years.

This process of change is not exactly subterranean, but it is not often signaled by spectacular effects. On the contrary, it is specific, differentiated, and gradual, and so can pass almost unperceived. Elsewhere I have characterized the process in terms of the conflictual decomposition of traditional forms of political brokerage and control, and the institutional affirmation of more centralized and concerted forms of political mediation[24]— in an effort to discern the direction of institutional change (Foweraker 1989a). But what matters here is that this is a general process underpinning more dramatic political initiatives, as well as giving the lie to more apocalyptic readings of Mexican politics.

Among these, Cammack's (1988) stands out for its radical assertion of the "Brazilianization" of Mexico. In this view, the PRI regime depends on a monopoly of resource allocation, and any reform that infringes the monopoly automatically destabilizes the system. Thus liberalization measures have had the opposite effect of those intended because they are incompatible with the fundamental nature of the regime; and, in particular, by opening political spaces to opposition activity without conceding positions of power, they have hastened the loss of legitimacy to the point of political hemorrhage. The liberalization project, says Cammack, is "self-contradictory."

At any time in the past several years this statement might have been dismissed as being too abstract, as contriving to ignore real processes of political struggle, and as leaping to general judgment from one particular area of political activity. But the general elections of July 1988 demand a reassessment of the liberalization of electoral politics, which is Cammack's focus and which was seen above as the strategic displacement of political representation from the corporative to the electoral arena. But now it is not simply a question of whether the PRI has shot itself in the foot. On the contrary, the vertiginous rise to electoral prominence of the National Democratic Front once again emphasizes the political dynamism of Mexican civil society. But in what sense? Was the front the privileged vehicle for the entry of popular movements into the electoral arena? If so, there is at least a theoretical possibility that electoral *neocardenismo* will overdetermine linkage politics across the range of organized popular contact with the political system and condense the institutionalism of popular movements into some version of party politics.

POPULAR MOVEMENTS AND ELECTORAL POLITICS

There is no doubt that the most recent (conjunctural) rise in the rhythm of popular organization and mobilization coincided with the emergence of the Democratic Current and its split from the PRI. Indeed, the election year was ushered in by the first mass mobilization of the National Front for Mass Organizations in Mexico City. Nor is there any doubt that the current itself was in some sense a response to popular mobilization, insofar as electoral protests in the north spawned the Democratic Electoral Movement (bringing together both left and right of the political spectrum), which catalyzed the formation of the Current. Moreover, most commentators (e.g., Tamayo, this volume) suggest that 1988 saw a crucial change in the response of popular movements to electoral politics. For the first time the movements were prepared to ally with political parties, if only to prevent the right wing from capitalizing on discontent in the electoral arena (Ramírez Saiz 1987c). Leaders of urban popular movements themselves ran as candidates to Congress and, in Mexico City, to the Assembly of the Federal District. Furthermore, the different movements' incursions into electoral politics coalesced around the nationalist and progressive platform of the National Democratic Front, which itself called for the electoral convergence of the popular opposition. Hence, by the time Cuauhtémoc Cárdenas himself admitted that the "popular response has overtaken the front," it seemed undeniable that the front had become the principal political expression of the popular movements.

Nevertheless, there are reasons to be skeptical of this conclusion. In the first place, the PRI had been suffering a secular decline in electoral support for many years before the arrival of the front. The PRI is now a conservative party, and in Mexico (Torres 1987) just as surely as in Brazil (Soares 1986) rising levels of industrialization, urbanization, and literacy had slowly eroded the social bases of conservative politics. In other words, the PRI vote is concentrated in rural areas that no longer carry the same weight in general elections, so by 1985, in conditions of increasing abstention, it won the votes of just 31.1 percent of the electorate. In the second place, in a "liberalized" electoral system that has increasingly offered "participation without representation," opposition voting in Mexico, just as surely as in the Brazil of the seventies, had taken on a plebiscitary character. In other words, voting did not take place in order to gain representation and influence PRI policies, but to protest against the policies; not to change the government, but to demand that the government change itself. On both counts, it seems plausible that the front captured an opposition vote that was "already there" among the disaffected middle classes of the major cities of the country rather than providing an electoral vehicle for the popular movements. Equally, the historically unprecedented abstention rate of almost 50 percent may have recorded the politicization of grassroots social actors through widespread popular mobilization.

In this connection, it is worth insisting on the corporative nature of popular movements, which have generally defended or extended sectoral or neighborhood interests rather than addressing general interests in the electoral arena (Ramírez Saiz 1987c). Although the politics of the corporative and electoral arenas are not mutually exclusive (as the PRI has long since demonstrated), the evidence for popular political "crossover" is still very spotty. Therefore it is likely that the impact of popular movements in the electoral arena is still indirect and achieved mainly by the wedge they have driven into the corporatist flank of the PRI's "corporatist democracy." In particular, it is almost certain that a decade of struggle by the teachers' movements has damaged irreparably the capacity of the SNTE to mobilize and deliver the vote in the way it always did in the past, and this made Jonguitud's promise of eight million votes for the PRI candidate appear completely unrealistic (*Proceso*, February 22, 1988). At the same time, the massive participation of popular movements in the campaigns of protest against electoral manipulation has raised the political costs of electoral fraud, and has made it more difficult. In this way, popular movements have dramatically reduced the PRI's ability to manage the electoral arena, but not necessarily because they have invaded it. In short, although the movements may not have found political expression in the front, they may indeed have created its electoral opportunities. To put it another way, free elections will be the result and not the starting point of democratic struggle.

There is no suggestion here that the front did not attract some votes from members of popular movements. The mobilizations that accompanied the campaign and the popular protests over the electoral results make it clear that it did. But it cannot be considered an organic political expression of the popular movements, and still less was it a grand popular movement itself (as some have suggested). On the contrary, in the narrow sense it is a PRI initiative, or at least a top-down initiative, which has responded to popular demands for a free vote and a nationalist response to economic crisis. Its project is therefore quintessentially populist insofar as it promises a return to the golden age of revolutionary politics, and this nostalgia confirms its populism. Lázaro Cárdenas has returned from the dead to purify the revolutionary project. This may or may not be a good thing. There is a clear convergence between the demands of popular movements and the program of the front (now the Party of the Democratic Revolution, or PRD) around opposition to PRI austerity policies and, in particular, the supine response to the demands of foreign bankers. But a populist project like *janismo* in the Brazil of the 1960s or *aprismo* in the Peru of the 1980s could lead the popular movements into a political cul-de-sac that would limit their hopes of institutional advance. No doubt the Party of the Democratic Revolution will aim to construct a permanent political force from the electoral conjuncture of July 1988, while the popular movements will remain engaged in a range of "institutionalist" struggles. But the relationship between them is still an open question. In the meantime we should exercise caution before canonizing Cuauhtémoc and "satanizing" the reform initiatives of Salinas.

NOTES

1. I have (mis)appropriated this term from the title of J. Rosenau's edited volume on *Linkage Politics*.
2. This is not only a question of *external* relationships. The role of political (party) groups *inside* popular movements has been a matter of intense debate within the movements themselves. In this chapter I shall be referring to the case of the teachers' movements, where the influence of such groups has been mediated by the action of the central struggle committees, which scrutinize all political projects and initiatives that then must be approved in open assembly. The movements' democratic procedures therefore mitigate the influence of party programs and prevent capture by partisan interests. Controls of this kind are never complete, however, and most movements have suffered from some form of factional infighting. I return to this particular question below, in the discussion of popular movements and war of position. The general question of party-movement relations is also relevant to later discussion of the rise of the National Democratic Front (FDN).
3. This is tantamount to divorcing the struggles of "particular peoples" from those of the "people in general" (or what Rousseau might have called "the general interest"). In popular-democratic theory these are the same struggle "since the extension of democratic control requires the creation of specific material and social conditions favorable to the exercise of various formal freedoms" (Jessop 1980).
4. Evers asserts that "the innovating capacity of these movements appears to lie less in their political potential than in their ability to create and experiment with different forms of social relations in everyday life. . . . Their potential is mainly not one of power, but of renewing socio-cultural and socio-psychic patterns of everday social relations, penetrating the microstructures of society." But Foucault would see this process as central to the question of political power, which always rests on the "moving substrate of force relations" (Foucault 1978), and which finally refers to "a complex strategical situation within a particular society." Compare chapter 15 of my *Making Democracy in Spain* (Foweraker 1989*b*).
5. Carr makes the point that with the continuing economic crisis the problem for

government is not how to include a greater part of the "working class," but how to exclude it (Carr 1983a). I develop the point in Foweraker 1989a.

6. As Manuel Hernández wrote in *Germen*, a publication of the Chiapas teachers movement (Hernández 1982), "we feel that present circumstances in Mexico and the correlation of political forces argue in favor of our negotiating with the government at the national and state levels, and that our position that the rank and file must hold the power of decision in our various organizational structures serves as a guarantee that the leadership will not enter into accords without prior consultation with the membership, especially if such agreements threaten the consolidation and advance of our movement."

7. Compare Salinas and Imaz Gispert (1984), who censure the first democratic leadership of the teachers' movement in Chiapas for their unilateral agreement of November 1980 with the National Executive Committee of the SNTE. Although the agreement ensured the election of a democratic sectional committee, it allowed the SNTE to control the mass mobilization and reassert its own agenda. Salinas and Imaz Gispert blame the dominant faction, Proletarian Tendency, and its strategy of privileging negotiation with the SNTE leadership. In my view, their critique is too "purist" and ignores key questions of tactics and strategy.

8. For information on the Revolutionary Vanguard, and detailed explanation of syndical *charrismo* in general, see the chapter by Francisco Pérez Arce in this book.

9. Only the main sections of Chiapas and Oaxaca actually got this far. In other states, sectional congresses to elect new sectional committees were promised but then denied.

10. "By 'political society' in a democratizing setting I mean that arena in which the polity specifically arranges itself for political contestation to gain control over public power and the state apparatus. . . . [A] full democratic transition must involve political society, and the composition and consolidation of a democratic polity must entail serious thought and action about those core institutions of a democratic political society—political parties, elections, electoral rules, political leadership, intra party alliances, and legislatures—through which civil society can constitute itself politically to select and monitor democratic government" (Stepan 1988).

11. Changing relations between the federal executive and the syndical corporations express important shifts in the terrain: In the early 1970s independent syndicalism meant parallel syndicalism (as in the democratic tendency of the electricians' syndicate), but after 1978 *charrismo* was constructed as consensual, and independent unions began to participate in the Labor Congress.

12. The CNTE, the STUNAM, Volkswagen, the National Retirees Movement, and many smaller independent unions came together on the Forum for Union Cooperation in order to make more effective use of the Labor Congress for their own purposes.

13. The reform came to damage the teachers' movements by the divisions it encouraged between nonpartisan central struggle committees and party political groups, which sometimes left the movements vulnerable to state offensives.

14. For example, the Ley de Servicios de Segunda Carrera, part of the grand plan of educational decentralization that seeks to destroy the cohesion of the teachers' movements by creating different categories of teachers with different wage levels and privileges. This initiative also conforms to the broad strategy of consolidating state-SNTE positions while isolating and dispersing local and regional struggles.

15. This phrase has no direct translation into English, but refers to the gradual "wearing down" or exhaustion of the enemy implicit in siege or trench warfare. It was precisely this kind of warfare Gramsci (1971) wished to invoke in his concept of "war of position."

16. Thus the teachers' movement in Morelos at first directed all its efforts toward the teachers themselves, to gain recognition as their legitimate representatives, before confronting the SNTE and affirming its own organization through what Touraine calls the "principle of opposition."

17. Compare note 2 above, which explores the opposite view that internal

democratic mechanisms work to prevent factionalism.

18. Some argue that a comparative approach to the teachers' movements reveals that moderate leaderships won important concessions more radical leaderships failed to achieve. Others reply that the relationship between moderation and concession is spurious and suggest that what really differentiates the success of movements is the varying strength and violence of the official response to democratic initiatives. In Sections 7, 9, and 11 of Mexico City, and in the Valle de México, the *charro* leadership reacted especially violently, and even carried out assassinations, to prevent the teachers contaminating other sectors of organized labor in the industrial heartland of the country; the harshly repressive reactions in Guerrero and Hidalgo were conditioned by the contingencies (Governor Figueroa in Guerrero) and specificities of those political contexts.

19. These years see the formation of the National Front Against Repression, 1977; the National Coordinating Committee "Plan de Ayala" (CNPA), 1979; the CNTE, December 1979; the National Coordinating Committee of the Urban Popular Movement (CONAMUP), May 1981; and the National Union Coordinating Committee (COSINA), January 1982. These national coordinating committees have organized joint demonstrations, such as that between the CNTE and the CNPA in May 1981, and between the CNTE and the COSINA in March 1982.

20. The internal organization of the teachers' movements encouraged the direct participation of their adherents and catalyzed successive mobilizations. Even where the movements had achieved some form of legal representation, it was nearly always through mobilization that they won their demands, and especially wage rises and bigger cost-of-living bonuses. (The official leadership of the SNTE continued to argue, on the contrary, that any such successes were the result of legal representation.) Documents of the FMIN (National Independent Teachers Front), which directed the movement in the Valle de México, suggest that this was a clearly conceived combination of legal and extralegal struggle, but the logistical limits of most movements anyway favored recurrent mobilization over increasing organization.

21. In Chiapas the movement was initially supported by interim governor Juan Sabines, who belonged to the clique of fellow *chiapaneco* Edgar Robledo Santiago, which had run the SNTE prior to 1972; the movement in Oaxaca also benefited from divisions within the sectional leaders of the SNTE and the state governor (and between these same leaders and the SEP delegation). In both cases, the political space at state level was reinforced by the minister of the interior, Olivares Santana, who was also associated with the Robledo Santiago group.

22. Reyes Heroles saw that any effective "political reform" would entail confrontation with syndical caciques, and he confronted not only Jonguitud, but also Joaquín Hernández Galicia of the oil workers' syndicate. His career now appears as a historical dress rehearsal for Salinas's present assault on the feudal bastions of syndical power, which is the beginning of the political battle he most needs to win. In this perspective, Salinas is something of a Henry VII figure, battling with feudal barons in order to achieve autarchy. Henry, however, had gunpowder that the barons still lacked; Salinas enjoys no such material advantage.

23. This point is worthy of emphasis. The newly democratic forms of organization within the teachers' movements, for example, changed the point of linkage from the supervisor and director to the teacher in the school, because now the democratic assembly takes syndical decisions, rather than the supervisor and the delegational committee. By extension, this changes the whole chain of linkage from bottom up, including the relations between SEP and SNTE at state level, while the institutional control of the SEP itself is undermined by increasing representation within the syndicate (Street 1983).

24. A perfect example of this is the educational decentralization project itself, which is in fact highly centralizing in its political effects. The old, decomposing syndical-administrative controls are substituted by others directly incorporated into state educational institutions (so reducing the distance between "rulers" and "ruled").

4

Legal Constraints and Mobilization Strategies in the Countryside

ANN L. CRAIG

In August 1936, early in the administration of President Lázaro Cárdenas, Mexican attention was riveted on a massive general strike in the Comarca Lagunera. After months of unsuccessful negotiations, agricultural workers struck against employers over a complex range of demands. Urban workers joined in sympathy strikes. Militant political party activists (from the Communist party) and state-linked organizations (such as the National Committee for Proletarian Defense, CNDP) also took part in the popular mobilizations that led to the strike.

How can we explain the formation of labor unions in the Laguna? Can this case help us to explain the occurrence of popular movements that cross the boundary between countryside and city, peasant[1] and worker?

The Laguna strike was not an isolated instance of CNDP mobilization of a broad working-class front, although it was clearly among the most dramatic examples of such mobilization (Carr 1987; León 1977). Moreover, political exchanges between urban and rural workers preceded the strike by more than a decade in this region as well as in parts of Veracruz (Salamini 1978), Tlaxcala (Buve 1975), and Jalisco (Craig 1983). My effort to explain these several occurrences of popular movements that combine rural and urban populations brought me to the Laguna as the best-documented case of rural-urban linkages that emerge autonomously within civil society, as well as under the aegis of national political institutions.

The Laguna may not be "typical" of Mexico, but it certainly has been politically important. There is no doubt that it is a key region for understanding the relative power of popular movements in Mexican politics in the 1930s as well as the 1980s (and the years in between). Before the revolution and since, the Laguna has remained a center of political resistance and popular mobilization. Although we must be cautious about generalizing from the Laguna about the intensity of popular movements elsewhere in the country and about militant opposition-party vanguardism in popular rural struggles, we can use the Laguna to explore strategic choices taken in particular rural contexts and the organizational form of some rural political struggles. Most especially, the Laguna affords an opportunity to develop an explanation for the conditions under which popular movements form alliances among rural and urban organizations, and between these and national political parties and institutions.

Given the distinctive political economy of the Laguna, one might be tempted to explain the union struggle and the alliance between urban and rural groups in the region as a case of class-driven conflict between relatively advanced capitalist enterprises and an increasingly "proletarianized" labor force. The economic context was important. It focused state and political leaders' and organizations' attention on the region. It influenced local resources for responding to popular movements. And economic crisis contributed to popular grievances. But I will argue that in the Laguna, as elsewhere in Mexico in the first third of the twentieth century, the choice of *form* of organization and statement of grievances is not primarily a reflection of class consciousness or group identity. Instead, organization form and stated grievances result from the interaction between local leadership and state policy, including legislation and state practices for administering laws. In this way, the establishment of formal union activity occurred as the result of changes in the political environment in which popular mobilization could occur. But, the selection of the Laguna as a locus of organization by the Communist party and reformist elements within the ruling coalition, and the rapid expansion of popular participation can only be explained as the result of the economic significance of the region, the strategic choices of the leadership (both regional and national), and the history of political mobilization there.

My argument emphasizes the legal and institutional context within which grassroots organizations emerged and took action in the Laguna between 1918 and 1936, but it is an argument I contend can be sustained in other time periods and regions as well. Regionally, these years circumscribe the emergence, consolidation, and peak strength of militant unions and the intermittent collaboration between rural and urban popular organizations. Nationally, this period could be extended to 1938, at which point national corporatist institutions (the Mexican Labor Confederation and the National Peasant Confederation) began to close the space for independent organization or double militance within parties of the left and official popular organizations.

During this period (referred to hereafter as the 1920s and 1930s), radical activists saw themselves engaged in the construction of a new tomorrow. Labor unions and peasant organizations hoped that they would be able to work independently of the controls of their employers, and they struggled for rights defined in law. In some parts of Mexico, these ambitions were reflected in mass mobilizations and horizontal alliances among workers, peasants, and low-income urban residents. In limited localities and for brief moments, they shared political projects they pursued through strikes, electoral mobilizations, and the formation of multisectoral organizations and one broad national front (the National Committee for the Proletarian Defense). This effervescence of organizations preceded the consolidation of a state corporatist project and capitalized on a divided political elite. This context provides some interesting parallels, but also some sharp contrasts, with the situation in which contemporary popular movements must struggle in Mexico. The comparisons are made throughout this chapter, and also in the concluding chapter.

LAWS AND POLITICAL INSTITUTIONS IN THE COUNTRYSIDE

After the revolution, changes in the federal and state government laws opened up political spaces that sanctioned the formation of labor unions and gradually broadened the national pool of peasants eligible to petition for land reform. Laws and the practices for administering them influenced the *institutional form* which popular organizations assumed, as well as the *discourse* or form in which grievances could be expressed. Grassroots movements emerged around particularized, local political and economic grievances. Legislation indicated which of the grievances authorities might be prepared to support. When grassroots movements became formal organizations, their agenda was often cast in language legitimized by law. Despite the legal inducements and constraints (see Collier and Collier 1979), however, rural and urban organizations did not encounter consistent state support for autonomous or state-affiliated grassroots organizations. The state's arbitrary use of law contributed to popular decisions to establish linkages with other popular movements for mutual support and protection. Local popular groups also accepted initiatives of individuals and institutions, some of them clientelist or cacical ties, where these might ensure support and respect for the law (see Craig 1983; Friedrich 1970; Katz 1988b).

For radical activists during the 1920s and early 1930s, legislative changes and governmental use of law established the fluctuating formal boundaries within which they tried to build relatively independent popular political organizations. Formal legislation did not translate *directly* into the expansion of popular mobilization, nor into the development of autonomous grassroots organizations. (Were this the case, we would find very similar patterns of political organization within sectors or geographic areas covered by the same laws.) Legislation helped to define the boundaries within which grassroots organizations mobilized, but laws would not by themselves have *created* popular movements in the absence of an available social base, a set of grievances produced in part by the economic structure, the extralegal policy of the authorities who protected or repressed popular movements, and the availability of leaders prepared to help coalesce and formalize local movements.

Although this chapter develops each of these elements for the analysis of the 1920s and 1930s, the same argument can be sustained for popular movements in the 1980s, not only in the Laguna, but elsewhere in Mexico. Clearly the legal and institutional contexts have changed, the social base is more diverse, economic grievances are now associated with state policy, and there is new individual and institutional leadership of the popular movements. None of these changes, however, undercuts the fundamental explanation for the form and discourse of popular movements, or the importance of supralocal leaders and institutions in facilitating alliances or coalitions.

The federal state's institutional presence was limited in the 1920s and 1930s, certainly by comparison with the 1980s. Branches of federal agencies and ministries were small and distant from the geographic base of many popular movements. Federal agricultural agencies had little visible daily or seasonal contact with communities or popular organizations. By the 1980s this had changed dramatically with the creation of state and local offices of agencies that intervened directly in production and marketing decisions in the countryside. Among these agencies we could number the Ejido Credit Bank (later the Banrural, or Bank of Rural Credit), the expansion of agricultural technical assistance and marketing programs, the CONASUPO stores and purchasing programs, the National Agricultural and Livestock Insurance Company (ANAGSA), the expansion of irrigation programs, and the extension of the Ministry of Agriculture and Water Resources, and so on (see, for example, Fox and Gordillo 1989; Otero 1989). As far as state-affiliated institutions claiming popular representation, in the 1920s the CROM was the closest one came to a state-directed instrument of popular co-optation and control. Its representational mandate extended to agricultural and labor organizations, although the militance with which it represented these populations waned considerably over the course of the decade and the early 1930s.

Since the federal state's institutions were not prominent instruments of local control or intervention in politics or the economy, local movements rarely targeted the federal state as the antagonist responsible for their grievances. When state-level agencies, governors, or military zone commanders abused their powers to make policy in the interest of adversaries of popular movements, the latter did not blame the federal state as much as particular officials or individuals for their travails. In my view these are the principal differences in the institutional context for popular movements in the first and last thirds of the twentieth century in Mexico.

The Regional Economic Context

By the time of the Revolution of 1910, and continuing largely until after the land reform of October 1936, the Comarca Lagunera was characterized by a highly capitalized, intensive, largely monocrop economy, producing a commercial crop that was partially processed within the region and marketed domestically by landowners; the owners of the most acreage were foreigners. Several different types of land tenure coexisted, along with considerable diversity in the terms of employment. Although cotton took up the greatest area of the land surface cultivated, wheat was becoming increasingly important, and guayule had made a gradual return as a third major commercial crop. This prevailing pattern of landownership and production was associated with a rural labor force, part of whose income was earned in wages, much of it for seasonal labor. Many workers congregated in the off-season in the towns and cities of the region or passed through on their way to work in Baja California or the United States.

There was also a substantial industrial labor force in the Laguna, despite its reputation as a commercial agricultural region (see Meyers 1980; Senior 1958). The earliest industry in the Laguna, located on the margin of the agricultural zone, was mining. Mining gave rise to a metallurgical industry, including smelters and foundries in the urban centers. Cotton textile mills were also large urban industrial employers, concentrated in Torreón and Gómez Palacio. The growth of cotton agriculture spawned a number of industrial investments in cotton-derivative products. There was also an important group of railway workers in Torreón. By the mid-1930s, other industries had been established in the urban areas, but they were characterized by more dispersed places of employment and smaller labor forces.

The rural and urban economies were characterized by insecurity, and it appears that "economic crisis" was endemic. The Laguna's economy was subject to periodic downturns depending on the price of cotton, weather conditions, and the availability of credit. Among the most consequential changes in the regional economy were the shift from cotton to wheat production, the shift from labor scarcity to labor surplus (except at harvest time), increasing variety in industrial and urban employment opportunities, the closing of the U.S. migration option after 1930, the closure of the frontier of cultivable land, increased pressure on water resources, and the stabilization of maximum labor force requirements in agriculture. Together, these developments did indeed affect the material circumstances of the rural and urban working class, not only by increasing their wage dependence, but by increasing competition for relatively more scarce jobs. They also changed the elite context for decisionmaking.

In this economic context, a range of potential economic and social grievances were created, as well as a social base of industrial workers in large and small factories, permanent and occasional agricultural wageworkers, and a few sharecroppers and dispossessed farmers. The highly industrialized urban areas and the commercialized agricultural zones were associated with a communications network that facilitated laborers' physical mobility and with a network of contacts and exchanges among workers. Large unions were limited to the economic activities linked to rural production of raw materials (cotton, wheat, rubber, and minerals). These industries linked rural and urban areas—sometimes under the same ownership of land or mine and industrial establishment—and through the labor force, which worked seasonally in the countryside and in the city.

Labor and Agrarian Reform Policies

For Mexican workers in the 1920s and 1930s, and for those in the Laguna's industries and agriculture, the weightiest changes in the legal environment for mobilization derived from the adoption of the Constitution of 1917 (of which Articles 27 and 123 were the most important), the passage of labor laws by individual states, and the Federal Labor Law in 1931 (on Mexican labor law, see Bensusan 1985.) The constitution established individual and collective rights for wageworkers. These included maximum hours of daily work, minimum wages, a seventh day of rest, the right to share in profits, the responsibility of owners for worker safety, and the right to strike and unionize. The constitution also specified the right to compensation for unjustified dismissal and the creation of tripartite local labor arbitration boards (Labor Conciliation and Arbitration Board). To balance workers' unions, it granted employers the right to form their own associations. The constitution left it up to the states, however, to pass labor codes and to provide administrative enforcement regulations for the law. This gave state and local government authorities considerable latitude and produced significant variability in the protection afforded to unions and the incentives for workers to organize. Among the states with labor laws that most favored workers were Michoacán, Veracruz, and Durango.

A number of urban unions formed in the Laguna, alluding to rights guaranteed under Articles 27 and 123 of the 1917 Constitution. Some of the unions formed part of federations that gradually expanded within limited domains from local town federations to municipal and finally regional federations (see Landsberger and Hewitt de Alcántara 1970:10, 126; Carr 1987:383–384; Adler 1970:64–65).

The Federal Labor Code was passed in 1931, in the wake of a series of labor actions to protest dismissals, shorter days, and lower wages resulting from the 1929 crash. The law reasserted the individual and collective rights granted under the 1917 Constitution, reaffirming workers' rights to security of employment and to protection from unfair dismissal. It also affirmed the right to unionize and to negotiate collective contracts and to be paid a regionally fixed minimum wage. The right to strike was confined to collective grievances.

As far as popular movements were concerned, the law's most important consequence was to place the state in the role of mediator and arbitrator between workers and employers. Workers were given the right to form associations, but unions were required to be registered and recognized by the state in order to serve as legal bargaining agents. Contracts negotiated by unregistered unions would have no legal standing. Favorable relations (many of them clientelist or cacical) between state officials and union locals might redound to the contract advantage of unions. Like the constitution and the state labor codes that preceded it, the national labor code had a further consequence for local political strategy. Grassroots organizations, urged on by activists, couched their grievances—their discourse—in appeals to the authorities for the application of the rule of law at the factory or hacienda.[2]

Labor's rights in the 1970s and 1980s remained substantially the same. What had changed was the institutional density of government agencies involved in the administration of the law and their much more widespread presence "on the ground," where popular movements are more likely to encounter them. Moreover, even the labor unions formed to secure labor's rights had become ossified institutions that failed to represent workers effectively. Consequently, the form of organization continues to respond to rights granted in law, but the issues and grievances have changed. In the 1920s and 1930s the popular struggle was to form unions and win the right for them to represent workers in negotiation with employers. By the 1970s and 1980s, labor's struggle was in part over income and social wage policies for which state agencies had (respectively) a major regulatory and funding responsibility, as well as for increased worker control over labor union organizations and leaders, that is, for more effective representation.

National agrarian legislation and policy passed through a number of phases that affected the eligibility of petitioners for land reform.[3] As far as the Laguna was concerned, very few communities in the region could claim a right to land based on the eligibility criteria in the presidential decree of 1915 or in the Reglamento Agrario in 1922. As a consequence, although a number of communities did seek land reform, their struggle for land was "dispersed, incoherent, and without appropriate strategy" (Liga de Agrónomos Socialistas 1940:30). In 1927, the new Law of Dotation and Restitution of Lands and Water, further modified in 1929, seemed to broaden the eligibility criteria, encouraging the establishment of ejido petitioning committees. As eligibility expanded, so too did the number of petitions for reform. The number of communities in the Laguna whose petitions for land were unresolved ("pending") tripled between 1928 and carly 1930 (Liga de Agrónomos Socialistas 1940:34). But as the eligibility rules became more inclusive, the position of landowners hardened as well.

The agrarian reform laws of 1922 and 1927 and their further amendment in the 1934 Reglamento Agrario were encouraging, but also problematic for peasants in the Comarca Lagunera and elsewhere in Mexico. There were few *peones acasillados* in the region—that is, agricultural workers employed full time by haciendas and who resided in hacienda-owned housing with special privileges of permanent staff. Instead, there were a large number of temporary workers, or *peones eventuales*, who lived on hacienda-owned land in settlements that had grown up over time. When laws were passed making a minimum number of residents in a community the key criterion for eligibility to receive land, *peones* who were irregularly employed, often on several different haciendas, were encouraged to petition for land. But foreseeing the possibility of rapid growth in petitioners and of communities whose size made them eligible to petition for land, owners were quick to expel agrarian activists and to forcibly remove residents of these settlements from hacienda lands. In this way, modifications in the law encouraged mobilization, but also led to confrontations with *hacendados*. In parts of the republic, local organizations called upon powerful regional caudillos to protect petitioners.

Responding to the new national agrarian legislation, which gave hope to petitioners for land, the National Agriculture Chamber of the Comarca

Lagunera in 1927 asked to have the region declared exempt from land expropriations. Their argument was that expropriation would have dire consequences for the economy of one of the richest agricultural regions in the country.[4] Responding to this request, the federal government named a study commission whose results were released in 1928. The report, by engineers from the Agriculture Department, argued for the subdivision of property of the region into privately held units of 300 hectares; it did not mention ejidos. The report also called for various changes to improve the well-being of agricultural workers (Liga de Agrónomos Socialistas 1940:33–37). Over the subsequent two years, nothing was done to implement the recommendations in the report.

In all cases, the impact of the legal framework on the institutional form and expression of rural popular grievances in Mexico came not only from grassroots awareness of the specific laws or policies but also from information about how the laws were interpreted and applied. Certainly they were not consistently implemented. Laws were used by state and federal agrarian commissions to justify decisions made on pending petitions for land reform. The disposition of these petitions then had a chilling (or heartening) impact on the pursuit of other petitions for land in the region. Petitioners used the law to appeal for state intervention in protection of their rights guaranteed in the law. Knowledge of the law and how to refer to it was one of the contributions made by leaders and organizations with which popular movements were affiliated (see, for example, Craig 1983:95–177).

According to the law, the settlement and employment patterns in the region made most peasants and agricultural wageworkers in the Laguna ineligible to petition for land reform until the eve of the labor strikes in 1935–1936. To improve their economic circumstances and to defend themselves against the landowners, they resorted to the formation of organizations labeled "unions," protected by the state labor codes. These organizations often pursued a dual strategy of defending workers' rights and seeking land reform. Residents of towns or villages—legally disqualified as beneficiaries of land reform despite their work in agriculture because the locality in which they resided could provide other (nonagricultural) means of subsistence—also turned to more trade-unionist demands. For most of the *laguneros*, the legal inducements to organize (such as they were) pointed toward the establishment of agricultural labor unions, not peasant organizations, and so the former were more common.

The formation of rural labor unions, asserting trade-unionist demands, must be regarded first and foremost as a reflection of strategic choices made by leaders and rank-and-file participants, given the prevailing legal-political space for mobilization. It does not necessarily mean that agricultural wageworkers' preference was to improve wages and working conditions more than to secure ownership of land. Nor does it mean that dependence on wages in capitalized, commercialized agriculture had developed a "proletarian consciousness" among agricultural wageworkers. This may have occurred, and it was certainly an objective of some movement activists, such as those affiliated with the Mexican Communist party (PCM), but the proliferation of trade unions must not be regarded as prima facie evidence in the argument.

By the 1980s the issues in the countryside had shifted, most clearly for the state. State policy has emphasized problems of credit, production, and marketing in the countryside. Presidents no longer issue even symbolic promises of land reform. The law now provides incentives directing peasants to organize around problems of production through credit societies, marketing cooperatives, and unions of ejidos. In the Laguna, because land has already been distributed, the key problem for the *ejidatarios* has become resistance to federal institutions' and agencies' contributions to the economic crisis in the countryside and to the abuse of power through corrupt banking and crop purchase practices. *Ejidatarios* continue to pressure for compliance with the law with respect to agricultural credits and marketing.

Political Parties and National Labor Organizations

Concurrent with changes in legislation affecting unions and land reform, there was a surge nationally in the number of local, regional, and national political parties. This, too, changed the context in which popular mobilization occurred. A number of supralocal institutions and individual leaders operated within the political space created by the federal and state laws affecting labor and agrarian disputes. For the Comarca Lagunera, as for other regions of Mexico (Michoacán, Veracruz, and Jalisco), these included, most significantly, first the CROM, then the PCM, the *lombardistas* and *cardenistas*, and finally the National Committee for Proletarian Defense (CNDP). Guided by ideology or central directives, and by their need to develop local affiliates as a social base of support, these organizations contacted some incipient local groups and were instrumental in establishing others (see Craig 1983; Salamini 1978).

Labor and political party leaders from outside the region did not create the popular movement in the Laguna. They tapped into movements that were emerging, sometimes amorphous and frequently informal. They contributed to the intensity and extent of popular mobilization and to divisions between popular organizations. They did try to influence agendas, to formalize organization, to build alliances through individual leaders or formal agreements between organizations. They extended movements beyond local, community boundaries and in this way increased the visibility and effectiveness of popular organizations' negotiating capacity. The alliances that endured the longest were those that resulted from a dialogue between outside institutions or leaders and the grassroots base—a dialogue that resulted in a compromise agenda and strategy. The result was not only a greater accountability of leaders (Hellman 1983b), but a process of political learning and network building.

In my view, much the same argument could be made about the contributions of individuals and movements active in independent grassroots organizing in the Laguna or elsewhere in the years since 1968. The linking agents are new (such as OIR-LM, Proletarian Tendency, PSUM-PMS-PRD, and CNTE). They are not necessarily political parties; in fact they may reject partisan affiliation and electoral contestation as a political strategy. They typically are *not* associated with corporatist institutions and claim to reject clientelist strategies of accommodation. The challenge they confront is strategically complex because now they must insert themselves into a much denser web of political institutions. In the 1920s and 1930s, organizations could participate in the surge of newly forming institutions to represent popular interests, and sometimes in contesting officialist institutions for the right to represent. Now they must nearly always contest.

The Mexican Communist party.   By early 1935, the single most important national institution that had promoted joint rural-urban mobilization in the Laguna was the Mexican Communist party. Communist-led trade unions in the urban centers of the Laguna would probably have had negligible impact in the rural sector had it not been that independent agrarian activism in the Mexican countryside was increasing at about the same time that the agrarian question was linked to Communist party mobilizational strategy (Adler 1970:66–67). The Mexican Communist party had already distinguished itself by early ties to the peasantry, especially in Veracruz and Michoacán (Carr 1987:385; Salamini 1978). It advocated a proletarian revolution, formed by peasants and workers, as the means to achieve agrarian transformation where this was conceived as cooperative ejidos and the socialization of all means of production. This made the Laguna a particularly important, but not exclusive, locus of PCM organizing.

Institutionally, the party's commitment to agrarian reform was reflected in close ties between the PCM and the National Peasant League (LNC), which it helped to establish in Veracruz. The LNC was instrumental in promoting new community struggles and organizations and supporting existing struggles in various parts of the republic. In the Laguna, the influence of the league was mediated by the peasant organization in Durango (the Union of Agrarianist Peasants of Durango) and by officials in it who were also involved in the LNC. The Durango union was quite militant in the defense of both workers and peasants associated with it (Adler 1970; Landsberger and Hewitt de Alcántara 1970). Nationally, roughly between 1919 and 1928 the PCM advocated an aggressive approach to the agrarian question, supporting land invasions and discarding the option of individualized parcels of land (Carr 1987:386). In the Laguna, grassroots groups with a history of grievances related to conflicts over land and water rights periodically joined forces with socialist or communist organizations. Together, they participated in at least one land invasion near Matamoros at the Vega del Caracol (see Carr 1987:384–385; Liga de Agrónomos Socialistas 1940; Santos Valdés 1973:277–281).

In 1929, however, the party was split over national political strategy and Comintern policy. As a result, its involvement in land reform and with the peasantry declined dramatically. Between 1928 and 1935, the party's rural strategy focused on the organization of the agricultural proletariat—a strategy most successfully executed in the Laguna region. As part of the turn to the left, the PCM had decided no longer to collaborate with the government; following that decision, the party was declared illegal in 1929 (León 1977:61). This accentuated the importance of political leadership provided by specific unions with a history of PCM activism, such as those in Torreón and Gómez Palacio. These organizations were particularly visible in the Laguna during the underground years and helped to build ties between countryside and city, often through party activists engaged with both urban and rural organizations. The combination of party strategy and organizational location of party activists further reinforced the pursuit of trade-unionist strategies and grievances.

The Communist party survived six years of underground life through its trade union and peasant league cadres. Cárdenas's legalization of the party coincided with a change in Comintern policy that encouraged a popular front strategy as part of the international struggle against fascism. This position was formally adopted by the PCM in October 1935 (León 1977:61). Thus, the more open political environment in Mexico and the new party doctrine together facilitated collaboration with Cárdenas in mass mobilization. For different reasons, the PCM, Lombardo Toledano, and Cárdenas were able to join in encouraging the organization of a united working class. The most important manifestation of this strategic priority was the formation of the National Committee for Proletarian Defense (CNDP) in June 1935. The policy was reflected down the party hierarchy, to the CSUM (of the PCM), which urged a united union strategy on the eve of the first call for a general strike in the Laguna (Carr 1987).

Communist party–affiliated unions were not the only ones active in the region, although they figure most prominently in studies of agricultural mobilization in the Laguna. Part of the strength within the national—and Laguna—rural-urban alliance must be explained by the degree to which the parties on the left and national labor organizations were able to agree on a common political project. Dissent within the official national labor federation was reflected in a regionally conflicted labor movement, but also in the proliferation of local organizations as national divisions were refracted through them.

Labor organizations.   When the CROM was founded in Saltillo in 1918, some thirty-six unions in Coahuila and one in Durango appeared on the list of founding organizations (Leal 1985:87–93). In Torreón this included textile workers, railway workers, employees of the tram company, carpenters, and metallurgical workers. Nationally, both the CROM and the Casa del Obrero Mundial promoted contact between rural unions and their urban counterparts and supported petitions for land reform in their early years. Many of the complaints filed by hacienda workers' organizations in the Laguna note the organizations' CROM affiliation. This national (corporatist) labor federation continued to be involved regionally in supporting both union demands and petitions for land reform (Carr 1987:384; and union petitions in Cajas 301, 302, 309, Fondo de Trabajo, AGN).

As the leadership of the CROM became more corrupt and more closely tied to the federal government under President Calles (1924–1928) and during the "Maximato" period (1928–1934), the organization became less militant in pressing workers' demands, more willing to accede to the mediation of an increasingly conservative and capital-supporting state, and more willing to support a national project of modernization of agriculture and industry. CROM affiliates became less willing to endorse peasant organizations and petitions for land reform. This produced a schism within the confederation and division within local organizations.

Ultimately the CROM split apart in the midst of intractable internal debates over leadership, corruption, and labor and peasant representation. Some of the more militant members, seeking greatest autonomy from the state, formed the Communist party–affiliated national labor and peasant organization, the Unitary Labor Confederation of Mexico (CSUM) in late 1928 (Carr 1987:388). Then in March 1933, Lombardo Toledano broke definitively with Luis Morones, head of the CROM, taking with him a number of unions that in October held the founding congress of the General Labor and Peasant Confederation of Mexico (CGOCM, later UGOCM). Lombardo, influenced by Marxism but never a member of the PCM, tried to build up labor and peasant organizations prior to the 1934 elections to give them a stronger negotiating position with the new administration. The CROM and CSUM each had affiliates in the Laguna.

As the incoming candidate of the official party, Cárdenas hoped to construct a party of peasants and workers. To accomplish this, he sought to expand the number of labor unions in Mexico, and in his campaign he encouraged the formation of workers' organizations, to which he promised the protection of the law and the government (see Cornelius 1971). Lombardo Toledano, seeking to strengthen his wing of the labor movement, supported Cárdenas and came to head the leading labor organization.

Finally, the opportunity to build a united mass movement was created by the political crisis brought about by the confrontation between Calles and Cárdenas in 1935. A dispersed and polarized group of labor and peasant organizations had developed since 1933. Lack of unity had kept these popular organizations from successfully pressing grassroots concerns onto the national political agenda. But the new PCM, Toledano's faction of the old CROM constituency, and the new Mexican Peasant Confederation all saw in the National Committee for Proletarian Defense the opportunity to influence the Cárdenas administration (León 1977:57, 59). The CNDP therefore was not simply the imposition of a paternalist state policy but rather the result of extensive popular mobilization.

This conflict within the national labor movement and between emerging parties and national institutions contributed to the intermittent proliferation of unions in the Laguna in the years leading up to 1935, most especially 1932–1935. Speaking in the Laguna during his presidential campaign, Cárdenas promised protection to labor organizations. However, it was not until the conflicts between Calles and Cárdenas, Morones and Lombardo Toledano, reached such proportions that they threatened the survival of the incumbent government that the program of more progressive labor leaders, a PCM willing to endorse a popular front strategy, and grievances at the grassroots level come together to facilitate the growth of the CNDP—a progressive, armed, militant alliance of peasants and workers. For a brief period, the political and economic objectives of national political parties, politicians, and leaders of peasant and workers' organizations came together to stimulate popular mobilization based on a multisectoral alliance, linked to parties on the left as well as to a faction of the political elite in control of the state apparatus.

POPULAR MOBILIZATION AND STATE POLICY IN THE LAGUNA

Throughout the preceding pages, I have argued that the form of popular political organization in Mexico and in the Laguna between 1918 and 1936 was shaped by federal labor and agrarian reform legislation and the state practices for administering the laws. The labor laws defined the rights workers could organize to defend and progressively came to specify the state's role in registering unions and mediating conflicts between workers and employers. These legal inducements to form unions were not uniformly administered over time or geographic space, so they posed inconstant incentives to organize. But they remained a steady point of reference that workers cited in justifying their demands, and they set the boundaries within which popular movements could form. National organizations (the PCM and the CROM especially, but the CTM and CNDP as well) used the laws to occupy open political spaces. They helped to encourage the formation of local unions and linked them together for mutual support and common strength (in the case of the PCM) and eventually for control (in the case of the CROM). The agrarian legislation prescribed the land tenure and employment eligibility of individual petitioners and the political eligibility of communities soliciting land. This legislation and the ways in which it was implemented shaped at least *how* claims for land could be put and *who* might legally mobilize to try to secure land.

For these reasons, by the time of peak organized popular mobilization in the Laguna (roughly 1932–1935), trade unionism had become the most common form of mobilization. Local organizations were linked through national labor organizations or parties with which they affiliated. Thus mass mobilizations and rural-urban collaboration were feasible by calling upon existing institutional and personal networks established through the experience of organization and struggle. Unions in the countryside were institutionally linked—not necessarily tied—to urban industrial unions. With this explanatory framework in mind, we turn to look at the intensification of struggles in the Laguna after 1930, and to the adoption of a general strike strategy in 1936.

The endemic economic crisis in the Comarca Lagunera intensified in 1930. Wheat and cotton production dropped precipitously, as did employment (Liga de Agrónomos Socialistas 1940:182–183).[5] More agricultural unions were formed (Restrepo and Eckstein 1975:25). The political climax came in midyear, with a demonstration in Matamoros on June 29, 1930, which provided the impetus for popular mobilization in the region. Unarmed and unemployed agricultural workers residing in Matamoros and nearby *ranchos* were fired on by the police, culminating in twenty-one deaths and the arrest and conviction of demonstration leaders affiliated with the illegal PCM (see Restrepo and Eckstein 1975:25; Adler 1970:72).

The Matamoros demonstration began as an attempt to publicize a number of accumulated grievances and demands. These included demands for higher wages, an eight-hour day, respect for individual rights (including the right to bear arms and to gather firewood), freedom for political prisoners (members of the Communist party–affiliated CSUM, twenty-one of whom had been arrested in two separate incidents), land for peasants, and relief from the high cost of living. Demonstrators were incensed by the arrest of their leaders and also by the more generalized repression of independent and militant activists, particularly from the Communist party (Santos Valdés 1973:293–301, 350–354).

The demonstration galvanized employers and landowners. In the wake of the confrontation in Matamoros, the National Agriculture Chamber of the Comarca Lagunera proposed the creation of two ejido districts, one each in the states of Coahuila and Durango. The proposal called for the establishment of ejidos on land outside the irrigation district, purchased from landowners by the Agriculture Chamber. In return for their cooperation with this scheme, landowners expected to receive perpetual immunity from expropriation. Signed in 1934, the agreement between the federal government and the landowners creating two such ejidos stipulated that no new petitions for land would be recognized. The proposal and agreement effectively closed the legal space for land reform petitions as a target for rural struggle.

Roughly between 1930 and 1936, most popular participation was channeled into trade unions and focused on trade-unionist demands. The use of law clearly contributed to the shift in strategy (see Restrepo and Eckstein 1975:26). We have already seen that this was also a period of PCM union mobilization in rural areas, of intensified competition for labor's loyalty within the splintering CROM, and of federal government resistance to land reform. As a consequence of all these changes, the number of labor unions in the Laguna, both agricultural and urban, multiplied. The initial membership of each of the new rural unions was probably small and represented only a minority of workers on any given hacienda (see, for example, Wilkie

1971:37).

By June 30, 1935, there were enough unions to establish the Revolutionary Union Federation of the Comarca Lagunera in Torreón. This federation coexisted with unions affiliated with the CGT and the Socialist League, both of which were more moderate. Initially urban, the federation soon moved into the countryside as well (Liga de Agrónomos Socialistas 1940:39–40). By late summer, it brought together several unions in order to establish a regional militia of workers and peasants affiliated with the national CNDP.

The popular militias in the Laguna included mostly urban industrial unions, such as the PCM-affiliated union of the de la Peñoles foundries in Monterrey and Torreón (the Industrial Union of Miners and Metallurgical Workers) and a few militant peasant unions (see León 1977:63). The urban unions that composed the CNDP represented mining and metalworkers, mechanics, railroad workers, bricklayers, electricians, textile workers, and members of the CGOCM unions, many of which were either controlled by the Communist party or influenced by socialist groups.[6] By September 22, 1935, they were joined by the Federation of Worker and Peasant Unions of the Comarca Lagunera (Adler 1970:78; Landsberger and Hewitt de Alcántara 1970:12; Rello 1984). Once established, the militias became the instrument for creating new unions in the countryside and for protecting additional groups of peasants who petitioned for land (see, for example, Wilkie 1971:36–38).

Several agricultural workers' strikes were called in 1935, with the support of industrial workers and the local Proletarian Defense Committee. They included a thirty-two-day strike on the Hacienda de Manila over a range of trade union demands, supported by urban workers in Gómez Palacio and Torreón (Liga de Agrónomos Socialistas 1940:40). Some of the leaders were members of the CROM and of the PCM and "had for some time been collaborating actively, along with rural teachers, in the ideological guidance of the workers on the haciendas" (Restrepo and Eckstein 1975:26).

More agricultural workers' strikes soon erupted (Liga de Agrónomos Socialistas 1940:41; Adler 1970:81–82), some as a result of a demonstration effect, some in solidarity with earlier strikes. The formal agenda of this second wave of strikes was to reinstate striking workers who had been dismissed by management and replaced by strikebreakers from outside the region. By the late fall of 1935, virtually all the workers in the Comarca Lagunera had formed either "red" or "white" unions (Liga de Agrónomos Socialistas 1940:41). Strikes on individual haciendas continued through April and May of the following year.

In the first months of 1936, with the unconditional support of the PCM and the CTM, the new national labor federation, agricultural wage workers, and the Revolutionary Union Federation joined together and began to prepare for a general strike, protesting mass layoffs of activists who tried to organize workers. Responding to the unity of the owners in the Employers'

Union,[7] workers looked to adopt a unified workers' strategy. The Proletarian Defense Committees had succeeded in bringing together workers and peasants but lacked legal status as a bargaining agent for workers in conflicts with employers. Therefore the Union of Agricultural Workers was established and claimed to speak for all the agricultural workers in the region, demanding better wages and working conditions and calling for a collective contract covering workers throughout the Laguna.

On May 26, 1936, the first call was issued for a general strike involving both urban and rural workers in the region (required by Mexican labor law as a prelude to a strike). The strike was postponed at the request of the president while a commission of experts named by workers and employers deliberated the case. The commission filed a report favoring the workers, which the employers refused to accept.

Finally on August 18, 1936, the region's agricultural workers struck, led by the Revolutionary Union Federation of Torreón, the Labor Congress of Torreón, and the Federation of Workers' and Peasants' Unions of Gómez Palacio, affiliated with the CTM. They were joined in solidarity strikes by urban unions although some of these had earlier issued independent threats to strike. All of these unions were formally within the national labor federation and were also affiliated with the Communist party. State labor agencies in Durango and Coahuila declared the strike illegal, and the leagues of agrarian communities still under the control of the state governors and not affiliated with the Communist party, declined to join the strike. Confrontations between workers, and some bloodshed, ensued. Military zone commanders sent in troops to protect strikebreakers.

Eight days into the agricultural strike, workers' representatives were again called back to Mexico City where they had met on several previous occasions with representatives of employers and the federal government. In the capital, President Cárdenas personally intervened in the settlement of the strike. He promised land reform if the strike would be terminated. This time the president's proposal was accepted, and the strike, which at its peak had involved 104 unions and some 20,000 workers, was suspended on September 3.[8] When the dust settled, the labor dispute was resolved by presidential decrees that established in the Comarca Lagunera the largest zone of collective agriculture in Mexico. The first presidential decree for the expropriation of land in the Comarca Lagunera was issued on October 6, 1936. A second decree was issued the following year on May 12, 1937.

These decrees did not bring down the curtain on popular mobilization in the Laguna. In fact, most of the literature on the region begins with the expropriation and focuses on the analysis of state intervention and on the gradual erosion of financial and political support for collective ejidos. Local management and control of the ejidos in the region, initially respected by the Cárdenas government, eventually gave way and were replaced with repression of progressive leaders and the imposition of controls, especially through credit and banking agencies of the state (see, for example, Hamilton

1982; Hellman 1983a; Martínez Saldaña 1980; and Rello 1984, 1987).

CONCLUSION

My objective in this chapter has been to develop an explanation for popular mobilizations in the form of agricultural unions as well as for the cooperation between rural and urban popular movements. I have used the Comarca Lagunera and the general strike there in 1936 as a case from which to develop a more general argument about the conditions under which particular forms of popular organization emerge (especially in the countryside), and the grievances these movements pursue.

The combination of economic crisis with the changes in political space and legal framework outlined earlier led to actions by employers and authorities such as the attacks on demonstrators in Matamoros, the removal of squatters in the Vega del Caracol, and the blacklisting of independent labor organizers and petitioners for land reform. These actions further worsened the material circumstances of some workers and violated a grassroots sense of justice and acquired rights, embodied in the law (see Moore 1978). This incursion on rights, combined with the law's sanction in principle of some forms of organization, propelled many activists to engage in sustained and militant political action. They pursued their grievances and formed associations within the parameters established by law. The legal context therefore established the boundaries within which popular mobilization would occur and shaped popular organization. The key to the rural-urban alliance was the availability of political institutions and leaders from the CROM through the PCM to the CTM and CNDP—which served as interlocutors between popular movements and the state, encouraged organization, and linked activists in countryside and city.

Over the last twenty years, some trade union and rural activists have shared with their forebears in the first third of the twentieth century the conviction that they are engaged in struggles to make their own history in ways that will reconfigure the Mexican political system. This time their struggles are against state policies and practices that prejudice popular welfare and in defense of an independent negotiating position vis-à-vis state institutions. In this respect, the legal and institutional context in which rural struggles are waged has changed considerably, although it continues to shape the organizational form of popular mobilization. In the countryside, state policies have shifted to encourage the formation of credit, marketing, and production cooperatives. The political space for land reform has, in effect, been closed and even reversed by the state's failure to favorably resolve petitions for reform. State corporatist institutions are now undertaking to organize agricultural wageworkers. The struggles again employ broad alliances crafted among sectors within a region (for example, COCEI) or among movements across regions (for example, CONAMUP). These often have an affinity for parties or organizations on the left (e.g., PRT or PRD, and Proletarian Tendency), although they have been suspicious of linkages between popular movements and parties. Some of these parties have moved to occupy the political spaces created by the political reforms after 1977.

In February 1988, midway through the presidential campaign, Mexican politics was again shaken by popular political mobilization in the Comarca Lagunera. While on a swing through the Laguna, the official PRI candidate, Carlos Salinas de Gortari, received the most hostile reception of his campaign when he was jostled and heckled by supporters of the opposition's Cuauhtémoc Cárdenas. The very next day, Cárdenas was welcomed by tens of thousands of supporters, who gave him his warmest campaign reception. Parties of the left and independent trade unions joined peasants and low-income urban residents in the demonstrations. This time rural demonstrators protested agricultural credit and purchase policies of the state bank and corruption of bank officials.

As a result of this regional opposition to state policy, popular movements were positioned to take advantage of divisions within the political elite. Popular movements in the Laguna and throughout Mexico must choose how to position themselves strategically between the modernizing neoliberal project of the Salinas administration and the populist nationalism of the emerging PRD. These divisions, created by the attempts to reform the political system and modernize the economy, are every bit as portentous as the confrontation between Lázaro Cárdenas and Plutarco Elías Calles.

NOTES

This chapter is part of a larger project on peasant-worker political alliances in Mexico. Research on the Laguna was supported by the University of California, San Diego Senate Committee on Research, as well as by sabbatical support from the same institution, and a fellowship at the Hoover Institution at Stanford University. Joe Foweraker, Judy Hellman, and Wayne Cornelius all commented on earlier drafts of this paper but bear no responsibility for the final product.

1. I have substituted "peasant" where Mexicanists would more commonly use campesino, to refer to people who make their living in agriculture in a variety of land tenure and employment arrangements.

2. See, for example, complaints from the Sindicato 30 de Obreros y Campesinos, Covadonga, Coah., October 5, 1921, Caja 301, Exp. 9, and the Sindicato 27 Santa Sofía, La Laguna, July 8,1921, who point out to the governor that Coahuila's labor law, passed October 25, 1916, should be applied throughout the state with the only exception of any provisions that might contradict the constitution, Caja 301, Exp. 14, Fondo de Trabajo, Mexican National Archives (AGN).

3. A general relationship between these laws and the fate of the land reform movement in the Laguna was first posited by the Liga de Agrónomos Socialistas (1940:30–35) and has been accepted by subsequent scholars. See, for example, Rello 1984; Restrepo and Eckstein 1975.

4. Right up to the time of the creation of the ejidos, the manager of the Tlahualilo Company continued to assume that the regional economy would be destroyed if the large holdings were broken up. See letters of J. D. Holby and Tom Fairbairn to

members of the British board of directors of the Tlahualilo Company, folios January–June and July–December, 1936, correspondence 1914–1963, Mexican Cotton Estates of Tlahualilo, Ltd, Kleinwort, Benson Archives, England.

5. Most of what has been written about the history of political mobilization in the Comarca Lagunera is derived from a very limited number of sources. The secondary literature draws most heavily on the 1940 report of the Liga de Agrónomos Socialistas, on Senior (1940, 1958), and on interviews of activists conducted by Landsberger and Hewitt de Alcántara (1970) and Adler (1970) as part of a CIDA project in the region.

6. For some time there has been general agreement among scholars about the Communist party–affiliation of leaders of this union movement. Barry Carr has begun the painstaking task of documenting this relationship (1987).

7. The Employers' Union was formed in late 1935 or January 1936 to respond to workers' demands for a collective contract. It negotiated with labor unions and government officials in the labor sector in the name of all producers. The Agriculture Union, by contrast, spoke for producers on the issue of agrarian petitions for land reform. As such it served as representative of landowners to agrarian organizations, government officials in the agriculture department, and ejido committees.

8. Liga de Agrónomos Socialistas 1940:43–45. See similar chronologies of the strike in Adler 1970:83; Landsberger and Hewitt de Alcántara 1970:13; Restrepo and Eckstein 1975:27–28; Senior 1958:65–66; and Wilkie 1971:19.

5

Historical Continuities in Social Movements

ALAN KNIGHT

It is a useful but difficult task to present a historical résumé of social movements in mid-twentieth-century Mexico.[1] *Useful* because, as I shall argue, the diagnostic "newness" of the "new" social movements is, at the very least, debatable; thus, some sort of historical perspective is required in order to place recent social movements within their broader context. *Difficult* because the phenomena are so varied in time, space, and character, and the relevant literature (though voluminous) is patchy and often noncommensurable. That is, we have an abundant literature focusing on social movements since the late 1960s, written (according to conventional academic criteria) by political scientists, sociologists, and (to a lesser degree) anthropologists. We have an alternative literature, written by historians and characterized by archival work, which deals with the revolutionary era (roughly 1910–1940). Between the two lies a chronological and conceptual gulf. The years 1940–1965 (to take approximate benchmarks) have not yet been thoroughly researched by historians, although the process is beginning. The work done by social scientists during this period—the period of the economic miracle and the peace of the PRI—tended to focus on the macropolitical system, on the secrets of the regime's stability, and on the political culture that underpinned that stability (Brandenburg 1964; Scott 1964; Hansen 1971; Almond and Verba 1963). The state rather than civil society absorbed academic attention.

Since the late 1960s, as a new generation of commentators has come to the fore, the focus has switched in Mexico and elsewhere. Social scientists working on Mexico now pay much greater attention to civil society; they are more interested in probing social movements than in measuring regime stability; like their historian counterparts, they display more of a bottom-up, less of a top-down perspective. In this, they form part of a broader trend, evident in European social science. A key underlying question is whether the shift faithfully mirrors reality (a reality in which civil society has somehow escaped from the constraining bonds of state control), or whether, in contrast, it represents a change in academic fashion, a response to intellectual currents (Gramscian, neo-Marxist, idealistic) that are to a considerable degree independent of "reality." Most social scientists would accept, I think, that changing research emphases respond to quite diverse and complex factors; they do not arise transparently from objective contemplation of the *explananda*. Given at least a degree of intellectual autonomy, of distancing from an elusive reality, it is possible for entirely new paradigms to emerge, unjustified by objective reality (consider, by way of example, IQ theory, modernization theory, and Freudian psychoanalytic theory). In the name of such questionable paradigms, intellectuals have claimed to reinterpret—and even change—the world.

Theorists of the new social movements, of course, do not usually operate at such a high level of theory, though Laclau (1985) and Evers (1985) come close. The contributors to this book have, in the main, produced exceptionally rich case studies, located within a more general theory that is often assumed. Because individual case studies can neither refute nor substantiate higher-level theories (at best they qualify or lend weight to such theories), it does not fall to these contributors to pass judgment on the basic concept of the new social movements. Nor, I would say, does the value of their analyses necessarily depend on the validity of that concept. In fact, to the extent that I criticize the concept, I do so partly on the basis of the evidence contained in these chapters. I do not, therefore, disagree with their contemporary analysis, but I question how far the situation they describe is genuinely novel, thus how far it represents a break with the past, and how far it points the way to a new future—questions raised, with greater theoretical subtlety, by other critics of the new social movements genre (Cohen 1985). To some degree, it seems to me, intellectual fashion has outrun reality. Or, rather, intellectual fashion has caught up with reality: civil society is now getting the attention it merited all along but that the social scientists of an earlier generation declined to give it. My quarrel, therefore, is not so much with my contemporary social science colleagues as with their predecessors, whose paradigm has been too readily accepted, to the extent that the "peace of the PRI" (with all its connotations of an all-powerful state, pervasive corporatist organizations, and an inert civil society) becomes a datum, a historical given against which to compare the political effervescence and contestations of today. Unfortunately, any critique of that historical given faces two major problems: the lack of serious historical research for the 1940–1965 period and the absence of any known methodology whereby the power or incapacity of the state, the inertia or effervescence of civil society, can be meaningfully measured over time. The first (historiographical) deficiency will gradually be remedied; meanwhile, however, it is clear to me that my thesis is riskily premature. The second (methodological) deficiency may never be overcome. In some instances, it is true, the weight of historical evidence is so overwhelming that confident broad comparisons can be made, largely on the basis of accumulations of impressionistic evidence. It is clear, for example, that the late eighteenth century witnessed appreciably more social tension and protest in Mexico than the late seventeenth. But this is a broad brush comparison, made with the benefit of two centuries of hindsight. To hazard a similar comparison of shorter blocks of twentieth-century history (1910–

1940, 1940–1965, post–1965) is much more difficult. Ultimately, we come down to informed hunches. My hunch, which underlies this chapter, is that the Mexican state was less powerful and less pervasive even in the years of its heyday (1940–1965), and that civil society was less docile, less amenable. The "new" social movements display more continuity than often imagined, and are not necessarily that new. By the same token, the degree of rupture— the potential for sociopolitical transformation—may be less than currently imagined. In presenting this argument, I shall begin with a brief critique of the underlying theory of the "new social movements"—a critique that arose from my attempt to grasp what the theory was trying to say. Next, I shall offer an alternative (but far from original) view, I then go on to address the key question of continuity as against novelty. And in the final section, I consider the question of periodization, relating it to forms of political control and incorporation.

A CRITIQUE OF THE THEORY

A brief discussion of the concepts and arguments put forward by theorists of the new social movements will clarify the phenomena under discussion, and the theory that purports to explain them. I am struck, at the outset, by certain ambiguities and obscurities. The literature is rich in suggestive but vague concepts. Analysts introduce terms that, it seems, are deemed self-evident: "modernity," "tradition," "autonomy,"[2] and "organicity" (Torres Mejía 1989:3–4). They describe the 1940–1965 period—the historical given against which the new era is contrasted—in terms of an "absolute" state and a pervasive "corporatism" (I shall later question the empirical validity of this interpretation: my initial point is that the very terms they use demand greater theoretical clarification). They are fond of mechanical metaphors, involving, for example, "space" and "escape valves," which form part of a larger universe of common concepts ("empowerment" is a favorite). These concepts and metaphors, currently in vogue, do not possess the theoretical lineage of, let us say, classic Marxist discourse, which has at least been refined by years of debate. There is also a good deal of ambiguity surrounding the definition of the central *explanandum*: Is the focus on *social* movements or *popular* movements—or are the two terms interchangeable? Semantic common sense would suggest that they are not. The mobilized middle class of Ciudad Satélite presumably constitutes a social movement but not necessarily a popular movement (Tarrés, this volume). The same could be said of *los tecos*, who are credited with organizing an "enormous variety of social sectors" in Jalisco (Romero 1986:47). Linked to this is the common, though usually tacit, assumption that popular movements might be conventionally placed on the left. Popular means progressive. But, as some recognize, this is not necessarily the case (Laclau 1985:33–34). Finally studies of the new social movements often oscillate uncomfortably between the analytical and the normative. They slide from "is" to "ought." It is sometimes quite difficult to pick up where objective analysis (of, say, the relations between the state and social movements) gives way to prescriptive recommendations.[3]

These are specific but recurrent problems. More important is the general theory that addresses the question of new social movements. Like most general theory, this is a diffuse, largely abstract corpus of ideas, the intellectual labor of many contributors, to be summarized at the reviewer's peril. According to these theorists, the contemporary period (post-1950s in Europe? post-1960s in Latin America?) has witnessed the development of new social movements that represent a significant departure from their historical predecessors. It is assumed that this applies, in some measure, to Latin America and thus to Mexico, as well as to Western Europe or the United States (much of the literature derives from and focuses on Western Europe; this is no mere coincidence).

Theorists have produced a variety of typologies, which make generalization risky. Some common features, however, are evident. The new social movements are new (qualitatively different from what has gone before); they represent a departure from previous class-based social movements (thus, they are premised upon different identities, which do not relate to socioeconomic or occupational identities); yet they are somehow causally derived from the development of advanced capitalism. On the one hand, therefore, theorists like Laclau boldly deny the old economism of earlier Marxists; on the other, they cling to a Marxisant discourse and show no readiness to relinquish their adherence to the Marxist canon (Laclau 1985). They want to stay in the club but rewrite the rulebook. This appears odd and illogical, as their departure from classical Marxism is so pronounced, their approximation to conventional "bourgeois" analysis so close. The Laclauian analysis of new social movements can very easily be accommodated within a pretty conventional bourgeois (that is, non-Marxist) analysis; indeed, the theoretical "Eureka!" accompanying such analysis is unlikely to thrill the conventional historian (or, I dare say, the conventional political scientist). The discovery that social actors do not faithfully conform to class imperatives—that, for example, a worker can be a socialist, a liberal, a fascist, a Catholic—need come as no surprise and represents no great theoretical breakthrough. Non-Marxists have assumed this all along; some Marxists (those who have remained closer to the letter and spirit of classical Marxism) have also come to terms with this rather obvious fact. If Laclau and others are just dissenting from vulgar economism, they are merely joining the crowd. Indeed, Evers comes close to recognizing this. Having proclaimed that "reality is changing . . . moving out of the realm of our modes of perception and instruments of interpretation," and having initially assumed that this *transformation of reality* necessitates a *rethinking of theory*, he has a moment of doubt (or glimmer of insight): "Has it not always been like this, perhaps, and is it just our perception [namely, that of certain Marxist social scientists] that is clumsily catching up with reality? . . . Yes and no" (Evers 1985:61).

At this point, the crowd might disaggregate itself according to several principles. Some might retain a basically Marxist position, albeit recognizing the sterility of vulgar economism. In terms of political science, this might constitute a Gramscian position; in historical terms, the work of Thompson (1962) or Genovese (1974) springs to mind. Some, on the other hand, might dispense with Marxism altogether (thus dispensing with concepts such as mode of production, the interrelation of forces and relations of production, the centrality of class conflict) and choose to interpret social reality in terms of multiple conflicts, functions, and identities. Such a stance might qualify as structural functionalism, Weberianism, elite theory, or whatever. What seems least useful is to mix classical Marxist terminology with garish neologisms, to eschew empirical investigation (while asserting the kaleidoscopic variability of the phenomena), and, while repudiating economic determinism, to insist that these phenomena are somehow causally linked to the historical development of capitalism—and/or bureaucracy: a Weberian contribution that further muddies the waters (Slater 1985a:2, citing Chantal Mouffe). Finally, the rather abstract, introspective character of this general theory (its indifference to research, its revolving of abstract concepts), combined with its pronounced Eurocentrism (which I shall refer to later), suggests that the theory derives at least in part from the ratiocinations of Western European intellectuals disengaged from—and averse to—practical, especially party, politics and captivated by the prospect of a new politics, vested in the new social movements, in which the historical working class plays a reduced role: intellectuals, "women," greens, and others come into their own, and political parties exit by the back door. No matter that the historical working class is still very much with us; that it was never solidly socialist; that women have played a part in diverse social movements throughout history; and that Western Europe is a far cry from Latin America. I begin, therefore, by suggesting that the very notion of the new social movement, heralding a new politics, must be treated skeptically; it may be more the subjective creation of intellectual navel gazing than the objective recognition of a genuine sea change in global politics.

LATIN AMERICA: TWO CHEERS FOR ECONOMISM

Even if the notion of new social movements has some validity for Western Europe (Offe 1985), where the shrinking of the industrial working class may be eroding traditional political alignments, its application in Latin America is another matter (for the moment, let us make the massive assumption that Western Europe and Latin America are each sufficiently homogeneous to justify mutual comparison). It does not require a profound historical knowledge to appreciate that Western Europe and Latin America have not marched in close political order, notwithstanding the ideological diffusion that has taken place—usually from east to west—since the conquest. Latin American Catholicism was not a carbon copy of the Western European; nor was its liberalism, socialism, or fascism. Laclau himself concedes that Latin

America may still retain a more strictly class-based society than Western Europe; that, in other words, a greater measure of economic determinism may be appropriate for the analysis of Latin American societies, at least for the time being (Laclau 1985:30).

This seems a refreshingly correct appreciation of reality. Analyses of recent social movements in Latin America (or, specifically, in Mexico) reveal a powerful underlying economic rationale. Judith Adler Hellman, who has worked on both sides of the Atlantic, argues that "in Europe, new social movements mainly represent a response to post-industrial contradictions, while in Latin America, the movements arise in response to clearly material demands" (Hellman 1989:2). The genesis of these demands may be sought at three levels of economic causality. First, the durable class structure of Mexican society generates familiar and recurrent conflicts between capital and labor, landowners and peasants. Such conflicts, structurally induced and amenable to broad comparative analysis along the lines of Paige (1975), Wolf (1973), Stinchcombe (1962), Moore (1969, 1978), and others, have a long and continuous history in Mexico. Neither that history nor the relevant comparative analysis should be lost to sight. But within this inherent continuity there are inevitable changes—shifts of emphasis, if not radical transformations. There are grounds for believing that recent social conflicts and social movements (roughly over the last twenty years) have involved such changes, which have brought with them greater mobilization, radicalization, and popular challenge to the regime, particularly in certain sectors, and particularly if the post-1968 period is compared with 1940–1968 (not with 1910–1940). The history of the last twenty years may therefore be interpreted in terms of certain important shifts in Mexican society, which have resulted in a social panorama different from that of the 1950s: the relative decline of the traditional peasantry; the bankruptcy of the ejidal program; the end of the import-substitution–industrialization model; the mushrooming of the cities; the growing importance of labor migration and of the U.S. economic nexus. Virtually every analysis of the new social movements takes the late 1960s or early 1970s as the point of departure (many, of course, cite the *annus mirabilis* of 1968). Third and finally, social movements are also seen to respond to the conjuncture of depression, unemployment, and declining incomes and living standards characteristic of Mexico at least since 1982 (hence 1982 is another much-cited date). The timetable of the new social movements is therefore strongly determined by economic structures and processes, which may be analyzed at these three levels; the relationship between the "new" social movements and Mexico's model of socioeconomic development is, in fact, remarkably close.

The overt demands of these movements, too, are often overwhelmingly economic; that is, they are concerned with the provision of basic subsistence requirements, with the material quality of life in some fundamental sense. This applies not only to the "economistic" demands of trade unions, but also to the concrete demands of neighborhood groups for water, drains, transport, electric power, and other basic amenities. Such demands are clearly economic (the more so if we hark back to Polanyi's [1957] definition of the economy as the "material means–provisioning system"). Furthermore, they derive directly from the pattern of Mexico's socioeconomic development, in both its structural (long-term) and conjunctural (post-1982) manifestations.

Because "new" social movements obey an economic rationale, both structural and conjunctural, does not of course mean that their demands are *invariably* economic or economistic. Again, it may be worth introducing an elementary distinction. The simple class-based economic identities (allegedly) underlying the "old" social movements and the "old" politics were never, in fact, as simple as all that. Working-class trade unions and socialist parties did not represent collective Pavlovian reactions to capitalist exploitation; on the contrary, they had to be constructed on the basis of distinct national and regional experiences, ideologies, and struggles. Nevertheless, their relationship to the development of the relations of production was crucial. Without large-scale industrialization (or, in some cases, large-scale agrarian commercialization), no such unions or parties developed. In the course of their development, however, parties and unions evinced demands that went beyond the strictly economic: they fought for the suffrage, for the legalization of unions, for international and "solidarist" issues. Sometimes these issues and demands possessed an overt economic rationale; sometimes they did not. The radical wing of the British Chartists saw the suffrage as a "knife and fork" question; Mexican workers in the 1900s also saw "liberal" rights as conferring distinct economic benefits (Anderson 1974). But demands for political representation were not purely instrumental and linked to economic benefits. Equally, demands for just treatment, for respect, for some kind of dignity, cannot be reduced to economic calculation, even if, at root, they derive from the economic (class) subordination of the group making the demands. We might recall—and generalize—Scott's well-known thesis concerning the moral economy of the peasantry (Scott 1976). It is on the basis of the peasant's (definitional) socioeconomic subordination and reliance on subsistence production that a moral economy arises, justifying certain forms of behavior, sanctioning others. Peasant protest does not, therefore, follow some crude stimulus-response mechanism; peasants differ from Pavlov's dogs or Skinner's pigeons; peasants (as both Aristotle and Gramsci would agree, and as some analysts of the new social movements would do well to recall) entertain political and moral notions about the world and act upon them.[4] Scott's point is that those moral notions are (often) derived from the logic of subsistence production. Economics and morality are inextricably intertwined.

What goes for peasants goes for workers, too. Working-class mobilization—of the classic, industrial, class-based kind—combines a distinct economic determinism (i.e., it is not random in its historical timing, regional location, or behavioral form) with no less clear moral and ideological expressions, which may be vital to the development of the movement (Moore 1978). These expressions, furthermore, may depart from the strictly "economic." *Pace* Lenin, the trade unions of tsarist Russia were debarred from taking narrowly economistic action; any strike was political. To a lesser degree, the same was true of Porfirian Mexico. Since the revolution, demands for syndical democratization have been frequent and insistent: the history of the major Mexican unions (and centrals) has been one of constant internal dissent, schism, breakaway, co-optation, and repression. This applies, as Maria Lorena Cook shows, to white-collar unions, such as the teachers', as well as to industrial, blue-collar unions (Cook, this volume). The endless quest for union democracy is not a narrowly economistic struggle, but it is inseparable from the position of socioeconomic subordination in which Mexican workers find themselves vis-à-vis capital and the state. It possesses a clear economic dimension, in terms of both its genesis and its purpose. Cook suggests that the early demands of the teachers' movement, indicate that it organized primarily as a workers' movement, fighting for better material conditions and more effective representation within the union. It soon became apparent, however, that the fight for material conditions was also a political fight.

This is not to say that all social movements, all popular mobilizations, are inherently economic in terms of origin and motivation; to do so would be to legitimize the vaporings of certain new social movement theorists by creating a convenient paleolithic economic determinism. Rather, we should continue to make distinctions. If demands for union democracy have a clear economic genesis and purpose, can the same be said of the demands of the *panista* middle class—or of its many historical precursors? This is an empirical question, though a tough one. The evidence casts doubt on the thesis that middle-class demands for democracy invariably have an economic basis (i.e., that they are impelled by economic considerations, that the middle-class participants in such movements are "constituted" by their shared economic position and interests). Such a thesis cannot, in my view, explain the first great wave of such mobilization, the *reyista/maderista* movements of 1908–1910 (Knight 1986, vol. 1:47–70). The PAN boom of the 1980s appears to correlate with the economic travails of the Mexican middle class; Tarrés stresses the significance of the 1982 crisis (Tarrés, this volume). But, as she also notes, the middle-class mobilization of the 1980s had many antecedents. There were PAN boomlets in the 1960s and 1970s, when that class was riding high. PAN strength has also been concentrated in the more prosperous, less depressed parts of the country, such as Chihuahua: here, the evidence is frankly contradictory (Tarrés, this volume; Aziz Nassif 1985:79, 82).

Studies of PAN mobilization suggest that motives other than the economic are important. (This is not to deny, of course, that some of the PAN leadership and the party's elite backers are dedicated to a forthright economic project, which serves their interest and which is in part a reaction to perceived economic threats, such as Echeverría's populism and López Portillo's nationalization of the banks; the point at issue here is the motivation of the party's mass electorate). On the one hand, *panismo* draws upon a powerful tradition of middle-class "democratic" opposition to the ruling party: we should recall not only the boomlets of the 1960s but also the long tradition of middle-class democratic mobilization that can be traced back through 1940 and 1929 to 1908–1910, when *reyismo/maderismo* burst on the scene as a pioneer movement of democratic middle-class protest. On the other hand, *panismo* is also a strongly Catholic movement, and we should avoid the trite conclusion that Catholic (and other religious) movements are fundamentally economic movements decked out in clerical purple. Attempts to reduce the Cristiada to basic economic interests have failed (Meyer 1973–1974, especially vol. 3:8–50). Other religiously inspired movements defy economic explanations: the LNDR, *sinarquismo*, the Movimiento de Padres de Familia. These, of course, differed according to their class (as well as their regional) base. But they cannot be reduced to class movements. The PAN may be best seen as a political quadruped, resting on four (unequal) legs: a monied minority; a traditional Catholic constituency (strong in San Luis Potosí or Jalisco); a more progressive, prosperous, urban middle class (Chihuahua, Sonora, Baja California, and the Federal District), the heirs of a long tradition of middle-class mobilization; and an economically afflicted middle class, victims of the 1980s recession (Zermeño, this volume).

Of course, the inclusion of the PAN among "social" (or, a fortiori) "popular" movements may be queried. PAN may not constitute a "popular" force; its character as a political party arguably disqualifies it from the "social movement" category. We return to the definitional queries I raised at the outset (how are social or popular movements defined?). One conclusion seems to be that social movements cannot maintain themselves in isolation of state and parties; and the latter—whether it be the PAN in Ciudad Juárez or the FDN/PDR in Michoacán—draw upon the energies of local social movements. While the modus operandi of parties and social movements may differ, they may share common motives, grievances, and memberships, in which case too rigid a demarcation of the two does not assist our understanding of either. Even if we choose to confine our attention to social/popular movements strictly defined (workers' and peasants' associations, barrio organizations, base communities, and certain issue-oriented groups) we find that the new social movements appear, if anything, to be even more firmly economic in their origin, motivation, and demands than many of their predecessors. The historian reviewing the broad sweep of Mexican social history could therefore advance three propositions, all critical of the new social movement thesis. The first, which seems to me irrefutable and hardly worth arguing about, separates Mexico from the (supposed) European stereotype of new, classless, antiparty, popular politics. The second proposition, comparing the Mexican present to the past, would cautiously suggest that things have not substantially changed, or at least that things have changed (that is what history is all about) but that change cannot be interpreted in terms of a departure from a class-based "old" politics to an alternative, "new" politics whose principal actors are social movements possessed of an alternative, nonclass rationale.[5] The third and boldest proposition would be that, on balance, class-based politics are more pronounced now than they have been in the past and that economic issues, related to Mexico's pattern of economic development and serving to constitute political actors in terms of their economic location, are more pressing, contentious, and "mobilizing" than before. If this proposition can be sustained, the new social movements thesis, as deployed by European theorists, becomes a busted flush.

MEXICO: NOTHING NEW UNDER THE SUN?

Propositions two and three lead us to the central question of historical continuity and to "the banal theme, there is nothing new under the sun" (Finley 1985:4–5). In other words, how new are the new social movements? The notion that the Mexicans are—as one revolutionary *político* put it—*un pueblo levantisco* seems to have some basis in fact. Since the later eighteenth century at least, Mexico has been affected by three major revolutions and numerous lesser insurgencies and social movements. In particular, Mexico's peasants (who made up the bulk of the population for much of this period) have displayed a propensity for protest and revolt that seems to set them apart from most Latin American peasantries (Coatsworth 1988:21–62). Mexico was unusual in producing an independence movement that was popular and revolutionary, a liberal movement that was mass-based and tested in the fires of civil war and foreign invasion, and a twentieth-century social revolution. Since that revolution, too, social protest has been recurrent and often decisive in determining the course of Mexican history (the 1930s offer the best example).

It is not difficult to review this impressive national curriculum vitae and to tease out impressive continuities. The insurgent peasantry is as old as the republic—or even the Aztec empire, according to Friedrich Katz (1988 *a*:65–94). Trade union activity can be dated to the mid-nineteenth century; it boomed during the revolution and has continued, in tense symbiosis with the revolutionary regime, ever since. The syndical insurgency of the 1980s has clear precedents in the 1970s (the SUTERM), the 1950s (teachers and railroad workers), the 1940s (railroad and petroleum workers), the 1930s (almost all major industrial sectors). White-collar unionization is nowadays more important than in the past, and traditional industrial unions (such as that of the railroad workers) relatively less important.[6] But the basic grievances, organization, and political impact of independent unions display remarkable continuity: "rank-and-file insurgency has been a constant feature of Mexican industrial relations," Roxborough notes, even during the supposedly placid 1950s (Roxborough 1984:24–25). Even the teachers' close involvement in popular local, especially rural, organizations has ample precedents in the 1930s, and in previous periods (Raby 1974). Similarly, the complex relationship between government and insurgent teachers in the 1980s had its precedent in the late 1950s.[7]

Residential organizations—sometimes seen as characteristic of the "new" social protest—are, of course, the oldest form of collective action, long antedating occupational organizations. Peasant rebellions often assumed a communal form (in the sense that they mobilized the bulk of the community), some communities were known to contain particularly militant barrios. Communal mobilization preceded collective mobilization; the insurgent pueblo preceded the peasant league. The welter of popular protests that punctuated the later eighteenth century—symptomatic of the incipient crisis of the Bourbon regime—were precisely local, communal, and (because political parties did not exist) "apolitical"; women also played a prominent role in the demonstrating, rock throwing, and shouting (Taylor 1979:chap. 4). Certain pueblos or regions acquired reputations for militancy and rebelliousness that have often displayed a remarkable tenacity over time. Juchitán was a troublemaker as early as the seventeenth century. Morelos (especially the Villa de Ayala district) was known to be a hotbed of dissidence long before Zapata, and it continued long after with Jaramillo and the PAOM (Bartra 1985:82, 90). So, too, with the sierra pueblos of western Chihuahua.

Recently, of course, communal organization has shifted from the countryside to the town. The pueblo protest of the past becomes the barrio protest of today. Land invasions become urban as well as rural phenomena, which is hardly surprising in view of Mexico's headlong urbanization.[8] By definition, the barrio organizations of new barrios must be new. But the manner of their demands and organization may not be so original. Urban protest has a long history in Mexico: the renters' movement of the early 1920s affected several major cities (García Mundo 1976; Perló and Schteingart 1984:109). Now protest has expanded from the center-city slums to the low-income neighborhoods. Even the base communities that have played such a key role in urban mobilization possess their historical pedigree: in the rabble-rousing priests of 1810 (and after), or in the social Catholicism Jean Meyer sees as underlying the Catholic revival of the late *porfiriato* and revolution.[9]

The reasons for this continuity of protest are various, complex, and often unresearched. At least two recurrent factors, however, seem relevant. First, traditions of protest were maintained by myth, legend, and symbol, passed down in the form of stories, ballads, and family memories from generation to generation. Ethnic identity clearly helped in the maintenance of such traditions in Juchitán and in the Yaqui Valley. So, too, did formal political movements, such as *cardenismo*. The enthusiasm for *cardenismo* evident in the Laguna or Michoacán, expressed by a population largely too young to have known Cárdenas's presidency, or even his administration of the Tepalcatepec Plan, attests to the durability of such political traditions. In the specific case of Michoacán, communal traditions of agrarian protest (and of clerical conservatism) run deep, and would repay further "microhistorical" investigation.[10]

Second, local sociopolitical structures helped sustain protest over long periods of time. Rebellious pueblos were often rebellious because they were locked in conflict with local haciendas (or with rival pueblos). The villages of Morelos were at odds with the sugar plantations long before Zapata. Matamoros, in the Laguna, battled local planters since its inception and thus acquired the reputation of being a radical—first liberal, than revolutionary—community (Craig 1989). Rival pueblos often constituted their political identities on the basis of ancient dyadic conflicts: radical Juchitán and conservative Tehuantepec; *cardenista* Jiquilpan and clerical Sahuayo; progressive Amilpa and backward Soyaltepec (Adams Dennis 1976). Since they could not escape each other, each tended to define new political trends and opportunities in terms of the old rivalry.

City-based opposition, as I have already suggested, also displayed long continuities over time. The middle-class liberal opposition that confronted Díaz in 1908–1910 rallied to Vasconcelos in 1929, to Almazán in 1940 and, we may hypothesize, to the PAN in the 1960s and 1980s. If these were the moments of greatest national mobilization, there was an almost constant undercurrent of local and regional mobilization, both multiclass in its social makeup and electoral in its political strategy. Thus, the notion that an old, intransigent, class-based politics has recently given way to a new, more pragmatic, multiclass (or "popular") politics is probably a myth.[11] *Navismo*, a classic regional citizens' movement, dates to the late 1950s in San Luis Potosí (Márquez 1987; Martínez Assad 1985). Juchitán experienced anticacical movements throughout the 1940s and 1950s, when the Front for Democratic Renovation won support in an overtly antimachine campaign, and comparable movements affected other *municipios* prior to 1968 (Rubin, this volume). In 1959, Genaro Vázquez and other opponents of the corrupt state government of Caballero Aburto founded the Guerrero Civic Union, which embraced rural workers, students, shopkeepers, and even government employees. The UCG staged a two-month *parada cívica* in Chilpancingo, which achieved the ouster of the governor; in 1960 it successfully ran candidates in municipal elections; and in 1962 it invited severe repression by vigorously challenging for the state governorship (Jacobs 1976). Though stronger in the provinces, such civic mobilization also affected Mexico City: Tarrés (this volume) dates the inception of Ciudad Satélite's lengthy process of social mobilization to around 1960.

In addition to these important civic movements, the Catholic middle class also recurrently mobilized: in support of the LNDR in the 1920s, of the Padres de Familia in the 1930s and after. Women were often prominent in these movements of Catholic protest. These examples remind us that, when we consider the historical backdrop to recent popular protest, we should not overlook movements that stand (conventionally) on the right or that defy any such neat categorization. (Although, as we have noted, Jean Meyer makes a bold attempt to depict the Catholic church of the 1900s and after as a major reformist force: for him, liberation theology finds a precursor in the "social Catholicism" of the late *porfiriato* and revolution.) The biggest popular mobilization of the 1920s was, of course, the Cristiada. Jean Meyer further stresses the mass appeal of *sinarquismo* in the 1930s and '40s (Meyer 1979). By the 1940s, *sinarquismo* was able to take advantage of a groundswell of popular discontent that, in general, failed to achieve organizational clarity and as a result has been largely neglected by historians. For Mexico, World

War II brought severely deteriorating living standards, which in turn provoked not only widespread strike action, but also hunger marches, food riots, and armed resistance to military conscription blended in with banditry, another old Mexican tradition (Niblo 1988).

If we seek to relate this rich history of popular protest to the contemporary scene and to the "new" social movements within it, we can discern numerous continuities but also some genuine innovations. We should try to be clear as to what continuities and innovations mean. There is little point in seeking obscure precedents in order to proclaim that there is nothing new under the sun. On the other hand, those who proclaim the novelty of the new social movements (and implictly or explicitly link it to major changes in Mexico's political economy) are under some theoretical obligation to demonstrate— not just to assert—this novelty. And there are different kinds of novelty. Let me offer three ideal types. First, some social movements may be genuinely new: examples would include gays and greens. They lack precedents and have sprung into existence in the very recent past.[12] Others may have tenuous roots in the past, which we historians can dig up, but their recent efflorescence is most striking—as much a sign of discontinuity as of continuity. One example would be the women's movement, by which I mean a movement premised on some kind of feminist ideology. Women have always played a part, often important, in Mexican social movements: village rebellions, revolutionary mobilizations, Catholic protests. It is another myth to believe that women have only entered politics in the last twenty years. Consciously feminist movements, however, have been rare and weak. Those that arose at the time of the revolution were narrowly based, somewhat elitist, and incapable of making much headway against the ingrained patriarchy of Mexican society (Macías 1982). Women's movements premised upon some kind of feminist consciousness are doubtless stronger currently than they once were. But the main contribution of women to social movements—now as in the past—has been to form part of broader movements, often communally based and lacking a specific feminist ideology. Logically, women have played a big part in barrio organizations, just as they did in village protests throughout history.[13] However, there have also been recent social movements, especially in the countryside, which have remained impervious to this trend: "gender equality is low on most political agendas in rural Mexico," as Fox and Gordillo (1989:156, n. 53) politely put it.

Perhaps the best example of genuinely new and significant mobilization would be the student movement of postwar Mexico. Mexico's students were never politically marginal. They demonstrated against Díaz, they provided recruits to the revolution, to its Catholic opposition, and to *cardenismo*. But in general the student body (especially that of the UNAM, the National University) was conservative rather than radical, and not necessarily conservative in an active, mobilized fashion. The indifference of most students (and, indeed, of many intellectuals) toward the armed revolution was striking (Garciadiego Dantan 1988). Again, in the 1930s, the National University was seen as an obstacle to the *cardenista* reforms: it was a "bourgeois," conservative ivory tower, which only made its commitment to socialist education and transformation as a result of a (minority) internal coup (Lerner 1979:148–164). There is, then, a clear contrast with the role of the UNAM since the 1950s. Of course, not all UNAM students and faculty have been politically active, still less politically active on the left. But the major part played by the UNAM in the politics of the 1950s and 1960s was something new, reflecting changes in the scale and character of higher education and in the course of Mexican political history; it culminated in the National University phenomenon of 1988 (Zermeño, this volume; see Romero 1986:47–48 for right-wing student movements). The same was true of several provincial universities, too. Students played a significant role in social movements in Guerrero, Sinaloa, Sonora, and elsewhere—and, it should be noted, they played their role in the 1950s and 1960s: student activism did not suddenly spring into existence in the late 1960s (Jacobs 1985; Terán and Inzunza 1985; Moncada O. 1985; Rubin, this volume). The story of student activism is therefore an evolutionary but important one, and 1968 should be located within a context of repeated postwar mobilization, which in major respects sets that period apart from the prewar (revolutionary) era, when students played both a less prominent and a less radical role. A quantitative shift—the expansion and concentration of student numbers—helped bring about a genuinely qualitative change. It was perhaps for this reason that the regime, confronting a new, unfamiliar, ideologically articulate protest movement, reacted with such brutality in 1968 (see Fagen and Tuohy 1972:59–60).

Third, we may discern genuine continuities—which should be deemed continuities and not, on the basis of historical amnesia, novelties—but these do not, of course, represent simple carbon copies of the past. You cannot step into the same river twice. Each village riot is distinct; each land invasion or syndical insurgency has its own particular character and cause. Is it legitimate to homogenize such phenomena, thus implying continuity? Were the Morelos land seizures prior to the 1910 Revolution substantially similar to those that characterized the early 1930s (and influenced *cardenismo*), or to those in the northwest in the early 1970s, paving the way for Echeverría's dramatic *reparto*? In each case, land was seized by land-hungry *campesinos*, and we are therefore entitled, I think, to see these phenomena as part of an enduring tradition, itself the product of secular conditions of land hunger and *latifundismo*. In other words, they reflect basic and durable structural features of Mexican society. We could also tease out particular continuities, of the kind already mentioned: the historic rebelliousness of Morelos, which produced Zapata in the 1910s and Jaramillo in the 1940s; the key contribution of the Yaqui Valley to Sonoran agrarian protest in the 1910s, 1930s, and 1970s. In Michoacán not only is the most powerful recent peasant (and strongly Indian) movement the Emiliano Zapata Union of Communal Landowners; in addition, a gang of *guardias blancas* "operates [in the coastal sierra] under the conspicuous name of 'Porfirio Díaz.'" As the source explains, "the pressure on peasant resources is not in itself a recent phenomenon" and "the peasants' response is simply the result of a long historical process of despoliation and exploitation, exacerbated in the last ten years" (Zepeda 1986:324–325, 338).

Of course, there are differences to which we should also be alert: the character of *latifundismo* and of peasant subordination has evolved (not least thanks to the agrarian reform), as has the political context. Peasant movements are not concerned simply with the acquisition of land *tout court*—but then they never were. *Zapatismo* stressed the interdependence of land reform and political autonomy. When contemporary peasant movements demand land and power they are updating but not transcending zapatismo.[14] The varied peasant demands and organizations of today (including the relatively new phenomenon of producer organizations, pressing for price supports) probably present a more complex picture than those of 1910 or 1930, but we should not homogenize and simplify the old peasantry, which, as recent historical research stresses, was also a complex mix of villagers, tenants, sharecroppers, and peons, possessed of different aims and allegiances.[15]Similarly, changes in landlord-peasant relations, though significant, may not alter the fundamental facts of that unequal duality. Transnational companies have supplanted the landlord families of the Bajío, corralled those of Sonora. Capitalism's penetration of the countryside has proceeded apace, especially since the 1940s. But it is not clear that the old, conflictual, landlord-peasant relationship has radically changed: capitalism's perpetuation of the peasantry—sometimes in its new role as a "disguised proletariat" (Paré 1977)—has also ensured the perpetuation of peasant protest and organization, which frequently follow historically familiar paths.

The peasantry's insertion into the political system displays regular continuities, too. Litigation, lobbying, and clientelism have been hallmarks of state-peasant relations at least since the 1920s, if not before. Peasants petitioned Díaz; they solicited the backing of Cárdenas in the 1930s, of Echeverría in the 1970s. They were also prepared to combine legal lobbying with extralegal demonstrations and shows of force, culminating in land seizures. Land seizures presaged the 1910 Revolution in Morelos (and elsewhere), the *cardenista reparto* of the 1930s, and Echeverría's 1976 *agrarista* swan song. The postrevolutionary state's response to such tactics has always been ambivalent. Frequent repression has been combined with occasional concessions. The nature of the state has changed; the personal *caciquismo* of Díaz gave way to the institutional *caciquismo* of the revolution, with its ever-ramifying rural bureaucracy (the Banco Ejidal, *indigenista* agencies, CONASUPO, and the whole bewildering barrage of today's official acronyms). Nevertheless, the old dialectic of negotiation and violence has remained a constant of rural politics. Peasant movements, however intransigent and committed to "autonomy," cannot avoid dialogue with the state. The *zapatistas*, under Magaña, came round to this view, which few or no postrevolutionary peasant movements have seen fit to challenge. "What the UCEZ is can be explained in many respects by the dynamic of its antagonistic relationship with the state" (Zepeda 1986:363–365). This reflects not some new, sophisticated pragmatism on the part of contemporary peasant movements, but rather a fact of political life which has molded Mexican peasant movements since the revolution. Again, therefore, the *continuity* of social protest is striking. The powerful social movements of the recent past rarely lack precedents, and these precedents often display notable similarities; genuinely innovative social movements (gays and greens, for example) are relatively few and feeble. This is true not only for peasant movements but also for syndical insurgency or middle-class democratic demands. There are abundant precedents for all these phenomena; the onus of proof falls to those who assert their striking novelty.

Yet it is undeniable that the sociopolitical context within which such phenomena arise has changed significantly. The Mexico of *neocardenismo* is very different from the Mexico of *paleocardenismo*. In socioeconomic terms it is more populous, urban, industrial, literate; in political terms it is more stable, civilian, centralized, and institutionalized. Does this contextual change denote an absence of continuity and justify assertions of novelty? Is it anachronistic to compare, say, peasant movements in the 1930s and 1980s? To compare Lázaro and Cuauhtémoc? To advance this final point, we must resort to that other favorite historian's pastime, periodization.

A SWISS CHEESE PRI?

Periodization carries an inherent temptation and risk. Periods are homogenized and labeled: the Renaissance, the Enlightenment, the Postwar Era. It is assumed that political, economic, social, and cultural trends obey common rhythms and can be subsumed under these grand headings. Without denying the interconnectedness of politics, society, economics, and culture, it is necessary to exercise a certain skepticism concerning this analytical homogenization. In the case of Mexico, there is the temptation of interpreting recent history in terms of broad swings: the revolutionary era to, say, 1940; the "preferred revolution"—the era of stabilizing development—from the 1940s to, perhaps, 1968; since 1968, "crisis." According to this scheme, the period from about 1940–1968 was the golden age of Mexico's political economy: it was the time when the "peace of the PRI" prevailed, when the economic miracle unfolded, when Mexico was held up as a model of political stability and rapid yet well-managed economic growth. It was a time, too, of generally rising real wages and, we are told, of a falling poverty index. It forms the bland two-dimensional backdrop against which today's images of crisis and mobilization are projected to dramatic effect. I shall argue that the backdrop is misleading and the contrast exaggerated.

First, consider the fall from grace. The late 1960s witnessed harbingers of economic affliction, coupled with an obvious political crisis that, for all its brutal "solution" in October 1968, had long-term consequences: the delegitimization of the system, Echeverría's attempts to recover popular support, the political reform of the 1970s, the diaspora of 1968 veterans who carried their message to differents regions and sectors of the country. These processes in turn provoked responses. The private sector, and much of the middle class, recoiled from Echeverría's supposed radicalism; the political reform focused greater attention on the electoral process; and López Portillo sought to placate both right and left by an oil-financed spending spree that was as short lived as it was ill advised. These interlocking events combined to generate the "crisis" that, according to many observers, has wracked the Mexican system at least since 1982 and perhaps since 1968, and out of which the new social movements have sprung.

This chronology is well known but, I am suggesting, a little too trite. It homogenizes the 1940–1968 period, exaggerating its stability and consensuality, and does likewise for the post-1968 period of crisis, exaggerating its novelty (and thus erring in the direction of apocalyptic prediction). It cannot be doubted that, since the late 1960s, Mexico's hitherto "successful" pattern of growth faltered, stalled, and entered a period of major redirection.[16] This, as I have said, represented in part a structural reconstitution, in part a conjunctural crisis, the product of the petroleum price collapse and the debt crisis (the relation of conjuncture to structure is, as usual, difficult to unravel). As might be expected, this dual economic crisis provoked protest and mobilization that displayed a clear economic and class rationale: the protagonists were "constituted" as economic actors and sought—whether by means of direct economic demands or indirect political demands, e.g., for syndical democracy—to achieve some kind of amelioration of and control over their precarious material destinies. Apart from the resulting domestic conflicts, the process also logically involved a reassertion of Mexican nationalism, which fed into *neocardenismo*. These movements, I have suggested, followed old precedents and revealed deep continuities. Very likely popular protest has been more vigorous in the 1980s than it was in the 1950s (the case would be weaker if either the 1940s or 1960s were chosen for comparison). I know of no attempt, however, to display this systematically; the point is usually assumed as obvious—a very risky historical procedure. But even the 1950s, the halcyon days of stabilizing development and presumed *priísta* hegemony, were not entirely tranquil: they witnessed major labor disputes (teachers and railroad workers), land invasions, peasant mobilization (notably the UGOCM in the northwest), civic protests against *caciquismo*, and the *henriquista* bolt from the PRI, which finally culminated in the "last old-style insurrection," that of Celestino Gasca in 1961 (Bartra 1985:85–89; see also Stevens 1974; Pellicer de Brody and Reyna 1981:44–62, 123–214). True, the more benign economic climate made concession and co-optation easier in the 1950s, but it would be a mistake to think that Mexico has shifted between polar extremes of social consensus and social strife in the last twenty-five years.

We should perhaps see the social protests of recent years chiefly as replications of earlier movements, now rendered more extensive, and perhaps more radical, by harsh economic circumstances. The majority of the new social movements would not, therefore, be considered strictly new, but rather as developed examples of historically familiar phenomena. The point at which such a *quantitative* increase can be said to produce a *qualitative* shift is an old, intractable question. But we should at least be clear that the hard historical evidence points, at best, to a quantitative increase, to more of the same.

Apart from the economic dimension, which I have stressed, there is an important political or institutional dimension. Again, the conventional wisdom refers to a long era of *priísta* hegemony (c.1940–1968), followed by delegitimization, the growth of opposition, the increased pluralization of Mexican society, finally translated into the vigorous political opposition(s) of the 1980s—the *panista* challenge in the north, in particular, and the *cardenista* breakthrough of July 1988. Again, this is true to a degree, but arguably exaggerated. It overemphasizes, above all, the strength and depth of *priísta* hegemony in the 1940s–1960s. Some caveats have already been mentioned: at the national level, the dissident unions of the 1950s and 1960s, the PAN boomlets of the 1960s, the student movement; locally, recurrent movements of political opposition (often involving PRI breakaways) in Oaxaca, San Luis Potosí, Guerrero, Yucatán, and elsewhere (Martínez Vázquez and Arellanes M. 1985:203–237; Márquez 1987; Jacobs 1976; Pellicer de Brody and Reyna 1981). The more one looks, the more the hegemony of the PRI resembles—in Jeffrey Rubin's felicitous phrase— Swiss cheese: it is full of holes. That being the case, the delegitimation of the PRI since 1968 (or whenever) looks less sudden and apocalyptic, more progressive and familiar. This *could* lead to the conclusion that the decline of the PRI is a longer, more debilitating process than often believed; or it could suggest that the PRI never exercised the kind of unblemished hegemony sometimes suggested, that inherent weaknesses and incapacities have been facts of party life, and that party and system have lived with repeated ups and downs, challenges and responses, since their very inception (say, 1946). Thus, talk of an all-powerful state, exercising almost absolute control, with its corporatist organizations, such as the CNC, serving as sole mediator between state and peasantry, is probably highly exaggerated; and, by creating a false backdrop, it overestimates the degree to which state control has eroded and popular contestations have increased (Tamayo, Harvey, Pérez Arce, all in this volume).

It is worth developing this line of argument further, considering whether, on the basis of history since about 1940, the PRI should not be seen as a more ramshackle institution than often supposed, albeit one that, having survived in ramshackle form for half a century, may continue to do so; or whether, on the other hand, the conventional image of a once mighty, hegemonic party, now facing a drastic and unprecedented hemorrhaging of its support and legitimacy, is closer to the mark. We might call these, respectively, the Hapsburg and Bourbon images of the PRI: the first chronically faltering but remarkably durable; the second, once lusty and able, fallen victim to dissent, schism, and breakdown. Indeed, these historical labels have an additional appropriateness. Hapsburg rule involved a kind of social pact between rulers and ruled (the latter including creole elites as well as Indian and mestizo masses); the Bourbons, in contrast, tried to railroad a modernizing project through a resentful colony. Hapsburg government mirrored civil society; Bourbon government strove to recast it.

My argument is that the PRI, for most of its existence, has been something of a Hapsburg institution. I am certainly not reviving the old notion of the PRI as a broad, aggregative and representative party (see Scott 1964). I would argue, however, that the PRI served to aggregate and represent a range of important elites (some of whom were linked to broader clienteles); it represented interests rather than ideology. It did so from its very birth: the PNR was a loose assemblage of caciques and bosses, and even the PRM, for all its radical rhetoric and genuine mass base, was constituted from above, by national and provincial elites. Thus it embraced a huge range of elements: radical *lombardistas* (who made a lot of noise and drew attention) and conservative caciques (who, maintaining a lower profile, successfully colonized the PRM and, in doing so, cannibalized *cardenismo*). Thereafter, through its various organizational, ideological, and nomenclatural shifts, the party has continued to reflect, aggregate, and embrace the interests of dominant elites. Business elites, it is true, have remained outside, but they have exercised abundant influence nonetheless. Provincial elites, too, have sometimes refrained from direct participation in the party—but chiefly because they rest content with party organization and activity (Schryer 1980:138). In many cases, however, the party has served as a direct representative of such elites, for example, in Los Altos (Martínez Saldaña and Gándara Mendoza 1976; see also Arreola Ayala 1985 for México State). Presidents may come and go, pendulum fashion; national *camarillas*, scrutinized by Rod Camp and Peter Smith, weave their clientelist webs in the UNAM and the ministries; but in the provinces elite control (direct or indirect) of the PRI has generally remained strong, premised upon the old mechanisms of *caciquismo*. *Caciquismo* has also continued to flourish in the unions, in peasant organizations, and in the sprawling cities (Pérez Arce and Harvey, both in this volume; Tamayo 1986:186, 196; Fox and Gordillo 1989:136–137; Cornelius 1972).

This is not, of course, a conflict-free system. On the contrary, it generates recurrent splits, factions, and disputes. *Caciquismo* is, by definition, a system defying institutionalization. Caciques owe their power to noninstitutional factors; cacical power is transferred by noninstitutional means. *Caciquismo* may be remarkably durable (Hapsburg style, it translates informal socioeconomic power into political clout) but it does not lend itself to decorous forms of political representation. Elections mask *caciquismo* but do not usually change caciques. It is often argued that recent socioeconomic trends have invalidated this entrenched political practice. Massive cities are, perhaps, less prone to cacical control: "build cities and they will take votes away from you" (Héctor Aguilar Camín, quoted in Márquez 1987:111). The urban middle class, the historic critic of *caciquismo*, has also grown in numbers and stridency. I am, however, skeptical of the argument that modernization, urbanization, and literacy automatically doom machine politics. Neither Mexican—nor U.S.—history proves this point conclusively. Boss politics endures in big cities and big industrial unions. It still dominates relatively developed regions, like the state of México.[17] Conjunctural economic change is perhaps more directly relevant. It is another standard argument that, in times of economic crisis, elites and bosses lack the resources with which to buy clients. Again, we should not overdo the argument. When times are hard, sparse resources may still get results. Furthermore, the PRI still seems able to stump up the goods when the stakes are high (for example, in Chihuahua [Lau 1989:27–28] or Michoacán). And if conjunctural economic crisis is the root problem, its passing may leave the system in being and ready to bounce back.

But there are also two important political factors at work. The more "technocratic" national elites of the 1970s and 1980s have shown a congenital dislike of *caciquismo* and have taken steps to mitigate it. The political reform infused new life into the electoral process; de la Madrid flirted with free elections at the beginning of his term; Reyes Heroles sought to clean up the SNTE; Salinas has shown a readiness to attack syndical *caciquismo*, or at least its commanding heights. Traditional middle-class concerns for good government (as old, at least, as the 1910 Revolution) seem to have infected the high *políticos* of the regime. Still, we may be skeptical about the commitment or, even more, the likely effect of these measures. Bourbon attempts to substitute high-minded and honest officials for corrupt tax farmers came to naught and Mexican history is littered with examples of political and administrative reforms wrecked on the flinty rocks of *caciquismo*. Such, in part, was the fate of Carrillo Puerto's reforms in Yucatán, or of Cárdenas's nationwide (Joseph 1988). Recent history, too, suggests a dogged resistance by local elites and bosses to the reforms of the center. De la Madrid's promise of free elections was confounded by the opposition of local bosses, particularly in the north; in the particular case of San Luis Potosí, Enrique Márquez notes, "one factor was fundamental: the retreat of the de la Madrid government in the face of forces as archaic as they are, apparently, indispensable" (Márquez 1987:118). (This suggests an interesting and neglected angle to the discussion: the role of the center as a force for reform and mediation, capable of bridling the worst excesses of arbitrary local power. It could be hypothesized that, but for the PRI and Mexico City, Chiapas would resemble Guatemala or El Salvador). At any rate, one aspect of the celebrated technocrat-*político* dichotomy would seem to be this: national technocrats faced strenuous, local, elite resistance in their attempts—perhaps rhetorical, perhaps real—to create a modern representative system.

The second point concerns the longevity of the system. It is a common anthropomorphic historical fallacy to believe that social systems (nations, empires, regimes) age in some inevitable and even predictable fashion.[18] Certainly, none is eternal; yet neither are they bound by the strict constraints of biological aging. This fallacy seems to underlie a good deal of thinking about postrevolutionary Mexico. The demise of the system (defined in terms of the hegemony of the revolutionary family and its official party) has often been predicted. Recently, analysts have stressed the incompatibility of a modern, urban, industrial society with such a centralized, one-party system (an incompatibility appreciated even by some of the leaders of the PRI). They have pointed to the decline of corporatist forms of control and representation, such as the CNC and CNOP, and cited "the conflictual decomposition of traditional forms of political brokerage and control" (see Foweraker, "Popular Movements and Political Change in Mexico," this volume). In short, they suggest that traditional *caciquismo* is coming to an end and that it will be replaced (presumably) by a functioning pluralist party system and/or by new forms of politics that transcend both liberal pluralism and traditional *caciquismo* (there is, in this latter prognosis, a certain rosy romanticism, which pervades quite a bit of the new social movements literature).

It seems to me much too early to write the obituary of that most durable figure in the Mexican political landscape, the cacique. In the past, reformist movements have perforce recruited and re-created caciques (among other things, this reminds us that not all caciques are standpat conservatives; the populist cacique is a recurrent phenomenon, local, regional, and even national). *Caciquismo* has flourished in urban settings, in trade unions, and in peasants' leagues. So long as *caciquismo* remains, of course, it will provoke both opposition movements dedicated to democratization (for which read "accountability")[19] as well as top-down ("Bourbon") attempts to create an efficient, centralized, impersonal bureaucracy. As a result of such efforts, cacical heads roll: local bosses are eliminated; trade union leaders are thrown to the wolves. Recent examples join a long list spanning the entire history of the postrevolutionary state. It is not clear that such periodic purges have any lasting structural effect. Rather, they reflect the system's capacity to absorb demands and offer modest concessions—but specific, ad hoc concessions rather than thoroughgoing democratic reforms. The latter, as Paul Cammack has convincingly argued, would scupper the system (Cammack 1988). Genuine liberalization would end the *pax priísta* as we know it. Qualified concessions—the removal of an unpopular governor, boss, *charro* leader— are recurrent and, apparently, quite effective.

Thus, Mexican political history, especially at the local and regional level, is one of constant, contained conflicts and changes. It is a myth to believe that change is a recent phenomenon, that a monolithic state once ruled impervious to popular protest, or that the concessions made to recent social movements are of a completely new order. Instead, we may posit a rolling cycle of renovation, stabilization, ossification, protest, and renewed renovation. *Navismo*—the celebrated *potosino* political protest movement, has been compared to a comet, returning every twenty years (Márquez 1987:120). Juchitán, too, has gone through its cycles of caciques. A cluster of local or regional cycles may or may not add up to a national cycle. Perhaps the 1980s has witnessed a clustering of such cycles, within localities, unions, and peasant movements (rather as the 1930s did). That can only be judged on the basis of hindsight and future research. But even a cluster of such cycles

of renovation—propitiated in some measure by the new administration—
may not yield genuine structural change.

In part, this may be because of the system's capacity to accommodate (as
well as to repress) movements of renovation. The PRI's capacity for co-
optation is legendary but well founded. The contributors to the workshop
from which this book emerged have cited numerous examples of regime
compliance in the face of popular demands. They have also debated at length
the question of political involvement and party activism, the rejection of
which has been seen, by a good many theorists, as the hallmark of the new
social movements (Evers 1985:45–46; Regalado Santillán 1986:139; Zepeda
1986:360–361; Cook, this volume; Foweraker, "Popular Movements and
Political Change," this volume). The debate, as I have suggested, is often
couched in normative as well as analytical terms: it revolves around what
social movements *should* do and what they, *in fact*, do. The first part of the
debate recycles (unwittingly, no doubt) the old wrangles of the Second
International, which pitted Kautsy against Jaurès (again, nothing new under
the sun). In the 1900s the debate was whether socialist parties should
participate in bourgeois parliaments and governments; now the debate is
whether social movements should participate in political parties; either way,
purists and utopians (and, some would add, hypocrites) confronted pragmatists
and realists. The latter seemed to predominate in the workshop: several
chapters in this book not only advocate party political activism (and query the
high-minded abstentionism of Evers et al.) but also point out (rightly) that it
is happening, inevitably and pervasively (Foweraker, "Popular Movements
and Political Change," and Harvey, both in this volume; Torres Mejía 1989).
Social movements are not just engaged in a dialogue with the state and with
political parties; the 1988 election brought home the extent to which electoral
politics are crucial for social mobilization and protest. This has always been
true to a considerable degree locally. With the political reform and the rise of
panismo and, a fortiori, *neocardenismo* it has become true at the state and
national levels, too. This makes the idea of an apolitical social movement,
eschewing politics, huddling in splendid social isolation, even more a
romantic figment of the European intellectual imagination. In a sense, this
empirical fact settles the normative debate, for it is clear that the apolitical
social movement is something of a myth. Even movements that start out, as
many do, with a healthy distrust of politics and politicians find that eventually
they have to come to terms with both. So it was with the Second International.

In the Mexican case, as several other chapters suggest, this carries the
risk, or likelihood, of co-optation. Autonomy is sacrificed for the sake of
results. From a historical perspective this is familiar, almost, it seems,
inevitable. Movements (like *zapatismo*) begin as isolated, abstentionist,
purist protests. They are either suffocated, or incorporated into the political
system. Incorporation need not imply a traitorous derogation of first
principles, and it may require substantial concessions on the part of the
regime (as in the annihilation of the Morelos planter class). But there is a
cyclical character to such reforms, as already suggested. Renovation gives

rise to a new status quo, to ossification, and to fresh protest. The challenging counterculture of the early protest is either stifled or subtly appropriated. The popular leaders of yesteryear (Cedillo, for example) become the resented caciques of today. It may be too strong to talk of an iron law of oligarchy, but a plastic tendency toward *caciquismo* certainly runs through Mexican history.[20] This must engender skepticism insofar as the transforming power of the (new?) social movements is considered. Change is occurring and will continue to occur, as it has in the past. Shifting social structures will induce different emphases within protest movements—as white-collar unions supplant blue-collar, as burgeoning city barrios generate local movements, as peasant grievances focus on prices instead of land. But these are manifestations of continuity within change. Genuinely new protest movements—greens and gays—are the exception, and hardly crucial. The women's and student movements, both of whose pre-1940 origins were tenuous, have exerted greater political impact. But, especially in regard to student mobilization, this development has been an evolutionary process, clearly evident during the "stable" 1950s. Student mobilization is not coeval with the post-1968 "crisis"; it coexisted (often unhappily) with the "hegemonic" PRI during the latter's supposed heyday. It is therefore too early and too risky to speak of a transformation of a political culture that, as Zermeño remarks, is so deeply rooted in the past. Thus, as is often the case, a historical perspective induces caution, even conservatism, not because historians are necessarily curmudgeonly conservatives who deny the possibility of change in history,[21] nor because there is nothing new under the sun. Rather, a review of Mexican history since the revolution, especially since 1940, suggests a regime that was never as strong, absolute, and decisive, nor a civil society as weak, cowed, and inert, as often supposed; and, against such a revised backdrop, the social mobilization of the 1980s, albeit greater than in the past, appears less threatening or, if you prefer, less promising.

NOTES

1. This chapter forms part of an ongoing workshop whose principal focus is the contemporary (roughly, post-1968) political scene. My job is to offer a historical perspective, stretching back to the Revolution of 1910, though concentrating rather more on the post-1940 period. "Mid-twentieth century" is therefore a loose periodization.

2. Autonomy is a recurrent concept that at least has received some definitional attention. See Fox and Gordillo 1989.

3. Weber's caution bears repeating: "What is really at issue is the intrinsically simple demand that the investigator should keep unconditionally separate the establishment of empirical facts and his own practical evaluations, i.e., his evaluation of these facts as satisfactory or unsatisfactory" (Weber 1949:11). See, for example, Prieto 1986:94.

4. Rural to urban migrants in Jalisco "are men and women from the countryside who bring with them no experience of previous struggle"; thus, the bulk of new recruits to the Jalisco working class "derived from the countryside, bringing with

them elements of the peasant psychology which obstructed the development of their class consciousness" (Regalado Santillán 1986:135; Tamayo 1986:187). Such assumptions of peasant inertia (in Jalisco) should be set against Craig 1983.

5. See Foweraker, who calls 1968 "a watershed year in Mexican political history because it marks a general shift from the politics of *class* antagonisms to the politics of *popular-democratic* struggle" (1989a:109).

6. Torres Mejía (1989) sees the electricians' movements of the mid-1970s as the last movement mounted by a major industrial union in defiance of the government.

7. Joseph Foweraker ("Popular Organization and Institutional Change," this volume) separates past from present, noting that the SEP at least occasionally recognized the teachers' movements of the 1980s as valid interlocutors, something inconceivable in the 1950s. But this is open to debate. See also Pellicer de Brody and Reyna 1981:131–155.

8. As Juan Manuel Ramírez Saiz correctly reminds us, land invasions were realized systematically from the 1930s in the principal cities of the country (Ramírez Saiz, this volume).

9. Meyer 1973-74, vol. 2:46-53, 212-231. On the late 1960s genesis of the ecclesiastical base communities, see Concha Malo 1986:233–292.

10. Note, for example, the participation of old *agrarista* communities like Naranja and Tarejero in the UCEZ of the 1970s and 1980s (Zepeda 1986:323–378).

11. Harvey (this volume) sees the formation of multisector organizations, which link campesinos to other social groups and region to region, and which, in doing so, raise consciousness (and even create a new sense of identity) as something qualitatively new in Chiapas. Perhaps this holds for the time frame he cites, but the prior history of social mobilization in Chiapas is rich and would appear to embrace most of these features (see García de León 1985, vol. 2:chap. 7, 228–235).

12. I take my universe of allegedly new social movements from Slater (1985a:1) and Evers (1985:43), although they neglect the gay movement. As regards the greens, I am suggesting that a formally ecological movement is a new phenomenon in Mexico, although protests against ecological abuses (which are not easy to distinguish from movements of economic self-defense) are far from new. Recent campaigns against Laguna Verde bear comparison with the early twentieth-century protests against the devastation wrought by the oil companies—notably the Dos Bocas blowout (1908) and the 1910 gusher, Potrero del Llano No. 4. Such protests were, in a sense, ecological *avant la lettre*. For want of space and expertise, I will not try to discuss either the ecological movement or the (nonstudent) youth movement, on which there is an interesting and growing literature (see Zermeño, this volume; Tamayo and Ladrón de Guevara 1986:105–120).

13. Taylor describes the role of women in colonial riots in strikingly contemporary terms: "perhaps because men were more often traveling outside the communities or working fields several miles from town, more women than men usually took part [in village rebellions]": (Taylor 1979:116; see also Ramírez Saiz and Logan, both in this volume).

14. Taylor 1979:348. See also Rubin, this volume. Early *zapatismo*, we might say, sought land reform with political autonomy and village self-goverment; late *zapatismo* (1919 and after) settled for land reform with political integration into the national revolutionary state/movement. Either way, the importance of politics was explicitly recognized. Of course, the shift from one stance to another was neither simple nor sudden.

15. On contemporary peasant differentiation, see Fox and Gordillo 1989:145–158. Recent scholarship has underscored the complexity and heterogeneity of peasant society and peasant demands during the Porfirian/revolutionary period. See, for example, Brading 1980.

16. According to Stephen Haber (1989), this successful pattern of development, the oligopolistic product of later Porfirian industrialization, was inherently flawed and, we may infer, bound to run out of steam.

17. Arreola Ayala 1985. As Fox and Gordillo observe: "*Caciquismo*, or 'bossism,' is not simply an archaic holdover from precapitalist forms of production. Traditional elites are often replaced by new concentrations of power, modernizing rather than eliminating *caciquismo*" (Fox and Gordillo 1989:136–137).

18. David Hackett Fischer terms this "the pathetic fallacy"—"the ascription of animate behavior to inanimate objects" (Hackett Fischer 1970:190–193).

19. Rubin raises some important considerations concerning the significance (for participants) of "democracy" in Juchitán. The implication is that formal electoral democracy is not a supreme goal and that political support/legitimacy depend on other than procedural factors. It follows that parties (such as PAN) that stress procedural democracy above all will enjoy limited popular support, whereas those— *including the PRI*—that can display responsibility and responsiveness to local demands will benefit. This seems to be borne out by the story of the recent (July 1989) municipal elections in, for example, Chihuahua (Rubin, this volume).

20. Cook, this volume, and Fox and Gordillo (1989:137) note how, with the agrarian reform, "ejido leadership, with state support, often became new caciques." Examples of such cacical formation are legion: Friedrich (1986), Azaola Garrido and Krotz (1974, vol. 3:129–144), and Rubin (this volume) deal with *caciquismo* at the local level; individual cases are analyzed by Márquez 1988 and Arreola Ayala 1988:385–393, 395–403.

21. On the contrary, I would stress the importance of change—for example, the sociopolitical change induced by the Revolution of 1910—against those ("revisionists") who stress the seamless continuity of Mexican history, from *porfiriato* to present. See Knight 1985. Part of that change, however, involved the establishment, over time, of an effective—but far from "absolute"—party/state, which has successfully reproduced itself, weathering political and socioeconomic upheavals, for some fifty years: a modestly Hapsburg achievement.

3

Political Organization in Mexican Civil Society

6

The Enduring Union Struggle for Legality and Democracy

FRANCISCO PÉREZ ARCE

NIGHT FALLS ON A DIFFICULT DAY

Take the twenty years since 1968. In my opinion the period makes sense, not merely for its point of departure—the student movement, generally accepted as a historical watershed—but also for the date of its destination, July 6, 1988, and the most important general elections in recent Mexican history.

Whether we take the official figures or the estimates of the opposition, the results of these elections reveal a profound change in Mexican public opinion, and this new electoral reality has changed the way of doing politics in Mexico. Whatever else, it has affected, perhaps irreversibly, the figure of the president. Unlike his precedessors, Salinas cannot appear infallible, and his legitimacy will continue to be questioned. Even if his policies win him personal prestige and political force, for the people themselves the figure of the president is no longer the unquestioned, unchallenged, because just and benign, court of last resort.

It is at least possible that the PRI will recover its unity and support in places where it was defeated, but it will never be the same as it was. In the collective imagination it is no longer invincible, and elections take on a whole new meaning. In the past the electoral contests where opposition parties fought real battles, as in the state of Chihuahua or the municipality of Juchitán, were really very rare. But by 1989 the government had to recognize the defeat of its party in Baja California and hand over the state government to the National Action party (PAN). In Michoacán it appears that the *neocardenistas* in the form of the Party of the Democratic Revolution (PRD) easily won the legislative elections, but here the government refused to acknowledge defeat and imposed a fraudulent majority for the PRI. In general, the PRI will now have to make wide concessions and build new alliances, or else it will lose out to powerful social forces in the regions—or have to hold onto power by fraud without winning the popular vote.

Suddenly the Mexican Congress stopped being a mere democratic facade, and its mannered and courtly pretense disappeared forever. A slim PRI majority faces a belligerent opposition that knows itself to be underrepresented. This "underrepresentation" is even more evident in the Assembly of the Federal District, where official recognition of its minority vote still gave the PRI a majority of the seats. In other words, the combativity of a healthy opposition draws its strength not only from the seats it holds but also from the sure belief that its real support was shrunk by computerized manipulation of electoral results. And as if this were not enough, the PRI majority has to deal with groups within its own party who feel slighted, and who can now threaten the PRI majority with a mere handful of seats. This has already happened with the "petroleum deputies," who sought political judgment for then-governor of the state of Mexico and ex-director of PEMEX, so reviving the accusations made by the left-wing opposition in the previous legislature. And it is not impossible that one day they may want to collect what is owed to them for La Quina.

The working-class sector of the official party grows weaker by the day and could finally lose its loyalty after a decade of complete submission. It is true that it again bowed the knee during the conflicts in the petroleum workers' and teachers' unions, but the restlessness of the bosses who feel their power threatened and of the masses who go on suffering the wage erosion, may reach their limit. Jonguitud Barrios, one of the old political bosses, was a silent witness to the concerted attack on his colleague Joaquín Hernández Galicia (La Quina). Some months later, faced with growing internal opposition, the government forced him to give up his political domain within the teachers' union (National Union of Workers in Education, or SNTE). But if his power has been diluted, it has not been eliminated entirely. Someday, somehow, he can still seek retribution.

In short, the weak congressional majority[1] tends to sharpen the struggles inside the PRI and to enhance the power of the groups controlled by traditional boss figures or groups at odds with the present leadership in the government. In this way the precarious congressional dominance hampers the reform of the PRI, which appears obliged to seek an all-inclusive unity and must avoid damaging internal confrontations. It faces a seemingly insoluble contradiction: unity or change.

As for the municipal struggles, the passing of the single-party system will have immediate and not so immediate consequences. The former are linked to the sharpening of electoral contests and the now vigorous defense of a clean vote (and insofar as this gives new meaning to electoral contests it is something new in the national political culture). The latter involve the emergence of regional- and national-level political alternatives, with more popular political platforms than the PRI, and with real prospects of winning elections. The PRI always based its predominance on its position as the party in power, the party of the government. This was what made it attractive—not the effectiveness of its policies, nor, still less, the appeal of its ideology, but the very quality of its hold on power. The PRI is powerful because it promises to keep power for ever. If it fails in this promise, it will grow weak. And therein lies the contradiction between the declared end of the "practically one-party" era and its open desire to recover its former strength. Its identification with the government loses it popular support because the government's neoliberal economic policies have led to a continuous downward pressure on the living standards of the population at large—and this pressure is bound to continue during the first year of the Salinas administration, or longer. But a real separation from the government would weaken the PRI. As was only too clear in the recent elections in Tabasco, overwhelming electoral victories for the official party can indeed be achieved by the government and from the government, when it follows the logic of the "practically one party." This was similarly demonstrated in the more resonant case of the local legislative elections in Michoacán, where the government brought all its influence to bear, and where it was not content to win a merely modest victory.

Natural Leaders

One of the most important aspects of popular mobilization is the recruitment of natural leaders. The PRI could count on its powers of co-optation because it could offer immediate benefits. But the government line of the last administration (highly restricted welfare policies alongside a permanent wage freeze) and the new prospects of the opposition (and especially the left, which is most easily identified with social welfare policies) have opened the door to a new generation of natural leaders who can hope to pursue their careers outside of the PRI. It is no accident that the message uniting the social forces in opposition carries echoes of the *cardenista* era. In the days of syndical insurgency, the words of Rafael Galván recalled the popular appeal of Cárdenas ("revolutionary nationalism" required a strong welfare state). In the recent electoral conjuncture, no one could better represent the popular and nationalist alternative to the neoliberalism of Salinas and de la Madrid than the son of General Cárdenas.

It is possible that the PRI will go on pulling apart. Many opposition candidates have emerged from its ranks and some, like López Obrador, the *cardenista* candidate to the governorship of Tabasco, have been PRI figures with huge support and prestige among broad sectors of the population.

The Unions

Until now, traditional working-class leaders could always negotiate certain political favors (congressional seats, municipal presidencies, and governorships); but in the elections of July 6, 1988, the majority of the PRI candidates who were "sacrificed" in the districts where the government recognized PRI defeats were in fact bosses in the corporate union system. This reflected not only their lack of popular appeal but also their declining influence within the official party itself.

Thus, the changes occurring in Mexican politics target the very heart of the political system and threaten the mainstays of institutional stability. At the beginning of the 1970s, Cosío Villegas concluded that the two main characteristics of this system were an executive power or, more specifically, a presidency of the republic, "with exceptional powers, and a predominant official political party" (Cosío Villegas 1972). These two mainstays are changing. Moreover, the "political pact" between government and the large corporations of the party has visibly weakened, and the Salinas project appears to require that it weaken still further. Perhaps this is the lesson to be drawn from the recent events in the petroleum workers' and teachers' unions. But it is a dangerous game because the weakness of official syndicalism can encourage democratic alternatives close to the opposition—unless the government chooses to depose the old syndical bosses to make way for different and more docile old bosses, while showing everyone that it means business (which is what happened in PEMEX). In this case the government leaves no doubt that it can get tough. Or, with the effrontery it displayed in the case of the teachers, it can replace an old dinosaur with a new and flexible leader quite capable of placating the democratic opposition within the union. These are just some of the parts of the "modernization puzzle" that continues to require antipopular wage policies.

This political picture is not simply the result of one bad day. The results were not unimaginable, although they were certainly unexpected. What happened on July 6, provoking the unforgettable "failure" of the computer in the Ministry of the Interior (Gobernación) was the climax to a history, or better to say different histories, of diverse and sometimes diffuse popular movements. None of them was able to establish itself as an organized and permanent political force, and the discontinuous history over the past twenty years has seen a few successful movements and many resounding failures. But this sporadic and labyrinthine history spawned groups of leaders and dissident citizens in every corner of the country. From the student movement of 1968 to the syndical insurgency of the 1970s; from the organization of popular neighborhoods in cities big and small to the teachers' rebellion of the 1980s, and to the uprising of the citizenry in September 1985.

In many ways the student movement of 1968 anticipated the economic crisis. It called attention to the limitations of the political system. The movement found its second wind in the mobilization of 1971. The unforgettable events of October 2 and June 10 are historically indissoluble. Beyond their political impact, which was clearly reflected in the discourse of President Echeverría and its central thesis of a "democratic opening," they also indirectly influenced many social movements. Hundreds, possibly thousands, of students opted for an intense political commitment as much in the countryside as in the city. They were the seeds of a new political culture. Students converted to political activism among the workers, peasants, and organizations of squatters served as catalysts of a new political perspective that was national in scope. More than mere carriers of political fliers and pamphlets, these student cadres would participate in all the important popular movements and in every attempt to build new parties and other political organizations.

Syndical Insurgency, 1970–1976

After the mobilizations of 1958–1959 (when the railroad workers led a movement that was finally repressed and its leaders imprisoned, and the teachers of the Federal District also played a salient role in economic and democratic struggles), the Mexican proletariat sank into a decade of almost total control by the official unions. It was the decade of corporatist consolidation, buttressed by continuing growth in industry and urban employment and by rising real wages. Protest in this period was left to the nonindustrial sectors such as the doctors and the students. During the student explosion of 1968, the workers remained on the sidelines (Pérez Arce 1980).

The 1960s

The workers looked upon the unions as part of the federal administration, and sometimes as an employment office more closely linked to management than to government. During this decade the use of the terms "*charro*" and "syndical *charrismo*" became general. The adjective was adopted by the working-class movement insofar as the struggle against "*charrismo*" lent a certain coherence to the period of the "insurgency." Notions of "independent syndicalism" or "syndical democracy" challenge the core of *charrismo*, but it must still be pointed out that *charrismo* is also a question of corruption, collusion with management, and subservience to the government.

> A *charro* is someone who has an office (the union's office) and has a political career (in the PRI) and will probably become a congressional deputy, or is one, or already was one. It is someone whom the workers never saw working as a worker (or they already forgot it because it happened so long ago), who dresses like the boss, and has a new car with driver. "Those from the union," in the language of the workers, are those who live from the Executive Committee (their power rests on the negotiation and control of the collective contract; it is bureaucratic power).

Union meetings and elections were rare occurrences in most factories. If it were possible to calculate the number of unions that held meetings as required by the statutes, the results might be surprising. Even a brief archival survey discovers a huge number of protests by workers who complain that the *charros* held such meetings "ten years ago," "twenty years ago," or "never that we remember." As for elections, if they happen at all they are for minor posts, and rarely do they renew national committees. There were hardly any exceptions to these rules in small and medium industry. All this explains why workers lost all faith in the unions as organizations for the defense of their interests. To give them back some meaning they had to reject them, and this was the motive of the working-class insurgency.

The 1970s

Working-class insurgency was a spontaneous outburst of popular discontent. Innumerable movements in small and medium industry struggled against *charro* unions and for independent unionism. It was an attempt not so much to clean up the unions they had as to build new unions. What characterized these unions, what made them attractive and gave them meaning, was that they were put together by the workers themselves, who ran them democratically. They called meetings and respected the outcome. They published the statutes. They rejected collusion with government or management. Most important of all to this young working class of the first or second generation was their participation in setting up the union. It was not a question of organizing unions formally distinct from those there before. They did not reject the existing legal framework, nor did they advertise different ideological beliefs. Very often even the statutes were similar to those of the old union. But the new unions stayed outside the discredited federations and confederations.

In the struggle for independent unions the new leaders had no overall strategy. It seemed more like a natural tendency of the movement, which followed logically from their attempts to achieve their immediate and rather limited goals. The Federal Labor Law (revised in 1970) had considered such a possibility and had seen it as real. From a strictly legal standpoint no more than twenty workers needed to request the registration of a new union. Once the registration was issued (an administrative matter the authorities had to execute within ninety days), the right to represent the workers was decided by a "recount" in the factory. Official recognition went to the union with the most votes. Although it seemed like a simple procedure, getting recognition by this route proved practically impossible. The business of the "recount" was always delayed. The collusion between management and the *charro* union led to repression (firings and threats). Numerous factory struggles had to be carried on by lawyers using due legal process rather than by political organizations.

This was what characterized many movements in small and not-so-small factories, furniture workshops, food-processing plants, bakeries, garment workshops, small and medium-sized foundries, and so on. In large industry the struggle led to the construction of national industrywide unions. The automobile industry (Spicer, Nissan, and VW, among others) was salient in this process.

A different story is told by the traditional unions, where syndical struggles were never entirely suppressed and where the insurgency led to demands for democratization. Sometimes such demands were advanced by nonlegal initiatives, such as the occupation of local union headquarters. This was the story of the Railroad Union Movement (Movimiento Sindical Ferrocarrilero), led by the famous Demetrio Vallejo; of the STERM during its fight to defend its contract, and later in the Democratic Tendency of the SUTERM; of the revolt in the telephone workers' union that brought Francisco Hernández Juárez and a new group of young leaders to the fore; and of the conquest of several locals of the National Mineworkers Union. The amalgam of these three distinct struggles (independent unionism, democratization of big national unions, formation of new industrywide unions) formed the core of working-class insurgency in this period.

Echeverría's Discourse

The populist rhetoric of Luis Echeverría aspired to respond to the political crisis created by the events of 1968, but served to catalyze the union movement.[2] The Confederation of Mexican Workers (CTM), the union confederation with the most autonomy within the apparatus of the PRI, was directly opposed to the presidential policy of a "democratic opening." Porfirio Muñoz Ledo was the minister of labor and social security at the time, and he granted legal recognition to several industrywide unions outside of the official confederation. This was the case of the National Iron and Steelworkers Union (SNTIHIA), which led the struggles in the factories of Spicer and the Zapata Consortium; of an autoworkers' union; and of a union of rubber-workers, affiliated to the UOI, the domain of Juan Ortega Arenas. The governing group sought new methods of worker control to undermine the dominance of the old labor bosses. Olivo Solís and the COR were seen as a possible alternative to the CTM, whereas outside of the Labor Congress, government was prepared to tolerate nonpolitical unionism in large and highly capitalized enterprises (such as the UOI in the automobile industry).

The "democratic opening" of Echeverría's first years meant that the independent union movement met with a certain tolerance. Nevertheless, the legal battles were stymied by the composition of the Labor Conciliation and Arbitration Board, where the labor representative nearly always belonged to one of the official organizations.[3] Judgments on which a union had the legal right to negotiate were systematically delayed. The only exception was when the "official" union had fallen from CTM favor, as was the case in the judgment against the FODF (later the COM), whose boss, Leopoldo Cerón, had been expelled from the CTM and was a sworn enemy of Fidel Velázquez.

Wage Policy

> Our strategy of shared development has served to correct the dire distortions of the real economy, which has been proved incapable of absorbing the growing labor supply. For decades the owners have failed to act and have systematically ignored labor demands .... The government therefore took two basic steps. On the one hand, it stimulated productive investment and took a direct hand in creating new jobs . . . on the other, it designed new procedures for a rapid response to workers' demands and streamlined those already in place.

These are the words of President Echeverría. But of course his version leaves out government repression of independent unionism in the later years of his administration, which was a key element of his labor policy (Echeverría Alvarez 1976).

Nonetheless, wage demands prospered during his administration: Annual wage increases were approved in 1975; the distribution of benefits was improved; FONACOT was set up in 1974 and INFONAVIT in 1972. Fidel Velázquez and the CTM pressed for the most important measure, the annual wage increases, as they did for the emergency increases of 1973 and 1974 that anticipated it. So from 1973 it seems clear that Echeverría's policies and official union aspirations begin to coincide. The government came to see that it could not set up an alternative unionism opposed simultaneously by the traditional unions and the employers. Hence its democratizing discourse was replaced by support for wage demands and reliance on these traditional actors. For his part, Fidel Velazquez sought to restore his image by a vigorous campaign for the emergency increases, so legitimizing Echeverría's policy. The contradiction appeared to be resolved.

The darker side of this reconciliation between the government and the dominant faction within official unionism was repression. The conciliatory attitude toward the democratic electricians' movement disappeared, and CTM supporters took the offensive in expelling Rafael Galván, who at that time was not just another union leader but rather a national figurehead of working-class insurgency. The "political class" closed ranks behind the union bureaucracy, and the policy that had begun by seeking to weaken the CTM ended up by bolstering it. Its image was refurbished, and it was made ready to maintain the control it had exercised so easily in the 1960s.

Diffusion and Core

Between 1971 and 1974 the insurgency advanced along innumerable roads. Not one sector remained unaffected. No doubt similar industries followed similar patterns, but the common denominator for all sectors and sizes of industry was the immediate adoption of demands for an independent union or a democratic union. A search through newspaper archives turned up some three hundred disputes, of which a third were explicitly directed against *charrismo*. But this sample does not reveal the true magnitude of the phenomenon. A more exhaustive search found 189 disputes in 1974 and 350 in 1975. Of the former, 126 involved wage demands and 63 political demands: the latter included 234 wage demands and 116 political demands (Ramos et al. 1979).

It appears that diversity and dispersion are characteristics of this surge: There is no sectoral or geographical concentration. Nonetheless, the surge appears as a single phenomenon, the insurgency. This is explained, on the one hand, by the uniformity of the demands and, on the other, more importantly, by the existence of a core organization that achieved a national network and a national projection. The democratic electricians, with their strong economic and structural base, constituted this national core. The diversity of the struggles found a principle of political unity in the demand for "union democracy" and coalesced into a real national movement around the electricians.

At the same time there emerged some regional groupings like the Cuernavaca Union Coordinating Committee, the Popular Front of Chihuahua, the Naucalpan Strike Coordinating Committee, and the Independent Union Front of Yucatán. These "frontist" organizations included small local struggles (which were already being waged and which otherwise would never have spread or won support) as well as movements actually promoted by the core organization. Therefore the core acted both as an organizational axis and as a catalyst to stimulate and support new struggles.

The key role the workers in the Spicer factory played in the Federal District is illustrative of the process overall. Sources indicate that these workers won the solidarity of 105 unions or union organizations throughout the country, most of them in the Valle de México, without counting university unions, the thirty student organizations, seventeen city-dweller organizations, and three peasant groups (Ramos et al. 1979). This list includes everything from large and important organizations like the Democratic Tendency of the SUTERM and factory unions in big industry, to groups of tiny workshops, often locked into long and debilitating struggles.

Without the permanent national nucleus, the convergence in *coordinadoras* and fronts would have been confined to the regional level and would probably only have lasted for the short periods when an important or spectacular struggle pulled different groups together. When the government repressed the combative electricians, it did much more than simply defend a single union and much more than simply suppress a single "democratic tendency."

The National Popular Action Front (FNAP)

This working-class insurgency was only part of a broader popular insurgency. At the beginning of the 1970s, at the same time the first symptoms of economic crisis appeared, a movement began to emerge from the factories and, as we have seen, discovered an organizational core and a common program of basic demands that gave it a national dimension. The zenith of this upsurge was the attempt to organize a "broad front" (the FNAP) around the vertebral column of the electricians' and the independent union movement, and bring in peasant and student groups and popular organizations in general. It even included an organization of cane-cutters belonging to the PRI (Flores Lua 1984).

The FNAP was the most important effort to unify the intense insurgency of these years. Its failure was mainly one of timing, insofar as it was set up when the movement had passed its high point and was already beginning to decline. It was on the defensive. But the disputes within the FNAP itself were not unimportant, many owing to the presence of factions that rejected the majority position of revolutionary nationalism. (Significantly, twelve years later all left groups managed to agree in their support for *neocardenismo* and for the person of Cuauhtémoc Cárdenas himself). The huge demonstrations of 1976 in Mexico City, which recalled the struggles of 1959, were, paradoxically, the sure sign of the movement's decline; after this date the tide of organization was on the ebb.

The insurgency left a record of innumerable battles on the shop floors, in the labor courts, and on the streets. The net result was more defeats than victories. But the workers who were defeated, repressed, unemployed, or simply silenced by the shriek of machinery had in their hands the Federal Labor Law, which was redrafted in 1970 as the last measure of the welfare state. They covered the city, and some the country, with their demonstrations, marches, meetings, and "brigades." They got to know the labor courts from the inside. They developed a critical view of production processes, assembly lines, and the time-and-motion regime of Taylorized industrial production. They became familiar with Marxist theory, or in some cases just the theoretical terms. They got to know a new way of doing politics, which had nothing to do with voting. Many who graduated from their defeats found refuge in other unions, and some were found in other popular movements. Many of the students of 1968, not so much the leaders as the middle-level cadres, the so-called activists (or "brigadiers," as they were known then), filled leadership positions in the insurgent unions, or acted as advisers or simply supporters. Many militants of the working-class insurgency were afterwards party organizers or nonpartisan activists in the urban popular movements. There is continuity. There is diffusion. This is the creation of a new political culture.

The working-class insurgency had certain characteristics. Its principal goals were the struggle for legality (raising as its banner the respect for the letter of the Federal Labor Law) and the struggle for internal union democracy (and against the interference of the government and the official party). And it achieved a national presence. Here I have been concerned to emphasize this projection, not only in the geographical range of the struggles on the shop floor, but also in the movement's own aspirations to a national presence, which are quite evident from its published platforms and from its attempt to organize the FNAP.

THE TEACHERS' INSURGENCY

We will be talking here of just one union (the National Union of Workers in Education, the SNTE), which, however, is both distinctive and of special importance. To start with, it is a huge union, the biggest in the country, and organizes some 800,000 teachers and probably another 200,000 workers who do not teach. This alone gives it enormous weight. Moreover, this union is present in every corner of the country. There is at least one teacher in even the most remote village of deepest Mexico; and there are many thousands in the great industrial centers. A single organization combines modern and ancient Mexico. The bilingual teacher of the mountain municipality and the technical teacher of the industrial valley confront the same boss, the same bureaucracy, the same corrupt union practices, the same top-down control of privileges. Both one and the other, the teacher of the countryside and the teacher of the city, probably went to the same teacher training school, or to the same summer courses of the same advanced school. Both one and the other, as we will see, have traditionally played a role in their communities that goes beyond the instruction of their pupils.

The making of Mexico's teachers has its origin in the educational projects of Vasconcelos in the 1920s. Their epic forerunners were the rural teachers of the Cárdenas era, who fought equally for literacy and agrarian reform, and sometimes paid the price of their ears.[4] More recently, they remember the days of union struggle in 1958–1959, when Section 9 of the SNTE (the primary school teachers of the Federal District) fought tooth and nail with *charrismo* (Loyo Brambila 1978); and more recent still are the struggles of trainee teachers during the movement of 1968 and in the defense of rural teacher training schools.

The leadership of the SNTE was vested in just one man, who emerged from the coup delivered against the previous leadership on September 22, 1972. In the intervening years until 1979 the new leadership built a parallel organization within the SNTE, composed of a network of corruption and sinecures and embellished by a language replcte with the kind of revolutionary nationalist ideology better suited to baroque eulogics than union debates. This parallel organization calls itself the Revolutionary Vanguard, and its leader-for-life (named as such in a national congress of the SNTE) was, until 1989, Carlos Jonguitud Barrios, presently a federal senator, ex-governor of San Luis Potosí, and eternal candidate to the post of minister of education.

The democratic revolt began toward the end of 1979 in the southern state of Chiapas. It seemed to be a hopeless effort to confront the extremely strong and well-consolidated Revolutionary Vanguard. But, surprisingly, the movement rapidly spread to other states (Oaxaca, Guerrero, Morelos, Hidalgo, Mexico State), and their mobilizations acquired an unexpected momentum. The teachers occupied Mexico City on more than one occasion and became the most difficult labor "problem" of the day. Jonguitud's control wavered. The mobilization lasted a long time, from 1980 until 1983, and this impression of continuity was mainly created by the staggered entry into the struggle of the different union locals. When one started to retreat, another reached the battlefield. It was a dynamic movement that constantly discovered new forms of struggle, such as sit-ins (*plantones*). The teachers also organized huge marches along the highways (from Cuernavaca, Chilpancingo, and Hidalgo to Mexico City) and carried out "mobile sit-ins" (temporary sieges of governmental offices that lasted all day, were lifted during the night to avoid violent eviction, but regrouped again the next morning). Some factions went their own way and occupied embassies, without prior consultation with the National Coordinating Committee of Workers in Education (the CNTE), which was the executive arm of the movement. They organized regional and national meetings and demonstrations, and even held hunger strikes, winning the sympathy of the parents. Some of the new forms of struggle were not legal, but the movement always insisted on the proper application of the law and was careful to see that its union demands had a secure statutory basis.

The movement gained democratic control of the locals in Chiapas and Oaxaca, but in the other states it retreated and the breaches it had opened were closed again by the official leadership. By the end of 1984 the Revolutionary Vanguard had recovered control of the main body of the union and set about wearing down the two remaining "dissident" locals by every means at its disposal. The movements in both Chiapas and Oaxaca were on the defensive from 1985 to 1988. But despite an offensive that included physical attacks (the Oaxacan teachers denounced tens of assassinations, presumably at the hands of *vanguardista* gunmen), the two locals succeeded in keeping their own committees and therefore democratic organization. In the other states, even though the movements had been defeated, there remained organized cadres of activists and natural leaders. The defeats had not been final, and some years later, in 1989, the insurgency was reborn, but this time with its considerable experience of organization and leadership.

Two Images

At this stage of the argument I wish to highlight two images of the teacher. First is the rural teacher—an important figure, whose importance increases in inverse relation to the size of the village where he or she works. His or her links to the community are all day and every day, and the job does not finish with the primary school, but multiplies to include the duties of amanuensis, legal consultant, and general adviser. Second is the big-city teacher—just a wage earner without vocation who has to seek another job. Probably a taxi driver, he or she lives in a working-class or squatters' district, where daily life links him or her with industrial workers and the urban poor.

The first teacher is tending to disappear. If in the past the teacher could become a local cacique, or fellow traveler of caciques (or, on the other hand, a reformer or adviser, or even peasant or community leader), today this same teacher feels attracted by city life and struggles to leave the village and get as close as possible to the city by moving up the professional ladder. The number of this second teacher is therefore multiplying. These trends are inconclusive, of course, and will remain so. There will always be rural teachers alongside peasants, despite industrial revolutions.

No doubt these are stereotypical images. But it is interesting to look at the experiences of different teachers' movements of the 1980s in light of these sketches, namely the movement in the Valle de México (Local 36 of the SNTE), and the movement in Chiapas and Oaxaca (Locals 7 and 22, respectively). In the first case the groups who initially set up and organized the Central Struggle Committee (the CCL) were teachers who worked in the north of the Federal District and were linked with the factory movements of the 1970s. Misael Nuñez Acosta, a famous leader assassinated by gunmen sent from the National Executive Committee of the SNTE, was a political activist in the organization of independent unions in his district. But as it expanded the movement showed its other face, its Indian face, its rural origins. For it was the Oaxacan teachers, with their first sit-in in Mexico City and the political brigades they sent from school to school, who spread, catalyzed, and stimulated the revolt. It is easy to understand how teachers from Nezahualcóyotl in the eastern part of the Federal District came to identify with these rural teachers. Many of them had begun their work in rural communities and had climbed the professional ladder to the city. Many had studied in rural teacher training schools and had participated in student struggles. Quite a few of the leadership cadres knew each other from those days.

An Oaxacan teacher reports on the sit-in of June 9, 1980:

> The political brigades set out with great difficulty because we did not know the city and were afraid that we would get lost in the urban jungle. On Monday we set out with difficulty, but on Tuesday the main problem was that there were not enough teachers from the Federal District to show us around. On Tuesday teachers from the Valle de México and the Federal District began to arrive. They offered to act as guides, and about a hundred brigades set out daily. The number was already huge by Wednesday. These brigades had a multiplier effect because in every school they visited the teachers there took on the task of spreading the word, and this spawned lots of support groups that brought in money and food. At that time we reckoned we collected some 200,000 pesos a day. (Pérez Arce 1987b:57)

A teacher from Nezahualcóyotl explains:

> The movements in Chiapas and Oaxaca had a decisive influence on us. We learned from the press and radio what was going on, . . . Moreover many of the teachers of the Valle had previously worked in the countryside, and had come to the Valle to study, or to get a double-shift job, or to work longer hours in the secondary schools. There is a big demand for teachers here, and educational services are expanding every year. In the countryside, on the contrary, the hours available in the secondary schools are very restricted, and there is a shortage of double-shift jobs, most schools working one session only. This explains why many teachers in the Valle de México feel very close to Oaxaca, to Morelos, to the countryside. Moreover, most of us have graduated from rural teacher training schools, and this also makes us what we are. I knew many of my comrades already, from 1968 and the movement in the training schools. I studied in the teacher training school at Atequiza. Today's cadres were formed back then, or a lot of them were. (Pérez Arce 1987b:69)

If the relations between parents and teachers is difficult in Mexico City, in the countryside teachers tend to be much closer to their communities. In the Montaña de Guerrero, where one of the first struggles took place, the teachers' demands went way beyond wages and union matters, and centered on community concerns such as schools and study grants. And in Chiapas, after several years of mobilization, Local 7 took up popular demands; one of its main leaders spent two years in prison for his support of peasant struggles. Looking from the other angle, this explains why parents, or the community at large, became so deeply involved in a movement that seemed confined to union struggles.

The National Coordinating Committee of Workers in Education

The organization of the movement took the form of central struggle committees, where the schools were directly represented. These committees, in turn, elected representatives to the National Coordinating Committee of Workers in Education, which met often during the times of intense struggle. The democratic teachers set up these central committees only in locals where they could count on an active and mobilized majority. They set up six such central committees, which were a true reflection of the real weight, the real mass base of the CNTE. The teachers also organized central committee "campaign" groups in locals where they lacked a majority, as well as democratic delegations and well-known political groupings with considerable influence in some locals, such as the historic MRM (the Revolutionary Teachers' Movement), the FMIN (which was very important in the Valle de México), and many others. But the major decisions were taken by the central committees (Hernández and Pérez Arce 1982).

Given this structure, no one political faction or group could achieve hegemony within the movement. The central committees retained their autonomy throughout, owing in large measure to their directly democratic character. This might well have reduced their political flexibility because, except in extraordinary circumstances, all decisions were taken in open assembly or after widespread consultation. But, in return, they managed to keep closely in touch with their mass political base.

The movement had no great leader or leaders. Instead, a large number of lesser leaders emerged in the different regions and subregions of the country. As for the character of this leadership, it is worth emphasizing its widespread antipartisan attitudes. The movement's documents and essays reveal an obsessive disavowal of parties and party-linked organizations—the movement and nothing but the movement. Perhaps this explains why the most frequent contradiction in the CNTE was between the trajectories of the regional movements and that of the national movement. The CNTE insisted on remaining the faithful reflection of the movement, and so its political life mirrored the highs and lows of this movement. When the movement is on the rise, the CNTE is there with it, but when the movement retreats, the committee disappears. The other characteristic to be underlined is the movement's strict adherence to legal forms. There is a systematic search for a legal basis for every one of its political initiatives. The teachers' movement always demanded respect for the law.

The Teachers' Insurgency Revisited

The nature of the SNTE made it a key element in the PRI's electoral machinery. This was the card Jonguitud played during the two previous general elections, trading the SNTE's ability to deliver the vote for political offices. For himself he got a governorship and a Senate seat (which he still holds). For his clique he got seats in the Chamber of Deputies and in municipal governments. They never gave him what he most prized, which was the Ministry of Education. Although he had not given up hope, by 1988 the SNTE's electoral machinery had run down. Jonguitud could no longer really offer the kind of electoral guarantees he had promised to the PRI candidate, Salinas de Gortari. Other parts of the PRI's machinery were also creaking, and the CTM and the other official labor confederations could not get the vote out either. President Salinas took note.

In 1989, while the incoming government settled its accounts with oil-union strongman, Joaquín Hernández Galicia (La Quina) by launching a careful military and political offensive, the SNTE was getting ready for its national congress (which was poor timing from Jonguitud's point of view). The insurgency took off again in the local congresses that elected representatives to the National Congress in Chetumal. Jonguitud for his part was careful to control everything down to the last detail. He made no concessions to the democratic teachers nor to anyone who sympathized more with the Salinas administration than with the Revolutionary Vanguard. The Executive Committee thus elected was uniformly behind Jonguitud. But the victory, as was soon apparent, was to cost him dearly. The insurgency grew stronger and spread further than before. The powerful Locals 9, 10, and 11 (representing primary school teachers, secondary school teachers, and nonteaching staff, respectively) took to the streets of the Federal District. Oaxaca and Chiapas followed their lead, and other states began to show signs of life. During the following months the movement for "democracy and better wages" spread throughout the country. The government responded very differently than it had in the case of La Quina. True, it removed Jonguitud and replaced him with Elba Esther Gordillo, who was better fitted to Salinas's new approach. But it also increased teachers' wages far above the ceiling imposed by its anti-inflationary policies. This was a double concession the teachers celebrated triumphantly on Teachers' Day, May 15, with a massive demonstration in the Zócalo.

The new official leadership faced the difficult task of building its own power base at a moment when the democratic movement was still growing, and when the Revolutionary Vanguard was just possibly waiting for the right time to return. Thus, in 1989 three political forces were fighting it out for the control of the biggest union in the country. First, the CNTE of the democratic teachers, which had the biggest mass base; second, a battered Revolutionary Vanguard, which yet maintains its presence in nearly every local of the union; and third, in control of the National Executive Committee and enjoying the support of the government, the Salinas supporters, led by the new secretary general (San Juan 1989).

Society Getting Organized

"Civil society has continued to progress and can count among its achievements the kind of democratization that changes people's outlook and attitudes. My optimism does not spring so much from improvements in political parties or corporations as from a universal reassessment of democracy" (Monsiváis 1987a:13). Monsiváis coined a very apposite phrase in the title of one of his recent books that refers to the "society that is getting organized." In just twenty years, from the movement of 1968 to the elections of 1988, Mexico has lived a popular insurgency whose labyrinthine path has reached every social sector in the country. In this essay I have discussed two such sectors at some length. But I have made no mention of the peasant struggles that swelled into a wave of land invasions and office occupations (over the years 1970 to 1976), besides building a series of producer organizations and setting up regional and national coordinating committees such as the National Coordinating Committee "Plan de Ayala," CNPA (Bartra 1979). Nor have I referred to the municipal battleground, where many important popular struggles have taken place. (Although some of these have been brought to national attention, they have been little studied by social scientists [López Monjardín 1986].) Indigenous movements have built organizations to defend their culture and set forth their political demands; city-dweller and squatter organizations have advanced from demands for services and infrastructure to address more general political issues. Finally, let us not forget the days following the earthquake of September 19, 1985, when, weighed down by the tragedy, the people of Mexico City yet showed themselves ready to organize and run their own lives in the face of the complete failure of government to find an effective response. For once the government was even at a loss for words.

With the benefit of hindsight, it is clear that these have been twenty years of intense popular mobilization. Popular insurgency discovered imaginative forms of struggle, and though these were sometimes illegal, one of the constant characteristics of these very diverse movements was the struggle for legality. Another was the fight for democracy—despite the structures of state and political parties.

These twenty years of social movements, which touched every sector and reached throughout the national territory—which had achieved little in terms of political organization, but which had diffused new ideas throughout the society—came together on July 6, 1988. In short, the new generation of popular leaders succeeded in changing the political culture of the country. Without any doubt at all, the political culture of Mexico is quite different today from twenty years ago.

NOTES

Translation by Joe Foweraker

1. The PRI no longer has the necessary two-thirds majority in the Chamber of Deputies for passing constitutional amendments.

2. On December 15, 1970, at the Twelfth Ordinary Assembly of the FTDF, President Echeverría asked, "How can we talk of democracy in Mexico, if the process for electing the executive committee of a union is not democratic?" (Tello 1979:49).

3. The Labor Conciliation and Arbitration Board, which acts as a court in labor matters, is made up of one representative each from labor, employers, and government.

4. The teachers played a key role in the struggle for agrarian reform. The "white guards" in the pay of the large landowners sometimes cut off their ears in reprisal.

7

Neoliberalism Encounters
Neocardenismo

JAIME TAMAYO

The year 1988 was a landmark year in the history of social movements in Mexico. A broad sociopolitical movement formed in response to the elections and the presidential candidacy of Cuauhtémoc Cárdenas. An electoral front was established uniting political parties and social movements. The politicization of social movements accelerated as they modified their positions on electoral contestation and political parties. Finally, the foundations were set for a party with strong ties to social movements and with the potential to articulate them politically.

DEFINITION AND TRANSFORMATION
OF SOCIAL AND POLITICAL MOVEMENTS

Social movements constitute "a dynamic created within civil society, which purposefully directs itself to the defense of specific interests. They may partially or totally challenge the prevailing structures of domination and their implicit objective is to transform the conditions for social growth" (Camacho 1987:8). Under some circumstances they experience a qualitative change through which, without abandoning their sectoral interests and demands, they become political movements. So, "when class conflict becomes organized at all levels, when the struggle against enemies once expressed as the resistance to exploitation and domination can be articulated as a new project, then we have a political movement." This process is not confined to political parties or organizations that are transmission belts for ideologies. It can also be found in sectoral interest groups such as trade unions, peasant associations, urban organizations, and student groups as well as in cross-sectoral organizations (Alonso 1988:246).

The transition from a social movement to a political movement does not necessarily involve the politicization of the movement. The shift may occur, not by design, but because the state may locate the movement's demands in the terrain of the political, even if the movement does not itself identify its demands as political. The neoliberal policies employed by the de la Madrid administration created the context within which most social movements—

121

regardless of the form of their economic demands—would simultaneously become political movements. Their demands became incompatible with the state's strategy for economic restructuring. "The reduction of real incomes is so central to the state's current policy that the struggle for the recovery of real wages becomes a challenge to power in the broadest political and economic terms. This striking politicization of limited material struggles thrusts workers and their organizations, willingly or not, into the political arena." Earlier, the revolution had turned trade unions into political organizations, but the state's contemporary policy of control over labor conflicts is unprecedented (de la Garza Toledo 1988:179).

In Mexico, the transformation of social movements into political movements was not a product of the 1988 federal electoral process. On the contrary, the transformation was itself a prerequisite for their insertion into electoral politics. There is now in Mexico a new way of doing politics. New forms of organization and struggle are expressed in the politicization of these movements, in their capacity to insert themselves into the electoral arena, to establish clear political alliances and, as a consequence, in their potential for broad, cross-sectoral articulation. These changes tend to lead in turn to growth of civil society and to the limitation of the state.

Social movements in Mexico had experienced a relative decline during the decade between 1975 and 1985, although during that period there were still a significant number of conflicts and demonstrations. They gathered strength and vitality once again at mid-decade in the aftermath of the 1985 earthquake and as a result of declining living conditions of subaltern classes and the inability of corporatist organizations to prevent further impoverishment of wageworkers. Despite this, the most detailed and sustained proposal for the creation of a new and stronger civil society in Mexico, prior to the 1988 elections, had come from the right, especially from business associations.

It is not surprising that the economically powerful business groups undertook the struggle to modify political structures in order to create a more restricted state, more suitable to a liberal model. Their decision was a response to the characteristics, origin, and structure of the Mexican state. Although the Mexican state retains some absolutist traits that undermine the very existence of civil society, nonetheless it is indisputably a mass-based state. From its inception, the Mexican state has relied on the participation of the masses for the organization and consolidation of political power and the state itself after the revolution. Even today, in spite of the contemporary political crisis, these masses constitute an important pillar of the state and a decisive resource for the political system.

Paradoxically, then, when the government began to dismantle this powerful and nearly omnipotent state apparatus, social movements emerged with increased strength and autonomy. When they confronted political power, they were no longer disconnected groups with sectoralized demands but rather an integral part of an evolving national political project that would transcend the sectoral character of previous popular struggles.

THE CRISIS OF THE QUASI-ABSOLUTIST STATE

In fact, the very nature of the modern Mexican state has permitted different forms of social pressure to lead the state into negotiation or repression and the imposition of solutions to conflicts. This has been true even in conflicts that should have been resolved through juridically established channels. Although these imposed solutions have often broken the law, the state's capacity for self-regulation is such that it has been able to represent imposition as keeping within prevailing law. This is possible because of a pyramidal legal-political structure established by the constitution that provides the state with the indiscriminate and nearly absolute power to interpret, apply, and even technically modify public law.

The state's capacity to mold the law is defined by the absolutist features of the state.[1] Absolutism does not refer to "a political system in which the sovereign authority has no constitutional limits." On the contrary, absolutism refers to "a constitutional political regime (in the sense that its actions are somehow subject to preestablished norms and limitations) that is not arbitrary and is above all secular and profane" (Schiera 1984:2) Although we may find it difficult to extrapolate from this to *define* the modern Mexican state, it is possible nonetheless to identify absolutist characteristics of the Mexican state, which by constitutional right has a nearly absolute power as compared with limited or liberal states.

The traces of absolutism concentrate and centralize power in the state, specifically in the executive branch. This limited absolutism was the result of the defeat of external and internal social forces (the church and local interests, respectively) that had prevented the consolidation of the absolute sovereignty of the state. With their defeat, and the subordination of the masses to the state, the centralization of power in the executive facilitated the manipulation of the law.

This state, with its absolutist features, emerged as a product of the Mexican Revolution, assumed its present form, and was consolidated quite clearly with the participation of popular movements. The explosive entry of the masses into politics during the revolution, and in the wake of the destruction of the oligarchic state, compelled the emerging dominant classes to incorporate some of the demands of the masses into the project for the new state. The making of the modern state clearly was determined in large measure by the popular struggles, demands, and demonstrations that gradually delimited the spaces for reform which the new state would permit, promote, or constrain.[2] The new state molded its structure and institutions to the demands and interests of these masses—although they were to be subordinated.

It follows, therefore, that the Mexican state and its party were not detached from the masses. In order to guarantee economic growth and political stability, the Mexican state maintained participation in social organizations, not only through power sharing, but also in policymaking. In spite of the flawed formal democratic representation in the Mexican political system, the existence of sui generis mechanisms for expression and representation of interests of subordinate classes allowed the state to achieve a clear consensus and a scarcely questioned legitimacy (Pérez Fernández del Castillo 1989).

Nevertheless, since the administration of Miguel de la Madrid, the adoption of a neoliberal strategy to try to resolve the economic dilemma has generated a crisis for the Mexican political system. The economic model required dismantling the state whose origins were in the revolution, substituting for it a more "modern" state. The subsequent political crisis has created the context for the separation of important social groups from the structures of political control. Moreover, it has raised the possibility of articulating social movements that emerge and/or expand as a result of the economic crisis and the policies developed to confront it. These movements can join around an alternative political project that, ironically, may reclaim the defense of the revolutionary state and its institutions. Yet this defense by emerging social groups assumes a new logic that does not imply a retention of traditional forms of control. Quite the contrary, it leads to the efflorescence of civil society, for theirs is not a defense of the quasi-absolutism of the state, nor of corporatism per se, but rather of the revolution's social achievements, which are being undermined by neoliberal policies.

Even more paradoxically, however, the conditions for the articulation of social movements into a common political project were created by the separation from the state of a small sector of the so-called political class. Furthermore, the movement generated by the Democratic Current and especially by the presidential candidacy of Cuauhtémoc Cárdenas in response to the regime's call for modernization, became the national catalyst for a diverse social movement whose caudillesque and messianic characteristics made it oddly reminiscent of the 1920s and 1930s. The rupture within the elite had its parallel, although the two processes were not related, in a less visible but real separation of urban and rural bases from the corporatist structure.[3]

ECONOMIC POLICIES AND POLITICAL CRISIS

The neoliberal policies adopted by the de la Madrid administration to handle the economic crisis also produced political consequences. The "ideological underpinnings of the adjustment policies departed from a radical critique of state management of the economy." The approach rejected state intervention in the economy as market destabilizing. Reforms were designed to secure monetary and price stability, trade liberalization, employment (assuming an inverse relationship between inflation and unemployment), and growth based on laws of supply and demand (Novelo U. 1989). The result of these policies was not only a streamlined state and a privatized economy but also a loss of regime legitimacy.

Specifically, the renunciation of national economic sovereignty undermined the nationalist image exploited by the state party from which all postrevolutionary administrations had benefited. In addition, the pact between the state and subaltern classes was broken by the dismantling of institutions that had guaranteed access for their social organizations to decisionmaking affecting these classes.

The "strategy the government has been pursuing systematically to discipline the country by demolishing and weakening the project and institutions born in the revolution" (Cárdenas 1988) was ideologically justified by the administration as the modernization of the state and the rejection of populist practices. But the strategy strongly affected the ability of organizations that had been social "shock absorbers" to negotiate and get a solution to their members' demands. For example, the trade union confederations not only lost their ability to win new benefits for union members but were even unable to maintain wage levels and employment. This thrust Mexican corporatism into crisis, weakening the state party's instruments for electoral control.

RESPONSES TO POLITICAL AND ECONOMIC CRISIS

Urban and rural workers were affected by the economic crisis itself and by state policies to deal with it. These policies depended on a drop in wages, a reduction in the government's budget for social programs, the elimination of subsidies, and the repudiation of union achievements. Coupled with the impact of natural disasters, especially the 1985 earthquake, these economic effects on workers created an opportunity for the emergence of new social movements. These movements, however, were not able to change the direction of economic policy. Heretofore, despite attempts to coordinate and even proposals for unifying political projects, the movement's demands were still largely syndical. Sometimes these were combined with a radical political discourse that contrasted with their actions or demands. They were unable to transcend sectoral struggles or to articulate a common project beyond statements of unity and solidarity.

The alliances and electoral strategies adopted by social movements emerged from the convergence of two political practices. The first related to the struggle in the electoral arena and the various positions maintained by the several political groups active in the collective leadership or political management of the movements. On the one hand, some sustained a principled opposition to electoral participation—a stance sustained by the majority of the organizations that identified themselves with the independent left. Others accepted the possibility of some limited electoral participation, rejecting the facade of political reform more than a strategy of electoral struggle.[4]

The other influence on the adoption of alliances and strategies of electoral contestation came from attempts to establish intersectoral fronts promoted by mass organizations. Among these one could cite the National

Popular Action Front (FNAP) promoted in the mid-1970s by the Democratic Tendency within the Electrical Workers Union, as well as the creation of the National Front for the Defense of Salaries and in Opposition to Austerity and Shortages (FNDSCAC) and its successor, the National Popular Assembly of Workers and Peasants (ANOCP), as well as the National Committee for the Defense of the Popular Economy (CNDEP) and subsequently the Forum for Union Cooperation. All were important in shaping broad political fronts which joined parties and social organizations in attempts to collaborate around shared interests transcending sectoral demands.

Although in some cases (FNDSCAC and ANOCP) they were able to bring together the most important sectoral organizations, all of these popular fronts not only failed to achieve their objectives, but even their demonstrations and stoppages had very limited impact.

THE POPULAR SHIFT TO ELECTORAL STRATEGIES

So at mid-decade a change in attitudes toward political parties and the electoral process began to brew within social movements. This was a shift from a marked "rejection of clientelist practices of political parties" (León and Marván 1984: 13) and a devotion to spontaneity and direct action that had predominated at the beginning of the decade (Tamayo 1986: 27). The change was toward electoral participation, partisan political projects, and even in some instances to a political pragmatism bearing little resemblance to a purist past.

Until their participation in the broad movement generated by Cárdenas's candidacy, social movements' participation in the electoral process tended to weaken their organizations. Electoral participation also reduced consensus within organizations to the extent that partisan and electoral politics corresponded very little to the sectoral interests that had initially given birth to movements and organization. This was the experience, for example, for such significant groups as the Committees for Popular Defense in Durango and Chihuahua, as well as for more limited but potentially important groups such as the Democratic Front for Popular Struggle in Guadalajara.

By the time of the federal and state elections in 1985, the decision to participate in electoral struggles became more important for various organizations that participated in or helped to lead popular movements, as well as for the movements themselves. In February 1985, the National Revolutionary Coordinating Committee (CRN) issued a call to all "registered progressive, democratic parties" in which they pointed out that

> It is well known that some regional organizations can challenge the PRI and win elected offices. COCEI is only one example among many. There are also other groups that could confront government parties and parties on the right with some chance of winning within a region, such as in Chihuahua (CDP), Guerrero (Groups of ACNR), in some districts of Puebla and Veracruz (UCI), as well as other states such as Nuevo León, Chiapas, Durango, Zacatecas, Michoacán,

Jalisco, and Nayarit. In these places there are strong and experienced popular organizations that have consolidated over more than ten years of promoting a revolutionary social movement. They can contest for a voting majority if the conditions exist to facilitate their electoral participation. The best help they can receive is from registered parties in coalition with the name and banner of the regional organizations: Our concrete proposal is that we should henceforth act more frequently in regional coalitions, adopting in each case the name and banner of local organizations (CRN, February 20, 1985).

Shortly thereafter, the Unified Socialist party of Mexico (PSUM), the Mexican Workers party (PMT), and the Revolutionary Workers party (PRT) cosigned a document with the organizations in the National Revolutionary Coordinating Committee, accepting the proposal to join forces to engage in regional electoral competition. They noted that "encouraging, consolidating, and legitimizing democratic popular regional movements are of great interest to progressive forces" and subsumed the possibilities for electoral coalition within the overall process of coordination sustained on other fronts "to promote the development of social and syndical movements" (CRN et al., February 26, 1985).

Although there had been precedents for the participation of social movements in electoral coalitions, from this moment forward their numbers increased, especially within regions. This is all the more remarkable because it included several organizations that only shortly before had proudly proclaimed their opposition to electoral contestation.

The electoral results of this agreement were not very significant. The important successful exception to this generalization were those cases in which the political-electoral struggle was closely joined to demands and interests of participating movements: the struggle against *caciquismo*, the struggle for control over municipal government or local public office, and others. One example would be the case of COCEI, which had a past history of successfully contesting elections (López Monjardín 1986).

There were, however, other profound consequences to the shift away from an antiparliamentary strategy and toward the public acceptance of a strategy of electoral contestation. The change created an even more unpredictable attitude toward the political process within social movements. With the exceptions noted earlier, not only did these experience electoral defeats that undermined the previously recognized mobilizational capabilities of the movement, but in some cases internal weakening, division, desertion, and demobilization clearly followed electoral participation.

The problem was that even when the movements' demands were included in the electoral platforms, this was not a clear response to the sectoral and syndical demands that gave rise to the movement in the first place, at least not from the viewpoint of the mass of the participants.

In effect, whether a social movement finds real expression in the political sphere or not depends much more on the kind of political struggle in question than it does on top-level agreements between leaders of social movements and political parties. In other words, the link to be forged between sectoral struggle and democratic struggle has more to do with the concrete goals of the struggle than with ideological positions. As a result, demand-led movements usually ally far more easily with political groups that directly express their sectoral demands than with groups engaged in broader struggles. A clear example of the former are the Neighborhood Councils, which have actively promoted the demands of urban popular movements across the country.

Furthermore, we need to consider to what extent electoral participation—which clearly responded to a political strategy adopted by the leaders of organizations and movements—really interested and motivated their rank-and-file members. The political organizations' objectives in seeking the electoral participation of social movements tended toward legitimating mass organizations and their leaders, articulating and joining dispersed political and social forces, legitimating and giving voice to protest and social discontent, utilizing the electoral process to organize and denounce and to spread socialist ideas, as well as to provoke meaningful political events and to accumulate political experiences of struggle and securing local power (*Boletín Interno Punto Crítico* 1985). In the absence of a strong process of politicization within the movements, these objectives were not easily shared by rank-and-file members in the movements.

The year 1985 was also important for another reason. The earthquake in September of that year and the social consequences of the economic crisis, expressed with increasing virulence, put the administration's political-economic project to the acid test. The administration was attempting to limit corporatism and to give voice to social discontent through the electoral process. This project had been in gestation since the reforms initiated by José López Portillo.

Official trade unions, reluctant to accept the policies of the de la Madrid administration that undermined the traditional pillars of the historical "social contract," were joined by newly emerging social actors, born of the crisis and the earthquake (Hurtado 1989). These new groups called for a redefinition of relations between the state and civil society along new lines differing from official corporatism of the past, but also dramatically in contrast with the neoliberal solution proposed by the government. Social organizations such as the National Coordinating Committee of the Urban Popular Movement were frozen in time and incapable of responding to changed circumstances. They were overtaken by new organizational forms such as the United Coordinating Committee of the Earthquake Victims, the Neighborhood Assembly, and others, and entered a period of decline during which they lost their prior hegemony. Shortly thereafter, local elections in Chihuahua would clearly demonstrate that the administration had not found a solution and, on the contrary, was losing ground in its political modernization project. With the electoral reforms, the political system had set a trap for the left and for social movements, miring them in electoral processes and limiting the arenas of struggle. Unable to offer a liberal democratic alternative, the political system began to slide into an even larger trap, schizophrenically speaking in support of democracy and against corporatism, but acting quite to the contrary.

The emergence of the Democratic Current within the PRI further complicated the situation. The initial demand of its members to democratize the state party further undermined the corporative forms of control and the whole system of domination that one way or another obstructed the emergence of independent organizations in civil society and assured the state of a virtual monopoly over mass politics through the state party. The Current also assumed a militant nationalist position in reclaiming and reasserting a historical project rejected by the ruling technocracy. The first document of the Current called for a change: reconstruction of national alliances to permit the direct participation of the social base in party decisions and to "defend the integrity and unity of the nation by means of the full participation of all social forces" (Corriente Democrática 1986). In the wake of meetings, debates, and discussions, the Current's second document reemphasized that "nationalism and democracy are the simultaneous objectives of a single struggle" (Corriente Democrática 1987a).

In the "Democratic Proposal" put forth shortly before the official PRI candidate for the presidency was unveiled and before the definitive break between the Democratic Current and the state party, the former presented a program that restated their position and prominently incorporated it into a national project. In the document they underscored the need to democratize national life and to recognize the existence of a plural society (Corriente Democrática 1987b). The Democratic Current's break with the PRI, the opposition candidacy of Cuauhtémoc Cárdenas, and Salinas's nomination as official party candidate for continuity of an antipopular policy all combined to raise great hopes within many social movements and opposition political groups.

In truth, although the dissidents who broke with the PRI were few in number, at the leadership level, their departure was viewed as portending a potentially much larger rupture of the social base from the official party:

> Cuauhtémoc Cárdenas's break appears as the fissure that opens the door to resistance and social pressure within the PRI. . . . There can be no genuine democratic change in Mexico without a crisis and a break in the PRI domination, that is, without democratization of the PRI itself. The Democratic Current is resuming the historical path of radical democratic currents that always existed within the PRI. (Gilly 1987)

Cuauhtémoc Cárdenas's candidacy opened a particular political conjuncture for the participation of social movements in an electoral process that would overcome the tendency of social movements to weaken when engaged in electoral struggles. The willingness to participate in elections, the electoral participation itself, and the alliance with parties and political organizations that had begun to develop beforehand among ascendant social movements coincided with the dramatic arrival of a candidate made more attractive by his break from the omnipotent state. His surname connoted a history and a project, and he explicitly adopted the most strongly held social demands and raised the banners of revolutionary nationalism and democracy in a direct assault on the state party.

POPULAR MOVEMENTS AND *NEOCARDENISMO*

Cardenismo, occasionally manifested but often latent, endured in Mexico as a memory and an ideology within large portions of the population. Much more than the state party, *cardenismo* permeated the mass public incorporated until then into the PRI through official organizations. But it had also taken root in the heart of the political organizations on the left.[5] With this legacy, Cuauhtémoc Cárdenas became the symbol, the redemptive myth, capable of reversing social decay, of resuming the abandoned path and promoting democratization, the defense of national sovereignty, and social equality. The social and political movement that began to build around his candidacy quickly overtook the parties that nominated him and in a way signaled a return to a country of caudillos. Quite obviously, the masses trusted him personally more than their parties, or even their own organizations. This situation forced the groups and political parties that had opposed his candidacy to throw their support in his favor or risk being abandoned by their social base. "He is the candidate of a historical memory and the emotions associated with it, not yet of a true political party" (Monsiváis n.d.; see also Gilly 1988).

Beyond a doubt, the broad movement generated by *cardenismo* and the several social movements affiliated with it are characterized by personalistic leadership (*caudillismo*). There is a historical explanation for this insofar as in Mexico all revolts and revolutions, along with the vast majority of mass movements, have needed strong leaders and political-military strongmen. Political movements in Mexico have also tended toward hipostasis, "personification," as "every political movement needs to 'hipostasize' itself in a person, or at least a symbol that takes on a comparable role. This symbolic individual becomes the magnetic center of the movement, giving the movement its name and defining characteristics. In the beginning, the individual carries so much weight that were he to disappear, the movement might founder and fail" (Alonso 1985:35).

Every movement, in addition, tends to generate "the illusion of equality," based on the identification of shared hopes, demands, and common needs personified in the leader who stands over and against a common enemy who defines the "otherness." In this way,

> the movement takes shape around a personification that must exorcise individualization of demands and thus avoid the disintegration of the movement. . . . In the early stages of the formation of a new social actor, without prior tradition or collective consciousness, one of the symbols or signals of the root identity, which enables the movement to define itself, is the image of a founding leader, a prophet, etc., who plays this role not so much because of his personal

characteristics as his conjunctural ability to embody a host of collective aspirations, needs, and frustrations. (Alonso 1985:38)

The first social organizations that joined Cuauhtémoc Cárdenas's campaign were the Committee for Popular Defense in Durango and the Federation of Workers Organizations of the Federal District, signatories of the common platform of the National Democratic Front (FDN) (FDN 1988). At that time, some of the most important social movements in the country had also begun to press for a single presidential candidate of the center-left. Among these organizations, the Neighborhood Assembly, leaders of the CEU, and the Urban and Peasant Regional Ecological Movements, and a varied group of trade-union activists all worked toward this end, finally supporting the candidacy of Cuauhtémoc Cárdenas.

In many cases, the rank-and-file members of popular movements were so eager to join the movement around Cuauhtémoc Cárdenas that they compelled political organizations to support him.[6] In other cases, the question of supporting Cárdenas produced schisms and breaks.[7] Finally, there were also instances in which the pressure from the mass base in movements whose leadership came from political groups opposed to *cardenismo* forced political parties to reexamine their alliances. They ended up supporting Cuauhtémoc Cárdenas's campaign.[8]

Neocardenismo reversed the tendency of social movements to sectoralize their demands by permitting their insertion into a national project that aggregated all criticisms of the economic and social policy of the regime and arguments for the defense of national sovereignty and the rejection of the state party and corporatism. In Cuauhtémoc Cárdenas's candidacy, popular movements and interest groups found a point of agreement around which they might organize, generalizing their demands and politicizing their struggles. They sat down together and agreed on joint projects that went far beyond electoral tasks and that strengthened and unified their struggles, organizations, and movements, which until then had sustained divergent and even opposing practices and visions. Syndicalists from different tendencies and sectors, urban popular movements, peasants and indigenous groups, ecologists, and student leaders passed through convergence in their support for Cárdenas and moved on to dialogue and unity in their sectoral struggles and linkage with the ensemble of social movements. The conflicts among them became secondary as the system of domination and the state party in the election came to be defined as the principal common enemy. The seeds were sown for improved coordination; novel proposals for organization and social struggle were put forth, ranging from syndical forums to the Cardenista Peasant Union; the Current of Workers in Art, Science, and Culture; and later the Convención Anáhuac.

This explains how in this exceptional conjuncture social movements overcame the negative consequences of participating in electoral processes, actually reversing the trend and turning it in their favor. They strengthened their capacity for struggle by taking on a project that not only responded to the expectations of the movements' social base but was in fact pressed on the movement in many instances by a base eager to support Cárdenas's candidacy without waiting for the leadership to call for an electoral struggle. This pressure from the social base sometimes even opposed the positions sustained by those who had some political leadership of the movement.[9]

POLITICAL SYSTEM CHANGE

It is difficult to determine how much change in the political system was wrought by the *cardenista* movement, and especially by social movements inserted into it in one way or another. Any notion of change requires some indicators against which changes can be measured. To that end, we might begin by simply reiterating some of the most important characteristics of the Mexican political system outlined earlier. This includes the quasi-absolutist characteristics of the Mexican state, the concentration of power in the executive, the centralization of national politics, corporatism, as well as what we might empirically label the *priísta* political culture characterized by elite decisionmaking, authoritarianism, vertical structures of power, clientelism, intolerance, and discipline to elite decisions.

Our assessment of the impact of *cardenismo* and social movement support for it is complicated in that popular forces are not the only source of recent attacks on the political system. The traditional mechanisms of domination also have been attacked from within the government itself. The attempt to change the postrevolutionary social authoritarian system into a liberal authoritarian system (given the impossibility of creating an opening for a liberal democracy) has directly affected corporatism. Given the difficulty of identifying legitimate and consensual mechanisms that would substitute for populist and corporatist practices, it appears that the government will seek a means to repair the system, creating further subordination of social organizations.

With these reservations, quick assessment of the *cardenista* movement and the electoral process allows us to highlight the following consequences for the political system. First, recall that the political crisis in Mexico was brought about initially by the renunciation of several aspects of national sovereignty; the accelerated dismantling of the Mexican revolutionary state and especially the institutions through which subordinated social classes expressed their interests and the state took account of them; the rupture of the pact with popular social classes, a pact that reflected a limited but real policy of social concessions; and, finally, the inability of the state party to reconfigure itself on a new foundation. This political crisis was deepened by the emergence of a vast social movement (*neocardenismo*) that extends well beyond the electoral arena but is constrained by the political system itself, which is unable to cede it a place.

In fact, the 1988 elections unleashed a broad social movement[10] that included various rural and urban sectors (intellectuals, university students, workers, residents of low income neighborhoods), as well as social and political organizations that had shortly before defined themselves in opposition to elections. Under changed circumstances, elections have become a new arena for struggle for these groups, not simply a conjunctural strategic option.

In this case, the electoral process assumed a new dimension, elevating the capacity for political response above the formal and legal questions that had until then determined the arenas for struggle. Thus, although the Electoral Law is written in such a way as to allow legalization of fraud, in 1988 the system had to concede electoral defeat in the cases of most obvious opposition victories and was unable to legitimize its own official victory. This led, among other things, to a considerable weakening of the president and, by extension, a reduction of the power of the presidency which had been associated with the myth of his infallibility and invulnerability.

In electoral terms, the 1988 elections gave birth to a new political geography. According to the official electoral results, the modernization candidate lost in the most developed cities and regions (except for Monterrey), and his victory was attributed to the most marginalized rural vote. The myth of the invincibility of the state party was undermined, and national and intersectoral response to the state's manipulation of elections was organized for the first time.

Perhaps the most important results of the electoral process for *cardenismo* are long term and directly influence political culture. Among them, we might note a rapid process of politicization among sectors of society that had traditionally been passive with regard to elections—especially important peasant groups. Moreover, a wide range of political and social organizations previously defined by their opposition, both to parties and elections, were incorporated into the electoral struggle. These generalizations must, however, be qualified. Civil society's much-proclaimed desire to establish a regime of parties must be questioned, as we see from the results of local elections after July 1988, in which participation declined abruptly. This decline in electoral participation tends to underscore the *caudillista* qualities of *cardenismo*.

The elections also produced the emergence of sectors representative of civil society that assumed the responsibility of monitoring fraud in the electoral process through organizations such as ADESE. Their moral weight began to constitute a new, noninstitutional form of electoral sanction. By the same token, for the first time the entire opposition came together in defense of the vote, irrespective of ideology and party. What stands out here are the massive demonstrations after the elections, which in number and militance surpassed even the most important demonstrations of Cárdenas's campaign. Social movements, mobilized in defense of the vote by their organizations (such as the CEU) rather than their leaders, were also important participants in these demonstrations.

Also, varied social movements and political groups formerly incapable of engaging in dialogue with each other were able to converge around a common struggle. Furthermore, the subordinated classes and parts of the bourgeoisie affected by the economic policies of the regime that favored the interests of transnational finance capital found interests in common. This created the possibility of electoral alliances in which small and medium entrepreneurs joined forces with syndical or socialist groups, *compañeros de fórmula*. The seeds of a genuine popular front were present in the FDN and could crystallize in a party with those characteristics in the medium term, possibly laying the foundation for a new hegemony.

Social movements have also been strengthened as instances of sectoral struggle, checking their past tendency to be weakened following their insertion into electoral contests. The sudden politicization of these emergent social movements and their inclusion in *cardenismo's* national project, has not so far affected their independence. Quite the contrary, it has allowed them to expand their intersectoral alliances without diminishing their autonomy. This applies, for example, to the Neighborhood Assembly, various peasant organizations, and several regional social movements that have made pacts and alliances specifically with the Party of the Democratic Revolution (PRD).

Critiques of authoritarian patterns of leadership have begun to emerge from within organizations in civil society. There is an incipient rebirth of internal processes of democratization.

New forms of political expression and organization have begun to take root as an outgrowth of the *cardenista* movement. This would include the Democratic Current, the Movement toward Socialism, and now the planning and founding committee of the PRD. The ground rules shaping their organizations are directly opposed to those of the traditional left as well as those inherited by political parties from *priísta* political culture. So far, these new organizations reject corporatism and recognize the autonomy of social organizations whose relationship with the parties is established through pacts and alliance agreements. Nonetheless, one part of the left retains a covert corporatist vision, and some of the *priísta* practices have been retained by sectors of *cardenismo.*

So far, some of the characteristics of these new political associations would include consensus, sectoral and regional autonomy, independence for social organizations and respect for their right to establish political alliances, pluralism, tolerance, and the search for broad representation on governing committees that change frequently, individual membership, respect for citizenship, and the creation of broad spaces for participation by members. None of this allows us to assert that centralist visions, clientelism, and other elements of the dominant *priísta* culture have been eliminated. Apart from anything else, *caudillismo* remains a weighty factor and in some ways the most important cohesive element in the new party.

The electoral process and the new correlation of forces in this arena have also had an impact on existing political parties. The official party found its network of control partly dismantled. Corporatism, especially in the urban environment, was unable to secure even a minimum of the projected electoral results. The PRI has been compelled to present a proposal that, if followed to its logical conclusion, could signal the end of a state party regime. The proposal for change has encountered skepticism in the absence of any clear alternative to the status quo.

Within the PAN, on the other hand, the real possibility of contending for local government positions has prompted one faction to reclaim some Social Christian banners. This faction has taken up a platform that includes social demands not recognized by this party in the past, as they were made against social groups on whom the party traditionally depended. As long as it appears that the "barbarians" of the north are in retreat, the failure of *neopanismo* that emerged clearly in the electoral results has provoked a crisis of conscience within the party, exacerbated by the spectacular growth of the FDN, regarded at the time as the principal enemy by a fraction of the PAN.

In truth, the de la Madrid administration's attempt to change a social authoritarian system into a liberal authoritarian system brings the PRI project closer to the PAN. The contradiction between the liberal democratic project and the social democratic project reclaimed by the PRD may become the principal contradiction for the *panistas* to the extent that the banner of democratization may be replaced by the interests of the class the PAN represents.

The leaders of political parties on the left retain many of the traditional vices—sectarianism, authoritarianism, centralism, opportunism, and political myopia. Nevertheless, parts of the left have begun to experience a process of "Chileanization" characterized by encouraging the formation of fronts and coalitions of the center-left that have an interest in governing and compete for power with a real possibility of winning. This contrasts with their conventional position as a small ally of the left or of the opposition. The process is hardly consolidated and is potentially reversible. Witness the internal splits and the disappearance of the FDN. Hope is kept alive, however, by the establishment of the PRD and the recent formation of the National Patriotic Front.

NOTES

Translation by Ann L. Craig

1. Absolutism "requires that state power be exercised without limit or restriction. The alternative, which characterizes liberalism, attempts to impose limits and restrictions on state power" (Abbagnano 1974:2).

2. Although popular movements have participated in the conformation of the modern Mexican state throughout its history, their greatest participation took place during the administrations of Alvaro Obregón and Lázaro Cárdenas.

3. This refers to more than the splinters (*desprendimientos*) the National Peasant Confederation (CNC) suffered during the electoral campaign and to the forces that abandoned the National Confederation of Popular Organizations (CNOP) under the leadership of individuals who shifted their allegiance to *cardenismo*. It includes as well a number of rank-and-file PRI supporters who much earlier had joined independent social organizations, for example the Neighborhood Assembly. "Some 75 percent of [the assembly's members] came from sectors of the PRI, such as small

tradesmen, renters, blue-collar workers, salaried employees, etc." (*Punto Crítico* 164 [July 1989]:24).

4. This was the case, for example, of the Revolutionary Organization Punto Crítico, which contended that, with the exception of particular cases, the appropriate conditions did not exist for electoral struggle. Yet they supported Valentín Campa's unofficial campaign for the presidency in 1976 as well as Rosario Ibarra's 1979 campaign and other congressional candidates in 1982. But they never proposed their own candidates for office.

5. For example, among the components of the most important party on the left, the Mexican Socialist party (PMS), the Mexican Workers party (PMT) and part of the Unified Socialist party of Mexico (the Popular Action Movement, MAP, within PSUM) had held a political position identified with the principles of revolutionary nationalism. But even the Patriotic Revolutionary party (PPR), also part of the PMS and composed of individuals who had participated in the guerrilla activities of the previous decade, was identified in an internal *cardenista* document as "an original path of social transformation through the renewal of socialism" (*El movimiento obrero y el PPR*, 1987, mimeo).

6. It appeared at first as if the CRPC planned to continue fighting for the single candidacy until the end, but it finally decided in March 1988 to join the Movement toward Socialism (MAS) composed of various social and political forces on the left to support Cárdenas.

7. Such was the case of the Party of the Socialist Revolution (PRS) whose leaders in Puebla and the Federal District—associated with the Universidad Autónoma de Puebla, the peasant movement, and the CEU—did not respect the agreement to reject the electoral process and joined the Cárdenas campaign. Similar breaks occurred in various parts of the country within the PMS before Heberto Castillo withdrew as a candidate.

8. For example, the Organization of the Revolutionary Left–Mass Tendency and the National Revolutionary Civic Association (ACNR), *Uno más Uno*, June 15, 1988.

9. This became clear in interviews conducted with leaders of various social organizations in Jalisco, such as the Forum for the Struggle for Housing, the Coordinating Committee of Popular Neighborhoods, and the Marcos Castellanos Fishermen's Organization, as well as in debates and decisions taken in the Second and Third Regional Workshop for Conjunctural Analysis organized by CEIDAR-EDOC and by participants in urban movements and organizations, trade unions, and peasant groups from throughout the state.

10. See Camacho's definition of social movements at the beginning of this chapter (Camacho 1987).

8

Middle-Class Associations and Electoral Opposition

MARÍA LUISA TARRÉS

The analysis of social movements has traditionally neglected the supposedly unheroic urban middle class and its demands and forms of action.[1] Consider, however, the political importance that collective mobilizations acquire when the middle class is involved (Moore 1978; Linz 1987), or the critical importance of collective action in Latin American cities (Kowarick 1985; Borja 1981; Coulomb and Duhault 1988).

Studies in Mexico and Latin America have demonstrated that social movements produce more than demands regarding labor relations or living conditions, and that they are not the monopoly of a particular class. These movements do organize various groups that share a set of needs and complaints, but the very process of allying to negotiate with or fight against a political system and its representatives also creates common identities, associations, networks, and social relations. If the social movement survives and controls enough resources, it helps create new forms of political participation (Tilly 1978; Kowarick 1985) and new relations between social sectors (Touraine 1973).

This chapter analyzes the conditions that produce collective action and the development of an electoral opposition among the middle classes in Mexico, paying particular attention to the perspectives of the protagonists in this process. It proposes that social conditions unique to urban life support the formation of a class identity through collective action. The central issue is the process by which an economic stratum develops social and political autonomy through mobilization.

The analysis is based on the case of Ciudad Satélite, a neighborhood with over 100,000 inhabitants located in the northern metropolitan area of Mexico City.[2] During the last two decades, the population of Satélite has organized a series of political protests, and since 1982 has actively supported the conservative opposition National Action party (PAN). In that year, the community elected the first opposition candidate from Mexico City to win a direct majority seat in the Mexican national congress.

Given the importance of the unique conditions found in Satélite, there are limits to the generalizability of this analysis. The relevant population belongs to the middle and upper classes and is self-employed or works for either domestic private industry or transnational corporations. The middle

137

class of Satélite falls outside of the regime's corporatist control and is able to create a social identity based on shared values and life-styles. Its electoral behavior and political attitudes are probably distinctly different from those of middle-class Mexicans who live closer to poorer areas or hold more binding professional ties to the state.

Nevertheless, the case of Satélite shares critical characteristics with those of Monterrey, Puebla, Guadalajara, and the urban centers along the U.S. border. First, the middle-class political opposition has developed a geographically distinct identity based on place of residence, as opposed to the sectoral organizations of the PRI or the professional and commercial associations sanctioned by the regime. The population of Satélite organized its political action through Neighborhood Associations and parishes, and its demands were initially oriented toward the improvement of urban living conditions. This indicates the separation or alienation of the political elite from the daily life of the population (Camp 1986; Smith 1986), as well as the creation of a new civic space outside the state.

Second, because the confrontation takes place in urban centers, opposition is directed toward the bureaucratic apparatus and the local representatives of the political system. The principal adversary for these groups is the state and its system of political control, not just the leading elites. Third, middle-class political opposition is closely linked to increasing support for the PAN in those areas with the fastest economic growth (Ramos Oranday 1985).

Finally, it is important to emphasize that the electoral opposition developed during a period of economic crisis. Although the relationship between economic growth and social and political behavior is not mechanically deterministic, it is worthwhile noting that in the Mexican case increased electoral participation and political mobilization occur during a prolonged recession.

The middle class, which for many years had left the management of the state to the so-called Revolutionary Family and neglected the exercise of its political rights, entered the public arena during the start of the economic crisis in 1982 (Lustig 1987; Tello 1985; Samaniego 1986). This historical parallel may help to explain the formation of an electoral opposition within a sector that had traditionally legitimated the regime in exchange for social mobility and increased consumption. The middle-class opposition, however, has not focused on the economic situation, but has criticized the rules of the political system and generated demands for greater democratization (Alvarado 1987; Loaeza and Segovia 1987).

The first section of this chapter describes the political and economic context in which the opposition developed. The second summarizes the results of the case study, emphasizing the socioeconomic characteristics of the area and the principal forms of collective action. Third, the chapter analyzes the results of a survey of electoral behavior taken in January 1987. A fourth section evaluates the principal demands of the opposition and the emphasis on democratization. The chapter concludes with a set of hypotheses regarding the formation of a political opposition within the Mexican middle class that will serve to guide further research.

THE NEW CONTEXT

The development of modern Mexican society is defined by the first successful social revolution of the twentieth century. The country has clearly changed dramatically since 1910. During this century, the economy has grown at an average annual rate of 6.3 percent, and significant numbers in the population have benefited from the accompanying industrial development and urbanization.

The process of economic development in Mexico is closely linked to the role played by the state and the corporatist organization of the official party. For many years, the state functioned as an agent of development and silenced opposition through economic growth and its distribution, and through negotiated participation in decisionmaking. The official party served as a mediator between government and society through the incorporation of the population in the three national sectors representing labor, the peasantry, and the middle or popular classes, as they are known in the official language.

The new opposition to the system partly originates in the incapacity of the government to continue fulfilling its historical role. By 1982, the economic crisis had weakened the state's ability to continue the policy of clientelism on which it based its relation with the society. Traditionally, politics was defined by the distribution of resources and benefits rather than by representation. The population supported the political leadership because it was able to mobilize and distribute resources. Without this distribution of wealth, the system lost its contact with and support from the majority. Without the promise of resources, the system could not incorporate and silence opposition.

These developments have been accompanied by important changes in the recruitment of cadres by the PRI. Meritocratic educational criteria have replaced political credentials as the key factors in determining access to power (Camp 1986; Smith 1986). Along with the decline of clientelistic relations and the difficulty in adapting to new electoral rules, the new recruitment mechanisms tended to further separate the political leadership from the society and blocked the participation of new actors in the system.

Despite these changes, political and social movements are still largely defined by the very system to which they are opposed, and this makes them particularly fragile. This is clearest in the case of political parties. The PAN does not have a concrete alternative proposal for the country's development, and its opposition is largely defined by nothing more than a rejection of the current ruling system. The same is true of the Cardenista Front for National Reconstruction, whose discourse consists of calls for a return to the populist project of the revolution.

Rather than an opposition organized along the lines of institutionalized electoral parties, there exists a proliferation of movements, groups, organizations, and networks of relations developed outside the state and the corporatist structure. This phenomenon is predominantly urban, not just in the Federal District, but also in the provinces. In the cities, social groups have developed enough experience to reclaim the exercise of their political rights.

This parallel set of citizens' organizations played a critical role during the presidential elections of July 1988. For the first time in the history of postrevolutionary Mexico, the official party lost both its absolute predominance on the national level and the majority of votes in Mexico City. The Cardenista Front for National Reconstruction, led by dissidents from the PRI, won the election in the Federal District, in part because of the support of various popular organizations. The PAN also improved its electoral performance within the capital thanks to the traditional support from the middle classes and a new influence among the poorer sectors of the population.

At stake in contemporary Mexico is the replacement of a regime that had resolved conflicts within a unitary and monopolistic institution by a new system of representative democracy based on competition between parties. It is possible that the Mexican regime may retain the capacity to reform itself and redefine the game in its favor. On the other hand, demands for influence over public decisionmaking now have a solid base in the society, and these can no longer be satisfied through redistribution. The analysis of the case of Ciudad Satélite represents an attempt to understand these demands and their politicization.

THE CASE OF CIUDAD SATÉLITE

Because of the high educational level of the population, the number of owner-occupied domiciles, and the predominance of a salaried nonmanual work force, Ciudad Satélite can be defined as a middle-class community (Tarrés 1989, 1987, 1986).[3] What is of interest in this case is not the socioeconomic characteristics of the population but the process through which it became politicized and the unity it demonstrated after 1982.

The election of a *panista* congressional deputy in 1982 placed Ciudad Satélite in conflict with local and national authorities who sought to control the opposition. Such efforts were stymied by the relative financial independence of the population, the strength of preexisting communal networks, the shared experience with previous movements for improving urban services, and the definition of a common enemy represented by the local government and state representatives. Each of these factors played a critical role.

Economic Independence of the Population

Although the heads of households in Ciudad Satélite had a wide variety of occupations, the majority (63 percent) worked for the domestic or international private sector or were self-employed. Of the other third of the population, which worked for the government, 56 percent also maintained positions in private industry or owned a share in a business or professional association. These figures indicate that we are dealing with a population largely beyond the reach of corporatist controls but that, on the other hand, has little opportunity to form a class identity in its workplace. Most importantly, the citizens of Satélite are relatively immune to state economic sanctions.

Communal Networks

At least two critical factors in the daily life of the population of Ciudad Satélite facilitate the uninterrupted creation of networks and the generation of demands. The first is linked to the acute gender division of labor that excludes women, no matter how well educated, from well-paid employment. Women therefore enjoy plentiful free time during which they can develop community activities (de Oliveira 1989). This allows them to create their own social space with its set of demands, activities, and relationships with other community groups, making them one of the most active agents of local politics (Tarrés 1988).

The second critical element in the creation of communal relations is the development of a local parish organization and a Neighborhood Association during the first years of Satélite's history. Both of these stimulate and legitimate the formation of local and regional groups and produce new values and norms.

The geographic isolation of the inhabitants in the early years of the community, the high proportion of nonlocals, and the fact that most of the households arrived in Satélite as newly formed families help to explain the critical importance of social integration within a population requiring new friendships, network links, mutual assistance, and a sense of permanence. The notions of an "intermediate" society and of a common good became generalized through these organizations. It is perhaps not a coincidence that these ideas are also central to the political discourse of the PAN.

The experience with the Neighborhood Association allowed the population to practice democracy on a communal level. For fifteen years, the association administered local urban services with a participatory organizational framework. The community became familiar with electoral campaigns and procedures and with the management of diverse interests that allowed it to develop a more open or—to use the preferred Mexican term—transparent local democracy.

Through its activities, the local parish reinforced local participation and the development of an ideological discourse parallel to that of the state. It appears that the parish priest encouraged religious practice to the point that Ciudad Satélite, along with Zamora, Michoacán, was considered one of the most religiously active communities in the country.

Relations with Authority and the Definition of a Common Enemy

Perhaps one of the most important factors in the development of social movements in Ciudad Satélite is its relation with local and provincial authorities. In the first years of the community, the municipality of Naucalpan was extremely rural and lacked an institutional, legal, and material infrastructure with which to meet the needs of the newly arrived, urban middle-class population. This provoked a series of problems derived from the multiplicity of authorities in the municipal and state government in charge of the area. Each service, such as postal delivery, water, or taxes, had to be arranged through a separate agency. The absence of an efficient municipal apparatus not only encouraged the development of the Neighborhood Association but compelled the relevant authorities to grant the area some form of self-administration.

This experience allowed the association to maintain contacts with local, state, and national governments. Through daily conflict and negotiations, the community developed a set of relations distinct from the clientelistic and authoritarian political system. From the early 1970s, government authorities were perceived as corrupt and inefficient because they were allied to individual factions and because they did not respect the local and regional urban development plans.

The community's perception of itself as both distinct from and better than the government produced a special local identity. The 1982 election made this perspective particularly clear: support for the PAN candidate came more from his position as a well-known and well-liked neighbor than from his formal affiliation with a party. Loyalty to the PAN developed only after the election, in response to the government's efforts to divide the community's voting bloc through geographical redistricting. The state's actions unified support for the candidate as Ciudad Satélite responded to what was seen as an external threat. This response further strengthened the community's already adversarial attitude toward the government.

In summary, one can see that the socioeconomic characteristics of the population, the presence of well-established communal networks, as well as the anarchic and inappropriate strategies of the government and the community's responses to them all played critical roles in the politicization of Ciudad Satélite.

ELECTORAL PARTICIPATION

Since the victory of the PAN in 1982, opposition organizations have been very active in promoting the integration of Ciudad Satélite into the electoral process. These activities have focused on demands to democratize the representational system and have included protests, strikes demanding respect for the ballot, and vigilance against fraud in the various elections held since that date.

The high level of participation by women and their associations, groups, and social networks is partly explained by the moral, as opposed to political, dimension defining *panista* discourse. The PAN and its National Feminine Civic Association (ANCIFEM) have also played an active role in the recruitment of female support.

Both local groups and those representing the government developed strategies for resource and vote mobilization in preparation for the elections of 1985 and 1988. In these, the PAN won two victories, capturing a congressional seat and the mayoralty of Naucalpan. These elections demonstrated an ambivalent attitude on the part of the population: intense interest and activity focused on events having to do with the community and a rejection of the system and electoral proceedings.

Democracy appears to be the central community demand, overshadowing other issues. A survey I administered in January 1987 to a sample of 114 heads of household demonstrates that the population considers fraud, corruption, and the imposition of candidates as the major obstacles to democracy. Respondents assigned responsibility for these problems to the very top leadership of the government, party, and political system in general.

These findings would seem to point to a legitimacy crisis if one referred only to the attitudinal data, without taking into account the high level of political participation. The respondents' opinions indicate a lack of confidence in the regime, but their active participation implies that the middle classes are seeking to reintegrate themselves into a political system whose traditional channels are closed.

The congruence of a democratic opening with an increase in local political activity has contributed to dramatic changes in electoral preferences. Although 42 percent of the respondents claimed always to have voted for the same party, 37 percent said that they had switched allegiances, and 10 percent stated that they had previously abstained from voting. Both of these shifts imply a realignment of electoral forces in favor of the PAN.

The distribution of electoral preferences is relatively polarized. Among the respondents, 43 percent claimed to have voted for the PAN, while 27.2 percent said they supported the PRI. Those parties that eventually supported Cárdenas were relatively marginal and remained so in 1988. The 20 percent abstention level is much lower than the national average (50 percent in 1988).

The votes for the two leading parties may be interpreted as reflecting either support for or rejection of the system. Very few respondents made reference to an ideological project or a party program when explaining their choices. If support for the PAN represents a protest from a group of voters "disenchanted and discontented with the Mexican political system" (Loaeza and Segovia 1987:78), the PRI vote is not linked to an ideological predisposition but to concrete personal interests. The latter would perhaps originate in defense of personal position and status as discussed by Garrido in his analysis of recruitment and militancy in the PRI (Garrido 1987:72).

The absence of an ideological socialization in Ciudad Satélite reflects the low level of politicization on a national level and is so common to both PAN and PRI supporters as to suggest a shared culture and life-style. This paradox requires a more detailed analysis of the electorate in order to explain the determination of political preferences in an ideological vacuum.

PROFILE OF THE ELECTORATE

Three factors appear to influence the electoral preferences of the population in Ciudad Satélite: social origins and socioeconomic status, religious and communal activity, and attitudes toward democratization and the political system in general.

The typical PAN voter comes from relatively humble origins (e.g., fathers were peasants or laborers with little formal education) and has experienced a high degree of social mobility. This voter's PRI counterpart tends to originate from a relatively privileged background. Some of the opposition's support comes from voters whose fathers were in the private sector and from the richest levels of the population, but in general there is a negative relationship between income and PAN support. At least in the case of Ciudad Satélite, the composition of the PAN electorate includes not only those in middle-income levels but also those who receive less than three or four times the minimum salary.

The predominance of working-class or peasant origins contradicts the commonly held view of the PAN as the party of privilege. A possible explanation for the relationship between mobility and voting for the PAN is that voters see their improved social status as a personal achievement not related to or dependent on the party or government. PAN support could also represent a protest from those on the margin of the middle class who fear that the economic crisis would push them into a lower status group. On the other hand, PRI votes may be read as the support by a dominant class for a system from which they have received considerable economic and social benefits.

Given that 82 percent of the survey respondents had medium to high scores on an index of religiosity, the relationship between voting patterns and participation in religious activities is quite important. Those respondents with high scores tended to vote for the PAN, whereas those with low levels voted for the PRI. The majority of respondents with intermediate scores also voted for the PAN.

It is not clear whether religious activity influences voting preferences or vice versa. In the case of Satélite, it is difficult to determine if religious practice reflects early socialization or a commitment to the values and historical political significance of the Mexican church. One also has to consider the critical role played by the local parish in the social integration of the community. The unique significance of the latter limits the generalizability of this analysis to the role of religion in political behavior for the Mexican middle classes. It would be worthwhile, however, to investigate the role played by local parishes in the creation and definition of political movements and orientations in other sectors of the population.

The respondents' relationship with the community as a whole is another critical factor in defining electoral behavior. Half of the sample population who identified themselves as members of the Satélite community and who claimed to have daily contacts with their neighbors voted for the PAN. Similarly, those who said that they actively participated in the Neighborhood Association (55 percent of the sample) tended to vote for the PAN. On the other hand, those who said that they would move out of Satélite if they could and who had *not* established a close relationship with their neighbors tended to support the PRI. There was no significant relationship between lack of participation in the Neighborhood Association and PRI votes.

As in most cases of popular movements, a set of shared experiences helped the population develop common goals and organizations that, in turn, allowed it to influence the distribution of resources by government bodies. What distinguishes the case of Satélite from those involving other social groups was that organizations such as the Neighborhood Association developed and redefined new projects that went beyond local concerns.

Mobilization contributes to the creation of a new community thanks to preexisting relations between families, the church, neighborhood associations, as well as to a set of values to which the population voluntarily adheres (Worsley 1985). In the case of Satélite, collective experience facilitated the formation of a group conscience or identity and the crystallization of common interests and political demands. The internal democracy of communal and religious organizations contributed to the development of a common experience and ideology that defined a new set of values. Local experience served as an agent of political socialization and helped determine electoral behavior.

THE DEMAND FOR DEMOCRACY: LIMITS AND DIMENSIONS

Demands for greater democratization became generalized in the 1980s and cut across all social structures. A superficial analysis of these demands among the various mobilized groups would lead to the possibly erroneous conclusion that they would create a generalized opposition based on the assertion of political rights.

Although the demand for democracy appears to unite various and varied sectors of the population, the definition of this concept changes according to social origin, ideology, and insertion into the process of economic development. The analysis of the content and dimensions of demands for democratization among the population of Satélite allows a more concrete evaluation of the possibility of creating a common project uniting all the opposition forces in Mexico.

Among the respondents there is a close relationship between electoral allegiance and attitudes toward the exercise of power in the current political system. Over 46 percent of the sample population said that Mexico was not democratic. But whereas 61 percent of PRI supporters believed that Mexico was democratic and another 16.1 percent said that it was a democracy of a kind, the figures for PAN voters were 18.4 and 28.6 percent, respectively.

It would appear that the population in Ciudad Satélite—familiar with democratic procedures in the community—elevated the demands for political rights to a national level. Does this indicate that such practices will generally lead to demands for national democratization? The results of the survey indicate there are two critical dimensions to this issue.

In Satélite, there is a widely held critical attitude toward the exercise of power in the current political system. The population demands clean elections, the alternation of parties in power, and an end to corruption. It is clear that democratic experiences in the community and the presence of the PAN, which bases its opposition on the principle of political participation, generate demands for democratization of the political system on a national level. The creation of a pluralistic legislature is a concrete example of this type of demand.

Democracy must also recognize the equality of groups and classes within the political system. In a society with the levels of inequality present in Mexico, democracy must include elements other than a more pluralistic electoral and governing system. For a significant minority of the population in Satélite, however, demands for democracy obscure an elitist conception of power and a desire to defend against political groups that would challenge their social and economic privileges.

Between 25 and 37 percent (depending on the sector to which the question referred) of the sample said that left-wing party militants, illiterates, the unemployed, and the indigenous population *did not* have the same political rights discussed above. According to these respondents, such groups should only exercise their political rights after developing to the level of the rest of society. Before they could be considered citizens, illiterates would have to learn to read, the unemployed would need jobs, and Indians would have to integrate themselves into the national society. Moreover, these respondents believed that the state should maintain control over radicals and left-wing opposition organizations in general.

The analysis above suggests several conclusions. First, the demands for democracy cannot be evaluated without some awareness of the various ways in which this concept is defined. Second, experience with local democracy does not necessarily generate democratic attitudes toward the nation as a whole. Democratic practices on the local level emphasize representation among members of the same social class. On the national level, however, democracy would imply the recognition of various social classes and the acceptance of their legal equality. Existing in a society with extreme levels of inequality, a considerable number of persons in the middle class have developed defensive attitudes toward those with less socioeconomic status and seek to limit the latter's participation in a democratic system.

CONCLUSIONS

The emergence of the middle class as a political actor is not an isolated event but coincides with that of other classes in a period of economic recession and crisis in the traditional mechanisms of political integration. The middle sectors' political opposition also originates in their increasing solidarity and cohesion as a class, with its own social and political identity expressed outside of those spaces controlled by the state.[4]

The experience of Ciudad Satélite illustrates the formation of a political opposition through participation in local collective activities. In various other cities, the middle classes also participate politically through a network of local associations and groups. This implies the existence of a new model of social participation, as previously the middle classes had functioned within the corporatist apparatus. The new model indicates the creation of a dual system of participation expressed through new groups and a change in the political culture of the middle class. These transformations originate in daily activities oriented to the resolution of local problems that, owing to national conditions, became specific policies expressed in electoral campaigns.

The significance of middle-class political mobilization in Mexico remains an open question. This is partly a result of the lack of research on this issue and the difficulty in relating the demands, strategies, and social project of this sector with those of other classes. The empirical limitations of the present study make any national generalizations difficult, yet the case suggests a series of working hypotheses, outlined below, which might inform future study of the relationship between local and national political processes as well as the role played within these by various social sectors.

The case of Satélite contradicts the general notion of the middle classes as consisting of individuals unable to generate their own organizations. The high degree of participation and the existence of communal identity indicates a well-organized social sector whose socioeconomic and ideological homogeneity will allow it to challenge the state whenever the mechanisms of political mediation break down. The creation of a community that for thirty years has administered its internal affairs and the distribution of resources, while maintaining its own means of communication, indicates the creation not only of a parallel form of participation but also of a new elite. The failure of the system to incorporate community leaders has led to their politicization and to their transformation into a competing alternative to local government. National conditions and the activities of communal organizations transformed negotiations between the community and local governments into electoral battles over the entire political system.

The ability of the middle classes to escape corporatist controls also supports expansion of new forms of association. The development of this relative autonomy is related to various factors. First, by working either on their own account or within the private sector, this well-educated population developed economic roles divorced from those controlled by the state. In turn, this work force finds it difficult to have their interests represented through the traditional network of official organizations. Second, the division of labor by gender allows well-educated women to devote their attention to the creation and defense of a unique life-style. Middle-class women are the unseen actors of the new social organization and emerge into the public arena with their own organizations and sets of demands. The obscurity of these groups, and the absence of any attempt, until recently, to represent the interests of women within the political system, favored the development of autonomous activities.

Despite the government's attempts to control them, local organizations have not only maintained their unique identity but have also transformed themselves into opposition platforms. In Satélite these organizations have undergone a civic apprenticeship and have developed new social practices and values, such as democracy and a commitment to the common good. Through this experience, local society replaces the party and the state and municipal government apparatus.

Although the government tried to coopt these organizations and has reached some agreements with them, the possibility of political control is remote given the well-integrated network of groups linked by a communal identity and the defense of a life-style.

Individual characteristics such as social origins, income, and socialization help define the electoral behavior of the middle-class population. Their participation in groups and associations based on the creation and defense of a style of life, however, also plays a major role in the definition of electoral preferences. In the case of Satélite, participation in the Neighborhood Association and religious activity is positively related to support for the PAN. The active local parish, daily personal contacts among the inhabitants, and the policies of the municipal and state governments have contributed to the formation of social actors linked through a communitywide system and united by opposition to a common enemy. Satélite voters support a party that presents itself as their ideological ally and, more importantly, as the enemy of the government.

This phenomenon is not unique to Satélite but is also evident in the organized sectors of the working and popular classes. Local associations are the bearers of a new definition of citizenship, emphasizing democratic participation and challenging the current electoral system. It appears that these organizations are responsible for the formation of a parallel political culture.

The case of Satélite suggests that the political orientation of the middle classes is partly defined by the interaction of structural position, exclusion from the political system, and the development of social participation not controlled by the state. The great differences in income and living standards between the middle sectors and those above and below them produce a social stratum intent on creating or defending an urban life-style within segregated neighborhoods. This makes it difficult for the middle classes to identify politically with the majority of the population. The social isolation of the middle classes supports the further development of organizations that expand the potential influence of members of this class and facilitates the definition of a collective consciousness linked to their specific interests and life-styles.

The demand for greater democratization includes class-specific dimensions informing the middle classes' relations with the state. The analysis of the political demands of the middle class in Satélite indicates that there are two dimensions to this call for democratization. On the one hand, these demands contain a subversive element calling for a competitive party system, modernization of the political order, and clean electoral competition.

With these demands, the middle class challenges the legitimacy of the authoritarian and archaic practices of the current system of domination. There is, on the other hand, a conservative dimension to these demands for democratization. An important group within this population supports a restrictive conception of popular or leftist political participation. The significance of such a perspective becomes clearer when one considers that this group believes that the state, against which they are united on most other issues, should exercise its control over these actors.

This double game, which includes demands for both   a political transformation *and* a defense of a social order, defines the activities of the middle-class groups studied here and establishes the limits to their ability to establish alliances with other groups or to create a wider social project.

NOTES

Translation by Miguel A. Centeno

1. Social groups will be defined as belonging to the middle class if they are: (1)concentrated in urban centers; (2) employed as nonmanual labor; and (3) possess a level of education above the national mean. This last characteristic is particularly important in underdeveloped countries where education is transformed into a form of social capital controlled by these same groups.

2. The research included historical analyses of protests since 1965 with special attention paid to the role of women in organizing these, and a survey of the socioeconomic characteristics and social, political, religious, and electoral life of a sample of the relevant population.

3. Ciudad Satélite has a population of 124,397 (Municipio de Naucalpan data, 1987). Built in Mexico State in 1965, it was the first community designed for the middle class and was originally conceived as part of a strategy to decentralize the Federal District. For the history of Satélite, see Tarrés 1986.

4. The case of Satélite indicates that certain groups within the urban middle class have created their own social and organizational spaces and socialization mechanisms. The migration and social mobility that initially defined the Mexican middle classes are today relatively rare. The tendency is for class reproduction to replace mobility as a structural process.

9

Women's Participation in
Urban Protest

During the past several decades, community-based mobilizations among the urban poor have become a new and important force on the political landscape of Mexican cities. In many cities, these residentially based movements have eclipsed all other kinds of mobilizations undertaken by the poor. Although there is considerable debate about how to interpret these movements, few observers doubt that they will have a significant impact on state politics for years to come.

A characteristic feature of many community-based movements is the notable presence of women. They are commonly the instigators and organizers of mobilizations. Women are involved as the rank and file, often constituting the majority of participants, and they have also formed their own subgroups within larger urban popular movements, as they have done in CONAMUP (National Coordinating Committee of the Urban Popular Movement). Their activism is evidence of the societywide emergence of women of all classes into the political arena as urban (Lozano Pardinas and Padilla Dieste 1988) and rural activists (Stephen 1989), feminists (Bartra et al. 1983), trade unionists, human rights workers (Sosa Riddell 1986), and activists within the political opposition to the dominant PRI (Tarrés, this volume).

The female activists who form the core of popular movements belie the stereotype of poor women as politically conservative, passive, or indifferent to the distribution of power and resources in their society. In fact, the formation of community-based movements in urban neighborhoods by poor women is only the most recent example of their political activism. Women of the popular classes have a long and involved, if only partially discovered, history of political engagement in such activities as peasant resistance movements, regional revolts against the state, and the Mexican Revolution itself (Macías 1982; Sosa Riddell 1986; Deutsch 1989).

If these instances of their activism are well known, it remains for historians to tease out from reluctant documents the complete account of poor women's political involvement and analyze the significance of their actions. Missing particularly from the historical record are the accounts of women's activities that occur outside the formal structure of state politics yet affect the policies of the state.

Although the historical analysis of poor women's political activities is incomplete, any such examination of the past will likely reveal that then, as now, gender is a critical variable in the politics of the poor. Contemporary community-based mobilizations undertaken by low-income women demonstrate that as political actors women differ from men and are linked politically to the state in dissimilar, and weaker, ways. As a result, the future of poor women in the politics of the Mexican state will also differ from that of low-income men because of the nexus of class and gender.

DEMAND-MAKING BY THE URBAN POOR: WHY *WOMEN* ACTIVISTS? WHY NOW?

As the population of Mexican cities grew, so did the magnitude and complexity of urban problems. Neither the state nor the private sector has allocated the resources necessary to make substantial improvements in the social, political, and economic conditions in which the urban poor live. Mexico's decade-long economic crisis has exacerbated conditions for the poor, whose meager resource base eroded further under increased economic pressure. Such problems are particularly acute in the new settlements of the urban poor, where the basic infrastructure for public services and institutions is inadequate or altogether lacking.

In response, low-income women—who as housewives and mothers are more deeply rooted in their residential communities than most men and whose skills as managers of the household economy determine family survival— have begun to organize collectively. Because of gradual, incremental improvements in education and public health since the Mexican Revolution and increased access to information via the mass media, poor women now have advantages in their efforts to mobilize that preceding generations of women of the popular classes did not. Consequently, women's collective demand-making has become increasingly common in low-income urban neighborhoods.

Working within the social context of the urban poor, women have formed a variety of organizations that have in common their base in the residential community: housewives' committees, consumer cooperatives, residential associations, and religious reflection, self-help, and self-improvement groups. The organizations in which women participate range from the large and complex to the small and simple. In Mexico City, thousands of women helped form cross-class, interneighborhood alliances to deal with the devastation of the 1985 earthquake (Hernández 1988b). On a more modest scale, a dozen women from a neighborhood housewives' committee in Mérida convinced the state to donate land on which the women could grow crops for market and as a supplement to their families' diets (Logan n.d.).

In addition to organizing as ongoing groups, women have also mobilized around single issues as community needs dictate. In Monterrey and Guadalajara, where there are chronic water shortages in outlying low-income areas, women have mounted protests again and again (Bennett 1989; Logan 1984). Despite the lack of established organizations to address the water problem, women succeeded in their mobilization efforts by forming networks that can be activated quickly whenever shortages occur.

The key to poor women's motivation to mobilize lies in their self-definition as mothers and their commitment to fulfilling the responsibilities attendant in the social practice of motherhood. Low-income Mexican women are socialized to assume motherhood as their primary adult role and identity. In Mexico, as throughout Latin America, motherhood is culturally idealized (if not necessarily always venerated in practice). For these reasons, motherhood has a centrality in the lives of women held by no other role.

As mothers, women are responsible for maintaining the household, caring for spouses and children, and distributing the economic and social resources of their communities. Unlike men, women cannot readily escape their familial responsibilities through alcohol, drugs, or desertion. Women do not easily resist the strong social pressure to be good mothers. Their ties to their children are especially strong and hold women to their familial responsibilities.

The material conditions under which the urban poor of Mexico live, however, prevent women from carrying out the duties and responsibilities involved in the social practice of motherhood. Because women come to view these conditions as obstacles to the proper performance of their motherhood role, they perceive the material conditions of their communities to be their concern. Since the most compelling problems women face fall squarely into what they regard as their domain of family and community, women consider it highly appropriate to mobilize around these issues.

The women who are involved in urban popular mobilizations possess a "female consciousness" that "centers upon the rights of gender, on social concerns, on survival." Such a consciousness arises from a culturally framed division of labor that assigns women the responsibility for preserving life. Under these conditions, women accept rather than rebel against the prescribed gender roles of their societies (Kaplan 1982:545).

But, by accepting these roles and their attendant responsibilities, activist women claim the rights that their obligations entail. As a result, the collective movements they mount to obtain their rights as family caretakers lead to a politicization of the networks of everyday life (Kaplan 1982:545). For the low-income female activists in Mexico's urban popular movements, what is familial and communal becomes political.

Urban poor women rally around the gendered role of motherhood as a base for their mobilizations. For men, the equivalent role of fatherhood does not possess the centrality, responsibility, or social significance motherhood holds for women. Consequently, men do not organize out of their gendered status as fathers; they are more likely to organize around economic and political issues linked to the workplace. As opportunities to mobilize in the workplace have decreased as a result of economic crisis, more men have joined community-based movements, but their concerns remain economic and political, not linked to or rooted in their roles as fathers.

GENDER-BASED MECHANISMS
AND TACTICS FOR MOBILIZATION

Just as women's motivation to mobilize arises out of their gendered roles, so, too, do their means and tactics. Faced with the worsening living conditions in their low-income neighborhoods, urban poor women turn to each other and inward to their communities to find the mechanisms and tactics to solve their problems.

The base from which women act collectively are the ties they have among themselves, linked, as they are, to each other by overlapping networks of kinship, *compadrazgo*, friendship, neighborliness, and mutual aid. Because extended family members often follow each other in rural-urban migration, they frequently settle in the same neighborhoods and thus create a potential kin network within new urban communities. Succeeding generations widen and deepen their kinship ties through marriages within the community and the formation of local *compadrazgo* relationships.

Women form the core of community life as the collectors and distributors of scarce resources. As such, they forge ties among themselves through reciprocal aid and social interaction. They exchange food and favors, lend money, and tend one another's children. Women visit, shop, and celebrate holidays and religious events together. From the shared routines of their lives, they create a sense of female community with other women.

These links are reinforced by a cultural pattern whereby women turn to each other for social support and companionship. Under such conditions, women share a camaraderie and form close bonds. Women come to rely on each other to fulfill many of their social needs and to see themselves as each other's allies. The longer a community's history, the more likely that extensive networks will form among its women.

Women's complex, many-stranded social structure also has its disadvantages. Within the community of women, the close attention to "*lo personal*" can become burdensome, especially when mobilization pressures are added. Perceived personal affronts and mistrust, especially about money, seem particularly problematic for women within their interwoven social communities of family and neighborhood. On occasion, interpersonal hostilities can override community concerns and forestall the realization of collective actions.

In Mexico's low-income urban neighborhoods, women are primarily responsible for mediating and maintaining the social world of the community through their networks. Consequently, women do not need to create a new social structure from which to mobilize; a structure is already in place from which they can act collectively. The base women have built, however, is not a firm, bounded social structure but rather a network of ties that can be activated and deactivated depending on particular circumstances. Therein lies both its weakness and its strength. The base for women's mobilization is less likely to produce structured organizations that have a continuous identity over time. As a result, the amorphousness and occasionality of women's organizing efforts reduce their visibility and allow analysts to overlook their importance.

Yet, the networks on which women base their mobilizations have the potential to spring into action when needed. Women's networks stand guard over community interests as a flexible and resilient response mechanism. The ebb-and-flow nature of women's mobilizing networks also protects them by making it less likely that they will be co-opted and absorbed by the state. This point is especially important because urban popular movements, in making claims to the state, become vulnerable to state control and thereby risk losing their project and identity.

Women in low-income communities come together initially as activists either because of their linkages to each other or because of the efforts of individuals working within the communities (especially clergy or social welfare workers). Regardless of how they come together, however, women meeting in groups soon realize that they are not alone in confronting inadequate public services, the increasing costs of maintaining a household, alcoholism, and family violence. For many, it is their first experience in reflecting critically upon the circumstances in which they live. Local group meetings also provide a new experience for women by giving them a forum for expressing their thoughts, a context where their ideas will be taken seriously.

In local group meetings, women develop their tactics for mobilization. They rely on time-honored mechanisms of protesting and demand-making long used by men, i.e., forming clientelistic ties with politicians, staging public demonstrations, petitioning government officials, and sending delegations to state offices. Their strategies differ significantly from men's, however, in that women mediate their demands and claims through gender. Women commonly employ the gendered role of motherhood in some way as a mechanism through which they can make demands on the state to improve the material conditions of their lives.

In Mérida, one such leader uses her position as a grassroots organizer for the PRI to get audiences with the state governor in which she can present her community's demands for new public services or convey complaints about already existing ones. Her talks with the governor are carefully orchestrated performances in which she presents herself as a humble grandmother simply acting on her community's behalf. She does not mention her history as a labor organizer, also part of her identity as an activist. In her requests, she emphasizes the devotion of the women in her community to their families. She asks that the state supply the services needed so that women can fulfill their traditional roles and remain loyal to the PRI. This leader's skillful presentation of her community's needs—and her nuanced understanding of when to approach the governor and what requests he is likely to grant—gives her community the edge over equally deserving neighborhoods and makes it one of the most successful in the city in making claims on the state (Logan n.d.).

Women have also been able to use their gendered status as mothers effectively in public demonstrations, especially when they can involve their children as part of the demand-making process. In Guadalajara, women from the northern *colonias* have repeatedly staged public protests over the chronic water shortage in their neighborhoods. In one particularly effective demonstration, women marched with their children in hand to the city center and bathed them in the splashing waters of the huge ornamental fountain in front of city hall. They made their point symbolically that they did not have enough water in their communities to carry out their ascribed gender roles as mothers. By using this strategy, the women reminded the state that, by allocating water as it had, it had chosen aesthetics over human needs and that they, as mothers, objected. For several months after this demonstration, the participating communities had water regularly (Logan 1984:79–80).

Using their children to mediate claims is common for activist women. When the state governor of Yucatán came to inaugurate a new housing project in a neighborhood adjacent to theirs, women had their children greet him with placards describing the plight of their community—no electricity, paved streets, or drainage system. The organizers made sure that the children were dressed in their best clothes and that the youngest and most appealing of them stood at the front of the crowd where they would not only be seen by the governor but would also catch the cameras of the assembled news media. Their careful planning met with some success—electricity was installed within weeks of their demonstration (Logan 1988:12).

To outside observers, what women achieve as a result of their mobilizations may seem modest indeed—electricity for some streets, water for a few months, an increase in elementary school classes by three, or a few plots of land distributed to a handful of families. Yet to people who have so few resources, and who have seen what little they have shrink to even less over the past decade, the bits and pieces of public infrastructure and services that women gain through their mobilizations are critically important. Women's popular organizing ensures community survival.

Women's motivation to participate in collective actions and the means and tactics by which they organize arise from their attempts to fulfill their traditional roles as mothers. It is ironic that in their efforts to maintain cultural tradition, they are part of a process bringing sociopolitical transformation to Mexico.

LINKAGES TO THE STATE AND POLITICAL TRANSFORMATION: THE IMPACT OF WOMEN IN URBAN POPULAR MOVEMENTS

It is important to note that in mounting mobilizations, low-income activist women have not yet seen a need to challenge their traditionally defined gender roles as mothers. They think of themselves as acting consistently within the confines of their role, such as Kaplan's (1982) model of activism within a female consciousness suggests. The female activists in Mexican urban popular movements are transforming the role of motherhood to include political activism in the public arena as an appropriate component of this role yet one that nevertheless remains congruent with the traditional definition of mothers as family and community caretakers. They have transformed the social practice of motherhood to become "activist mothers." Similar "activist" interpretations of motherhood have also been reported by observers of popular movements in Brazil and Nicaragua (Alvarez 1989; Molyneux 1985).

The potential for bringing political transformation through an activist interpretation of motherhood is obvious. As Kaplan (1982:565) notes, taken to its logical end, women acting out of a female consciousness would demand that the state place human life above all other goals—surely a change in the political project of the Mexican state that would lead to profound transformation of its conduct of state policy.

The success of poor women's efforts to bring transformation by means of an activist motherhood, however, depends heavily upon state responses to them. Unfortunately for the female activists, and ultimately for Mexican society, the state does not define motherhood in the way that women do, nor does it recognize their interpretation of this role. As a result, regardless of their participation in various kinds of urban popular movements, women are only weakly articulated with the state.

Just recently have the state and its supporting political party begun to turn their attention to women and women's issues. Their responses to date are discouraging in terms of allowing women the voice in public policy formation that women would choose for themselves. State celebrations to honor women as mothers (such as International Women's Day or Mother's Day) employ an interpretation of motherhood that limits women to the most basic home-centered aspects of this role. In programs involving women at the national and local level, the state and the PRI continue to conceptualize motherhood within a much more narrow framework than activist women apply.

The DIF (Family Services Agency) program is a case in point. For twenty-five years this nationwide state program has sought to bring social welfare assistance to those most in need of it, accruing support for the state and the PRI from those it helps. DIF goals include strengthening the family and participating in community development (O. Rodríguez 1987). Consequently, most of the DIF constituency are women seeking benefits for themselves or their children. Although this state welfare agency undoubtedly does much to aid some of the most needy of Mexico's citizens, its conceptualization of women's roles as mothers does not allow women actively to shape their participation in family or community life. Nor does it permit any evolution in the definition of motherhood.

At its most basic level of involvement with low-income women, the DIF clearly conveys its notion of their appropriate roles as mothers. Agency programs exclusively emphasize developing women's traditional skills as housewives. To ensure achieving this goal, women must participate in classes that emphasize their responsibilities within the home (primarily child care and food preparation) in order to receive the powdered milk supplements that the DIF sells at low cost to the poor. Repeatedly, women are told that the proper practice of their roles requires adapting to the conditions of their lives regardless of the problems they face (Logan n.d.).

State programs do little better at the local level in recognizing women's potential for bringing transformation through activist motherhood. A program run by the Mérida municipal government to increase the earnings of low-income women trains them to make hammocks and tablecloths for sale to tourists. Yet there already exists a well-established hammock and textile industry that has saturated both the local and tourist markets. Besides its economic inappropriateness, this program fails to confront the needs of low-income women because it does not allow for the possibility that women could increase their financial resources by learning skills less directly linked to homemaking (Logan n.d.).

In no case does a state program build on the concept of motherhood that women have made for themselves as community activists or teach skills that would enhance their capabilities as activists. Women are in fact allowed no voice in shaping the programs designed to help them.

It is not only that the state tries to channel women into restricted and unchanged interpretations of their roles, but also that the state has difficulty recognizing women's own activist definition of motherhood when confronted with it. Women throughout Mexico have been successful in gaining services and resources for their communities from the state, but there seems to be a structural blindness that prevents the state from recognizing the organization, activities, and achievements of low-income activist women. The state makes little effort to incorporate the women of urban popular movements within its project despite their political successes.

During the last dozen years, the PRI has responded to critics of its dominance by allowing new opportunities for political expression. As part of an internal reform effort, PRI party leaders have opted to set aside a certain percentage of party offices for women. Although some women may benefit from this opportunity, it is unlikely that they will be low-income women. Given the nexus of gender and class, it is doubtful that both these variables will be considered in the allocation of the reserved party offices. They are likely to be occupied by women from upper income groups who already have a notable presence in the PRI's lower and middle tiers. Poor women will remain linked to the PRI, as they are now, at the very lowest levels, as grassroots organizers with very little hope of upward mobility within the party. The current Mexican state appears unattuned to the needs of poor women and unaware of the talents that female activists from the popular classes possess.

With the appearance of new political openings, opposition parties have formed and sought alliances with urban popular movements. During the last presidential election campaign, many neighborhood movements coalesced into pan-urban organizations that spread beyond their original base in the northern cities to embrace popular organizing groups in other parts of Mexico. Some worked on behalf of the FDN (National Democratic Front), the leftist opposition to the PRI in the elections. Since the PRI's controversial victory, however, the shifting and complex realignment of power within opposition political parties and their allied movements leaves it unclear and unpredictable what openings they offer for the women of urban popular movements.

The rise of pan-urban supermovements such as CONAMUP has drawn more low-income men into urban popular mobilizations. The influx of men into the movements has diminished women's power as men take leadership positions and relegate women to roles as followers (CONAMUP 1983). The mobilizations thereby become "movements of women led by men." Issues of gender and leadership pose a dilemma for women and men in urban popular movements because it is difficult for women to rid themselves of life-long learned patterns of subservience, and for men to rid themselves of those of dominance.

How will the women of urban popular movements be linked to the state as Mexico upholds its process of political transformation? If the Mexican state continues its current policy of strategic reform coupled with selective suppression, it will do little to improve the lives of the majority of the urban poor. Should low-income women become too troublesome in their mobilizing efforts, the state will undoubtedly rely on proven means of undermining popular movements—co-opting movement leadership, splintering movements into quarreling factions, turning activist communities against each other, and, if these fail, increased use of violence.

Should the state exercise its harshest option in dealing with urban popular movements, the mobilizations will become so limited in their courses of action that they will be unable to exert influence beyond their individual communities. They will cease to be popular movements and become community-based strategies for survival. Were this to happen, Mexican popular organizations would likely follow the Chilean model of popular mobilization during the most severe years of the Pinochet regime, when urban activists focused their efforts inward to community survival while they waited for a change in state leadership (Friedmann and Salguero 1988).

Regardless of the possibilities, or lack of them, for women within the formal structure of Mexican politics, women will continue to mobilize in their communities because the material conditions of their lives remain unimproved or improved in only the most piecemeal fashion. Ultimately, the potential of the women involved in urban popular mobilizations to effect *political* transformation lies in their ability to first bring about *social* transformation. One option for changing Mexican politics lies in women's capacity to alter their roles within the family and community with an activist interpretation of motherhood.

Women's influence on the next generation of urban poor is one mechanism for such a role transformation. Within many families, the young are growing up in households where mothers are community activists. For them, it may become the norm for women to include political activity as part of the social practice of motherhood. For young women particularly, activist mothers serve as role models for adult behavior. It is also important to note that many children and teenagers participate in popular mobilization alongside their mothers and are consequently creating their own history as community activists.

Another option for low-income activists is to develop a popular (i.e., class-based) feminism that would address their needs as women as well as their responsibilities as mothers. Through it, they could work for class as well as gender interests. Popular feminism would allow women to continue to work collectively for improvements in the lives of the entire community as opposed to improvements in the lives of individuals. A feminism so defined would also permit low-income women to address issues that symbolize their subordination as *women*, such as male violence, institutionalized discrimination, and the lack of reproductive freedom.

Whether as activist mothers or popular feminists, poor women must continue to address the issue of class in their political activities so that their capabilities are realized and they are able to have a place in the political life of the state. If they are successful in bringing about such class and gender-role transformations, low-income women would create new societal norms that would incrementally impact the distribution of power and resources in Mexican society and women's position within it.

10

Crisis, Neoliberalism, and Disorder
SERGIO ZERMEÑO

This essay proposes a hypothesis: that the crisis of progress of the 1980s (and 1990s and beyond?), combined with the neoliberal actions of the Mexican government, has provoked a strong social disorganization—and, moreover, that a similar phenomenon is taking place throughout Latin America. An important question presents itself: Does this panorama of disorder and atomization bode well for the return of great national-popular leaderships in Latin America?

In considering recent trends in the conceptual evolution of the social sciences in the region during the last two decades, we find that the broad social sectors of Latin America—seen as classes, masses, peasantry, or people— once capable of giving a progressive sense to our history have become atomized, polarized, impoverished, stagnant, and disordered. In extreme cases, they have fallen into patterns of disorganized violence or defensive anomie.

This dynamic of disorder can and should be understood on three different social levels. The first level is the *organizational*, that is, that of the basic organizational referents of people in society, such as family, work, school, religion, neighborhood, community, sport, and recreation. The second is the *institutional*, that is, the level of the basically political aspects in the broadest sense of the word, which allow for the aggregation of the socially disperse in a way that it can be expressed, in either a conflictive or nonconflictive manner, at the more general level of collective subjects or social identities, through political parties, trade unions, parliaments, business organizations, ecclesiastic communities, confederations of ejidos or dayworkers, neighborhood organizations, and so on. The third and final level is that of the *state*, that is, of the relation between state and society.

FROM UNITY TO FRAGMENTATION: THE ROAD OF PESSIMISM

Consider the way in which the images used by students of Latin America have changed since the early 1970s. Once the so-called dependency theory of Cardoso and Faletto revealed clearly that the Latin American economies were developing in spite of (or thanks to) their growing articulation with the world

160

economy, the central preoccupation shifted from external aspects (imperialism, dependency) to domestic ones, and from the economy (investment, profit transfer, exports, outward growth) to "the social." Authors such as Gunder Frank, Dos Santos, and Furtado became outmoded, and a euphoria for characterizations of the social structure took over.

But this defection away from economics was not devoid of atavistic implications. Underlying this shift was a hope that, with development, leading national actors—true classes in the European sense—would be formed. Simultaneously, the issue of marginality of the reserve army of labor, or relative overpopulation, emerged in debate. Social scientists dedicated themselves to the question of whether what they saw in the periphery was or could become the same as what was found in the center, and to the problem of the revolutionary potential of the urban poor.

Alain Touraine spoke of the popular class and the "high" class, and how, in the struggle for appropriating the spaces and the instruments that orient the historicity of a society, they would give some coherence to development through their complex dialectic. The images of a dual society were displaced, apparently forever, by the idea of a combined development, by the illusion of a growing articulation of inequalities under the dominant logic of capital. Deep down, there was an assumption in the "conceptual imaginary" of Latin Americans that they were guaranteed entry into the "kingdom of the West," something akin to the unstoppable process of modernization. The emphasis on coherence surfaces in the very concepts used: mode of production, articulation of modes of production, fundamental classes, subordinate classes, structure, superstructure, dominance, and predominance. Twenty years later, however, references to common concepts that previously assumed such a degree of order in society are scarce.

FROM THE CLASSIST AND STATIST HEGEMONY TO THE COLLECTIVE WILL

It soon became apparent that in societies in transition, as they used to be called, the dynamic agents were not actors on the social terrain (social classes, in other words) but actors at the level of the state. On this point Barrington Moore and Touraine made decisive contributions. The debate shifted to the state level along three trajectories. The first, and probably the earliest, was linked to orthodox Leninist concepts. In this case, an external conscience converts the mass into a victorious revolutionary party, which, resting on the centrality of the working class, guides the social whole as it takes over the privileged instrument of transformation in societies developing along the capitalist path: the state.

The other two trajectories are related to the first and seem to respond directly to the failure of its revolutionary voluntarism and to the political tendencies associated with it, mainly the path of armed struggle. In the second case, then, the rise of dictatorships is analyzed by unearthing the implications of Friedmanite neoliberalism, the doctrines of national security, the seclusion of the private, and the freezing of collective participation and of the political system (trade unions, political parties, parliaments).

In the third trajectory, the problem of the state and politics finds fertile ground in the Gramscian conceptualization of hegemony. Within the hegemony problematic, the centrality of the working class, the accumulation of forces, the party, and the wars of maneuver as strategy to gain power cede their place to other tasks. Essential instead is intellectual and moral reform, the search for a "higher synthesis" capable of fusing all class, mass, and other elements into a "collective national-popular will." Latin American conceptions, centered on orderly visions of "class" and the "substructure," turned to the less pure notions evoked by terms such as "popular culture," the people, and the nation. It is necessary to point out, however, that important ordering concepts remained. Thus, we still find notions such as those of civil society–political society, wars of maneuver and of position, historical bloc, ruling and dominant class, consensus, and passive revolution.

FROM THE LABOR MOVEMENT TO RESTRICTED IDENTITIES

The blurring of actors and scenarios is also apparent in the important analysis of Latin American social movements. Here we see that the euphoria of analyzing the labor movement gave way to the study of the revolutionary potential of marginal masses, and later to an interest in the defensive actions that proliferated during the military dictatorships and the economic crisis of the 1980s. That is, there was a shift from class struggle to social movements, then to historic struggles of a national-popular profile as suggested by Gramsci and Touraine, which ends in the current concern with the "restricted identities" of movements organized around the urban setting, human rights, ecclesiatic communities, trade unions, youth, and women.

The Latin American scenario displayed the signs of hardship that resulted from being simultaneously hit by dictatorships and economic crisis. Faced with the fragmentation, the disarticulation, and the heterogeneity of historical actors, of modern classes and their political manifestations, the visions of defensive confinement and restricted identities—in a word, community-centered visions—became the ethical and conceptual ordering principles with which Latin Americans began to think about their reality in the first lustrum of the 1980s.

As the 1980s advanced, however, the matter lost its humanist and solidary dimension as the scenario become even more somber and excessively negative. Thus, the imagery that had centered on the community was replaced by concepts deriving from research in more marginal environments. In these contexts, it became necessary to talk of anomie, decadence, destructiveness, disintegration, barbarism, chaos, negativity, antisociability, and deterioration.[1]

TOWARD A SOCIOLOGY OF DECADENCE?

The most recent and dramatic proposal coming out of Latin America goes as far as asking whether we should not develop a "sociology of decadence" in place of a sociology of modernization. Thus, Eugenio Tironi argues that the current reality of Latin America is better understood through concepts of Durkheimian inspiration, which refer to the dissolution of social cohesion, the disintegration of intermediary identities, and the particularization or the retreat into the individual and atomized sphere of members of a society. These notions, it is argued, correspond more closely to the panorama of acute anomie, of generalized disaffection with regard to social order, and the weakening, fusion, or disappearance of basic social units. Classes, groups, and stratums are seen as giving way to delinquent and individual forms of adaptation (Tironi n.d.*a*).

Touraine agrees with Tironi's references and considers them to be effectively grounded in the world of the excluded, of the marginalized. He adds, however, that this line of argument should be put into context. To talk of the excluded is to talk of the majority, which accounts for the return of "the marginal" as a concept of central importance, so that, paradoxically, we must refer to "the centrality of the marginalized." This, however, is a destroyed centrality, because in the poor and marginal Latin American environment we find a bit of everything: communitarian, delinquent, anomic, populist, and consumerist values and attitudes; a longing to belong to a proletarian class; and so on. Touraine writes, therefore, that "they are negative and separate images. This means that what would be a social actor, or, in an extreme form, a social movement, is destroyed" (Touraine n.d.:218). Within this context, he argues that it even makes sense to talk of social antimovements.

Now, we must be referring to disintegrated forms of something, which allows us to imagine a principle of unity, to attempt to find integrating and analytical principles, in terms of actors and even of social movements. There is no doubt that here is the rupture point in the conceptualization of the last twenty years, that is, since Latin American thinking in the social sciences last adopted as an unquestioned point of reference both the continuity of development (in spite of dependency) and the inexorability of the distribution of society into social classes. In effect, in spite of the panorama of decadence, negativity, and destruction of "the social," the cited authors insist that we must search for "something" that will give meaning and a center (a principle of unity) to the scenario. This could be understood (amidst the chaos) as the formation of actors in a struggle to control a historic sense (historicity) of Latin American societies, of social movements, and of collective identities.

The point is that, for the social sciences in general, a social model without some future better stage is unthinkable. The idea that history must have some sense cannot be renounced, because in so doing one would have to renounce all humanist content in history and the very principle that history is or should be oriented toward the satisfaction of the necessities of human beings and toward an order that will empower their highest qualities, such as rational communication, the equality of opportunities, harmony, the growth of culture and the cultivation of the arts, or the care of the body.

ANOMIC DESPAIR AND THE YEARNING FOR WHOLENESS

The debate over the search for unifying principles and some sense of history, on the one hand, and fragmentation, opacity, and stagnation, on the other, has been the topic of several recent meetings of Latin American social scientists. It is hard to say what the conclusions of these discussions have been and, indeed, to determine if there are any conclusions, but we can risk the following assertions. There is an apparent shift from an analytical vision conceptualized in terms of actors and social movements toward one in which the preoccupation is centered on collective identities, or, better said, on the difficulty of ascertaining persisting identities of more or less organic identities. Previous collective identities—not only class identities but also national-popular, communitarian, gender, and generational ones—are seen as undergoing a kind of deconstruction, becoming denaturalized by the unstoppable spread of poverty.

Another noteworthy point is that the idea of transition is rejected, as social scientists refuse to see the prevailing disorder as some passing phenomena, or merely as necessary misfortunes on the road toward modernization. What prevails, then, is a synchronic approach to the social sciences, but one that refuses to be classified as an openly *negative sociology*, which deals with stagnated forms and the loss of meaning. Rather, there is an effort to coherently reconstruct the world of the excluded, in terms of social movements and of recreation of collective identities, taking as a central axis the yearning for wholeness (*anhelo de integración*).

The marginalized are not to be reduced to an anomic mass, unintegrated into society and barely redeemable

> through faith and the churches, with purely expressive and affective standards of action, easily influenced by prophetic leaders of any ideological sign. To the contrary, what one observes is an instrumental logic sharpened by the requirements of survival. . . . The *pobladores* show a strong cultural adherence to the system and an irreversible incorporation into the urban world to which they have belonged for more than a generation. Therefore, they demand *participation*, not rupture; more support from the state, not more autonomy; access to industry, not self-subsistence workshops; a place in modern culture, not the reduction to folklore. (Tironi n.d.*b*:78)

We can openly say that as Latin American sociology reaches this point it is in an ambiguous position. To find a way out of this quandary, no doubt, an adequate interpretation of the developmental crisis the region is experiencing will have to be found.

THE DOUBLE DISORDER

The current situation in Latin America is widely recognized, and there are facts to illustrate certain trends. I shall summarize the crucial facts.[2] In 1970 the percentage of poor people in the region was 41 percent, and in 1980 it was 35 percent; but in the first five years of the 1980s there was a return to the 1970 level. In absolute figures, in 1985 there were 25 percent more people in poverty than at the beginning of the 1980s; 44 percent of the labor force was either unemployed or underemployed, a situation that hit young people hardest. During 1980–1985 the GNP fell from an annual growth rate of approximately 6 percent to less than –3 percent, and GNP per capita declined 9 percent. A similar trend appears in levels of investment, which fell from 29 percent to 19 percent of GNP in Brazil, from 28 percent to 17 percent of GNP in Mexico, from 23 percent to 15 percent in Argentina, and, even more dramatically, from 22 percent to 4 percent in Bolivia and from 17 percent to 6 percent in Chile, all during the 1980–1983 period. Latin American participation in world trade has declined; technological innovation is practically nil; unionization rates are in decline; the domestic market is shrinking as wages are lowered in a vain attempt to pay the foreign debt and simultaneously become competitive in increasingly protectionist international markets. The only things that show an exponential upward trend are insecurity in all cities, financial speculation, and capital export.

All this is well known, so that the fundamental question within Latin American paradigms is another. Are we faced with a passing crisis, no doubt as drastic as that of the 1930s? Or is this bleak situation, marked by chaos and a profound deterioration, to last until the end of the century, as suggested by some forecasts? Or, rather, are we confronting a harsh change that entails a general shift leading to a quickening of events, i.e., a matter of much longer term, which will show the rationalist pretension of man's subjection of nature to be merely a utopian illusion?

The historical trends we face are such that they are hard to grasp; by considering a medium-term time frame, however, the task becomes more manageable. We can say that Latin America is living a *double disorder*. First, there is the disorder involved in the transition from a traditional order and in rapid growth rates, higher than those in the United States, for example. The United States grew at a rate of 4.8 percent a year between 1870 and 1906, whereas Latin America grew at a rate of 5.5 percent a year between 1950 and 1980 (Víctor Tokman and Norberto García, quoted in Touraine 1988a:32). We are dealing here with the modernizing effect in urbanization, in industry, and in society, within a context totally different from the European one in which industrialism was born. As a result, in Latin America we find a demographic explosion, savage urbanization, and ecological degradation.

More brutal still is a second form of disorder deriving from the stagnation that hit Latin America without warning, just when it had adjusted to a logic of dynamic growth. There is variation in the reaction across countries. On the one hand, Argentina, which industrialized early and had a population resembling that of a modern country in the European sense of the word, entered a period of stagnation several decades in coming. At the other extreme, we find Mexico, following its traditional heritage well into the current century and then, in only three decades, moving to the cities, where the offspring of yesterday's countryside inhabitants demand education. The tensions that such rapid changes create were more or less harmonized thanks to a populist system based on high levels of participation and public resources coming, until 1982, from the oil boom. The disaster represented by the conjunction of the double disorder thus hit Mexico over the period of only one six-year presidential administration. Seen in this light, it makes sense to say that the phenomenon we can call "Mexican late populism" lasted too long.

To sum up, whether we are dealing with a global crisis of the West or not, the double disorder discussed above will not be reconstructed or redirected in a few years. The acceleration of growth rates and the subsequent stagnation have been harsh; to understand what has happened and to invent a new order out of the broken pieces, regardless of the type of order it may be, will demand from Latin American social sciences a kind of thinking that may not be all that different from the pessimism and the negativity referred to above. Current efforts try to encapsulate this situation with a term that is elegant, harmonious, aesthetic, and culturally aseptic: postmodernism. The notions of anomie, heterogeneity and disarticulation are also invoked. But maybe we should utilize a different concept to talk about the phenomenon that takes place when a society undergoes double disorder in a short period of time, and suffers as well something akin to the 1985 earthquake in Mexico City.

EXCLUSION AND ANOMIC INDIVIDUATION:
THE ORGANIZATIONAL LEVEL

Our discussion points to the importance of referring to disorder as a central category in our understanding of Latin American societies as they approach the turn of the century.[3] No doubt the double disorder will have harsh repercussions on the disarticulation of the basic organizational references of society and that it will generate "sick" reactions, which will significantly affect ethical principles to the point of provoking confusion regarding cultural values. This very trend is beginning to be evident among popular sectors of Mexico City. The affected groups are increasing in number and becoming poorer and poorer, and no matter how many discourses about an integrated society are elaborated in their name, they remain subject to a rigid cultural and political exclusion.[4]

Youth between the ages of twelve and twenty-four represent, according to the 1980 census, more than one-fourth of the population: a little more than fifty million of Mexico's total population of eighty million are under twenty-four years of age. Thus, not only are we talking of a representative group in terms of sheer numbers but also in terms of Mexico's future. In the metropolitan area approximately five million youth form part of the popular sector and, based on a gross estimate, one out of ten belongs to or is in close proximity to a youth gang, which carries a name and operates in a demarcated territory. Some further data on the magnitude of the phenomenon relate to the labor market. Between 1985 and 1990, eight million youth tried, without much success, to enter the labor market. Meanwhile, the country as a whole saw its economy shrink in absolute terms between 1982 and 1988, although the contribution to the GNP of the so-called informal economy reached 40 percent. Investment in education dropped from 3.9 to 2.0 percent between 1982 and 1986, and per capita public expenditures in education, health, and social security fell, in 1984, to 60, 70, and 75 percent, respectively, of their 1982 values (Lustig 1988).

Given these conditions, expectations of forming part of a collectivity of wage earners, gaining access to a particular trade, and belonging to a labor union that engages in negotiations and confrontations become extremely rare referents. The same occurs with regard to secondary education, which is proving more and more unable to orient this growing mass of young people. In the process, youth become skeptical about the benefits of a form of schooling that is not based on knowledge of immediate experiences and is thus progressively seen as characteristic of sectors of the population better integrated into society. For their part, political and cultural groups and government agencies lose their appeal as channels of integration because their resources and influence have decreased, reduced to little more than the organization of a sports event or a musical concert. Not even religious groups, which usually find a favorable context for their message in marginal environment, seem able to find an audience among young people.

The situation of Mexican youth stands out in comparison with other Latin American cases. It is marked by the absence of a clearly defined adherence to a religious collectivity, the impossibility of reconstructing an ethnic identity counterposed to a racially differentiated oligarchy, and a low degree of adversity toward the state. All these factors hinder the establishment of an identity of the excluded. It follows that an extreme situation of economic exclusion does not necessarily translate into an identity of the excluded vis-à-vis an adversary.

The behavior of the marginalized and, in particular, of the youth in an urban popular environment thus does not tend toward confrontation, toward a rupture with the more integrated aspects of society, government authorities, or some state apparatus, nor toward the recreation of a communitarian refuge. Rather, their behavior tends toward the withdrawal to a small group, to a gang—or, in the extreme case, to withdrawal within the individual self: Having no hope in the future, no place to fall back on within the community, no clear adversary or ethical principle of identity, Mexican youth tend toward a situation of decomposition. This all leads to introversion, to personal crises, to the destruction of the capacity for social integration of the subject, to indifference, and to oblivion. The situation is not far removed from a "delinquent conformism" aided by drugs and other toxins.

The confusion of values is extreme, as things coexist in a disarticulated and contradictory manner. Youth simultaneously associate experiences based upon very dissimilar visions, leading to an overlap of values that stress: (1) an egalitarian group solidarity, which is a product of threatening surroundings; (2) an individualist imagery, fed by the mediums of mass communication that feature heroic and epic figures (Mad Max, Rambo); (3) a utopian vision of the Great Community, as in the images in the minds of young people who attended the Avándaro music festival fifteen years ago, with their stories about concerts in provincial cities and evocations of Bob Marley; and (4) a fascination with the leader of a dissident populist sort, such as Cuauhtémoc Cárdenas or, at another level, Alejandro Lora, singer and composer of TRI (the most influential rock group among Mexican popular youth) and Andrés Castellanos, leader of the Popular Youth Council (Consejo Popular Juvenil, a broad front of gangs). This chaotic imaginary, however, lacks a class or proletarian reference, the reason being the open rejection toward forms of work that imply confinement, defined rhythms, and set hours, and the greater inclination toward self-employment in open spaces.

INTERMEDIARY COLLECTIVE IDENTITIES: APPARATUSES, ORGANIZATIONS, MOVEMENTS, ASSOCIATIONS

We move now from our consideration of the extreme situation of youth to address the level of global society. It is commonly argued that sharp cutbacks in the state apparatuses and budget allocations oriented toward social welfare would leave enormous spaces to be filled by a "new sociability," new forms of social organization to face the crisis, and new collective identities. The power, the centrality, and the historical authoritarianism of the Mexican state would be exposed in all its nakedness. Thus, drawing upon the proliferation of poverty, an adversarial government-people relationship would emerge, leading to the loss of legitimacy of the whole political system. This hypothesis must be given closer consideration.

The Proliferation of the Excluded Without the Emergence of a Popular Subject

Though the struggles of the middle classes are not exempt from discontinuities brought about through the co-optation of their leaders and the atomization of their social bases, one could probably say that the crisis has provoked some strengthening of their forms of social participation. The increasing importance of elections and political parties among Mexicans during the 1980s, the greater visibility of the legislature and some labor unions, and, most importantly, the role of the mass media as a channel of contestation, all point in that direction. One could even argue that a similar situation occurs among certain popular groups. Their participation sometimes takes the form of fights for the legalization of occupied lands, or reactions to a catastrophic situation, as in the aftermath of the 1985 earthquake. At other times, their activities are based in neighborhoods, towns, or *colonias* with a great communitarian tradition, where activities of a productive and commercial nature are conducted in a cooperative fashion or entail a shared defensive position with respect to the growth of a great urban center (e.g., in the case of organizations of victims of the earthquake, organizations of recent or irregular settlements such as San Miguel Teotongo, commercial neighborhoods such as Tepito, the towns and *colonias* of the south of the Federal District, the Popular Youth Council of Santa Fe).

But one must ask whether these are isolated bright spots, few and far between, in a broad situation of exclusion. Indeed, this seems to be the case when we verify the enormous problems faced by the organizations and coordinating bodies of earthquake victims, settlers, and others and when we see how they become weaker and divided, establishing contacts with figures in high positions while the compelling situation of their real and potential constituents becomes more acute. Exclusion cannot be seen to generate an identity of the excluded. In other words, one can talk of the proliferation of "the popular," of "the people," of the informal economy within an urban setting (on street corners, in subway exits, in the main square, in the municipal administrative offices, in the parks, or on the campus); but this does not mean that we can verify an identity of the excluded. Thus, the emergence of "the popular" without a popular subject is a real possibility, because the presence of impoverishment, social polarization, even dualization, does not lead to two clearly defined poles. The poverty-stricken marjority of the population lives in the absence of an identity.

The Political System and Emergency Solutions

Within the current context it is crucial to note that the great apparatuses of the golden age of populism no longer articulate the relationship between the state and the excluded. That is to say, neither the institutionalized arenas of *concertación* that typified the welfare and paternalistic state, nor the PRI, the party-government system, and the labor federations and confederations provide mediation channels through which the demands of broad sectors of the population are met. All these apparatuses, and particularly the party system and congress, seem to function as places where integrated sectors, such as the middle classes and organized workers, express their complaints and resolve some of their demands.

For the world of the excluded, on the other hand, ad hoc specialized government apparatuses negotiate with organizations generated in situations of emergency. For example, after the 1985 earthquake, special housing programs and technical teams, which were trained to concert, mediate, delay, divide, provoke confrontations, co-opt, and repress were dispatched to the scene. Orders descend from the ministries to certain subministries, and from the Federal District Department to its delegates and assistants. The reverse direction is more common in action involving the more integrated sectors.

There is a tendency, which I shall call "*buropolítica*" ("bureaupolitics"), for organizations and leaders to project themselves upward, to gravitate toward the legislature, the party leadership, ministry offices, university deanships, and advisory boards. Like a vacuum, it draws from above and from below—"bureaupolitics" and anomic atomization—so that between the two, where we should find consistent intermediary identities, there is nothing but deserted space. Most political parties are incapable of operating at this intermediary level, and even the PRI itself appears unprepared for the specific and highly technical task of attending to popular demands, thus retreating to its merely electoral function. In this manner, and because of the neoliberal contractionist zeal, throughout the 1980s an "exclusionary state" was formed as a substitute for the "populist state" that had characterized Mexico until the end of the oil boom.

But we shall see that the decline of the populist state does not signify the end of the populist relationship with the state. The dismantling of paternalistic agencies of the state, rather than modernizing the articulation between society and state, has created a vacuum in the political system, that is, in the intermediations between society and state. The effects of this on the excluded are not inconsequential. The excluded, who have a weak relationship with political parties and the government bureaucracy, tend to move, with no intermediation, from a discussion about the diameter of the water tap to the support of Cuauhtémoc Cárdenas. The practically nonexistent tradition of political parties and intermediary identities makes this a prodigious act in the Mexican case. We could say that the excluded do not value the representative or "liberal" dimension of democracy; rather, they appreciate the participatory, substantive aspect, the direct relationship with the holder of executive power. The phenomenon of *neocardenismo* can thus be understood as the emptying of the president and the PRI of their ritual content and centrality, which is then displaced toward a new leader. Here we are entering into the terrain of state-society relations, which I shall expand upon below.

BUREAUPOLITICS, ATOMIZATION, AND THE DESTRUCTION OF INTERMEDIARY IDENTITIES

Probably the most important mechanism by which identities in the world of the excluded have been destroyed is the absorption of leaders by the higher bureaucratic circles of politics, what I have called "bureaupolitics."[5] In effect, in societies like the Mexican one, where conflicts and leaderships are constantly generated because of atomization—and especially the absence of intermediary identities and organizations (be they located on the plane of the political system, of social movements, or on the communitarian and associational level in general)—the privileged mechanism to ensure stability and order consists of the (likewise constant) destruction of these alternative constellations, these diffuse eruptions. Accomplished by dividing, encarcerating, killing, and co-opting, the result is the destruction of the local systems of authority and the centralization of a highly hierarchical and disciplined bureaucracy on an unquestioned leader.

At this point the direct connection with the theme of the state, seen as a form of articulation specific to each society, becomes obvious. It is more suitable, however, to develop a definition of the state around the "bureaupolitical phenomenon." The exacerbated form of this phenomenon in Mexican culture allows us to elaborate a hypothesis that sees bureaupolitics as the most important mechanism of governability in Mexico. Put briefly, intermediary identities blur as a result of a double and iterated mechanism, which combines an *upward-drawing dynamic* with a *downward emptying*.

The upward-drawing dynamic characterizes the various steps of the bureaupolitical path and underlines a problematic that goes beyond the simple will of leaders. The problem lies in a series of displacements that respond to deep psychological-cultural mechanisms and that are recognizable in the following four forms of collective behaviors displayed in sociopolitical action. First is the fascination with little understood "causes," which allows the displacement of individual responsibility toward some minimally shared symbols and images. Second is the fascination with the leader, that is, the adoption of a personality seen as responsible for the cause. This is another instance of displacement of individual or group responsibilities. Third is the fascination that leads to labeling any dissidence as treason, and any intermediary and societal identity as suspicious. In other words, any third truth is denied, because its recognition entails the possibility that one may be mistaken in embracing a cause; and any intermediary terrain, between hierarchies and the disciplining of "us" and our adversaries, is swept aside. The obligation to establish the underlying principle of one's behavior is thus displaced. Fourth is a fascination for forgiving leaders and reconciling with them, even after they distance themselves from the rank and file, as they are absorbed by bureaupolitics. This signifies a displacement of leaders' responsibilities, even when they make their project compatible with that of their adversaries.

A second and complementary mechanism by which societal identities disappear is downward emptying. In effect, the bases of a social struggle are again atomized by the repression and/or by the distancing of its leadership toward bureaupolitics. When this happens, divisions tend to appear between moderate and radical leaders, between basist and removed leaders. Confusion, demoralization, and discontinuity of the social action spreads. This is all facilitated by the broad and usually heterogeneous nature of the alliances forged in the process of struggle, as a result of the need to accumulate forces to have a fighting chance when facing an adversary as powerful as the state in societies without a vocation for social democracy.

Working out this double and iterated mechanism has crucial implications for the prospects of *neocardenismo*. Indeed, because of the marked natural propensity toward schisms, toward the dispersal of forces, and toward atomization, we can assert that *neocardenismo* will be strong only in the measure that it becomes the state. Though this statement may appear tautological, it remains true that "only by being stronger will it be strong." By negotiating and remaining as a long-term oppositional force, *neocardenismo's* centrifugal tendencies, its divisions, and its reconciliations represent enormous dangers, especially now that the PRI is moving to purge itself of its neoliberal sin. We are faced, in other words, with the general problematic of intermediary identities, where the logic of action tends toward confrontation, to positing all-or-nothing choices, and to an obsession with the here and now. The key point is that there is no identity without the state.

In the present context we witness a prodigious blooming of alternative orders. This is partly a result of certain current processes jeopardizing the role of bureaupolitics as a mechanism of governability. The modernization processes, seen as voluntaristic acts of planners, weaken this mechanism. At the same time, when the constant and defining characteristic of *repression* is not associated with its indispensable counterpart of *co-optation* (by way of the natural inclination of leaders toward bureaupolitics), *exclusion* becomes a reality, not only at the base level but also at the level of leadership and elites. Further exacerbating problems of governability is the deep crisis of progress and the popular deprivation in economic terms and in terms of future life chances, within which bureaupolitics as a mechanism of governability must be put into effect.

THE STATE ORDER

Only within this context is the recent phenomenon of the return of a kind of populism to be understood. It has been experienced by Mexicans and other Latin Americans yet remains largely incomprehensible. As with interpretations of the developmental crisis facing Latin America, we must find a precise form of conceptualizing the phenomenon, in a way that will both avoid the pitfalls of old debates and enable us to avoid falling prey to the unsuccessfully anathematized images created by neoliberalism. The primary fact is that although the ascent of "the popular" and its accompanying leadership has been observed with great clarity—first in Peru, and then in Mexico with Cuauhtémoc Cárdenas—there are many signs that allow us to hypothesize that we are witnessing a phenomenon that covers all of Latin America. Alfonsín is overtaken by Peronism in Argentina; Carlos Andrés Pérez returns triumphantly to Venezuela but is immediately vetoed by a disorderly and atomized mass as he puts his first neoliberal measures into effect; and other populist leaders, some of them in frank decline, are able to win elections against the candidates of modernization, as witnessed in Sao Paulo and others areas of Brazil. And among the Chilean *pobladores* there is a clear preference for distributive authoritarian leaders such as Frei (and not so much for his successor, Allende), rather than for representatives of political parties or for trade unions or other forms of intermediation.

No doubt what is happening is a weakening of the precarious intermediary orders, and a move toward a more direct leadership-mass relationship. The masses are inorganic aggregates of individuals and atomized manifestations integrated in a weak, contradictory, and discontinous manner.[6] Faced with economic stagnation and the absence of global mobilization, there is a prevalence of anomic forms of integration and a retreat toward the individual and the small group. Constituted as such, and given the fascination with leadership, the masses can be very easily and uncritically linked to any "cause."

The emergence of the popular, then, does not have an organizational correlate. Rather, it is linked to weakly integrated intermediary orders and a faint feeling of belonging to a group. With this panorama, it becomes difficult to construct and maintain communitarian and associational bonds in the environment provided by the neighborhood, the ejido, the cooperatives, the union or popular-urban coordinating groups, the ecclesiastical base communities, or the organs for the defense of the quality of life. Furthermore, even the concerted efforts of political parties and political and cultural groups aimed at the more needy sectors of the population produce few results. For all these efforts have to confront the widespread faith in the strongman, the belief that the highest leader will have to find a solution, and that to bet on him is the best option.

The unavoidable question, then, is whether the populist route, or the rebirth of the national-popular relationship, remains the only "sane" form of integration in the context of the crisis. No one would have said this fifteen years ago, but today it does not sound as bad or, at least, as unrealistic. We would be hard pressed to find any center outside the mobilizing state that could possibly articulate the diverse series of manifestations found in Latin America, from atomization and a threatening explosion of violence, to restricted identities and middle-class consumerism. Therefore, within a context of disorganized violence, anomic retreat, atomized apathy, and the tendency of Latin American societies to exacerbate the inequalities among the world of the excluded, a middle class in decadence, and a privileged minority, the surprising return of the authoritarian-paternalistic monster responds to a very real need. Indeed, it is beginning to reveal itself as a much more reasonable solution to the problems of national cohesion and reconstruction of identities than the one provided by the excluding neoliberal state. The latter has simply abandoned any hope of reconstituting the splintered social scene characteristic of Latin America, obsessed as it is with halting inflation, restructuring industry, servicing the foreign debt, and making the economy competitive in protectionist markets. The neoliberal view draws upon elaborate arguments to show that the immediate price is worth paying to fuel economic growth, but then simply assumes that GNP growth will automatically erase social inequalities and contribute to a saner integration of Latin American societies.

No doubt Latin Americans would be better off with a type of society with strong intermediary organizations that would facilitate the self-realization of each individual—the interactions of individuals at the highest level of rationality, as Habermas would like it, or the collective interest of the polis as evoked by Castoriadis—that would make socioeconomic aggregates correspond to organizations or political parties and to ideologies or projects of future societies; that would cultivate, in short, stable institutions both on the social plane and that of political representations. But what has happened is that Latin America is not moving toward either a democracy based in civil society, even if as a result of the struggle between classes, or a democracy based on the predominance of political society, which would include political parties, legislatures, and the large corporate forces (business, labor). Rather, in the most promising cases, the balance seems to be tilting in favor of what could be called either a popular massive, statist-popular, or national popular logic. It would even be deceiving to think in terms of a harmonic image of a popular democracy with its Jacobin correlate. The reality of Latin America instead is ordered in a way that draws upon all the organizational referents touched upon in this section, but in such a way that the state-masses relationship becomes central.

THE AGGREGATES AND THE NUMBERS

The argument thus presented can be strengthened by responding to two series of criticisms. First, we must consider the thesis according to which *neocardenismo* is the result of a reordering of civil society against the PRI-state, made possible by a better articulation between social movements and intermediary popular organizations, on the one hand, and political organizations (mainly political parties), on the other. Secondly, we must respond to the question that, even if *neocardenismo* was not a result of the precise factors considered in this first thesis, what matters is that its spontaneous orientation did result in a reordering in civil and political society, of which a first landmark is the creation of the Party of the Democratic Revolution (PRD). Regarding the first point, we must ask to what extent Cuauhtémoc Cárdenas was the candidate of a disorganized society. Without pretending that electoral returns correspond exactly to social categories (indeed, the great mass of PRI and *cardenista* voters is the same), some indicators are highly revealing. On this basis, we can assert that if Salinas was the candidate of the traditionally poor society, and Cárdenas was the candidate of the disorganized society, then Clouthier was the candidate of the integrated society.

The Traditionally Poor

With respect to Salinas, we recall the conclusion of the electoral analysis by the Fundación Rosenbleuth: "It is not far from the truth to say that Carlos Salinas was essentially 'the candidate of the poor.' The greater percentage of votes for this candidate and the ones that were decisive in his victory came from areas dominated by agricultural activities, a low degree of urbanization, low incomes (below the typical rural minimum wages), and a lack of basic services (housing, water, electric power, education, and communication and health facilities)." No doubt this trend reflects a fraudulent manipulation of the electoral returns. In the urban and semiurban areas, however, Salinas got close to 50 percent of the votes, although he garnered only 34 percent in the metropolitan districts.[7] This alone would have assured Salinas of victory, but "it would have been a relative majority" (Fundación Rosenbleuth 1989:13, 16–17, 46).

One could conclude, however, that the PRI is beginning to display signs of polarization. On the one hand, it is strongly embedded in rural-traditional-poverty aspects; on the other, it is composed of a highly influential nucleus represented by the high-level bureaucracy or political class, leading economic groups (not the middle-level business class, which is more inclined to the PAN), and labor leaders (not the rank and file in the industrial zones, which gave 16 percent of their votes to Salinas, 22 percent to Cárdenas, and 26 percent to Clouthier). The PRI thus seems to include both the most modern aspects of society (the great apparatuses of public and private domination, to use a Habermasian term) and the most backward aspects, connected to poverty, tradition, and a lack of culture. This represents the dominant tendency of the official party.

The Disorganized Society

Neocardenismo, and in particular the leadership of Cuauhtémoc Cárdenas, attracts the enormous and increasing sectors that a modernization process in crisis fails to absorb, in either objective or ideological terms. Cárdenas gained a majority in 100 of the 300 electoral districts, half of which were located in Mexico City and its surrounding areas. (Within the Federal District, Cárdenas took no less than thirty-seven out of forty districts.) The remaining districts, as underlined by the Fundación Rosenbleuth, are strongly linked to the figure of General Lázaro Cárdenas. In those areas touched by the reforms of this former president—such as the Laguna, Michoacán, Baja California Norte, Oaxaca, Guerrero, and some oil-producing zones of Veracruz, Guanajuato, and Hidalgo—Cuauhtémoc had strong showings. Noteworthy in the fifty electoral districts in Mexico City and its surrounding areas carried by Cuauhtémoc is "the approbation that Cuauhtémoc Cárdenas received from young people in the urban areas that helped tilt vast sectors of the urban population, including those with high incomes, in his favor."[8]

We must remember that the bulk of votes (60 percent) for Cuauhtémoc Cárdenas were cast in areas in which he did not obtain a majority. Indeed, a detailed analysis of the electoral returns allows us to uncover the following trends:

- The vote for Cárdenas was predominantly urban (70 percent urban in areas in which he obtained a majority, compared to Salinas's 33 percent); nevertheless, Salinas obtained 4.15 million votes in urban zones, against Cuauhtémoc's 3.8 million votes.
- The areas in which Cuauhtémoc won had an annual demographic

growth rate of 4.2 percent, whereas this rate measured 2.5 percent in areas carried by Salinas. This is important within the context of the "double disorder."

- Thirteen percent of Cuauhtémoc's victories were scored in areas based on agricultural production, and 22 percent in industrial areas. These proportions were 38 and 16 percent, respectively, for Salinas; and 4 and 26 percent, respectively, for Clouthier.
- Although 83 percent of the electorate that voted for Salinas had an income of two minimum wages or less, for Cárdenas this percentage fell to 69.
- Fully 92 percent of Cárdenas's votes came from people whose homes had electric energy, which was the case for only 61 percent of Salinas votes; likewise, 87 percent of Cárdenas votes came from people who had drinking water in their houses, but only 45 percent of Salinas voters did.

The social base of *neocardenismo* comprises the following groups:

- The great and growing number of people affected by the process of social distintegration and exclusion. These supporters are predominantly urban based:
- The historical beneficiaries of *cardenismo*, located primarily in the Laguna, Michoacán, and the oil-producing areas.
- A significant group of middle sectors. Although these need to be studied more carefully, we can say with certainty that they would include the most educated groups (intellectual workers, professionals, and students) and, very likely, some groups of public- and private-sector wage earners whose standards of living have been hard hit by the crisis and budget cutbacks (theirs would be a case of a protest vote against the PRI government).

Integrated Society

There can be no doubt that the PAN is the party of the integrated society. Furthermore, its 17 percent of the total votes is a fairly accurate reflection of the size of Mexican society that can be thus characterized, though a distinction should be made between two forms of integration. One is the integration with the modern world of consumption, fashion, and electronics, reflected in particular by the high support for the PAN in the three large metropolitan areas of Mexico, as well as in Sinaloa, Baja California, Sonora, and Chihuahua. But there is also integration with the traditional world around clearly defined values, which translates into the good PAN showing in Guanajuato, San Luis Potosí, Jalisco, and Yucatán.

The electoral returns support this judgment:

- Urban and metropolitan areas account for 90 percent of the PAN's total votes, but only 33 percent for Salinas and 72 percent for Cárdenas.
- Electoral support for the PAN has remained stable in comparison with

voting patterns three years earlier.

- The 3.5 percent average growth rates in heavily PAN areas are lower than in those areas inclined toward Cuauhtémoc.
- PAN support in agrarian areas was extremely poor. Thus, PAN candidate Clouthier received just 4 percent of his vote in rural areas, whereas Salinas garnered 38 percent, and Cárdenas 14 percent.
- The electoral districts where the PAN received greatest support were areas with industrialization levels (20.5 percent of the economically active population engaged in industry) far superior to those in areas where Cárdenas and Salinas scored their victories. A similar correlation occurs with regard to more heavily service-oriented areas, though here the trends are somewhat erratic (Fundación Rosenbleuth 1989:29).
- Clouthier received only 23 percent of his votes from individuals with an income of less than one minimum wage, against Salinas's 48 percent. There was no difference, however, between support for the PAN and for Cárdenas as a function of access to basic services, such as electricity and drinking water.

BUREAUPOLITICS AND SOCIAL ATOMIZATION

The second objection to our argument in positing a reordering in civil society and in political society asserts that *neocardenismo* has resulted in organizational and identity forms that could constitute a "saner" alternative to the social fragmentation provoked by the crisis and by neoliberalism, despite its status as the inheritor of this social disorganization and the loss of intermediary identities. The great "visibility" gained by opposition parties, the unusual protagonism of congressional actors and forces, the daily activities of certain social movements, all seem to point in the direction of a growing social order in Mexico and, therefore, support this criticism. A few clarifications are needed, however, to assess this argument.

First, a high percentage of the votes received by the opposition political parties were cast in favor of the person of Cuauhtémoc Cárdenas, rather than in support of his party.[9] Thus, the congressional "visibility" in the period after July 6 should be seen more as a surprising consequence of electoral legislation than as the product of an organic relationship between legislators and a society conceptualized as electorate, social movements, and organizations.

Second, one of the most serious problems in the leader-mass relationship deserves mention. When the leader is not in power, he faces the difficult task of holding together a wide and heterogeneous alliance, which has usually emerged in a rapid and spontaneous manner. To turn the *cardenista* phenomenon that peaked on July 6, 1988, into a political party is a delicate task. There are many elements to be balanced, and each choice necessarily entails a cost. This is particularly so because the alliance is weak and composed of forces not clearly defined ideologically. There is a constant threat of reconciliation with the state in exchange for small quotas of power. Thus, splits and the dispersal of forces are beginning to appear in the *cardenista* movement.

Third, the generalized autonomy of political actors (groups, political sectors, parties) with respect to the social base they purport to represent and their concomitant identification with the power of the state are accentuated in the Mexican case by the phenomenon of bureaupolitics. The "bureau-politicization" of Mexican social action historically functioned as an exchange. The leader offered to deliver his social bases, which were then disorganized and disarticulated, in return for his ascent within the state bureaucracy. Each time a social actor opposed this rule of obedience, trying to maintain autonomy and identity as an independent social entity, the state reverted to repression. Some of the better-known examples include the electrical, transport, and oil workers in 1948–1949, the rail workers in 1958–1959, the doctors in 1965, students in 1968, the electrical workers again in 1976, university unions in 1977, provincial universities and regional movements in 1983, and oil workers again in 1989.

It would be ridiculous, then, to talk of Mexico as a corporatist state, because the very co-optation of the top leadership of unions and other movements works against the constitution of an organic relation between these leaders and the bases they are supposed to represent. The contrast between Mexico and Argentina is instructive. In Argentina Perón fell, yet the trade unions continued to fight for the interests of their members under several adverse regimes, retaining a certain degree of coherence and continuity over time. In Mexico, on the other hand, the state can simply displace the top leadership of one of the most autonomous and better-organized unions—that of the oil workers—and put a new leadership in its place while the rank and file look on helplessly. The idea of corporatism should therefore be substituted by that of bureaupolitics.

These comments are pertinent because deeply rooted cultural practices do not change overnight. Within *neocardenismo* we see the same lack of organic links between the majority of important forces within the movement and social actors. And even when such a linkage does exist, these leaders spend most of their time in political meetings, discussing the future composition of the state, complete with hierarchies and posts to be occupied. To make matters worse, the top leadership of the PRD participates in a wide number of forums organized by the very government they oppose. This new reconciliation, which in Mexico is now called the "ideology of *concertación*," is really one of the privileged mechanisms of destruction of the collective identity of mobilized groups, and is turning into a new channel of bureaupolitical ascent. In brief, the practice of *concertación* without an accompanying practice of linkage with the social bases is nothing other than an act of pure bureaupolitics.

The danger represented by *neocardenismo*, then, is that we may be seeing the creation of a second channel of bureaupolitical ascent that would work alongside the one already in place. The function would be the same: to draw the leaders of social forces upward, and to draw groups of intellectuals into different public and prestigious forums, until they would become alien to the social arena and the collective identities from which they arose. From the perspective of the state, this is one of the cheapest forms of ensuring governability. From the perspective of *neocardenismo*, it would imply that the identity, continuity and consistency of the *cardenista* phenomenon is not, in any way, guaranteed. *Cardenismo* would continue basically as an expression of the disorder in Mexican society, and of the relationship between a leader and his atomized social constituents. As such, its capacity to propose a way out of the unhappy state of anomie is certainly wide open to question.

NOTES

Translation by Gerardo Munck

I would like to express my appreciation for comments from Joe Foweraker, Alan Knight, Sara Gordon, Alejandro Masolo, Ignacio Marván, Francisco Pérez Arce, and Jorge Cadena.

1. Fernando Calderón and Elizabeth Jelin reflected this feeling when they asked if it was still possible "to think about a global theoretical model of social action in the region starting out from the fragmentation and heterogeneity of the social movements; whether we are confronted with the emergence of a new system of historical action and the creation of subjects with a globalizing capability by means of the symbolic transformation of the meaning of common identities on the basis of the recognition of differences; or if we are entering a *gray phase* in the rationality of social action" (Calderón and Jelin 1987).

2. This information was summarized by a group of Latin American specialists during the Encuentro de Políticas Sociales para la Erradicación de la Pobreza, which met in Montevideo in July 1988.

3. It should be underlined, however, that we are not thereby attempting to provide a characterization of an exceptional situation but rather to describe the normal state of the global functioning of "the social." Three examples will help to clarify the point:

a. Our argument does not necessarily contradict, for example, the spirit of Carlos Monsiváis's essay "La sociedad que se organiza" (in Monsiváis 1987*a*). In it Monsiváis analyzes the origins of some of the main social struggles and emergency situations during the 1980s, such as the organizations, identities, and solidarities that sprung up as a response to the 1985 earthquake, the COCEI in Juchitán, and the "*ceuísta*" student movement. It is a characteristic of social struggles and of extraordinary situations that they lead to the definition of an adversity principle, and to the organization of a struggle against the perceived enemy and in favor of objectives that provide cohesion to the collective identity generated in the process. These situations arise here and there in all societies, but this should not lead us to assume that the normal state of the global society shared the same parameters of exceptional situations within which social struggles develop, unless we faced a generalized crisis of order.

b. The proposition of anomic disorganization cannot be refuted by the argument that we are witnessing a proliferation of organizations and political parties, because this argument is cast at a different level. As we shall see later in this chapter, it is very probable that a hyperactivity on the level of the political system (political parties, legislatures, trade unions, and so on) is associated with, hides, and even occasionally generates, demobilization, atomization, and false basist identities.

c. The proposition of increased social disorder cannot be refuted by an argument that focuses on the appearance of "the popular" within an urban setting. As we shall see, there can be an unstoppable proliferation of poverty, spreading throughout all aspects of urban life, without this necessarily having a clear impact on the identity and organizational forms of the excluded. The rise of "the popular," or, better said, the greater "visibility" of "the popular," does not guarantee that a "popular subject" will be formed.

4. These comments are based on the results of a study on popular youth sectors in Mexico City's Federal District (Castillo, Zermeño, and Ziccardi 1988).

5. Gramsci (1971:243–245), writing about a very specific historical context, referred to a similar phenomenon, calling it *tranformismo*. Gramsci was referring to the phenomenon of the separation of southern intellectuals from the subaltern classes. Lucio Kowarick writes, along similar lines, about the interest of the state bureaucracy to increase certain conflicts and demands that would allow it to exert greater influence within wider political spaces (Kowarick 1985). Joe Foweraker points to a strategy of institutionalization on the part of the PRI government toward popular struggles, accurately encompassing phenomena that are also referred to under the terms transformism, co-optation, and bureaupolitics. (Foweraker, "Popular Movements and Political Change," this volume).

6. It is better to talk of a leadership-mass relationship or of national-populism rather than of populism because, as Joe Foweraker correctly reminds us, in many South American cases populism signified the strengthening of intermediary forms of representation (political parties, trade unions), side by side with the disorder of the oligarchic crisis.

7. The distribution was: metropolitan, urban, semiurban, and rural and disperse.

8. This is not the place to develop this theme, but there can be no doubt that the student movement that emerged in 1986, growing out of the disorder produced by the 1985 earthquake, developed a discourse that broke with a trust in science, in technical and efficiency-driven kinds of solutions, all of which figured prominently in the modernizing discourse of Salinas in his 1988 electoral campaign. In this sense, we can talk of a CEU *cardenista* phenomenon (Fundación Rosenbleuth 1989:19).

9. The one possible exception is the electorate of the PMS. But even this party, which had a stronger self-identity than other members of the *cardenista* coalition, received a lower percentage of votes in comparison to previous elections.

4
Challenging Traditional Forms of Representation

11

Peasant Strategies and Corporatism in Chiapas

NEIL HARVEY

Since the early 1970s the Mexican countryside has seen the emergence of a large number of regional peasant organizations that have mobilized outside the channels of the PRI and the CNC. Despite several case studies that examine the interaction between such groups and the state, few authors have investigated the precise impact of rural opposition movements on the political system. This chapter, drawing on evidence from Chiapas, examines such impact in terms of the changing relationship between the state and peasantry in Mexico and the emergence of new forms of representation.[1] In this respect, I argue that the main change in state-peasant relations since 1970 has concerned the crisis in the corporatist form of representation, embodied by the failure of the National Peasant Confederation (CNC) to adequately represent the interests of its members at the level of the state and by the emergence of new forms of representation.[2] This process has had several ramifications, which I present as five related assertions concerning the changing nature of state-peasant relations in Mexico:

• The functions of the CNC have become less inclusionary and more exclusionary in its relations with dissident peasant groups.

• The state's intervention in the political and economic functions of the social sector (ejidos and *comunidades*) has become more direct, as reflected by the expansion of state agencies in the countryside, the promotion of *uniones de ejidos*, and the decline of the CNC as a mediating institution.

• Opposition groups that have continued to press for further land distribution and recognition as autonomous organizations have been marginalized politically through the use of law (especially in the legal protection of private property) and violence (both public and private).

• Marginalization has not meant demobilization but the development of more sophisticated popular responses based on political alliances and less confrontational actions.

• The impact of these movements on the political system has been to render ineffective the continued use of clientelistic and corporatist forms of representation among their constituencies. Evidence from other states, such as Michoacán, Oaxaca, and Guerrero, tends to support these findings (see Zepeda, Torres, and Palacios in Tamayo 1986; Durand 1988; Bartra 1985).[3] Consequently they present a challenge to traditional forms of political control

183

in the countryside and constitute alternative forms of organization based on horizontal networks of solidarity and leadership.

CORPORATIST STRATEGIES:
LESS INCLUSIONARY, MORE EXCLUSIONARY

How was it that the CNC went into decline in the 1970s, and why did new, autonomous organizations emerge? There are four main reasons. First, unlike the CTM, the CNC was never a privileged sector vis-à-vis the government, but had to compete for favor with state agencies and landowners' associations (Gordillo 1987). From 1970 onward the state's economic agencies became the most important channels for absorbing peasant demands as the CNC went into decline. Second, the CNC had become increasingly ineffective in achieving land redistribution as a result of the legal protection provided by the government to private owners. Two mechanisms used were the granting of titles that precluded expropriation (certificates of nonaffectability) and the acceptance of landowners' injunctions against redistribution, known as *amparos*. Third, there was the perception among many land-claimant groups that the legal channels for distribution had been exhausted and that new strategies (including direct action) were necessary. Already in the late 1940s and early 1960s two dissident groups had formed at the national level (the UGOCM and CCI), and in the early 1970s many regional organizations began to engage in land invasions.[4] The unwillingness of the CNC to confront the government with different methods was increasingly seen as a sign of weakness, and even of collaboration against the membership's interests. Finally, CNC leaders were perceived by members as less interested in achieving solutions than in furthering their own political ambition. A related criticism was that the leaders did not promote active participation of the member's and were unaccountable for their actions. Worse still, leaders were denounced for their collaboration with landowners and government officials in assuring that land was *not* redistributed.

Such dissent was thus responsive to the organizational efforts of leftist groups, church activists, and sympathetic state functionaries to promote grassroots participation in the resolution of the problems afflicting peasant communities. The development of such links helped consolidate independent organizations that began to struggle for land, services, control over marketing, and access to credit. In Chiapas, several of the communities that would play an important part in the formation of independent organizations were originally members of the CNC. For example, in Simojovel workers on coffee plantations, tired of the lack of solution to their petition for land redistribution, left the CNC in 1974 and decided to invade areas they had been claiming for several decades (Pontigo Sánchez 1985). In response to the question, "Why did you choose to join an independent organization?" almost all of my informants in Chiapas responded with some reference to the ineffectiveness, corruption, or plain unrepresentativeness of the CNC. Echeverría's attempt to revive the official confederation had a limited impact in the areas of greatest confrontation with agribusiness sectors (Sonora and Sinaloa) but was not enough to appease all the independent organizations, such that in Chiapas it continued to lose members to autonomous groups.[5]

The transformation of the CNC was accelerated by the shift in agrarian policy after 1976. The government of López Portillo entered office seeking to regain the confidence of agribusiness sectors who had reacted with hostility to Echeverría's attempted revival of agrarian reform. As a result, the new president declared that land distribution would be brought to an end in his *sexenio* and that emphasis would be placed on creating wage employment and boosting productivity in rural areas (Sanderson 1981:200–202; Bartra 1980:47–48; Canabal Cristiani 1981:280–281; Paré 1982:61–62; Rubio 1987:26–27). Thus, the CNC could no longer maintain even the rhetoric of land reform and was obliged to take on a new role in the countryside. Whereas previously it had attempted to incorporate communities through its "agrarian community leagues" in a single mass confederation loyal to the ruling party, it would now be used as a mechanism to contain, and in some cases physically repress, the influence and development of the newly formed autonomous groups. An example of this new role was its attempt to pull support among landless agricultural workers away from an independent confederation, the CIOAC.[6] This effort coincided with opinion within the ruling party that the CNC should place greater attention on this rural labor force, which was estimated at some three million workers. In the words of Ramírez López, "The CNC is obliged to play the role which corresponds to it in the transformation taking place in our society. Therefore, the unions that have been formed, and those in the process of formation, have publicly declared their militancy within the PRI, as a strategy to be incorporated in the achievement of the great objectives of Mexico" (1981:14).

Consequently, a contest developed between the CNC and the CIOAC to gain recognition for their respective unions, revealing a number of legal and bureaucratic mechanisms that independent organizations have had to confront. In January 1979 the Ministry of Labor granted official registration to the CNC-affiliated National Peasant Union of Agricultural, Livestock, Forestry, and Allied Workers of the Mexican Republic, which claimed automatic representation for three million workers. The same ministry simultaneously refused to grant registration to the CIOAC-promoted National Union of Agricultural Workers (SNOA), which suggests that the political objective of the government's corporatist strategy was to weaken the independent peasant organizations and exert tighter control over the rural work force. In April 1981 the CNC secretary general, Víctor Cervera Pacheco, claimed that the official union had organized 400,000 seasonal workers in twenty states, although the CIOAC denounced the CNC for seeking to take over, or *charrificar*, the seventeen unions it had organized throughout Mexico (see *Uno más Uno*, April 16, 1981). In the same month the CNC union was renamed the National Confederation of Agricultural Workers of Mexico, and the president of the National Executive Committee of the PRI, Javier García Paniagua, expressed his hope that the efforts of the new confederation would "strengthen our political institution" (*Uno más Uno*, April 22, 1981).

In Chiapas, this process came to the fore in an area that comprised both land and labor demands, namely Simojovel (see map). Here the administration of state governor Juan Sabines (1979–1982) had to respond to the creation by the CIOAC of the National Union of Agricultural Workers in October 1980 and the wave of strikes on the coffee plantations beginning in April of that year. Part of the government's corporatist strategy to regain control of the former plantation peons was the continual refusal by the Labor Conciliation and Arbitration Board (JLCA) to grant legal registration to the CIOAC union (successive applications were rejected in April and June 1981 and in June and October 1982). The JLCA argued that the relationship of the *peones* to the *finqueros* was not one of worker to employer because of the absence of formal wage relations and the renting of a plot of land inside the plantation in exchange for their labor. Consequently, the JLCA claimed that they were really tenant farmers and therefore had no legal right to organize as workers (Pontigo Sánchez 1985:97). This strategy was clearly illustrated when, at the same time, the JLCA granted registration to a CNC-affiliated union of agricultural workers, named Solidaridad, which had been created precisely to confront the CIOAC union by organizing strikebreakers.

Similarly, in Venustiano Carranza the CNC was used in an attempt to isolate the demands of a land-claimant group known as the Casa del Pueblo. Since 1965 this group had been involved in an intense struggle to recuperate communal lands from local ranchers who refused to hand over 3,000 hectares that had been included in a presidential resolution in the community's favor. Its leadership was arrested in 1976, and one of the prominent activists was bought off while he was in prison. On his release two years later, he called for the abandonment of the land struggle and the acceptance of government assistance in raising production on the lands they held. The majority rejected this policy, and a division occurred, with a minority joining the CNC. This faction's leader was named regional secretary of the CNC in 1979 and immediately sought to take over the community's affairs. The division created several practical problems for the Casa del Pueblo as the Ministry of Agrarian Reform (SRA) refused to recognize its elected authorities, although it did recognize the CNC faction. As a result, access to credit and inputs was denied the independent group, whereas its rival benefited from the new subsidies provided by the SAM program. The CNC also used an ideological campaign against the Casa del Pueblo, denouncing its leaders as Communists and terrorists and provoking fear among local inhabitants. The extent to which the CNC was used as a means to restrain independent opposition is further revealed by its participation in acts of violence against the Casa del Pueblo.[7]

STATE INTERVENTION AND NEW FORMS OF REPRESENTATION

The closer ties between ejidos and state in Chiapas had already begun to form

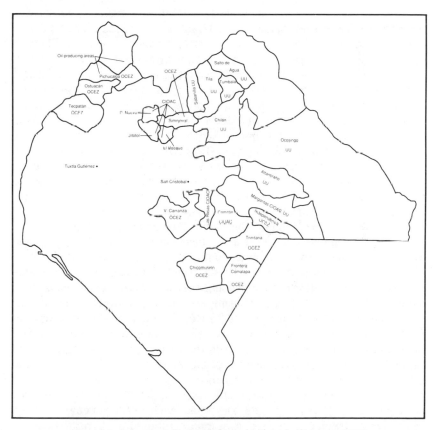

Map of Independent Peasant Organizations in Chiapas, 1988

during the Echeverría administration. In response to a national crisis in food production, the state began to intervene more directly in the organization of the ejido sector through new legislation, increased funds, and an expansion of bureaucratic agencies. One of Echeverría's first acts was to implement a new Federal Agrarian Reform Law calling for the collectivization of adjacent ejido plots into a single, productive unit that could count on state support in the form of credit, inputs, and access to marketing. Financial support was concentrated in the hands of the National Bank of Rural Credit (Banrural) and its regional branches (Bancrisa in Chiapas). Public investment in agriculture was increased to 17.3 percent of total federal expenditure in 1974 and to 20 percent in 1975, and a new Plan for Peasant Organization and Training was established. Finally, several state agencies were created to direct production and marketing, such as the Mexican Coffee Institute (INMECAFE), the Mexican Tobacco Institute (TABAMEX), the National Coordinating Committee for Support of Popular Consumption (CONASUPO), and the National Fund for Ejido Development (FONAFE).

Despite the limited impact of these measures on relieving the food crisis, one result was that the CNC began to lose importance as a form of representation, opening the way for more direct relations between state agencies and newly formed *uniones de ejidos*. In Chiapas this occurred in the context of a modernization plan that sought to displace local intermediaries and caciques, who were regarded as obstacles to regional development and integration. In response to demands from *ejidatarios* for greater control over marketing and access to credit, the state government of Velasco Suárez assisted in the formation of several cooperatives and *uniones de ejidos*.[8] One of these was formed by twenty-six communities of migrant colonists who had settled in the Lacandón jungle and had been organized with the help of students and church activists. One of its main demands was for the withdrawal of eviction orders brought against them so as to leave the area clear for the commercial exploitation of mahogany and cedar. This group, known as the Quiptic,[9] also called on the government to support its efforts to overcome problems in coffee marketing caused by geographical isolation and the low prices paid by private purchasers. Taking advantage of the opening of some room for maneuver to independent producer organizations during the subsequent *sexenio*, the Quiptic negotiated favorable agreements with INMECAFE, including a subsidy for transportation costs and a better purchase price. It also came together with two other *uniones de ejidos* and a total of 180 communities from fifteen municipalities to form the Unión de Uniones (UU) in September 1980.

In response to the formation of the UU, Governor Sabines moved to strengthen the official confederation in the region and pull support away from the independent movement. Leaders and the most active members were offered money and material rewards if they joined the CNC. Such attempts failed, and a division between state and federal government became apparent. Although the state government opposed the consolidation of the UU, the federal government proved more flexible and open to negotiation because of the declining capacity of the CNC in the region. This flexibility can also be explained by the UU's reluctance to criticize the agrarian policy of the López Portillo administration, calling for support from state agencies, such as INMECAFE and COPLAMAR, to help it raise production. For example, in a statement published in February 1981, it declared:

> We are organized to increase and improve our production and to market it in a freer way at better prices, contributing in this manner with the Mexican Food System (SAM). Proof of this are the two Agreements on Production and Marketing that we have established with INMECAFE and the support that we have given to the presidential assistance programs for marginal areas: CONASUPO-COPLAMAR and IMSS-COPLAMAR. We are willing to collaborate with the different institutions, with the state government and the federal government, in the solution of our problems of production and marketing.

Its emphasis on matters of production and marketing was a strategic choice that allowed the UU to exploit a margin of maneuver opened to *uniones de ejidos* but denied to land-claimant groups. The leaders of the UU were aware of divisions between Sabines and the federal government and successfully isolated the intransigent position of the former by developing an alternative solution to a land tenure problem that gained acceptance within the SRA in Mexico City.[10] This strategy was called "fighting with two faces" and was developed by intellectuals who had promoted the Maoist "mass line" and had participated in the formation of the Proletarian Tendency (LP).[11]

Although the regularization of tenure constituted the major concern for the communities threatened with eviction from the Lacandón jungle, the adoption of other demands in this conjuncture provided a space for the growth and consolidation of the UU. Furthermore, the land issue was largely resolved by the end of 1981 following a positive response from federal authorities to the demand for the withdrawal of the eviction orders. This moment allowed the UU to advance in the formation of its own credit union, established in May 1982. Despite an internal division in January 1983, the credit union has provided a basis for successful grassroots development. For example, at the end of 1983 a permit was won from the Ministry of Commerce allowing the UU to export its coffee directly for the first time. Profits have been reinvested in the provision of services by the credit union and in the construction of a coffee-processing plant in 1987.

In this case we see how a new form of representation emerged as a result of the federal government's interest in promoting low-cost, grassroots solutions to the crisis in small-scale production. As such it provided the state with a more efficient alternative to organizing rural producers and gave the members of the UU the chance to raise their own socioeconomic condition. Its impact thus appears to have been greater for the members concerned than for the political system. In the words of one of its representatives, the UU is still nothing but an "ant" in relation to the agribusiness and commercial concerns operating in Chiapas (interview with UU Credit Union secretary, October 1987).

THE MARGINALIZATION OF LAND-CLAIMANT GROUPS

As already noted, one consequence of the shift in agrarian policy after 1976 was that the demands of land claimants were relegated to a secondary level. As Fox and Gordillo have pointed out:

> López Portillo's agrarian policy began with generous compensation for landowners who had been expropriated and official rhetoric stressed the importance of bettering rural incomes instead of distributing property. This shift meant that peasant mobilizations previously considered legitimate would no longer be tolerated and many of the newly formed independent groups found that their tactics met with repression rather than negotiation. (Fox and Gordillo 1989:143)

In Simojovel, for example, where land invasions by workers on coffee plantations had begun in 1974, local landowners called on the state government to deploy public security police in the eviction effort. Taking advantage of the presidential succession in December 1976, they formed what they themselves called "counterinsurgency militias" who supported the army in mass evictions of summer 1977 (see Marion S. 1984; *El Día*, October 3 and 10, 1977). In 1978 and 1979 the army continued to patrol Simojovel and the neighboring municipalities of Huitiupán and Sabanilla and was reported to have harassed communities and made arbitrary arrests. At the same time, the policy of resettlement of land petitioners in other areas of the state continued, undermining efforts to rebuild an autonomous organization that had arisen in 1974–1976.

During the governorship of Sabines, the use of violence became more selective as particular leaders were targeted for repression (see Marion S. 1984:29, 39; *Uno más Uno*, February 25–26, 1982).[12] The imprisonment of one CIOAC leader in December 1981 and the arrest of four more in February 1982, together with the multiplication of arrest orders against prominent activists, sought to demoralize the movement and break the indefinite strike that in 1981 had spread to all plantations in the municipality. The murder of two CIOAC members in Simojovel in October 1982 served to confirm the persistent use of violence right to the end of the Sabines administration (*Uno más Uno*, October 30 and November 7, 1982).

In Carranza, the Casa del Pueblo faced attacks from the group affiliated with the CNC. In fact, the incorporation of this latter into the CNC presented the Casa del Pueblo with its greatest obstacle to gaining solutions to its demands and helped keep it in a defensive position from 1979 onward. In 1980 two of its activists were killed, allegedly by members of the CNC faction (Renard 1985:174–178). The implications of these actions and the practical difficulties the division has meant for the Casa del Pueblo were expressed by one member thus: "It was better when the struggle was directly with the rich. Now the rich stay out of it and put the Coras in the front line."[13] In October 1984 nine members of the Casa del Pueblo were killed in an ambush by the Coras. Additionally, the municipal and state governments attempted to demobilize the movement by arresting and imprisoning five of its most prominent activists between 1981 and 1984. Their release was usually made conditional on agreement to affiliate to the CNC and accept the division of communal lands, which the Casa del Pueblo rejected.

The continued struggle for land was further restricted by the use of law. For example, protection for private owners against expropriation accelerated during the presidency of Miguel de la Madrid, tending to confirm my assertion that the goals of land-petitioning groups continued to be marginalized. This can be seen in Table 11.1:

Certificates of Nonaffectability Issued in Chiapas, 1934–1988

Presidency	Period	No. of Certificates	
		Agriculture	Ranching
Cárdenas	1934–40	26	1
Avila Camacho	1940–46	82	0
Alemán	1946–52	315	57
Ruiz Cortines	1952–58	461	47
López Mateos	1958–64	107	6
Díaz Órdaz	1964–70	123	44
Echeverría	1970–76	5	46
López Portillo	1976–82	61	45
de la Madrid	1982–88	2,932	4,714
Total	1934–88	4,112	4,960

Source: Secretaría de la Reforma Agraria, *Concentrado de certificados de inafectabilidad por período presidencial* (Mexico: SRA Databank, 1988).

From this data we can see that the de la Madrid administration granted almost 75 percent of the total number of agricultural certificates of nonaffectability issued since 1934 and over 90 percent of certificates for ranchers for the same period. According to the same source, the amount of land in Chiapas protected against distribution during this *sexenio* was 1,142,881 hectares, almost 50 percent of the total amount protected since 1934. The figures also reflect a clear bias in favor of cattle ranchers, as 1,090,139 hectares were protected by new certificates of nonaffectability in the period 1982–1988, which coincides with the agrarian policy of the federal government to support large-scale livestock production. Similar trends were revealed by national-level figures. The implications for peasant movements are obviously serious: Many land petitions will now come up against the legal arguments of ranchers and large holders that their properties are covered by certificates of nonaffectability.

At the same time the number of cases of violence against independent land-claimant organizations suggests that such groups are unlikely to give up their efforts to take land back, nor has the government been able to control the activities of private gunmen at the service of landowners. According to a report compiled by the PMS (based on data from Amnesty International, the Mexican press, and various peasant organizations), a total of 814 peasants were killed in rural violence in Mexico between December 1982 and December 1987. Most belonged to independent opposition organizations, including the CIOAC and OCEZ. Significantly, 74.6 percent of the killings occurred in states with high indigenous populations and the most contested in terms of land struggles, namely Oaxaca, Chiapas, Puebla, Guerrero, Michoacán, and Veracruz. The majority were believed to have been carried out by private gunmen (see Grupo Parlamentario del PMS 1987; Amnesty International 1986).[14]

MARGINALIZATION VERSUS PRAGMATIC POPULAR RESPONSES

The attempted marginalization of the land-claimant groups has not meant their demobilization but their persistence and the sophistication of strategies. They have responded by forming alliances with other groups, promoting horizontal forms of leadership and organization, and developing struggles in the electoral arena. Whereas their marginalization previously implied just that—i.e., their limited capacity to produce changes in the political system— they now present alternative forms of representation that the government has so far been unable to co-opt.

In Carranza the strategy of dividing the community did not destroy the independent movement nor did it undermine the principal objective of the Casa del Pueblo, namely the restitution of communal lands held by private cattle ranchers. Instead, the movement was obliged to seek support at both regional and national levels. A commission from Carranza participated in the founding congress of the National Coordinating Committee "Plan de Ayala" (CNPA) in October 1979. There it came into contact with commissions from other communities throughout Mexico, including Chiapas, and in the following months contacts spread with land claimants in the northern and border areas of the state, culminating in the formation of the Provisional Coordinating Committee of Chiapas in August 1980. Contacts were also made through church lay preachers, or *catequistas*, who had been involved since the early 1970s in the formation of peasant cooperatives in several parts of the state. In 1981 marches were held in Tuxtla Gutiérrez and Mexico City, which allowed the coordinating committee to consolidate its position in the CNPA and make alliances with two other coordinating committees, the CNTE (the National Coordinating Committee of Workers in Education) and the CONAMUP (the National Coordinating Committee of the Urban Popular Movement). In July 1982 it renamed itself the OCEZ and made known its strategy of combining mobilization with negotiations. This strategy was popular with all member communities and no divisions occurred. On the contrary, new members from the municipalities of Tecpatán, Ostuacán,

Frontera Comalapa, and Ocosingo joined between 1983 and 1988, suggesting that continued marginalization of its demands did not result in its demobilization.

In fact, the OCEZ has been the most combative of the independent organizations in Chiapas. Between April 1984 and October 1988 it held nine marches (some to Tuxtla, some to Mexico City), staged several hunger strikes, and occupied municipal palaces, roads, and PEMEX installations to support its various demands. These concerned land distribution, the release of jailed activists, the dismissal of an allegedly corrupt municipal president, and compensation for damages caused to farmland by oil exploration. Mobilization has had some positive results for members, even if the most difficult demands have not advanced. For example, entitlement to ejido lands in Frontera Comalapa and Simojovel has been granted to OCEZ groups, compensation has been won from PEMEX, and prisoners have been released. Furthermore, the CNPA won the right to regular talks, or *audiencias*, with the SRA following a march and demonstration in Mexico City in May 1981. Similarly, the elected officials of the Casa del Pueblo in Carranza were finally recognized by the state delegate of the SRA in May 1987, marking a partial acceptance of the presence of the OCEZ as a representative social force in Chiapas. These gains are not seen as reformist initiatives by the government, but as the concrete result of struggle and a vindication of the need to sustain a strategy based on mobilization with negotiations.

Another outcome of this activism was the extension of alliances with nonpeasant sectors. In 1985 the OCEZ joined with teachers, *colonos* from Tuxtla, transport workers, and students in the formation of a new front of opposition organizations, the Coordinating Committee for Struggles in Chiapas (CLCH), the first multisector coordinating committee to operate in the state and an illustration of the increasing capacity for achieving unity. The second demonstration led by the CLCH in October 1985, however, was violently broken up by security police, and the CLCH was formally disbanded following the arrest and imprisonment in May 1986 of the leaders of the *colonos* group. Nevertheless, the experience helped consolidate contacts that will most likely be important in reconstructing such alliances in the future.

Sustainable mobilization such as this depended on broad participation and trust in leadership. In the case of the OCEZ, the promotion of horizontal forms of organization had its roots in the responses of the Casa del Pueblo in Carranza to the loss of several leaders and mass arrests in May 1976. The survival of repression and the frustration of the attempts by the rival CNC group to take over leadership were brought about by the cohesiveness of the organization and the broad participation that had been encouraged. In consequence, a rapid process of political learning took place as many members gained experience by attending meetings with state functionaries and acting as elected officials of the Casa del Pueblo itself. Every Saturday assemblies were held in each of the eight districts of Carranza, with general assemblies held the following day at the Casa del Pueblo. In this way problems and proposals were discussed by all members, making the decisionmaking process more open and hindering the emergence of caudillo-style leaders. The other communities which joined in the formation of the OCEZ also rejected vertical structures of decisionmaking in favor of more horizontal ones. For example, communities in Frontera Comalapa, Chicomuselo, Trinitaria, and La Independencia (the border zone of the OCEZ) already had experience of organizing transport and food cooperatives by the time they joined the OCEZ. Their activities and struggles over land were also based on broad participation, providing a point of convergence with the Casa del Pueblo with which they came into contact via the church *catequistas*.

Another dimension to the concern with achieving broad participation and politicization has been the development of cultural activities and awareness of popular struggles outside Chiapas and Mexico. Every year since 1984 the OCEZ has held a week of political/cultural events in each region and invited peasants, students, teachers, workers, and journalists to attend. These meetings have provided a forum for denouncing acts of repression and cases of corruption, as well as for exchanging opinions on how to take forward the respective struggles. Community members in each location participate with speeches, protest songs, and poems, and—with the help of the popular theater group CLETA—short satirical plays. OCEZ supporters also carry a portable projector from community to community and show films from Latin America. In short, there is an awakened interest in political change beyond the immediate community, and the cultural activities help to broaden participation, establish contacts between regions, and create a new collective identity.

The CIOAC similarly used a combination of mobilization with negotiations between 1983 and 1988, but also participated in the electoral arena in support of PSUM (later PMS) candidates. It led five marches between 1983 and 1986 and, like the OCEZ, extended its area of influence in Chiapas to other municipalities. Its main achievements concerned land tenure and official recognition. By July 1987 the SRA had authorized the entitlement of CIOAC members to disputed *fincas* in 50 percent of the cases in Simojovel. This achievement was made possible by the prior recognition given to the CIOAC as a representative of peasant interests in the area. As had the OCEZ, the CIOAC won recognition only after mobilization, in particular a highly publicized march to Mexico City in October 1983.

But whereas the OCEZ rejected alliances with opposition parties of the left in favor of links with the CNPA and CLCH, the CIOAC continued to support the PSUM and, after its fusion with other parties in March 1987, the PMS. In fact, the strength of the PSUM in Chiapas owed much to the CIOAC. Together the party and the CIOAC have published reports denouncing the use of repression that have received national attention, both through the press and in the Chamber of Deputies in Mexico City. For the CIOAC such links are important in its strategy to gain acceptance as an autonomous organization in Chiapas. Furthermore, the CIOAC mobilized its membership to support the 1988 PMS presidential candidate Heberto Castillo, who visited the state in

February of that year. Castillo spent time in communities affiliated with the CIOAC and called for an effective redistribution of land and the abolition of the *amparo* law by which large landowners protected themselves against expropriation. He also urged the audience to vote for PMS candidates at the national elections on July 6 (Castillo 1988:32–36). With the decision of the PMS to support the single candidacy of Cuauhtémoc Cárdenas for president, the CIOAC in Chiapas organized its membership in support of the National Democratic Front (FDN). Marches and demonstrations have continued to be used to lend weight to negotiations, but, like the OCEZ, the CIOAC has not engaged in acts of open confrontation with the state, preferring to develop simultaneously its economic and political base through cooperatives and its own credit union, and by promoting participation within member communities.

CHALLENGE TO CLIENTELISM AND CORPORATISM

Despite the limited, albeit important, gains of peasant-based opposition movements in recent years, an overall assessment of their achievements would reveal few areas in which they have advanced. Private landowners are now more protected than ever, repression continues to be used against land claimants, guarantee prices have fallen in real terms, and financial support has been cut by the economic crisis itself. The responses of the movements in question, it should be remembered, are also attempts to survive the impact of the crisis in the countryside.[15]

The evidence from Chiapas, however, shows that the continued use of corporatist strategies by the PRI to achieve political control are no longer effective. Despite the often violent pressure exerted against independent opposition, resistance to co-optation has characterized each of the movements discussed in this chapter. The political significance of such resistance is felt most at the local and regional levels. Here, the capacity of the CNC to successfully channel peasant demands has been gradually eroded by the combined effects of state policies and popular mobilization. As agrarian policy was diverted away from land redistributon to increased productivity, the original base of support of the CNC was undermined as the formation of independent movements provided more representative alternatives for land claimants. The erosion of corporatist control has met with different responses, from negotiations to repression, but the control of many peasant communities in Chiapas can no longer be guaranteed through their vertical organization from above.

A related impact of this challenge to corporatism has been the rejection of the clientelistic practices of CNC leaders and local caciques. Representation was not only selective, it was also conditioned by the use of favors, loyalties, and threats. Demands were resolved not in accordance with their legality but through benevolent patrons with privileged access to the state apparatus. Clientelism and the related arbitrary use of law and bureaucracy thus came to be seen as synonymous with the restrictions of corporatist representation. The critique of clientelism by organizations such as those in Carranza, Simojovel, and the Lacandón jungle went to the root of political control and political culture in Chiapas.

Independently of the peasant movements' impact on the political system, the struggles fought by the UU, OCEZ, and CIOAC inevitably helped the formation of new political subjects with a different perception of political process. First, demands were rapidly politicized in the general context of exclusionary forms of mediation. Access to land or recognition of autonomous unions were no longer simply petitioned for, but were demanded as basic rights upheld by legal arguments and the provisions of the 1917 Constitution. Awareness of these rights was facilitated by the courses in agrarian and labor law given by outside activists in the early 1970s. In each of the three cases studied, the government was called upon to respect labor and agrarian rights, to implement presidential resolutions for the distribution of land, to punish those responsible for violent attacks on peasant leaders, and to release others illegally imprisoned. In short, from petitioning favors, the participants in these movements began to demand respect for their labor, land, and human rights. In so doing, they effectively challenged the arbitrariness of the government's rule while recuperating a tradition of peasant resistance in Mexico that had found its maximum expression in *zapatismo* between 1911 and 1917.

Finally, this appreciation of the need to mobilize in order to gain respect for rights can be interpreted as necessary for the achievement of citizenship. As such, the movements provided schools for political education that, in the general context of exclusion and repression, developed at the margins of the political system. In village assemblies, negotiating committees, and coordinating bodies, peasants began to participate as citizens, in defense of rights won through previous struggles but whose realization had been denied. In the course of time they came to know and work with teachers, workers, students, and others engaged in similar struggles for union autonomy, labor rights, and democratic elections. In this respect, the formation of subjects is never a passive outcome but can only be achieved through struggle. In short, resistance has had an impact not only on the political system but also on the formation of new political subjects and the spread of a new political culture.

NOTES

1. By "political system" I mean the combination of the forms of mediation and representation linking state and civil society. Mediation refers to the political interventions that attempt to institutionalize popular struggle and contain it within specific legal and institutional margins. The forms of representation, or the ways in which interests are organized and represented at the level of the state, are licensed by these margins such that mediation does not refer to the actions of a neutral state that oversees conflict between contending social forces, but rather to the embodiment of power relations within civil society. By challenging the use of clientelistic forms of

mediation and the imposition of corporatist forms of representation, popular movements seek to change their relationship to the state and thus press for changes within the political system. These struggles are therefore always conditioned by their location within the political system, which I refer to here as the "legal and institutional terrain."

2. The CNC was formed in 1938 and constituted one of the four sectors of the Party of the Mexican Revolution (PRM), the forerunner of the PRI. Land petitioners and ejido members who had been armed in the struggle for land against their former bosses were integrated into local agrarian committees, which, in turn, came together in "leagues of agrarian communities and peasant unions" (*ligas de comunidades agrarias y sindicatos campesinos*) in each state. The CNC was the national confederation of these *ligas*, and its main objective was to achieve further land distribution. At the same time, however, its affiliation to the ruling party meant that it would be dependent on the latter for subsidies and political favor. Thus, in the post-Cárdenas period after 1940, the antidistributive policies of successive governments and the support to private, large-scale agriculture meant that the CNC's initial promise of achieving effective land reform for its members became increasingly difficult to deliver (see Huizer 1982).

3. It may be argued that Chiapas constitutes an atypical case given the relative persistence of the landed oligarchy and the historical resistance to land reform and peasant organization, including that of the CNC. But if the absence of strong corporatist institutions in Chiapas may be a differentiating feature, it is also the case that when opposition movements emerged in the early 1970s they first had to contend with CNC leaders who were unwilling to take on their demands. Nevertheless, the survival of regional caciques and their close links to the state government meant that clientelism underpinned corporatist representation, which did not occur in more developed areas of the country. Therefore, if it is true that the struggles in Chiapas are not representative of those in northern Mexico, I maintain that similarities can be found in other southern and central states with high indigenous populations that did not see significant agrarian reform or have in recent years seen the reversal of earlier peasant gains.

4. The General Union of Workers and Peasants of Mexico (UGOCM) was formed in 1949 and led important land invasions in the northwestern states of Sonora and Sinaloa in 1958 and 1959. In 1963 another division within the CNC led to the formation of the Independent Peasant Confederation (CCI), the peasant wing of the National Liberation Movement (MLN), an opposition alliance including dissenters from the PRI, most notably the former president Lázaro Cárdenas, and members of the Mexican Communist party (PCM).

5. Concerned that it might lose the initiative to the independent organizations, in 1973 the government unified the CNC with three smaller officialist groups in the Permanent Agrarian Congress (CONPA). A year later they pledged their support for Echeverría in a document known as the Pacto de Ocampo.

6. The Independent Confederation of Agricultural Workers and Peasants (CIOAC) was the new name taken in 1975 by a radical wing of the CCI. As its name suggests, it was concerned with organizing landless rural laborers but also insisted on the continued need for land reform in Mexico.

7. The Casa del Pueblo would later form links with other peasant communities in the state to form the Emiliano Zapata Peasant Organization (OCEZ) in 1982. (See also Harvey 1988, 1989; Renard 1985.)

8. The demands of the four largest indigenous groups in Chiapas (Tzotzil, Tzeltal, Tojolobal, and Chol) were presented at an Indian congress in San Cristóbal de las Casas in October 1974. The congress was called by the state government and organized by the bishop and priests of the diocese of San Cristóbal, with help from students and

intellectuals.

9. Its full name is Union of Ejidos "Quiptic Ta Lecubtesel," meaning "united by our strength" in Tzeltal. For an analysis of its development, see Rubio López 1985.

10. This struggle concerned the fate of twenty-six communities of Chol and Tzeltal peasants who had migrated to the Lacandón jungle area in the 1960s because of the lack of adequate land in other parts of Chiapas. Their tenure was threatened, however, when a government plan to exploit the region's forestry became known in the early 1970s.

11. The LP grew out of an earlier Maoist grouping that emerged at the time of the 1968 student movement. Its main presence was among urban squatters in northern cities and in branches of the miners', telephone workers', and teachers' unions (including the Chiapas branch in this latter case). By 1980 it had disbanded as a formal organization, but its activists continued to promote a strategy of "fighting with two faces" within labor and peasant organizations (see Unión de Uniones 1983).

12. It appears that repression was not confined to the areas of greatest mobilization (Carranza, Simojovel, and the Lacandón jungle). According to one source, over thirty peasant communities in Chiapas were attacked by the army or "white guards" in 1980, often in collaboration with landowners (*Punto Crítico* 115 [February 1981]:54). One of the most publicized incidents came in May 1980, when *ejidatarios* involved in a land dispute with landowners in Golonchán (Citalá) were allegedly fired upon by municipal police and soldiers of the 31st Army Batallion, resulting in the deaths of at least four people (*Uno más Uno*, June 2, 1980). The commander of the batallion at the time was Gen. Absalón Castellanos Domínguez, who would become state governor in December 1982.

13. Coras is the name given to the CNC group in reference to the alleged collusion of Cora Indians in the state of Nayarit with the Spanish conquerers (interview, V. Carranza, June 17, 1987).

14. Although Amnesty International could not provide detailed evidence of direct government involvement in killings, it did note a lack of investigation into such crimes, suggesting that perpetrators may have enjoyed effective immunity from legal prosecution. But it should be noted that in historical perspective suspected human rights violations in Mexico were higher during the Echeverría and López Portillo administrations. According to data collected from Amnesty International, the press, and the National Front against Repression (FNCR), Concha Malo argues that of all the violations committed between 1971 and 1986, 30 percent corresponded to the first *sexenio*, 36 percent to the second, and 22 percent to the third, the de la Madrid adminstration. The rest occurred in 1976 and 1982, which are considered separately because they were years when presidential power was transferred (see Concha Malo 1988:140–141).

15. According to José Luis Calva of the Institute of Economic Research at UNAM, fixed public investment in agriculture fell by 68.2 percent between 1982 and 1986, whereas agricultural credit declined in real terms by 53.2 percent between 1981 and 1988. Guarantee prices for staple crops such as maize fell in real terms by 41 percent in this same period, forcing many poorer peasants to abandon cultivation. Since 1981, over one million hectares of a total of fifteen million have gone out of cultivation in Mexico (*La Jornada*, May 24, 1989).

12

Organizing Opposition in the Teachers' Movement in Oaxaca

MARIA LORENA COOK

*What was won must be judged
by what was possible.*

In the second half of the 1970s, dissident unionists in Mexico directed their efforts to organizing within official labor unions and confederations (San Juan 1984:120). This move was influenced by both strategic and structural considerations: Most workers were located in official organizations, and the government was no longer as willing to recognize independent unions. Still, given union leaders' strong opposition to internal dissent, their government support, and superior access to resources, dissident organizing within official unions was tantamount to organizing "in the belly of the beast." The effort required to organize an opposition movement in this context was enormous, the costs high, and the gains limited. Teachers in Mexico nevertheless managed to sustain one of the largest and longest-lived opposition movements of the last twenty years in Mexico's largest official union, the National Union of Workers in Education (the SNTE).

The rank-and-file teachers' movement in Mexico emerged in 1979–1980 within union locals throughout the country. It arose in response to declining real wages,[1] serious paycheck delays, outdated regional wage differentials,[2] poor health services, corruption, and the lack of democracy within the union. In 1979 several regional teachers' movements formed the dissident CNTE, the National Coordinating Committee of Workers in Education. In 1980–1981 movements in the states of Oaxaca, Chiapas, Morelos, Guerrero, and Hidalgo, and in the Valle de México fought for economic demands and for the right to elect new local committees, ridding these of leaders linked to the Revolutionary Vanguard, the group that had exerted control over the union since 1972. Whereas all of the regional movements shared this political goal, only the Oaxacan and Chiapas movements obtained official recognition and control over their locals.[3] Chiapas Local 7 maintained this control until 1987, when the executive committee was decertified by national union officials, and Oaxaca retained control throughout the decade. In 1989 the teachers' movement reemerged nationally and democratic control of locals was again extended to Chiapas as well as to primary and preschool teachers in Mexico City (see Arriaga 1981; Hernández 1986, 1989; Hernández and Pérez Arce 1982; Peláez 1980–1984; and Salinas and Imaz Gispert 1984).

This essay examines the continuing struggle of rank-and-file teachers to democratize the SNTE, a union of between 800,000 and one million members linked to the PRI. In particular, the essay analyzes the dissident movement's strategy of organizing to hold and win elections in union locals, and assesses the advantages and limitations of this strategy over a ten-year period (1979– 1989). What were the implications of organizing within an official union for the movement's internal organization, demands, strategies, and ability to achieve its goals?

This essay is divided into three parts. The first looks at the official union as an institution that structured the protest movement within it. The laws, procedures, organizational structure, and leadership of the union set boundaries for the movement's actions, shaping, though not fully determining, its demands, strategies, organization, and what it was able to achieve. The second part examines how the movement overcame some of these constraints in pursuing a legal or institutional strategy to democratize the union. This part also analyzes the gains and limitations of the movement's legal strategy as experienced by those sections of the movement that obtained legal recognition. The last part looks at how changes in the movement's political environment affected the ability to achieve its goals. This section focuses on the Oaxacan case and argues that the relations between government and union officials were crucial to understanding the movement's important breakthroughs, as well as the limits to organizing within official unions.

THE OFFICIAL UNION AS STRUCTURING INSTITUTION

The CNTE's decision to organize within rather than outside the union was the outcome of both a political struggle among leaders of the movement and an encounter with legal and political barriers to independent union organization (Hernández and Pérez Arce 1982). Public-sector employees were governed by a separate section of the labor code that permitted only one union in each sector. Most dissident public-sector workers therefore organized factions within their unions, in some instances winning local or delegation executive committees. At the time the dissident CNTE was formed, it had the support of approximately 15 percent of the SNTE membership, far below the majority it would have needed to force the government to recognize an alternate union. As a result, the CNTE remained within the union and pursued a legal strategy that involved organizing to win control of local executive committees through elections. Union positions could then be used to support and extend the democratic movement (Hernández and Pérez Arce 1982:41).

The fact that the movement emerged and remained within an official union shaped its composition, demands, and organizational structure. Movement participants came together by virtue of their profession and their membership in the union (which included manual and administrative workers as well as teachers). The movement's organization closely paralleled the levels of organization within the union locals (delegations, local committees), and the union local was the principal unit of organization for the movement. The CNTE thus represented an alliance of regional (local) movements within the union, rather than an alliance across sectors between popular organizations, and it was structured as a loose network of local movements that retained regional autonomy.

The professional membership of the union shaped the movement's demands as well. In spite of the peasant and working-class origins of many teachers and the important role they played in poor communities, the demands of the teachers' movement corresponded to the specific economic and professional needs of union members. Nevertheless, many teachers participated in peasant struggles for land, in opposing municipal elections, and in organizing for basic services in communities (Hernández 1988a). The CNTE was also instrumental in forging alliances with other popular organizations to oppose government austerity policies and repression against the organizations in the mid-1980s (Prieto 1986:89). The union's primarily female membership did not appear to have shaped the movement's demands in a central way. The leadership of the movement, as well as of the union, was overwhelmingly male dominated, and even some of the most militant women participants felt that to introduce "women's" demands would be to risk dividing the movement. Recently male and female attitudes toward the role of women in the movement have begun to change as a result of several years of men and women participating equally in the movement, if not in leadership positions.

The teachers' movement maintained a position of autonomy with respect to political parties. According to the rank and file, union leaders' commitments to the government party were responsible for their failure to represent members. The party-union separation, however, was also an effort to curb party factionalism and maintain unity within the teachers' movement. Because of widespread rank-and-file mistrust of political parties and party activists, further restrictions were placed on the participation of political parties and currents within the movement, even though the most active movement participants typically belonged to some political organization. Members recognized political organizations' contributions to the movement, yet they rejected attempts to place party interests above the interests of the teachers' movement.[4]

The centralized structure of the union inhibited expressions of dissent. The National Executive Committee (CEN) authorized all electoral congresses at the local level, controlled the distribution of finances to the locals, and held important powers of intervention at local and delegation assemblies (de la Garza Toledo 1982:40–43). Nevertheless, officials regularly denied authorization of electoral congresses for political reasons, and finances normally allocated to local committees were withheld by national union authorities as a way of pressuring dissident locals. Union officials could also draw on the statutes to suspend or expel workers for "disloyalty, lack of discipline, and treason," and for activities said to "threaten the unity and integrity of the union," charges used to control the activities of dissidents within the union (de la Garza Toledo 1982:41). The history of labor conflict within the union was also marked by the use of violence—the intimidation, beating, kidnapping, imprisonment, and murder of union dissidents. In 1989 the Mexican news agency Notimex estimated that 150 union dissidents had been killed since the beginning of the movement (see *Uno más Uno*, April 24, 1989).

The SNTE was dominated by a faction that came to power in 1972 after illegally expelling the secretary general of the union. The act was a coup by one faction, led by Carlos Jonguitud Barrios, against another that had been in power since 1949. The support of the Echeverría administration for the new leadership was evident in the economic, material, and institutional concessions the union obtained throughout the remainder of the president's term (Hernández 1982b:48–49; Peláez 1984:166). Jonguitud used the considerable resources of the union to raise his and the union's political profile (Greaves 1980:91). He also set about to consolidate his control of the union by creating the Revolutionary Vanguard, a political-ideological instrument of the union leadership. Jonguitud was named president-for-life of the Vanguard, enabling him to circumvent union statutes that prevented reelection and to retain control of the union after his term as secretary general ended.

The Revolutionary Vanguard developed an impressive membership network. In the states, *vanguardistas* occupied administrative positions and controlled school districts and the careers of teachers through clientelism and corruption (Hernández 1982b:49–50). Union officials also held government and party positions at national, state, and municipal levels, blurring the boundaries between union and state power and providing *vanguardistas* with external resources to extend their control. Jonguitud himself became a member of the PRI's National Executive Committee, president of the Labor Congress, director general of the ISSSTE (the social security agency for public employees), and governor of the state of San Luis Potosí. Opposition to the Vanguard and its practices became one of the defining elements of the teachers' movement. As one teacher from Oaxaca put it, "People may not be very clear about what they're fighting for, but they're clear about being against the Vanguard," (personal interview, February 1987).

CONSEQUENCES OF THE LEGAL STRATEGY

The movement's pursuit of a legal strategy to democratize the union had several implications and consequences. In pursuing this legal strategy, the movement was forced to adopt extralegal and even illegal tactics. The clearest expression of the use of both was evident in the organization of the movement. By controlling the statutory or formally recognized structures of the union, the movement could officially claim to represent its members and legally bargain on their behalf. But the movement also created alternative organizations that derived their legitimacy from member support and use rather than from official recognition. One document from the movement noted, "We should learn to make broad use of legality, but we should also create our own forms of organization and struggle, even though these may not be legal from the point of view of the *charro* statutes or the repressive government" (SNTE, Sección 7 1983:16).

The first organizations of the movement were strike committees (*comités de lucha*), organized roughly by delegation or several delegations together. Committee representatives then made up the central struggle committee, which made decisions for the movement. Central struggle committees formed in most of the insurgent locals during 1979–1981. In most cases, the organizations of the movement existed alongside the legal structures of the local. After legality, both the Oaxacan and Chiapas movements made additional changes to the parallel and statutory organizations, in a conscious effort to increase member participation in decisionmaking. A state assembly composed of representatives from each delegation (including the rank and file and delegation officials) took primacy over the local executive committee in making decisions that affected the entire local. Important proposals presented at state assembly meetings were taken back to the delegations and schools for consultation with the membership. These issues were discussed at workplace and delegation meetings, and the decisions reached were taken back to the next state assembly meeting, where a vote was taken. In general, workplace, delegation, and regional problems were resolved at the corresponding organizational levels within the local. In the delegations, five-member coordinating committees were formed in addition to the statutory executive committees. These coordinating committees were in charge of the more political aspects of union organization at the delegation level, such as promoting member participation and education. Coordinating committees were also created at sectoral and regional levels to improve communication within the local and to decentralize the resolution of problems.

Legal status, however, did not guarantee that the movement's demands would be met or even heard. As a rule, the movement presented its demands through the established channels. Movement participants tried to get local and national union officials to spearhead or respond to demands, before attempting direct tactics that ranged from ousting the officials to bypassing them in order to appeal directly to higher authorities. Often, however, the locals were forced to rely on their ability to mobilize supporters and their capacity to disrupt. Mobilizations were typically combined with legal appeals and negotiations. That members decided the actions they would take strengthened the membership's ability to engage repeatedly in collective action; members had control over, and therefore some commitment to, movement activities. As a result, the mobilizations were often a reliable gauge of the movement's strength.

The membership of the democratic locals developed a degree of autonomy that enabled it to resist continued attacks. Members questioned and challenged their elected leaders and eventually selected new representatives whom they perceived as being closer to their own interests; these were usually people who had less contact with union and government officials. Members frequently insisted on sustaining mobilizations longer than their leaders did; in Oaxaca in 1985–1986 and Chiapas in 1987, members demonstrated that they were willing to mobilize for political demands alone—for democratic elections in their locals. These and other developments signaled that members were increasingly unlikely to accept the paternalism and clientelism that were pervasive in other parts of the union.

The electoral renewal of the local committees highlighted the central dilemma of the movement's legal strategy. Continuity of the movement's legal status depended on the CEN's willingness to authorize the elections. Union officials used their power to authorize local elections in order to pressure the movement into giving up seats on its executive committee. When this strategy failed, officials withheld authorization in an effort to divide and weaken the movement. Fighting the CEN on this issue called for a tremendous mobilization of resources, and the failure to advance on the election issue generated tensions within the movement. Differences developed between some members of the executive committee and the state assembly over tactics: the leaders' excessive reliance on negotiations against the use of mobilizations, and whether to focus on the election issue exclusively (a regional issue) or broaden demands to include other sectors in joint mobilizations.

Executive committee leaders were often in the contradictory position of having to appear radical to their membership and moderate to government and union officials. Union and government officials pressured leaders to accept compromise solutions without consulting their membership. Members, in turn, suspected leaders of negotiating behind their backs or of concealing information, causing them to challenge leaders openly in the state assembly. These internal relations were complicated by the stipulation that a new executive committee could not be elected without authorized elections, for fear that the union would use the event of unauthorized elections to impose its own committee.

This lack of trust between members and some executive committee leaders threatened the unity of the movement. In Oaxaca, however, members adopted creative solutions in response to the election debate and to the internal strains developing from it. The state assembly rejected the option that the CEN was trying to impose—negotiating *vanguardista* representation on the executive committee. At the same time, the assembly voted to develop member participation in rank-and-file organizations, expand the executive committee with rank-and-file assistants, improve relations with parents (which were strained due to the strikes), and work closely with other members of the CNTE in an effort to break out of isolation (FMIN

1985:23). The movement therefore reacted to the pressure not by centralizing decisionmaking, but by extending "horizontally"—developing its alliances and its democratic features.

CENTRAL CONFLICT AND REGIONAL MOVEMENTS: OAXACA

After the formation of the SNTE in 1943, the union played an important part in its support for the government party and for presidential candidates, particularly in its role as a party electoral machine during elections. In exchange, union leaders occupied positions in the party and government, becoming senators, federal deputies, party presidents, and directors of federal agencies. This alliance between the union and the government-party was not new when Jonguitud came to power, but it reached new dimensions under Echeverría. Still, the growing political and economic power of the union, which had made it an effective ally of the government, became an obstacle to government efforts to reform Mexican education in the late 1970s.

State-Union Conflict and the
Emergence of the Movement, 1978-1983

The successes and limits of the teachers' movement cannot be fully understood without taking into account the larger context of the union's relations with the government. At the beginning of the movement, conflict between the SNTE and officials in the Ministry of Education (SEP) under López Portillo led state officials to tolerate the movement in order to pressure the SNTE (Hernández 1986:66; Pescador and Torres 1985:4–5). Particular events contributed to an overall climate of conflict that benefited the dissident movement: the formation of the National Education University (UPN), changes in the requirements for the training of teachers, the union's demand for more deputy and senate seats and for greater participation in the formulation of education policy, and the deconcentration[5] of the administration (Peláez 1984:207; Pescador and Torres 1985).

The particular ways in which government-union conflict was expressed had different implications for rank-and-file teachers and for the opposition movement. The struggle over the formation of the UPN reflected deep differences between the government's technocrats and the more traditional union politicians (Kovacs 1983; Pescador and Torres 1985), but this conflict was relatively contained within an institution of higher education based in Mexico City. In contrast, the deconcentration of the SEP had an important impact on rank-and-file teachers. It affected practically all union members at once; it disrupted regional relations of power within the union without providing a strong substitute authority in the SEP delegation, and it forced union leaders to turn to the mobilization of their members rather than fall back on the more traditional forms of bargaining with SEP officials. As a result, SEP-SNTE conflict was displaced from the arena of high-level negotiations, unleashing rank-and-file mobilizations that later became difficult to control. Moreover, members were mobilized in support of the specific interests of their leaders (e.g., removal of SEP delegates) but not in support of member needs, such as wage increases. These conditions enabled groups of dissident teachers to emerge and organize, and facilitated the formation of a *national* opposition movement within the union.

In 1978 officials in the SEP initiated the administrative deconcentration of the ministry in order to address the problems associated with the enormous size and centralization of the system. Among these problems was the lack of information about and control over the availability, use, and distribution of resources in the states, and severe delays in the issuance of employee paychecks. The goal of the administrative reform consisted of modernizing educational planning and the personnel administration by substituting technical criteria for the personalist criteria that had thus far prevailed in the allocation and distribution of resources (Street 1984:18). A related, though unwritten, objective of the deconcentration was to launch a surprise attack on the power base of the union in the states, in order to "cut the octopus's tentacles" (personal interview with SEP official, September 1987). The ministry thus set out to undermine the union's pervasive influence over SEP personnel in the states, which was seen as the main obstacle to reform.

Before 1978 the union's power was based on its control of the assignment, administration, and promotion of personnel, through a chain of command that linked school directors and superintendents with federal directors and directors general of education in the states, many of whom were loyal to the union (Street 1984:18). The deconcentration tightened central control over these processes by establishing one delegation in each state and granting the SEP delegates—who answered directly to the education minister—control over the programming of resources and matters relating to teaching personnel, undermining the authority previously enjoyed by the directors general (Street 1984:15–16).

These measures threw the SEP into "a brutal confrontation with the union" (personal interview with SEP official, August 1987). Union officials responded by refusing to cooperate with the new delegates. In many cases, strikes and building occupations were organized by the union in order to pressure the SEP into removing delegates. The conflict over the deconcentration thus took place in the states, upset regional power relations, and directly affected rank-and-file teachers. At the same time, the creation of SEP delegations increased the autonomy of union locals vis-à-vis the National Executive Committee by making the channels of communication between the SEP and teachers more direct, and also by making the delegations more vulnerable to pressure from union members at the regional level (Pescador and Torres 1985: 50–51).

The SEP also planned to decentralize the system of payment to SEP employees in response to a severe payments crisis in which employees typically received paychecks months behind schedule. The payments problem spread discontent among rank-and-file teachers and was used by union officials as a mobilizing tool to protest the administrative reforms. In Oaxaca, prior to the emergence of the movement, local union officials mobilized members around the payments issue in a campaign to oust the SEP delegate. Their call to strike backfired, however, when rank-and-file teachers moved beyond the demands of their local officials in May 1980 and called for wage increases and the removal of the local executive committee (Yescas Martínez and Zafra 1985:105–106). Many delegation officials, dissatisfied with the way the new secretary general had been selected during a local congress held earlier that year, also joined the emerging movement.

Delegation committee representatives voted to reject the executive committee on May 13, 1980 (Peláez 1980:72; Yescas Martínez and Zafra 1985:94). A commission tried to negotiate with national union officials to hold new elections, but national authorities threw their support behind the rejected secretary general. The dissident teachers then went to Mexico City in order to pressure the National Executive Committee to spearhead their demands and to authorize new elections. Both the CEN and the Ministry of Education promised to address the movement's demands, but negotiations with the Oaxaca commission were abandoned after verbal agreements led Oaxacan teachers to lift their strike and return to their state. Finally, a day-long work stoppage was called by the CNTE on June 9, 1980, and approximately 70,000 teachers—including contingents from Chiapas, Morelos, Guerrero, Querétaro, Mexico City, and the Valle de México—marched and then camped out in front of SEP and SNTE offices in Mexico City (Peláez 1980:78). After twenty-four hours and the CEN's refusal to negotiate the movement's economic demands, the Ministry of the Interior intervened and led the CEN to the negotiating table with the Oaxaca commission. The CEN was forced by the Ministry of the Interior to accept a transitional executive commission in Oaxaca, in which all twelve members except for the president would be elected by the dissidents, and the president would be appointed by the CEN. This arrangement represented a structural change in the union local's government that opened the possibility of democratic elections. Other regional movements reached similar agreements in the ensuing months.

The reasons for the Ministry of the Interior's hard-line position with officials of the SNTE probably ran deeper than the union's inability to keep its members from erupting onto the streets of Mexico City. The government may have been interested in curbing the SNTE's power in the context of the presidential succession, particularly given the union's demands for political appointments and for the position of education minister in the next administration. The interior minister had also been an executive committee member in the SNTE in the late 1950s, when it was dominated by the faction that Jonguitud later ousted in 1972.

Although an interim commission was established in Oaxaca, CEN officials dragged their feet in authorizing elections. Repeated mobilizations, together with pressure on the part of the governor of Oaxaca, finally enabled

Oaxacan teachers to elect a new local committee in February 1982.

The State-Union Alliance, 1983–1988

The 1982 change in administration and the economic crisis altered the context of government-union relations and affected conditions for the dissident movement. The new SEP minister, Jesús Reyes Heroles, still came into conflict with the union over the decentralization of education, but the government was also harsher on dissident movements. The labor movement's initial militant reaction to the economic crisis was halted by the de la Madrid administration's firm response to labor protests in 1983. The new administration also dealt a blow to the CNTE by decentralizing the National Teachers College in Mexico City and closing its main campus. The school had been operating as the unofficial headquarters of the CNTE and was a meeting place for movement leaders from all over the country who attended its summer courses. The economic crisis also marked the beginning of a period (1982–1989) in which teachers' real wages would fall by 63 percent (Guzmán Ortiz and Vela Glez 1989:47). The crisis generated discontent but also limited the possibility of winning economic demands, and it reduced the amount of time teachers could devote to the movement as many teachers were forced to seek additional income.

The pressure of a mass movement on the government had also largely disappeared. The CNTE's last large national mobilization was during the June 1983 strike wave. By 1982–1983, the CNTE was fighting its battles regionally rather than nationally: Oaxaca and Chiapas already had their democratic executive committees, and Morelos, the Valle de México, Hidalgo, and Guerrero had been weakened.

By 1983 union officials of the SNTE had had time to reorganize (Hernández 1986:69; Prieto 1986:79). The reduction of substantive conflict with the state by the end of 1983 also released the CEN to focus on the dissident movement in the states. In their strategy to recover old losses and preempt new ones, CEN officials sent top cadres to Oaxaca and Chiapas in order to organize opposition to the democratic locals. In October 1983, *vanguardistas* occupied union headquarters in Oaxaca and took several democratic members hostage. A large crowd of teachers and supporters gathered outside, and eventually police were sent in to remove the occupants. Days later, *vanguardistas* in the state formed a parallel executive committee in an effort to take over executive functions and win members away from the democratic local, but the attempt failed. In addition, union officials had already begun to lash out at the dissident movement in other states, violating agreements for electoral congresses with movements in Hidalgo, Morelos, and the Valle de México.

After Reyes Heroles's death in 1985, Miguel González Avelar was appointed to head the SEP. The new education minister adopted a conciliatory position toward the union; his interest in the presidential nomination appeared to weaken his resolve to delimit the power and activities of the union. The

SNTE was able to negotiate the appointment of directors of the delegations, now called Educational Services Units to be Decentralized, or USED (Martínez Assad and Ziccardi 1988:37–38).[6] Union resistance to SEP delegates had already given way in many states to a greater *vanguardista* presence in the delegations, the removal of unpopular delegates, and power sharing in some areas (Pescador and Torres 1985:50–51; Street 1984:20–21).

This alliance between state and union officials greatly narrowed the Oaxacan movement's access to political and economic resources and limited the effectiveness of its mobilizations. National union officials began a campaign to wear out the movement by extending, then retracting, authorization for local elections to renew the executive committee. Union officials withheld authorization of the Oaxaca local's elections every year between 1985 and 1989 until after Jonguitud's removal from the union. Leaders that were to have remained in office for only three years, according to union statutes, were forced to remain at the head of the movement for seven. According to movement leaders, after 1985 the USED began to employ *vanguardistas* who blocked petitions coming from the local. National union authorities also cut off the local's share of dues remissions in May 1986. *Vanguardistas* were sent to work at schools without appropriate credentials and in violation of earlier agreements the movement had forged with the SEP on the criteria for transfers and hiring. National union officials attacked the movement on all fronts, threatening simultaneously its ability to bargain and petition on behalf of its members, its legal status and formal continuity, its access to resources, and its unity. The movement's few resources were diverted to fight battles in the schools, and conflict with the local SEP offices increased. The limited autonomy of the democratic locals—their vulnerability to the actions of national union officials—was never more evident than during this period.

Months of mobilizing with limited results placed the Oaxacan organization under tremendous pressure and strain. Nonetheless, it remained unified between 1985 and 1988, managing to avoid the divisive factionalism that had become public in the Chiapas leadership (Campa 1988). In February 1989 the Oaxaca local elected a new executive committee during its precongress, for the second time since 1985, and again national officials postponed the congress date.[7] After the teachers' movement gained strength nationwide in April and May and Jonguitud was removed from the union, the executive committee was finally ratified in the presence of the new secretary general of the SNTE, Elba Esther Gordillo.

The Renewal of Conflict, 1989

After the presidential elections of July 1988, national political conditions in Mexico changed. For Mexico City residents in particular, the success of Cuauhtémoc Cárdenas's presidential campaign (the *cardenistas* won the capital) provided a needed boost to popular organizing efforts throughout the city and eroded the authority of the Salinas administration. At the same time, the dramatic arrest of the leader of the Mexican oil workers' union in January 1989 was a sign from Salinas that traditional labor bosses were no longer inviolate, rekindling old demands for union democracy in a number of areas. Meanwhile, the SNTE reverted to its traditional methods of manipulating delegation assemblies throughout the country and obstructing the opposition in the selection of delegates to its national congress in February. The discontent generated by these maneuvers and by Jonguitud's tight control over positions of union power revealed dissension among former allies of the union boss. Severe wage erosion had also spread the discontent to locals throughout the country.

These factors converged in the spring of 1989 to produce one of the largest teachers' strikes in the history of the SNTE. The dissident movement encompassed far more than the traditional CNTE centers of support. It included rank-and-file members who had never participated in the movement, as well as disgruntled *vanguardistas* and other factions of union officials. The Salinas government seized upon this moment to displace a union boss whose internal support and benefit to the political system had seriously deteriorated. In the wake of this removal, the striking teachers succeeded in extending democratic union local committees to Oaxaca, Chiapas, and to the union's largest local—Local 9 of primary and preschool teachers in Mexico City. In other locals, dissidents gained representation on temporary executive commissions and obtained agreements to hold elections. In spite of later setbacks, the dissident teachers achieved more during this period than they had at any point since the founding of the CNTE in 1979.

Prior to the reemergence of the dissident movement in 1989, the general refusal of union and government officials to respond to the movement's demands—and in particular, to requests for elections—appeared to signal the effective containment of the movement. The events in early 1989, however, offer the clearest evidence of the difference that changes in the political environment make for popular movements, particularly for those contained within official institutions. The movement's successes during this period reflected a decade of CNTE activism and experience and the consolidation of the democratic movements in Oaxaca and Chiapas. But the closure of union and government authorities and the limited gains of the movement between 1983 and 1988 contrasted sharply with the movement's advances of 1989. It took the convergence of state-union conflict with the massive mobilization of discontented union members to achieve breakthroughs similar to those of the 1979–1981 period.

CONCLUSIONS

The democratic teachers' movement in Mexico highlights the limits and possibilities of organizing opposition within official unions. The institutional and legal context in which the movement emerged precluded some strategic choices from being adopted; instead of organizing as an independent union, the movement remained within the union. As a result, the movement had to confront the constraints to dissident organizing inherent in the union's statutes, organizational structures, leadership, and political ties. In employing both legal and extralegal measures to circumvent some of these constraints and gain a foothold within the union, the dissident movement used legality but was not bound by it.

The legal strategy pursued by the movement had positive consequences, but it also presented the democratic locals with a dilemma. During an initial period of increased autonomy for the movements, internal structures and procedures were altered to broaden member participation in decisionmaking and to increase the accountability of leaders. Legal status facilitated the democratization of the movement, which in turn influenced a new generation of teachers that entered the movement in the 1980s. But continuity of the movement's legal status depended on its securing the permission of its enemies—national union officials. This was the dilemma and central constraint of the legal strategy.

Changes in the movement's larger political environment, and the way the movement took advantage of these, were therefore crucial to its development. State-union conflict aided the emergence of the national teachers' movement, and government intervention in negotiations produced important changes and advances for the movement (representation on interim committees and election timetables). On these occasions, pressure by the dissident movement converged with a government interest in applying leverage against SNTE officials. In contrast, when union officials were not constrained or had the cooperation of government officials, they succeeded in changing conditions in the states so that opposition locals found it more difficult to manage and gains were increasingly limited.

The lack of a political opening rendered the movement's mobilization strategy ineffective and placed strong pressure on movement leaders to negotiate and compromise without mobilizing their forces. At the same time, however, the democratic organization of the membership kept pressure on leaders and forced them to remain accountable to members despite the lack of elections. As a result, the movement was able to survive intact in spite of its hostile environment. The dissident teachers' movement thus draws attention to the opportunities presented by conflicts within official institutions and to internal democracy as important elements in the organization and survival of popular movements.

NOTES

This essay is based on research supported by the Inter-American Foundation in 1986–1987. This write-up of the research was supported by a fellowship from the Center for U.S.-Mexican Studies, University of California, San Diego, during 1988–1989. I want to thank Paul Haber for comments on an earlier version of this paper. I alone am responsible for the errors or misinterpretations that remain. The results of this larger research project, as well as details on the points presented in this chapter, can be found in Cook 1990.

The epigraph at the beginning of this chapter is taken from Piven and Cloward, 1979:xiii.

1. Real wages for teachers began to fall after 1976, recovered slightly during the peak of the movement (1979–1981), then plummeted after 1981. On teachers' wages see Aboites 1984 and 1986, and Guzmán Ortiz and Vela Glez 1989.

2. These differentials were calculated as a percentage of the base wage. The percentages varied from one region to the next, reflecting differences in the cost of living. At the time of the Chiapas movement's emergence in 1979, the regional differentials had not been adjusted in thirty years.

3. In Chiapas two locals, one of federalized teachers (Local 7) and one of state teachers (Local 40), obtained this status. Both belonged to the SNTE. This essay focuses on the federalized teachers.

4. The formation of the Party of the Democratic Revolution under Cárdenas (PRD) has since led some groups to reassess the movement's relationship to political parties.

5. Deconcentration was the first phase in the planned decentralization of public education in Mexico. Deconcentration referred to the delegation of authority to a lower level of the SEP, whereas decentralization referred to the transfer of responsibility and resources for education to state governments. For an excellent analysis of the deconcentration of the SEP and its effects on the union, see Street 1983 and 1984. On decentralization see Martínez Assad and Ziccardi 1988, and Pescador and Torres 1985.

6. See also "Carta de la CNTE a Bartlett" in La Jornada, October 23, 1987: "The majority of ministry positions have been turned over to them, so that almost all of the educational services units and the regional services coordinating committees in the states are occupied by bureaucrats who belong to the Vanguard."

7. The official events were presided over by representatives from the CEN, so prior events were held to elect congress delegates and executive committee slates, so as to avoid confrontations and divisions at the official congress. In Oaxaca, delegate selection had taken place in 1985, but the precongress was postponed; in 1986 the precongress was held. On both occasions, the CEN rescinded authorization for the congresses at the last minute.

13

Women and Independent Unionism in the Garment Industry

TERESA CARRILO

Researchers have noted the predominance of women in Mexican popular movements, but few have delved into a more complete gender analysis. We know, for example, that in the territorially based urban movements, between 80 and 85 percent of the active participants are women. Labor unions with a high proportion of women in their rank-and-file membership often make headline news, as did teachers', telephone operators', nurses', and garment workers' unions in the late 1980s. We know little about women as movement participants and leaders, and even less about how gender is significant for popular movements. Although women are participating at an unprecedented rate, they rarely hold leadership positions in popular movements. One of the few cases of popular organization that highlights both female leadership and an orientation toward gender-based demands is that of the garment workers' movement and the new Nineteenth of September Garment Workers Union.[1]

The Nineteenth of September Garment Workers Union rose from the rubble of the 1985 Mexico City earthquake. The earthquake damaged or destroyed 400 centers of production in the central garment district, leaving an estimated 800 garment workers dead and 40,000 unemployed. In the midst of this tragedy, garment workers demanded official recognition from the Ministry of Labor as an industrywide, independent union. After just one month of intensive mobilization, the newly organized garment workers received the official recognition they sought and the Nineteenth of September Garment Workers Union was born.

This union is unique for a number of reasons:
- It emerged from a crisis situation—economic and natural.
- It is the first independent national union to gain official recognition since 1976.
- It is a women's union—women-led with a predominantly female membership.
- It is a product of collaboration between garment workers and feminist advisers.
- It is a multifunctional organization—and the organizational base of a social movement.

Although these characteristics differentiate the Nineteenth of September from other trade unions in Mexico, they also reflect similarities—in social bases, demands, and modes of political action—between the union and a growing number of popular organizations in Mexican civil society. These unique characteristics have influenced the demands, strategies, and tactics defined and pursued by the union's leaders, advisers, and members.

This essay focuses on the women active in the garment workers' movement and the patterns of leadership and collective action that emerged from 1985 to 1989. Garment workers employed three patterns of collective action—informal collective action, mass action tactics, and infusion of feminism—in attempting to create institutional linkages within the corporatist structures of the state. Despite obstacles encountered, the garment workers' movement influenced both the garment industry and the "official" labor bureaucracy that once monopolized trade unionization within the industry.

Although the union's impact is limited externally vis-à-vis the industry and the state, internally the union's transformative potential can be assessed through its patterns of leadership and the leaders themselves. What is new about this union is its leadership: women who have carved out a space in both the male-dominated realm of the Mexican labor movement and the broader realm of popular movements. Garment workers and feminist advisers, in sometimes uneasy partnership, have moved from dissatisfaction with existing organizational structures (official unions and political parties) to a collaborative effort that surmounts political differences in a move forward as a single union.

Labor organizing in the garment industry has been hindered by the "monstrous collusion"[2] among state labor authorities, "official" union leaders, and garment industry employers. To counter this force, Nineteenth of September activists have sought out new areas of leadership and collective organization, established new forms of collaboration between feminists and working-class women, and developed alliances with other movements. This chapter describes the union's leaders and takes a close look at the key role feminist advisers have played in the movement. Feminist participation brought to the movement an extensive network of support and solidaristic ties that broadened the base of the union's alliances, adding to its diversity. Garment workers and advisers alike have been challenged to resolve or to manage fundamental differences among factions in an effort to establish a collaborative practice of leadership. In this chapter I describe the way in which this union has proceeded in its attempt to improve working conditions and to link women's labor organizing activities to the feminist movement, the labor movement, and the predominantly female popular urban movement.

The analysis suggests that the unique gender configuration and the innovative leadership in the union have expanded its unionist boundaries. Constrained by garment industry troubles and the state's policies of austerity and labor control, garment workers have nevertheless defined and pursued alternative strategies for collective organizing, extending their struggle beyond the workplace and work-related demands. I argue that the multifunctional nature of their union has allowed the organization to survive despite opposition from labor officials and garment industrialists. A collective identity based on both class and gender has broadened the basis for collective action among garment workers and diversified the organization's functions. When the obstacles to effective collective bargaining have proven insurmountable, the union moved ahead in other areas, developing internal projects and programs; establishing links with other women's groups, independent unions, and popular organizations; and taking a leading role in coordinating mobilization around popular, gender-based demands. The combination of gender- and class-based demands and interests has worked to fashion the union's functions and goals to resemble a combination trade union/social movement/women's organization. This combined agenda allows the union to flourish in some areas but weakens it as a labor bargaining unit.

"OFFICIAL" UNIONS IN THE GARMENT INDUSTRY

Although the "official" union presence in the garment industry is uneven and decentralized, the official labor bureaucracy has effectively blocked Nineteenth of September's efforts to win contracts away from PRI-affiliated union centrals. Even though only a fraction of the garment industry's work force is unionized,[3] at the time of the earthquake there were some 2,000 garment worker unions (*Proceso* 469:30). A fraction of these were *charro* unions of the CTM, CROC, CROM, or COR—all PRI-affiliated union centrals. The majority were "white unions" that exist only on paper in a protective contract signed by a union leader and a factory owner. These unions have no history of union activity or communication between union leaders and rank and file. Often white unions do not collect union dues and workers are unaware that they work under union contract. In a 1984 survey among garment workers, 77 percent of the respondents worked under union contract although the majority (62 percent) were unaware of the purpose of the union. Moisés Gómez Guzmán reported, "Of the 150 garment workers interviewed, 116 of them belong to unions, but the majority don't know what a union is nor the rights that the union should protect. During the interviews, we observed that many of the unionized workers didn't know whether there was a union in their shop" (Gómez Guzmán 1984:93). In the same survey, in answer to the question, "How are union leaders elected or chosen?" 90 percent of the workers answered that they are named by the business. The majority didn't know who their union leader was, and of the minority who had actually attended a union meeting, 79 percent understood that they could not talk or vote in the meeting.

The unions that operate in the industry have little contact with workers and rarely take action in defense of worker's rights. Even though the majority of the unions belong to union centrals, they exist in isolation from one another. One analysis, based on findings from a survey of 36 garment factories, explained,

> The isolation of the various groups of workers in different sections of the centrals or in different company unions creates a dispersion that reproduces the same situation of chaos that characterizes production in the industry. This

allows for an arbitrary and speculative management of labor relations and salaries for garment workers; a situation that benefits first, the employers and second, the *charro* union representatives who profit from selling contracts without a single effort to defend labor rights of the union members. (Taller de Investigación Obrera 1987:66)

Although the existence of a union in no way guarantees regulation of employer-employee relations, unionized shops are more likely to hold collective work contracts than factories without a union. Of the thirty-six factories surveyed, only seven—all with CTM, CROM, CROC, or COR unions—held collective contracts with their workers. Thirteen had no contract at all, and the remaining sixteen had individual contracts.

The norm in the garment industry is that official union leadership is appointed by the owner, not democratically elected by workers, and worker participation is extremely limited. Most unionized factories are organized as isolated union locals and not as part of any network of activism or alliances on a national or regional level. In part because of the small scale of union activity and influence in this particular industry, garment workers make no great distinction between the labor bureacracy and the employers. Union leaders work in conjunction with owners to avoid labor conflicts. Within this context of labor control through official unions, the Nineteenth of September's efforts are that much more difficult and extraordinary.

FROM DISASTER RELIEF TO LABOR ORGANIZING

During the first six months of the union's existence, the garment workers' movement evolved apace with the sudden political opening that followed the earthquakes. With well-publicized but temporary cooperation from state authorities, it quickly consolidated as an independent union and pressured individual factory owners to pay indemnity to over 2,000 members who were earthquake victims.[4] When the indemnity period came to a close, the union reoriented its activities toward the longer-term goals of gaining and enforcing new work contracts. By early 1986 the pressure of public opinion had eased, and labor authorities reverted to a policy of ambivalence if not aggression against the union. The union's resources dwindled to an all-time low, emergency relief goods were scarce, membership fell as workers with claims were paid off, media coverage decreased, and public awareness and support could not be sustained. Nevertheless, it was clear that this new organization would outlive the crisis of the earthquake to become a permanent fixture among Mexican trade unions.

In the months that followed the earthquakes, *charro* unions lay low while media and government attention focused on union corruption in the industry and the collusion between union leaders and garment industrialists. But when the Nineteenth of September began to work for new contracts, employers and official unions reverted to traditional means of labor control to defend their positions within the industry. They pursued a two-fold strategy combining a more active role in factories where they held contracts with steps to prevent the union from gaining new contracts and winning contracts held by PRI-affiliated unions. These steps included threatening workers, electoral fraud, illegally firing activist workers, and using their position on the Labor Conciliation and Arbitration Board (JLCA) against the Nineteenth of September (Taller de Investigación Obrera 1987). At the this time it was extremely difficult for any union in the industry to negotiate for increased wages and benefits. The cost of materials, administration, and finance skyrocketed in the late 1980s, yet the available work force far exceeded the number of jobs, and the government called for a wage freeze as part of the national Economic Solidarity Pact (Brooks 1987).

When the union shifted its focus from one-time indemnity payments to collective work contracts, employers, official unions, and the state also modified their responses. Recount elections became the forum for confrontation between the Nineteenth of September and official unions. The Nineteenth of September leadership complained that labor authorities from the JLCA (the principal state agency with which the union must interact) who were responsible for presiding over recount elections and other procedures related to the enforcement of contracts, had reverted to their "monstrous collusion" with employers and corrupt union leaders. A Nineteenth of September leader explained,

> What we've seen from the beginning when they gave us our registration as a union is that the labor authorities thought this was an organization of earthquake victims who had lost their jobs. They assumed that as those people were paid off, the union would fade away. They never thought we would go on to fight for collective work contracts. We see clearly now that labor authorities are deciding in favor of the factory owners and the *charro* unions. (Personal interview by the author)

Filing for a recount election or a strike was a drawn-out process; months would pass before decisions were made and election dates set. And when a recount election was finally scheduled, multiple tactics were used against Nineteenth of September.

Ideally, the organizational process in individual factories follows one of two trajectories. The first applies when a factory holds no union contract and has no union. The initial formal action would be to submit to labor authorities in the JLCA, a petition to affiliate to a given union, assuming this move had majority support among the work force. If the petition were accepted without resistance, the incoming union would negotiate a contract and then seek to enforce it. The second trajectory is followed when a factory already has a contract with an existing union. Workers would petition for a recount election (overseen by JLCA officials) in which one or more challenging unions would bid for title to the contract and the right to represent worker's interests in negotiating a contract. In this case, if workers and organizers could garner enough support for the union challenging the existing union's claim to the contract, they would petition to initiate the recount process. In either case, once the challenging union won title to the contract, formal organizing work at the factory level would focus on enforcing the contract and renegotiating it every two years.

During the first weeks of its existence, the union was invited to join the Forum for Union Cooperation, a national coordinating committee for independent unions. The forum was instrumental in pulling the union into a network of shared services, resources, facilities, and advisers centered on the Electrical Workers Union, one of the oldest independent unions in Mexico. Through the forum, the new Nineteenth of September leadership received one-on-one training with leaders from other independent unions, although training fell off after the first six months. The Nineteenth of September's secretary of external relations especially benefited from her training with an adviser from the Electrical Workers Union. Working through the networks maintained by the forum, she developed a contact list of unions and union activists and used those contacts to establish solidaristic ties and to gain access to resources, services, and legal advice. As a voting member of the forum, the Nineteenth of September was pushed to develop positions and policies on an array of issues on the independent union agenda.

The union's first attempt to organize in a large factory (Organizaciones Roberts, with 700 employees) was countered by an attempt leveled by CROM—which held the official work contract at the factory—to nullify the union's registration. When the Nineteenth of September submitted a petition to hold a recount election in December 1985, member unions of the CROM submitted similar petitions and prolonged the process for months on end. Lawyers representing CROM and the factory then filed a law suit claiming that the union's registration should be nullified, a suit initially rejected but later appealed in a higher court.

During the months following the earthquake, state agencies and the official labor bureaucracy followed a policy of nonintervention toward the new union. The first change in this policy came on International Workers' Day (May 1), 1986. On this day, following Mexican custom, PRI-affiliated union leaders staged a massive labor march through the central plaza in Mexico City. The "official" union centrals (CTM, CROM, CROC, COR, CTC, and others) along with the *charro* industrial unions (PEMEX, SNTE, TELMEX, and others) orchestrated the march, which was televised and observed by invited international guests. On the morning of May 1, 1986, approximately 700 garment workers and supporters lined up behind a brightly colored banner and set out from the union local to join the march to the plaza, only to be met by a blockade of police and antiriot forces and ordered back to their union local. Marchers who resisted were threatened with billy clubs, and four were detained by police. Once back at the union local, they were detained for two hours by fifty officers on motorcycles, twelve patrol cars, 500 antiriot police, and a helicopter (Fuentes et al.

1987:24). Many garment workers were surprised by the repressive reaction of the police to their attempt to march on Workers' Day. As one commented, "We never expected anything like what happened—I don't know what we expected, but not that. After that, I think we became more alert and we thought a little harder about who our friends were."

On the day following the violent confrontation between police and garment workers, appeal proceedings against the union resumed and the judge requested proof of the union's existence. The union responded by presenting collective work contracts, membership lists, and other union documents in court while embarking on a national publicity campaign outside the court. This campaign in summer 1986 in defense of the union's registration included appeals to other unions and social organizations for solidarity; an extensive poster and flyer distribution in and around Mexico City; cultural events at the union local; and a mass mobilization on September 19. The campaign culminated in a march that drew 60,000 participants from a coalition of neighborhood associations, housing groups, women's groups, unions, political parties, and student organizations. Just five days after the march, the court decided in favor of the Nineteenth of September. Unwilling to drop the case, lawyers for the CROM and the factory once again appealed the case, and it remains unresolved, leaving open the possibility that the union may be declared legally "nonexistent" in the future (Góngora 1987). Commenting on the court's decision, a striking garment worker said, "With or without legal acknowledgment of our existence, we are now a fact of history known to practically all the Mexican people."

GARMENT WORKERS AND FEMINIST ADVISERS

From the outset, the garment workers movement has had two sets of leaders—garment workers voted into positions of leadership in the union's National Executive Committee (CEN), and feminist advisers who played an integral role in promoting the union's survival. It is difficult to imagine the movement without advisers; they influenced the movement's discourse, strategic choices, and alliances. They also contributed to factionalism within the union by carrying over longstanding divisions between different orientations and groups within the feminist movement and the Mexican left. The unique style of leadership that resulted from the combination of these two sets of leaders merits a closer look.

The ten former garment workers who became members of the union's National Executive Committee experienced a drastic change in their daily lives. Their routine of long, monotonous hours at sewing machines shifted to the extremely varied and demanding tasks involved in creating and running a new union. Some of these new leaders had never before spoken with bosses or labor authorities or before a crowd. The garment workers' efforts to know and understand their rights as workers and the laws that regulated the work relationship were stymied by their limited formal education and training. To overcome this obstacle came offers for training and advice from all corners of the Mexican feminist movement and the left, and the workers had to strike the difficult balance between the desire for autonomy and the need for training, experience, and expertise. This is a continuing dilemma, not only for garment workers but also for advisers and activists in other popular movements.

The advisers, on the other hand, had some training and expertise in legal and political aspects of unionism but lacked the garment workers' job experience and practical knowledge. The feminist advisers, who had studied and critiqued the patriarchal order and the sexual division of labor, now sought an opportunity to apply their knowledge on a large scale. Advisers expressed an interest in "creating a feminist political project," "forming an autonomous working women's political organization," and "pushing for demands as both women and workers," but most lacked the experience of living in working-class neighborhoods and supporting a family on working-class wages.

There was a great deal of disagreement between advisory groups on appropriate strategies and tactics, differences that still divide the union. Feminist advisers introduced conflicting strategies for dealing with employers and the state and contributed to factional splits within the union, but they concurrently introduced a feminist discourse, promoted a feminist agenda, and brought to the union a wide range of alliances and support networks with other women's groups and social movements (Lau Jaiven 1987; Comisión Organizadora del Encuentro de Mujeres et al. 1987). In spite of the differences between advisory groups, it was the joint effort on the part of garment workers and advisers and among advisers that allowed for the establishment of the union and its long-term survival.

SIXTEEN LEADERS

Two of the most notable characteristics of the ten elected members of the union's national executive committee are that all are women, and all have a recent work history in the factories or small shops of the garment industry. And as a group they tend to differ from the general garment worker population. For example, in educational attainment, eight of the ten elected leaders completed eighth grade or higher—substantially above the third-grade level for garment workers in general (Gómez Guzmán 1984:78).

But their major distinction is their history of participation in workplace collective action. Six out of ten had participated in a strike or some form of collective action in their place of work prior to the earthquake. Of these, five had taken leadership roles in those actions. Of the four not involved in prior workplace collective action, two had held leadership positions in other organizations—one in a church group, the other in a tenants' organization. This compares with an average of only two out of ten in the general garment worker population who had participated in workplace collective actions.

Immediately following the earthquake, all ten leaders were involved in some form of collective action in the garment district directed at employers, former employers, the Chamber of Garment Industrialists, or labor authorities. Although the majority had experience in leadership, workplace conflict, or both, all expressed a feeling of being pushed by their peers into something completely new. The leaders felt they were unqualified to hold positions but explained that they had been placed on the slate "out of necessity" and because "there was no one else."

From the movement's outset, feminist advisers and support workers, legal and political advisers, abounded, each identifying a specific niche in garment worker–related activity. As workers with claims either won or lost their cases, membership in the union dropped off, and advisers were weeded out, leaving a core group of six principal advisers who devoted their full attention to the union. These advisers worked with two different groups of organized garment workers, and over the course of the first three years of union activity two distinct factions took shape, each corresponding to a particular triad of advisers, leaders, and factories. Although there are few advisers in the union, their role can be disproportionately significant to their numbers because of their training, expertise, and access to information and resources.

The six advisers that constitute the core of the advisory leadership earned their posts through sheer perseverance—making decisions, training, and advising the ten executive committee members; persisting with organizing work in the factories; and attempting to negotiate collective work contracts or to enforce existing contracts. Their profiles show similarities on four counts: education, marital status, feminist activism, and prior organizational work with garment workers. All six completed at least two years of university-level education, and four completed a four-year degree or higher. All are single women with no children. Five have a history of organizational activity among garment workers that predates the earthquake and the 1985 garment workers' movement. Five of six had been active in leftist political parties or organizations, and three of those five ended their formal affiliation with the party and/or organization to rechannel their participation into specifically feminist organizations.

Although all six advisers identified themselves as feminists and their political work as feminist activism, they had different interpretations of what a feminist political project might look like and they differed in what they considered appropriate strategies and tactics for garment workers. Even before the union was formed, two factions had taken shape within the movement: advisers from a group called Women in Union Action (MAS) worked in central Mexico City, and advisers from the Integral Revolutionary Collective (CRI, or Colectivo Revolucionario Integral), worked in the San Antonio Abad area, where two other of Mexico City's garment districts are located. Between the MAS and CRI advisers, there are differences in ideology and class origin. MAS advisers generally come from a middle- or upper-class background, whereas CRI advisers tend to be from working-class families. MAS advisers view themselves first and foremost as feminist activists whose activism is directed toward the concerns of wage-earning women. CRI advisers identify themselves as labor activists with a focus on sectors that employ a high proportion of women.

The CRI was founded in 1981 by six women with experience in leftist political parties and popular grassroots organizations who wanted to create their own specifically feminist political project. There are two full-time CRI advisers currently working with the union. They carry out intensive training with a core group of garment worker leaders, who are presumably CRI members also. The two identify what they do as "training in labor rights," but they fulfill an all-encompassing role as advisers, mentors, strategists, and leaders with the narrowly defined objective of winning and enforcing collective work contracts in garment factories. Both advisers concentrate their efforts in teaching and training, writing documents and materials, promoting new and continuing sectional organization in the factories, and overseeing activity among the majority of the National Executive Committee who identify themselves as CRI affiliates.

A third adviser, working in collaboration with the two CRI advisers, described herself as "a labor lawyer for three factories and for the union in general" and characterized her role as both political and legal adviser. Prior to the earthquake, she worked in litigation of individual labor conflicts with garment workers and other wage laborers. She is a member of the MRP, the Revolutionary Movement of the People, one of the political parties that merged in 1987 with the coalition of left parties in the PMS (Mexican Socialist party). Of her party affiliation she commented, "From the moment we arrived, we didn't hide the fact that we were lawyers or that we were members of the Revolutionary Movement of the People. From the moment we started, we defined ourselves as people from political organizations." She became involved with the garment workers' movement when she realized that the momentum set in motion by the earthquake and the high level of mobilization could transform their short-term struggle for material benefits and disaster relief into a more permanent political organization. She added,

> I was the one who threw out the idea of a union in front of the people in San Antonio Abad, and I criticized the fact that they were waging a struggle for only material benefits —where they gave only emergency aid: water, food, used clothes, etc. Everyone knew that we had to form permanent organizations. Maybe it was this experience that kept me from getting lost in materially based struggle. Immediately after arriving, I started to formulate the criteria of a union, and the idea stuck.

The MRP labor lawyer and the two CRI advisers work with the majority of the executive committee members in the union.

A smaller faction within the union works with three advisers from MAS who, during the first year of union activity, dedicated their full attention to the garment workers' movement. Two were salaried employees of CIDHAL, a feminist organization whose central activities are education and training, and promoting organization among women. The organization's general objectives are to promote consciousness-raising among women in targeted sectors and to impel or help create autonomous organizations of women. CIDHAL had targeted garment workers as early as 1980 with an intent to "help groups of women workers, whether they had a union or not, to analyze alongside the workers certain themes that would help to raise their level of consciousness and that would offer resources for participation in union organizations." CIDHAL employees were involved in two of the more publicized strikes in the garment industry in the 1980s—against PIC S.A. and Levi Strauss—and in a number of smaller conflicts as well. After the earthquake, five CIDHAL employees organized a center for free legal advice and disaster relief for garment workers, which they set up on the site of a building destroyed by the earthquake. The five CIDHAL organizers, along with six other feminist activists, went on to form MAS as a feminist political organization in February 1986. As one CIDHAL organizer explained,

> CIDHAL is an institution—but the five [CIDHAL employees] in Mexico City decided to build a feminist political organization—along with these other feminists that joined us, or that we joined. Independent of CIDHAL, MAS is totally apart from CIDHAL. I would say that MAS is my place of political militance, although my work could also be easily confused with my militance. But I work in CIDHAL and my militance is with MAS.

The CIDHAL-MAS alliance was firmly grounded in a feminist tradition, CIDHAL being one of the most established feminist organizations in Mexico. The three advisers from MAS spent less time at the union than the two CRI advisers but maintained a consistent presence, running education and training programs, carrying out organizing efforts in factories, and promoting feminism in the union.

A third influence comes from the Authentic Labor Front (FAT), a national confederation of small, independent unions that has a long history of garment-worker affiliation in the small industrial town of Irapuato, Guanajuato. Garment workers from three factories organized by FAT in Irapuato provided an essential element for the Nineteenth of September's 1985 demand for a national union, as there is a proviso that requires affiliates in two or more states of the republic. FAT is represented on the Nineteenth of September's National Executive Committee by an ex-garment worker and salaried FAT staffer who holds the position of secretary of organization. Although there have been differences between the positions advocated by FAT and those of the other two factions, the FAT does not have enough of a constituency in Mexico City to become a third faction at the national level.

The adviser's role in the union has been a sensitive issue. In April 1987 the union divided over an issue involving advisers and decisionmaking processes. The controversy began when the union initiated an all-day, all-night sit-in in front of the National Palace in Mexico City's central square to demand reversal of a series of unfavorable decisions handed down by the JLCA. The MAS advisers complained that CRI advisers alone were making critical decisions for the union—planning the sit-in and proposing a hunger strike. In their bimonthly publication, MAS complained that "advisers are acting and deciding for the leadership of the union" (MAS 1987:9).

Differences between advisory groups deepened just prior to the Second National Congress in 1987, when the issue of proportional representation in the CEN was heavily debated among the union's factions. The debate was over the fate of the MAS-led minority within the union and how it would be represented in the new leadership. Union statutes specified that an entire slate had to run against another slate, and the slate with the majority of votes wins the election. In order to ensure a minority presence with a voice in the union's leadership, MAS advisers proposed a system of proportional representation in which a number of seats would be filled with representatives from the minority slate, according to the proportion of votes each slate won. The CRI faction, knowing they had a clear majority, opposed the proposal and won the election.

The factions represent two different political styles: MAS relies heavily on negotiation whereas the CRI favors a more confrontational style. One adviser commented on the difference, saying that between the two groups "the clash was great; in terms of political practice and method . . . we didn't coincide at all. We formed a separate organization, and when the union was formed we worked together to secure the union's registration, but always separate in terms of the tactics we used with garment workers in our groups." MAS advisers strategy called for patience when employers and labor authorities tried to repress the union's efforts to gain new contracts, firing workers identified with union activity, bringing "thugs" to recount elections, or closing factories once a contract had been awarded to the union. According to MAS advisers, a more gradual process could avert such repressive reactions. This cautious strategy has been criticized by the faction that works closely with the CRI and the MRP; they hold that the initial reaction of the owner will always be one of rejection. A CRI adviser outlined two stages of the union-management relationship: an initial stage of outright rejection of the union and repression by the management is followed by a second stage in which the union establishes a relationship of "discussion and respect."

The two contrasting styles of doing politics generate constant tension within the union. The factions are constantly differing in their preferences for political strategies and appropriate tactics when dealing with employers, the official labor bureaucracy, and the state. At a national level, the factional split hinders union efforts to present a united front. The factions also differ in styles of discourse and in the alliances they establish with other movements and organizations. The CRI advisers lean toward other working-class and popular organizations such as the Electrical Workers Union or the CONAMUP in building solidaristic ties, whereas the MAS advisers fall back on a network of feminist groups and independent unions of university employees for support and solidarity. Although these differences broaden the union's base, they also detract from its ability to define and pursue an agenda for national-level action.

COLLECTIVE ACTION AND STRATEGIC CHOICES

The sixteen leaders identified here (ten elected members of the CEN and six advisers) constitute the core of the union's leadership at the national level. Beyond these sixteen women there is a wide network of garment workers, advisers, supporters, and collaborators who are active in the union. Within this broader network of union activists, it is more useful to outline patterns of "collectivity" than patterns of leadership, where collectivity is the manner in which a collective identity is formed, a collective decision is made, or a collective action is taken.

Individual activists, many of whom are wage-earning garment workers, seem reluctant to pursue or be pushed into leadership roles. When asked about the reluctance to accept leadership roles at the factory level, workers expressed a fear of being fired and/or stated their lack of leadership experience and ability. One factory worker explained, "I would like to be part of a union that really functions as an independent union, but you know what happens to those who dare to get mixed up in politics. They get fired; they lose their jobs." In large part because the risk involved in individual leadership, a more collective form of action has prevailed in the union's everyday activities. At the factory level, the organizational process usually unfolds as a group of several workers begins to meet on a regular basis with one or more union organizers.

During the course of the first four years of union activity, the garment workers in the National Executive Committee have become key to factory organizing work and have expanded their own knowledge and experience in organizational work. Presently, the bulk of the actual organizing work (education and training, factory meetings) is carried out by CEN members, although advisers still play a central decisionmaking role. The formal organizational process at the factory level is directed through "training" sessions led by advisers and CEN members. At the national level, CEN members receive at least five hours a week in "leadership training" from their advisers. In these training sessions, CEN members report on their progress in the factories, address specific problems they are experiencing, and lay out a course for future action in their sectional work. They spend another ten to eighteen hours per week with small groups of activists working within the factories to promote the Nineteenth of September Union. The most critical decisions pertaining to organizational work are made in training sessions at either the national or the factory level. It is in those meetings that each factory decides how to proceed in its organizational efforts and each CEN member decides how to proceed with her sectional work. There is a fine distinction between being trained in and directing sectional work; both take place in the training sessions. This is one way in which advisers play a central leadership role in the union.

The groups of garment worker leaders and advisers work in separate factories, competing to gain collective work contracts through which each faction builds a constituency of union members working under contract in one of the factories organized by the individual faction. Although each factory's organizational process is unique, patterns of collectivity can be gleaned from a comparative look at separate attempts to organize new factories during 1986 and 1987. These attempts followed three distinct patterns: informal collective action, mass action tactics, and infusion of feminism. The first pattern, informal collective action, is widespread in the garment industry, even among workers in factories not affiliated with the new union. I refer to collective actions that take place in the workplace on an informal or de facto level but that have no corresponding documentation or bureaucratic process with labor or union authorities. Although informal collective actions may not be documented in any type of written agreement or contract, they often produce the most concrete results.

An example of an informal collective action can be found in the organizational history at Viva, a medium-sized factory. In 1987, after approximately six months of preparatory meetings, training, and organizational activity with seven of the fifty-five garment workers employed there, the Nineteenth of September won a recount vote against a white union. During the six months of organizational preparation, sixteen workers were illegally fired, of whom nine successfully demanded that they be rehired and, once rehired, became some of the most active members of the organizing committee. Even before the union negotiated a contract with the factory, the Viva organizing committee held its first talk with the factory owner. Committee members complained that one of the supervisors was causing problems that affected productivity in the factory: that he was drunk on the job, sexually harassing workers, and requiring workers to put in extra hours on Saturdays only to appropriate what they produced for his own profit. Once the committee produced evidence of the supervisor's abuses, he was fired, productivity and working conditions improved, and a collective work contract was eventually signed.

These gains were hard won. During the initial six-month organizational effort, seven of fifty-five workers went through a training and analysis process in which they studied unionism and the everyday functioning of their factory: the production process, employer-employee dynamics, and time and movement (*tiempo y ritmo*) with CEN members and advisers. Their preparation paid off twofold. The organizing committee was able to demonstrate that the supervisor had a negative affect on productivity and working conditions, and factory workers persuaded the owner to fire the supervisor. This was something the organizing committee had trained for with union organizers from the Nineteenth of September and had actively promoted in their factory. Even before a collective work contract was signed, a new sense of collectivity combined with a new awareness about the work process; planned collective action resulted in improved working conditions at Viva.

In interviews, garment workers involved in informal collective action repeatedly referred to the "new atmosphere" in their workplace or the "different attitudes" of their bosses and supervisors once they had taken collective action. One garment worker added, "It was as if a veil of intimidation was lifted and we knew things would never be the same." Respondents emphasized the need for unity and solidarity to address the widespread problem of harassment and to combat the high risk of management firing workers or closing the factories. Feminists have also been instumental in pushing forward internal union programs oriented toward the specific needs of women, such as child care, training, education programs, and health care services. Even before submitting formal petitions for recount elections or contracts, union members were able to create an atmosphere of solidarity in the workplace that decreased the incidence of sexual harassment by bringing the problem out into the open. One garment worker in training commented on the importance of worker solidarity in changing attitudes, expectations, and actual conditions in the workplace:

> When we talked with the *compañeras* of the Nineteenth of September, about how our workplace functions, we could see how the supervisor was playing with us; he divided us—pitted us against each other. I'm not saying that we hadn't seen this before, but in our meetings we could finally quit laying the blame on everyone else . . . . Before, we didn't complain when the supervisor treated us without respect. Now we defend ourselves, because there is solidarity among us.

In the interview process, I asked about the workers' initial decision to accept the risk involved in pressuring for changes in the workplace, but few could pinpoint a moment in which they made that decision. Respondents conveyed a sense of being pushed or forced by circumstance into collective action. Most stated that a specific event—such as unjustified firings, mass layoffs, a threat of factory closure, or an attempted cut in wages or benefits—had demanded a factory-level response.

In contrast to the successes attained through informal collective action is the case of Comercializadora, an illustration of formal collective action gone awry. The ninety workers at Comercializadora complained regularly about illegal and substandard working conditions, including pay by piecework that often resulted in a salary below the minimum wage, lack of legally mandated benefits, hiring of underage workers, and sexual harassment. At the request of a group of workers, the union began training and organizational work in the factory in early 1986. Following months of preparation, a group representing Comercializadora workers presented a petition to the JLCA to name the Nineteenth of September as their union. Within days, twenty-six workers were fired and those sympathetic with the union who remained in their jobs were harassed and threatened with layoffs. Workers were unaware at the time that Comercializadora held a contract with a CTM union and that a recount election was needed to win title of the contract from the CTM union. When the recount election was finally held after months of delay, fifty unidentified workers from other factories were brought in to vote against the Nineteenth of September; another fifteen votes were invalidated by false letters of resignation; and a group of fired workers waiting outside to vote (because their votes would count if the Labor Conciliation and Arbitration Board decided in favor of their petitions to be rehired) were harassed by CTM agents and three were beaten. Despite the intimidating environment, the Nineteenth of September won fifty-four votes but officially lost the election to the CTM union, which counted eighty votes in their favor. Following the elections, the Nineteenth of September presented evidence of wrongdoing to the JLCA and the fifty extra votes were nullified, but the contract was never transferred to the new union.

Obstacles to successful formal collective action encountered at Comercializadora and elsewhere have discouraged union activists from relying solely on formal legal tactics such as petitions, strikes, and recount elections. Garment workers have employed a number of informal tactics at the factory level that bypass the petition process in the Labor Conciliation and Arbitration Board and the like. Informal tactics include anything from consciousness-raising meetings, to slowdowns, to work stoppages. One union adviser commented, "For every legal procedure, there are a thousand ways that it can get derailed. We don't have the time or the resources to carry on in that kind of a struggle, and, anyway, we will never win if it is a legal battle fought within the offices of the government. We find our strength in how organized we are, and we are always trying new things."

Another pattern, mass action tactics, can be described by drawing on the example of how the union protested their defeat in Comercializadora. At the April 22 sit-in, the union presented a set of demands to labor authorities and government officials that called for the transfer of the Comercializadora contract to the Nineteenth of September, immediate reinstatement of twenty-one fired workers, and resolution of two conflicts in other factories. For ten days, between twenty and thirty people—workers fired from Comercializadora, the Nineteenth of September leadership, CRI advisers, and supporters—continued with the sit-in. In the afternoon, the crowd gathered around the garment workers would swell to one or two hundred, and the physical presence of a large, loud group of people in front of government offices increased the pressure on authorities. Before dawn on the tenth day, May 1, significantly, city police removed the garment workers from the public square, just hours before the massive government-organized labor march was to begin there. The union subsequently decided to establish a weekly presence in the central square every Thursday afternoon for the entire summer in order to prolong their protest. The sit-in is a good example of the mass action tactics the union and other popular organizations employ to exert pressure by sheer force of numbers and to raise consciousness about their struggles. Other tactics—including marches, demonstrations, and mass meetings in the government offices—are used frequently by the union.

One garment worker reasoned, "We go where our strength is—on the streets where the Mexican people are our witnesses."

The third pattern, infusion of feminism, reflects the active participation of feminist advisers in the garment workers' movement. From the start, advisers introduced a distinctly feminist discourse and promoted a feminist consciousness in the movement, especially in reaction to the widespread problem of sexual harassment. Garment workers quickly incorporated parts of a feminist vocabulary into their discourse, although most garment worker leaders do not identify themselves as feminists. This overlay of feminist ideology, experience, and orientation has put the new union on the cutting edge of women's labor organizations. Other unions with high proportions of women in their membership have looked to the Nineteenth of September as a pioneer organization and have drawn on the union's gender-related discourse, literature, programs, and objectives to begin developing a women's agenda of their own. The importance of the new union cannot be measured by its gains alone; its linkages with other movements are also important.

The "instant" feminism of the Nineteenth of September jump-started a growing popular women's movement among women in unions and territorially based neighborhood organizations. The union local became a meeting place for various popular women's organizations, including nurses', teachers', metro ticket-takers', and telephone workers' unions, and the women's sector of the National Coordinating Committee of the Popular Urban Movement (CONAMUP). Together, women in unions opposed potential changes to the labor law that would eliminate the need for union approval when changing production processes. They also fought a proposed reform that would allow new businesses to choose a specific union before opening and union presidents to veto strikes over the votes of the members at large. These reforms would have had a detrimental effect on women's unionization, especially in the *maquiladora* industries.

Nineteenth of September has played a central role in coordinating women at the national level, organizing events such as the National Women Wage Earners Conference, which brought together 400 women from thirty unions and organizations to address women's labor problems and propose changes. In 1989, women from the new union participated in a coalition of women's groups pushing for revised legislation on abortion and rape and became active in the formation of the Popular Women's National Coordinating Committee "Benita Galeana."[5] Coordination on a national level has been difficult because of the wide array of political orientations represented within this body. This is to be expected in a movement as broadly conceived as the popular feminist movement in which a sense of collective identity is based on gender and not built around a single issue or a specific interest group. The Nineteenth of September has been especially successful with one form of collaboration among popular women's groups: mass mobilizations. The union promotes three days of national protest and mobilization for women's rights: March 8, International Working Women's Day; May 10, Mother's Day; and November 25, the Day of Protest Against

Violence Against Women. During the mid-1980s these traditionally feminist forums have been transformed as popular women's organizations have "taken over" the three marches. In 1980, for example, the March 8 mobilization drew only 800 participants, mostly middle-class feminists. By 1986 the march had swollen to 7,000 participants, and in 1988 the march drew 10,000 with an overwhelming majority from popular organizations, including the Nineteenth of September, the CUD, the women's sector of the CONAMUP, the Neighborhood Assembly, and various unions. Middle-class feminists were a marked minority. Across the top of the poster announcing the event, class-based and gender-based demands were equally prominent: "No! to the Government's Economic Pact" and "No! to Violence against Women." The changing face of the women's movement is reflected in the growing numbers and popular character of the March 8 mobilizations, and garment workers have been a central part of that change.

The new union has multiplied its allies by defining a collective identity based on both gender and class. Through the gender link, the union has tapped into a broad network of women's organizations, informally building alliances that have resulted in free training, legal advice, material and financial support, and solidarity. Many of the advantages afforded the Nineteenth of September came from feminist groups, including funding and assistance for internal projects and programs, months of continuous material support as earthquake relief, ongoing legal and political advice, facilities, resources, and educational materials and programs. But these advantages are not without costs—the feminist groups also brought with them the factionalism that has divided the feminist movement and feminists in opposition political parties since the 1970s. Many aspects of these divisions are mirrored in the MAS-CRI split in the union, such as the class difference and the differing orientations toward confrontation or negotiation.

CONCLUSIONS

The new union, like other organizations that grew out of the post-earthquake period, is a product of collaboration between a network of forces and actors. This network, or hammock, as Esteva would call it,[6] extends in its furthest reach to other unions and independent organizations that have established ties of solidarity with the Nineteenth of September (Esteva 1987; Monsiváis 1987a). In the center of the garment workers' movement were, of course, the garment workers themselves, many of whom were awakened by the the collective action that followed the earthquake. Alongside the garment workers were advisers and supporters of the union, most of whom took part in the movement as women and feminist activists.

Some of the patterns of leadership and collectivity observed in the Nineteenth of September may be particular to this union and the conjunctural moment in which it took shape, but as a popular women's organization the union fits into a growing network of independent organizations in which women make up a large proportion of the active participants. In many of these movements, the role of the adviser has not been sufficiently explored. The case of the garment workers' movement suggests that advisers play an important role in the overall decisionmaking processes, often under the guise of "training." The relationship among advisory groups can also be very important to the functioning of the union, especially when advisory groups differ in their political orientations and strategies and bring those differences into internal union politics. The garment workers' movement, like other popular movements, is a product of collaboration between garment workers and their advisers and supporters. The advisory role is often neglected in analyses of popular movements, perhaps for fear of detracting from the movements' "autonomous," "democratic," or "grassroots" characterization. But if the garment workers' movement is representative at all, it demonstrates that the advisers cannot be extracted from the analysis without leaving large gaps in our understanding of how the movements emerged and how they operate in the Mexican context.

Of the patterns of collectivity outlined above, two—informal collective action and mass direct action—are common to other new social movements in Mexico. The third, infusion of feminism, is not widespread in popular movements in Mexico although the popular urban movements have mobilized around what Kaplan has called "female consciousness," a product of the sexual division of labor that assigns women the responsibility of preserving life (Kaplan 1982). In the garment workers' movement, feminist advisers have promoted a feminist discourse that attempts to move from "female consciousness" to a type of popular feminism, an idea just beginning to take root among garment workers and other popular women's groups (see Stephen 1989).

As a trade union, the Nineteenth of September has remained on the margins of the Mexican corporatist state. If the organization's success is measured in terms of contracts won or numbers of active members working under contracts, the union appears small and relatively weak, with only seventeen contracts and a membership of less than 1 percent of the estimated garment worker population. In most instances where the union has faced opposition from factory owners who hold protective contracts with a PRI-affiliated union central, the Nineteenth of September has been unable to gain title to the contract or to prevent factories from closing when the contract was awarded to the new union. During its initial phase, the union was extremely successful at bargaining for individual indemnity payments for garment workers affected by the earthquake. Much of this bargaining was done through the JLCA, with government authorities mediating between garment workers and employers. But beyond this initial phase, the union's success rate with petitions in the JLCA dropped dramatically and this legal and bureaucratic process became progressively less effective as a means to improve working conditions and resolve labor conflicts. As an effective collective bargaining unit, the Nineteenth of September faces many obstacles: an industry that relies on low wages as one of its few competitive advantages in the world market; production from the unregulated and nonunion informal sector; a small-scale labor bureaucracy in the few factories that are unionized; and opposition from the tripartite Labor Conciliation and Arbitration Board (with representation from industry, government, and the "official" labor bureaucracy). Many of these obstacles have proven insurmountable.

Where the union has been unable to move ahead in the legal-institutional terrain, it has branched off into other areas and activities and broadened its basis of collective identity and support by developing a combined class-based and gender-based agenda. A number of successful programs and projects have been sponsored by the Nineteenth of September, including a day-care center, a training center for women over forty, a popular education program, health services, a job bank, and some food distribution. The union has maintained high visibility on a national and international level through ties of solidarity with other unions and women's organizations. In some factories organized by the union, the incidence of sexual harassment has been reduced and employer-employee relations have improved. The new union has taken a central role in initiating communication and collaboration among unionized women in Mexico and has extended those linkages to neighborhood associations and other independent organizations.

The union's broad basis of support has left it open to factionalism among its many different supporters and advisers. But like other social movements in which the basis for collective identity is much broader than a single issue or interest, the union has tried to make this work in its favor. The Nineteenth of September illustrates that independent organizations are likely sites for political struggle as they provide arenas in which new political identities are forged.

In the case of the Nineteenth of September union, efforts to create an independent trade union fashioned a women's organization that is breaking new ground for popular female leadership and collective action. Elected union leaders and advisers alike are gaining valuable leadership experience while grappling with the ongoing challenge of balancing the need for advice and expertise with the practice of autonomous leadership. Although the collaboration among feminist advisers and between garment workers and advisers has been conflictual, it has moved ahead at an unprecedented rate, prompting innovation and change for women in Mexican unions and pushing the garment workers' movement toward an integral role in an emerging popular women's movement in Mexico.

NOTES

1. This essay touches upon many of the topics I explore in greater depth in my doctoral dissertation, titled "Women, Trade Unions, and New Social Movements in Mexico: The Case of the Nineteenth of September Garment Workers Union" (forthcoming), Department of Political Science, Stanford University. I would like to thank the Fulbright Foundation, the Dorothy Danforth Compton Fellowship Program, and the Chicano Fellows Program at Stanford University for supporting

this research. I would also like to thank Sonia Alvarez, Ann Craig, Richard Fagen, Joe Foweraker, and Terry Karl for their many helpful comments.

2. In October 1985, just one month after the earthquakes, Secretary of Labor, Farell Cubillas appeared on television to denounce the "monstrous collusion among inspectors, labor authorities, and unions in the garment industry." His televised speech is part of a 1986 documentary film on the birth of the new union, called "We're Not Asking for a Trip to the Moon" (produced by Mari Carmen de Lara, distributed by Macondo, Mexico, DF).

3. Only 52 percent of operating garment industrialists were registered with the Chamber of Garment Industrialists in 1985, and of these, less than half held contracts with unions. These 1985 figures are reported in Ortega Aguirre (1986:94).

4. Indemnity payments included a combination of severance pay, bonuses, benefits accumulated through seniority, pensions, and, in some cases, compensation for injury or losses.

5. For a more complete analysis of the Popular Women's National Coordinating Committee "Benita Galeana," see Maier 1989.

6. Esteva uses the image of the "hammock" instead of the "web" or "network" to represent a pattern for building grassroots institutions while avoiding an internal or external center (political, ideological, or administrative). He wrote, "Like the web, the image of a hammock holds the idea of horizontality and lack of center. But it opens other possibilities. The hammock is there, where it is placed: one is not inside it, nor part of it, nor a member of it. It can be used or not used when necessary, and for whatever purpose . . . . The hammock, above all, has the quality of adopting the shape of its user" (Esteva 1987:129).

14

Urban Struggles and their Political Consequences

JUAN MANUEL RAMÍREZ SAIZ

Urban popular movements in Mexico are one of the country's three principal independent mass groupings.[1] These movements, which have appeared since 1968, have taken root in the majority of cities in the country. In 1981 they successfully united a large part of their forces within one national coordinating committee—the CONAMUP, made up of *colonos*, tenants, land and housing claimants, and independent associations of retailers and self-employed workers. These organizations are particularly strong in Mexico City,[2] where, in the aftermath of the 1985 earthquake, they made significant political gains and succeeded in many of their demands (Ramírez Saiz 1986b).

Until recently the MUP were understood by theorists and political parties alike as spontaneous mobilizations around immediate demands, which lacked a political vision. But in the twenty years since they began to appear they have gained in social strength, in practical experience, and in organizational coherence. They continue to struggle to solve land and housing problems and to get urban services for their members, but their demands have now broadened to include the defense of neighborhoods and the inner city, on the one hand, and, on the other, participation in urban planning and city government. They now operate in a wider political and territorial context. Moreover, the deterioration and precarious material quality of *colonos'* and tenants' living conditions, along with the legitimacy of their demands, have made the movements representative of a broad consensus within civil society overall. The MUP's capacity for dialogue and their increasingly well-defined view of the state have been decisive factors in the achievement of their objectives. The literature on the different social movements has stressed their reactive and disruptive character more than their ability to take constructive initiatives. This is a valid characterization, but in the case of the MUP it should include recognition of their ability to use the government's legal and technical language to propose viable alternatives corresponding to their demands. It is true that this has only been possible at the level of neighborhoods or locally targeted plans, and not for entire cities or regions, nor for the country as a whole. Nonetheless, it does represent an advance in the forms of the urban movements' struggle.

Although jealous of their own autonomy, the MUP must maintain relationships with the government because the government underpins the sum total of social reproduction (which includes the MUP's own members). Furthermore, the government levies taxes and channels the social wage of the workers, and so is responsible in some degree for providing for collective consumption and guaranteeing the reproduction of the labor force—through social security and health, education, and housing benefits, amongst others (Ramírez Saiz 1987*a*:126–129). The MUP's understanding of these governmental responsibilities does not resolve the ambivalence of their relationship with the government. The MUP reject clientelism and subordinate relationships with the government, but they still expect government to be responsive to their demands. Increasingly they demand not only certain concessions or a response to their needs but also respect for their rights. In other words, they no longer plead for favors so much as demand their rights. The MUP have become a social and political force capable of challenging both the PRI government's clientelist, corporative, and patrimonialist practices, as well as its ideological hold over the majority of the urban population. As a result, they have won the respect of the different political parties, and even the government recognizes them as the legitimate representatives of both *colonos* and tenants.

Let us now look at the overall impact the MUP are having on the political system, through their forms of struggle and through the relationship they have achieved with the government. Two areas deserve special attention: domination and control, and legitimacy and hegemony. With regard to the first of these areas, the MUP's broad social support and the pragmatism of their demands have not prevented state institutions from using repression against them, even if the state's margin of maneuver has been considerably reduced. Furthermore, the rise of independent MUP and the disengagement of co-opted tenant and *colono* groups from the PRI demonstrate that the apparatuses of control are no longer as effective as they once were. The foundations of corporatist and clientelist relations are eroding and giving way to advances in alternative forms of social and political action. Structures of government control are under strain, and the mechanisms of political domination are being undermined. With regard to legitimacy and hegemony, the MUP's twenty-year history and recent resurgence suggest that the state's monopoly on representation is breaking down. The MUP's rejection of the political practices that characterize government's relationship with civil society affects the classic forms of mediation used by government. This means that the general consensus in support of the system is also eroding, and as the system exhausts its legitimizing resources, so also does it lose its ideological hegemony.

The principal elements of the Mexican political system (patrimonialism, clientelism, corporatism) remain, but they are under attack. As yet no profound changes have taken place, but nonetheless political relationships are different from what they were before. For example, the government has found it expedient to open up new areas of negotiation with the MUP and seek to integrate them. Consequently, it has partially modified urban policymaking and implementation. These developments are not so much government concessions as changes won at the margin by MUP mobilization. The changes are small but not insignificant.

The central argument of this chapter is drawn from the political lessons learned from the main struggles of the MUP. The analysis is based on the central areas of contention as defined by the accumulated experience of the MUP in Mexico City: (1) urban land tenure; (2) housing; (3) urban services and infrastructure; (4) neighborhoods; (5) the old city center; (6) urban planning; and (7) metropolitan government. The first three issues correspond mainly but not entirely to the activities of popular organizations on the urban periphery. The remaining four issues have been the special but not exclusive province of movements that mobilize around housing developments and rental housing in the inner city. I have looked at the movements' demands, proposals, and struggles elsewhere (Ramírez Saiz 1987 a:46–51, 73–78; 1987 b:423–476), so here I concentrate above all on their political consequences.

URBAN LAND TENURE

One of the central characteristics of the MUP's operations is the struggle for land. With respect to *colonias* born of land invasions prior to 1980, the MUP have been crucial in defending hard-won gains (by fending off evictions and wholesale resettlement of *colonos*) and in obtaining and registering legal title to urban plots. They have also blocked improper property taxes and managed to reduce the rest. Their main tactics have consisted of strong internal organization in the *colonias* and strong defense of de facto claims to land. These tactics changed after 1980. From this point on, groups of land claimants begin to form and obtain government credits to set up cooperatives for constructing housing and installing urban infrastructure. Urban land is now won through legal means and is collectively negotiated and administered. These practices demonstrate the evolution of the MUP's land claims, from de facto forms of struggle through invasion to legal negotiation and proposals—although never abandoning mobilization and political pressure.

One of the most important results of MUP proposals and struggles over land include their success in challenging and exposing the ambivalence of patrimonialist government policy and practice. It is especially notable that even though land in Mexico is constitutionally the property of the nation, government has controlled it in patrimonial fashion in both city and countryside. Urban land has been used to legitimate and secure government and to co-opt opposition. Such manipulation was not unknown, but it has been repeatedly revealed by the MUP. Faced with a government masquerading as a liberal donor of land, the MUP have proved its complicity with real estate companies that hinder or block the distribution of land to the majority and appropriate (on a greater scale and more often than occurs in popular land invasions) land that rightly belongs to the nation. At the same time, they have countered official arguments about the unavailability of land, particularly ejidal land, for low-income housing. The MUP have been able to show that if the Mexican government has favored numerous groups with urban land, other government practices have become part of the problem and actually work against its solutions (Asamblea 1987).

Moreover, it was unthinkable in patrimonialist terms to grant land to anyone who refused to join the PRI system. The MUP has broken this rule in a growing number of cities. Today the Mexican government has no choice but to keep part of the land for nonofficial popular organizations, even in land reserves the government itself creates.

A similar situation can be seen regarding distribution of financial resources for the purchase of urban land. The MUP have won considerable social support for their right to these resources, forcing the government to grant credit to those independent organizations that can mobilize most support. It takes this course reluctantly, as a lesser evil that may prevent sharper conflicts with the MUP and even achieve a degree of legitimation. The government's basic argument appears to be that it is preferable to help these organizations resolve problems of urban housing, even using government resources, than to confront them.[3]

In the area of urban land-use policy, the government is clearly abandoning laissez-faire tolerance in favor of regulation and planning, e.g., through the creation of land reserves. Because the government prefers to tolerate a *colonia* that it can thus regulate than to have to deal with one that is independent and uncontrollable, it has become less intransigent toward autonomous, popular urban settlements. In other words, it is sometimes easier to accept viable popular demands than always to reject them. Just as the government ultimately accepted the large-scale expropriation of private property demanded by victims of the 1985 quake via the National Coordinating Committee of Earthquake Victims (CUD), the government's 1987 housing program proposed that housing be constructed on the many vacant lots in the city (SEDUE 1987). This was the same proposal made by the Neighborhood Assembly, which the government adapted and called its own.

It is thus evident that the government's patrimonialist land management has been discredited, and that official policy has no choice but to embrace MUP positions. In other words, the government is losing legitimacy, and autonomous popular organizations are finding more room to move in. Both trends could change, but to date they are advancing to the detriment of the political system.

HOUSING

Fewer MUP demands concern housing than access to land, and for a long time the greater number of these concerned rental housing rather than new owner-occupied housing.

The tenants' movement, like that of the *colonos*, has taken extralegal action when legal channels failed to get its demands met. It has also drawn on group and cultural values and so achieved a strong degree of cohesion and a large membership. Cooperation and collective labor for housing construction were commonplace in independent *colonias*. Today such programs for independent construction are commonly replaced by planned self-management, bolstered by lines of community credit. The MUP have set up new organizational and operational mechanisms to underpin the self-management process. Demands and struggles for both tenancy and collective construction gained strength in the most important battles for housing in Mexican history—those of the victims of the 1985 earthquakes and, contemporarily, those of the Neighborhood Assembly.

To appreciate the political impact of these collective experiences it is important to keep in mind that the Mexican government has managed resources for housing programs—both construction credits and mortgages—in the same clientelistic fashion as it has managed urban land. One aspect of this strategy was to grant permits for housing cooperatives almost exclusively to official organizations such as the CTM and the CNOP. Such cooperatives have long served as both an instrument of control and a source of corruption.[4] The MUP challenged the clientelist character of government housing programs and won both credits and authorization for cooperatives without the help of official organizations—so maintaining their own autonomy.

The government's actions with respect to the victims of the 1985 earthquake is a special case in recent housing policy. The national and international news media hailed the government response as a technical, social, and cost-effective success with positive consequences for government legitimacy. This view, however, ignores the exceptional resources available to the government through international aid and financing. More importantly, it ignores that the main points of the reconstruction program were proposed by the National Coordinating Committee of Earthquake Victims. The government's initial plans were both illegal and insensitive to the victims' dearly held traditions and rights. When they were rejected the government had to take on board the MUP proposals. It was a clear victory for the movement.

Some independent victims' organizations chose to build their own housing, without taking part in the official reconstruction program. In spite of the low number of housing units constructed by these independent organizations relative to those built within the framework of the official program, the results indicate that they constitute a significant precedent not only for the cost and quality of the housing but also for the empowerment of the organizations that carried out the construction (Schteingart 1987:14).

In short, government intervention in housing is important but quite limited relative to demand. But clientelism in this terrain is weakening. Housing policy may still act to legitimate the government, but it is a policy in crisis. Moreover, on key points of housing policy like reconstruction, the solutions no longer come from government. On the other hand, independent popular projects are winning social support, even in government-subsidized housing projects for public-sector workers, where there is occasional resistance to government clientelism and manipulation of neighborhood organizations.

URBAN SERVICES AND INFRASTRUCTURE

In a wide variety of ways, urban services and infrastructure contribute to the reproduction of labor and thus form part of the indirect wage intrinsic to the social contract between labor and the state. The MUP mainly push to get services and infrastructure through their own collective efforts combined with pressure on the government—which is anyway responsible for providing them from the resources extracted through indirect taxation, tariffs, and so forth—and hence through their participation in planning and supervision.

In the popular *colonias* on the periphery of Mexican cities, demands for urban services and infrastructure tend to emerge later than struggles related to land and housing. In central neighborhoods where rental housing is the rule, these demands often arise at the same time as demands about rental conditions. In cooperative housing projects, such demands are voiced from the beginning.

In Mexico, as in other countries, as several studies have shown, "state provision of urban services has been one of the most powerful and subtle mechanisms of social and institutional control of everyday life" (Castells 1986:73–86). In the popular *colonias* and neighborhoods, the use of clientelism, on the one hand, or ideological control, on the other, has depended on the particular service provided. Although the two forms of control are not mutually exclusive, the former predominates in water supply, drainage, electric power, markets, road construction, public transportation, and garbage collection; the latter is seen in the provision, or absence of provision, of schools, health services, cultural and recreational resources, and postal or telephone services. On this assumption, every service provided by the MUP's own resources, or by government without loss of MUP autonomy, means a reduction in the government's sphere of influence.

It would seem that such a reduction matches the neoliberal expectations of present government policy. Nonetheless, government clearly wants to withdraw from or reduce its economic commitments in this area without losing political power. But as the services at issue are paid from taxes, the MUP have to insist on continuing participation in policymaking, despite the "slimming down" of the state, just as they exposed the duplicity of the so-called subsidy-reduction policy that stopped certain subsidies or services to households but kept them on those that benefited industry (such as water and electricity). Moreover, the increasing number of MUP-managed schools, pharmacies, stores, consumer cooperatives, and so on suggests still more areas where the social control achieved through service provision is more limited and imperfect (Ramírez Saiz 1988:2–6). In this way the government is losing some of the support generated through the calculated distribution of these services. In other words, the government's neoliberal, antipopular policies are damaging its legitimacy and weakening its capacity for ideological control.

THE CENTRAL AND PERIPHERAL NEIGHBORHOODS

Unbridled expansion in the cities is leading to the breakup of their spatial units, and hence to the fracturing or breakdown of the communities identified with them. In Mexico City, the neighborhood is one such space and community where personal and group loyalties predominate within its boundaries. Neighborhood identity is based on a strong sense of belonging and a distinct local culture, often resulting from the organization and cohesion of the community (Mesa Redonda 1986; Nivón 1988; Mercado 1986; Hannerz 1986; Castells 1986:428). On the urban periphery, neighborhood defense means resistance to expulsion; in the city center it takes the better-known form of fighting attempts at "urban renewal."

Efforts to block evictions of independent popular settlements have been a constant feature of the history of the MUP, not only in cases of organized land invasion but also where claims to land are legalized. One of the most recent attempts at mass eviction involved the victims of the 1985 earthquakes in the center of Mexico City: The government's initial reconstruction plans were based on relocation—removing the quake's victims from their inner-city neighborhoods to the periphery of the metropolitan area. This attempt not only denied popular values and traditions but also infringed on the legal rights enshrined in the certificates of property ownership in the case of the residents of the Nonoalco-Tlatelolco housing project.[5] But the government was forced to change much of the plan by the legitimacy of their demands and their growing support among the population at large. The earthquake victims stayed in their neighborhoods, and reconstruction proceeded according to their own plans. Today neighborhood defense is a central MUP principle, and one that the government includes—or at least pretends to include—in its own plans.

Neighborhood defense is a complex struggle that involves many of the collective practices and demands mentioned above and has many possible political results. Here I will only look at the impact on political culture, and especially on the attitude toward the president in the wake of the 1985 quakes. In this connection it must be admitted that the MUP have sometimes overestimated the role of the president both in the economy and in politics—which is understandable under a presidentialist regime and in a strongly statist political culture. As a result, the MUP's position has been ambivalent, looking on government as the enemy but also making demands based on the understanding that, in the end, it is the government that meets those demands and bestows favors. In this way, the class contradictions implicit in the exploitative mode of accumulation in the city are set aside; thus they underestimate the limitations such contradictions impose on the state's ability to regulate the economy and its class relations or to administer the cities (Navarro 1986:18). Even so, it must be recognized that the mobilization following the 1985 earthquakes constituted "the most important collective questioning of the government, and of its failing paternalist system, in the history of Mexico" (Lazcano 1989). Likewise, recent actions in the Neighborhood Assembly challenge the traditional presidentialist and statist political culture. The MUP no longer act so much to petition the executive as to insist that their rights be respected throughout the administration, along with the governmental responsibilities to which they refer. These initiatives insist that government recognize the organizations of civil society, which are the root of all governmental authority. The Mexican government accepts this principle in theory, but in practice it has governed on the basis of subordination rather than the complementarity that should exist between state and civil society. Thus, the struggles of the MUP and the earthquake victims, as well as of the Neighborhood Assembly, contribute to the belated, difficult, but real consolidation of civil society, and to the assertion of citizenship.

THE OLD CITY CENTER

In Mexico's main cities, including Mexico City, the center is chiefly characterized by the broad range of functions it fulfills (political, administrative, religious, cultural, commercial) and the provision of services, recreation, housing, and even industry and warehouses (Villavicencio 1988). After the 1985 earthquake, the federal government and various environmental groups proposed that the affected inner-city areas be reserved for parks. For its part, the metropolitan government, in its 1984 Federal District Urban Organization and Environmental Protection Program (PRUPE), sought the economic recovery of the center.[6] Without denying the importance of the environmental question, the victims' movement fought to keep a diverse center available to the people, which meant rebuilding what was there before. In effect, the PRUPE of 1986–1988 did preserve both the historical heritage and the residential function of the center. In other words, the combination of mobilization and negotiation culminated in the official adoption of the MUP's position. Today the housing has been rebuilt in the center, where the MUP also organize cultural activities, popular fiestas, and political demonstrations.

There are probably many political repercussions of the adoption of the popular plan for the old city center (and the consequent but possibly only temporary demotion of the government's approach),[7] but it is difficult to calculate their importance for the MUP. The most immediate was the government's recognition of the validity of the MUP's cause, and the need to alter its own plan (as a temporary expedient at least). This indicated a partial victory over official urban policy for the MUP, as I will argue in the following section.

ALTERNATIVE URBAN PLANNING

MUP challenges to official urban planning have been mainly concerned with showing the lack of a technical competence in the official plans (one example being the hasty eviction of the victims of the 1985 earthquake), and with working to slow the implementation of such plans and their related measures. Examples of such measures include the Delegación Cuauhtémoc's 1970 "Plan Guerrero" neighborhood relocation project, the Delegación Tlalpan's limited plan of 1983, the 1984 Ajusco Conservation Project, and the 1985 "Reconstruction Project."

The positive side of the struggle has taken the form of popular urban plans. The MUP have set about this through local and neighborhood projects, cooperative programs of low-income housing that may include urban services—depending on the number of housing units. The first kind of project includes, for example, the Guerrero Cooperative's 1976 improvement plan for the Los Angeles neighborhood, the Movement of Neighborhoods of the Southern Federal District's suggestions for the Local Plan of Urban Development in Tlalpan, as well as the Productive Ecological Colonia Plan and the 1984 Renewal Plan for the villages of Coyoacán. The most important of the cooperative housing projects is the El Molino Housing Program of 1985, with 452 of a total of 1,087 housing units already built. The drawing up of alternative local projects, or counterproposals to official plans, is a relatively new experience for the MUP but one that is growing alongside the founding of independent housing cooperatives.

As a general result of the MUP's successes in showing the limitations of official urban planning, and in blocking some plans and forcing substantial changes in others, this planning is losing both power and legitimacy. In fact, after the planning setbacks following the earthquake, the government has tried to change the process and achieve the kind of corporative agreements (*concertación*) that may recover some social support, and, in lesser degree, underpin past projects. Nevertheless, the proliferation of "popular consultation" at the end of the last and especially the beginning of the present administration, and the creation of councils and commissions (which often have the same role as existing government agencies) does not suggest newly democratic forms of administration and planning so much as a state search for legitimacy and social support.

THE METROPOLITAN GOVERNMENT

The government of Mexico City is unlike that of other Mexican cities.

Between 1917 and 1928 the Federal District contained independent municipalities, but in 1928 the municipal governments were replaced by the metropolitan government (the Federal District Department, or DDF). As a consequence, Federal District authorities are not elected but appointed by the president, and the Federal District has no local legislature. All laws concerning the Federal District are promulgated in the Federal Chamber of Deputies and Senate (Rodríguez 1987). The newly created House of Representatives of the Federal District has no more legislative or executive power than "neighborhood and citizen groups" such as street committees, residents' associations, neighborhood councils, or Mexico City's Advisory Board (Consejo Consultivo).

The MUP have amassed considerable experience of land management and self-government in the Federal District, but not as much as in the independent popular *colonias* of the northern part of the country. The number of MUP-controlled street committees and residents' associations is still relatively small but is increasing at the microlevel of popular settlements. From 1985 on, and especially at the time of the 1988 elections, there was a significant change in the scale and intensity of this sort of collective action. MUP demands and struggles no longer have a merely local (neighborhood or *colonia*) or sectoral (for the benefit of the MUP themselves) character, but rather reach the whole Federal District. Moreover, MUP participation in the 1988 elections, which got many popular candidates elected, was important insofar as the MUP confronted the official party at the polls. Following the elections, neighborhood groups mobilized to defend the results and prevent electoral fraud.

In addition to taking part in elections, the MUP was working to set up the state of Anáhuac in the Federal District. The Neighborhood Assembly played (and continues to play) a leading, unifying role in setting up Anáhuac through a formal convention and is continually pressing to get this project off the ground. It is worth noting that a project of this magnitude is being promoted by a formally nonpolitical sectoral organization.

MUP initiatives have had several effects within the popular *colonias*. In the first place, they have neutralized the influence of the National Confederation of Popular Organizations (CNOP) in an increasing number of neighborhoods and *colonias*. Then, they have broken the PRI government's control over neighborhood organizations in a growing number of *colonias*, and this trend is strengthening. In this way, the MUP are challenging the monopoly representation of the government on the boards of parent associations and other collaborative arrangements at the local level. Finally, civil society and political parties have come to recognize the MUP as independent representatives and advocates for the interests of numerous tenants and *colonos*. All this adds up to an erosion of official forms of urban administration.

The MUP have had a less notable impact on the metropolitan government. In some degree, this is owing to the uncertainty surrounding future political developments in Mexico City. In effect, the crisis of the PRI metropolitan administration does not allow the PRI regime to cede any political spaces in a city besieged by social and electoral mobilization.

CONCLUSION

This analysis of the impact of MUP struggles on the Mexican political system yields two mutually reinforcing conclusions. On the one hand, MUP struggles disrupt traditional patterns of presidentialism, official-party dominance, patrimonialism, clientelism, and corporatism across the whole terrain of government urban planning and policy. Until recently, these traditional patterns provided guaranteed means for buttressing and legitimizing the government or, even in the worst case, for co-opting and controlling neighborhood and *colonia* residents. But now they are no longer so effective. The government is losing its ideological grip on independent popular settlements, and its area of influence is shrinking. Its support is weakening, leading at times to a complete loss of legitimacy. In short, the government has increasingly lost control and monopoly representation of urban popular organizations, which were central to the overall pattern of domination.

On the other hand, the MUP are winning partial victories against both the guidelines and the implementation of official urban policy. They act independently of the government and political parties, and just as they have won recognition and social support for their struggle, so they have increased their capacity for organization, mobilization, self-management, and policy formulation. Much of their legitimacy and strength is derived from the validity of their demands and from their success in resolving vital needs and problems for a large segment of the urban population.

Nonetheless, these trends do not yet compose a clear picture. In many ways, the entire process is only just beginning. On the one hand, the lasting impact of the MUP partially depends on the response of the left, and especially the Party of the Democratic Revolution (PRD), in the present conjuncture. On the other hand, the political system itself is showing its ability to respond and adjust to the MUP and is changing its modus operandi. There are a fair number of isolated events that together suggest that the Salinas administration intends to encourage new initiatives and perhaps even some changes in the rules of the political game. Examples are the administration's moves against the leadership of PEMEX and the managers of the stock market. Still, it would seem that the administration is not so much trying to eliminate the old union and entrepreneurial corporatism as to reconstruct it to fit the new political reality, i.e., to decorporatize by recorporatizing with different rules.

This is also the context for the modernization of the PRI. On the one hand are the forces and interests that want to keep the corporatist structure as it is; on the other hand are those who leave this question aside and focus on the party's links to popular needs, its push for representative leadership and grassroots mobilization. Jesús Salazar Toledano, former PRI secretary in the Federal District, was demoted for favoring the latter view. This demotion was congruent with Manuel Camacho Solís's position during his brief moment as secretary general of the PRI (he is now regent of Mexico City), and that of Silvia Hernández, the secretary of the CNOP, in support of the sectoral structure and corporatist system of the PRI. Their position suggests that, despite the supposed changes, the Mexican political system is in fact reinforcing its corporatist arrangements.

As far as patrimonialism goes, the growing influence of technocratic criteria in government seems to suggest an effort to replace it with rationality and bureaucratic efficiency. But other signals suggest that this tendency is limited. Perhaps the most notorious is the continuing and illicit use of public resources in the PRI's electoral campaigns. The record of recent federal, state, and municipal elections shows that the government is willing to use even the most hackneyed patrimonialist and authoritarian methods in order to recover lost political ground.

The response of the government to the MUP in granting access to housing credits, to urban land reserves, and to local "corporatist pacts" (such as the agreement with the CUD in the Federal District and with the Committee of Popular Defense in Durango) seems to suggest a willingness to change its traditional clientelist practices. Without wanting to downplay this response, I would point out, however, that it only occurs where independent movements have shown considerable cohesion and organization as well as electoral mobilization in support of parties of the left. In other words, the government only cooperates when clientelism is unlikely to work. Nonetheless, the system still uses clientelism within PRI organizations as well as trying to condition the provision of all urban services to independent *colonias* and neighborhoods on the affiliation of their organizations to the PRI. (There is still no consideration that these organizations have a *right* to these services.) In short, clientelist practices persist, as many MUP experiences testify.

In conclusion, it is clear that the government is holding onto and trying to refurbish presidentialism, patrimonialism, clientelism, corporatism, and the official party. But on the evidence assembled here, it is equally clear that these mainstays of the political system are facing serious challenges in the cities.

The MUP reject any link or any agreement with government based, explicitly or implicitly, on these mainstays. They call for a new relationship grounded in reciprocity between government and civil society—as opposed to the subordination of civil society to the government—and in recognition of and respect for civil organization and representation. The MUP arose at the same time as the initial symptoms of Mexico's political and economic decline and are offspring of the crisis. Although this has weakened some of the movements, it has strengthened others whose struggles are challenging all the established ways of doing politics in Mexico.

NOTES

Translation by Joe Foweraker and William B. Heller

1. The others are the teachers' National Coordinating Committee of Workers in Education (CNTE) and the peasants' National Coordinating Committee "Plan de Ayala" (CNPA).

2. Outside the Valle de México, the MUP have strong bases in Durango (Committee for Popular Defense), Monterrey ("Land and Liberty" Popular Front), Tijuana (Committee of United Urban Residents of Tijuana), Chihuahua (Committee of Popular Defense), Guerrero (General Council of Popular Districts of Acapulco), and Tepic (Organization for "Land and Liberty") (Ramírez Saiz 1986a:76–85).

3. One example was President Salinas's pact (*convenio de concertación*) with the Committee of Popular Defense of Durango on February 14, 1989.

4. Most Marxists considered cooperativism as a reactionary utopia and saw self-managed housing as a way of getting popular organizations to take on what was really a basic governmental responsibility (Borja 1988:147).

5. There were some 78,518 persons in this one project prior to the quakes.

6. To this end a management board was set up, overseen by the banking sector, the commercial sector, and the Federal District Department itself, whose real estate interests did not favor keeping popular housing in the area.

7. On February 13, 1989, the Assembly of Representatives of the Federal District declared that it would consult the public over its view of the refurbishment and economic development of the old city center.

15

Popular Mobilization and the Myth of State Corporatism

JEFFREY W. RUBIN

Much of current discussion about popular movements and regime change in Mexico makes two assumptions about Mexican politics: that there has been a breakdown of the corporatist state and that recent popular movements constitute new forms of political activity. Those who make these assumptions look toward an end to the current system, with the PRI disintegrating in the face of a competitive regime (Reding 1989), or to renewed ability on the part of the PRI and the state to outmaneuver oppositions (Zermeño, this volume). Still others look toward the possible consolidation of some arenas of popular movement activity—through a combination of grassroots struggle and state policies—as a potential path for progressive social change (Fox 1989b). All of these analyses evaluate current political conflicts with the view that Mexican politics has changed completely since 1968, and especially in the 1980s; the terrain is new and will yield either a complete disintegration of the once-hegemonic ruling party or a set of negotiations that bear little or no resemblance to those of the past.

In this chapter, I challenge the corporatist state and new popular movements framework. The Mexican state has been considerably less monolithic and corporatist than observers have suggested, and current popular movements are quite varied in their strategies and share important characteristics, with regard to internal structure as well as external relationships, with popular movements of the past. A close examination of the history of the city of Juchitán and the surrounding Isthmus region of southern Mexico since the 1930s supports this alternative view. Because of its focus on a particular—and unusual—region, this chapter is suggestive, not conclusive. It demonstrates that the history and recent politics of Juchitán—the site of one of Mexico's strongest and most enduring grassroots leftist movements, as well as a commercial and transportation center for Mexico's southern states—do not fit with the corporatist state analysis. Although Juchitán's political forms and outcomes are in a number of ways unusual, its divergence from the generally accepted analysis of the Mexican political system is a characteristic it shares with many other regions and sectoral organizations (see Guadarrama S. 1987; Guadarrama 1987; Márquez 1987; Roxborough 1984). My analysis of Juchitán suggests an alternate way of thinking about postrevolutionary Mexico that emphasizes regional and local analysis and suggests that there can be no one national picture.

After discussion of the corporatist state, the essay compares the peasant-worker movement in Juchitán, other post-1968 popular movements, and grassroots movements from earlier in this century. It argues that rather than seeing current popular movements as new political forms operating in a transformed political context, all of these twentieth-century movements are better understood as balancing similar sets of concerns in somewhat similar contexts—changing, nonhegemonic states in perpetual conflict with regional elites and popular movements. This is not to suggest that Mexican politics has not changed since the 1930s—clearly it has—but rather that it has changed numerous times, that it has consistently involved popular challenges, and that the choices available and appealing to the state and to popular movements, if in part new, also resemble those of the past. Thus, it is not accurate to see present conflict primarily in terms of new organizations and state breakdown. This is a distortion that obscures the long-term nature of the conflicts, the uneven presence of official organizations in Mexican society, the regional and local sites of political struggle, and the degree to which popular groups have consistently been initiators of political action (see the introductory chapter, Stern 1987). Furthermore, by obscuring these characteristics of Mexican politics, a focus on state breakdown and new organizations limits our ability to envision and understand the forms of conflict or resolution likely to occur in coming decades.

The corporatist state literature emphasizes the development of a smoothly functioning, one-party, authoritarian system that remained relatively unchanged after 1940 (see Hansen 1971; Bennett and Rubin 1988). The regime exercised social and political control through state-sponsored mass organizations of peasants, workers, and middle-class groups, on the one hand, and through a set of implicit agreements regarding the state's role in stimulating private-sector growth, on the other (see Reyna and Weinert 1977). The regime responded to dissent, within and outside of official mass organizations, with a combination of concessions, co-optation, and repression (see Stevens 1974), and acted to prevent the development of autonomous organizations that could define and represent interests differently from the way the regime itself carried out those tasks (see Eckstein 1977; Montes de Oca 1977). Between 1920 and 1970, the power of several major forces of revolutionary and prerevolutionary periods—regional bosses, the church, and the military—gradually diminished, giving way to institutionalized party rule (González Casanova 1970). Elections were of negligible importance, serving primarily to ratify decisions made from above. According to the corporatist state analysis, this system began to break down in 1968 because the arrangements that had worked so well for so long could no longer deal effectively with a changing economy or with growing demands for greater political accountability. As economic crisis worsened, the Mexican regime showed considerable strain in carrying out the tasks of governing (see Whitehead 1981; Hellman 1983a).

WHAT'S WRONG WITH THIS PICTURE?

There are many important characteristics of postrevolutionary Mexican politics and history that contradict the corporatist state framework. The state coexisted with regional bosses from its beginning, right after the revolution, its unchallenged authority stopping where most political activities started—in the states and regions. The establishment of mass organizations was considerably more uneven than the usual picture assumes, and the formation of the PRI as a political party occurred much later than is generally suggested and was a contested, incomplete process. In addition, elections (though not necessarily fair elections) have been important in Mexican politics, particularly at the regional level, throughout this century.

The interaction between the regime and popular movements of the 1970s and 1980s, in part a response to new economic exploitations and oppressions, is also directly related to conflicts and accommodations that originated in the 1930s or before and have been played out since then in various forms, including but not limited to electoral competition. Mexican politics has been conflictual and turbulent throughout this century. It has not been characterized by successful centralized control but rather by popular and elite challenges bringing about unforeseen crises and resolutions. Furthermore, these matters have been actively debated by Mexicans at local and regional levels throughout the postrevolutionary period, with ordinary citizens and local leaders evaluating and reevaluating claims about economic development, political democracy, violence, and radicalism.

In sum, although there has been a centralized state, an official party, and powerful mass organizations affiliated with the PRI and the regime since the Cárdenas period, these institutions and organizations were established only partially and unevenly. A focus on a corporatist state maintaining political control through mass organizations is only one of several ways to identify the political in Mexican life. The character and course of recent popular movement activity—and of the changes in Mexican politics—are better understood in light of ongoing regional, national, and sectoral conflicts over forms of economic development, political rule, and social life, rather than as the direct outcome of the establishment and breakdown of Mexican corporatism, the establishment of new forms of political organization, or the onset of democratic electoral competition. The following discussion of the history of Juchitán will demonstrate the inadequacy of the corporatist state approach in understanding regional political conflict, Zapotec cultural defense, grassroots mobilization, and regime transformation.

THE COCEI IN THE 1970s AND 1980s:
DIRECT-ACTION ORGANIZING AND ELECTORAL
PARTICIPATION

The Coalition of Workers, Peasants, and Students of the Isthmus (COCEI) formed in Juchitán (population approximately 60,000) during Echeverría's democratic opening in the early 1970s. Through direct-action organizing, *concientización*, and electoral participation, the COCEI established a powerful and militant grassroots movement that succeeded in defending claims to land, credit, wages, benefits, and municipal services. The COCEI withstood periods of fierce police and military repression in the 1970s, including the killing of approximately twenty-five supporters at demonstrations between 1975 and 1977, repeated military occupation of the city, and the arrest and harassment of COCEI leaders and their families. The participation of women—not as leaders but in the process of political *concientización* and organizing, as well as indirectly in the form of maintaining and shaping Zapotec culture was central to this opposition activity. The strength of this culture—including language, dress, elaborate ritual celebrations, residential patterns, music, painting, poetry, beliefs, and historical memories—was in turn central to the COCEI's ability to mobilize people and foster solidarity in the face of repression.

In the 1980s, the COCEI succeeded in pressuring the Mexican government to recognize its victory in the 1981 municipal elections, making Juchitán the first and only city in Mexico with a leftist government. During the COCEI's two and one-half years in municipal office, the movement continued to achieve gains for the city's poor majority, and it began to reshape the nature of public and political life in Juchitán, bringing Zapotec language and culture, as well as the city's peasants and workers, into the town plaza and into public politics. This continued until the COCEI was thrown out of office by the state legislature and the military in 1983, an intervention that resulted in large part from the formation, among the city's politicians and businesspeople, of new organizations that placed increasing pressure on the regime to remove the COCEI, as well as from changes in the national political climate away from recognition of opposition victories in elections.

After 1985, while the army stood guard on the balconies of the city hall, the COCEI was able to emerge from a period of repression, resume its organizing around agricultural and urban workplace issues, and campaign in elections for federal deputy. In 1986 the COCEI once again participated in municipal elections and subsequently joined a coalition municipal government, headed by a *priísta*, in an arrangement overseen by the governor of Oaxaca (see Rubin 1987). In 1989 the COCEI was declared the winner in municipal elections, returning it to control of city government, this time with the PRI forming the minority in a coalition municipal council.

The 1986 coalition government was a startling outcome in a situation characterized by militant class conflict for a period of thirteen years. The way it came about illustrates well the relationship between elections and other forms of political negotiation and conflict in Juchitán. In May 1986, Mexico City authorities had surprised Oaxacans by designating Heladio Ramírez, the most progressive of the precandidates and a longtime supporter of peasant claims within the CNC, as the official candidate for governor of

Oaxaca. This choice represented a clear effort on the part of national authorities to recognize some leftist claims in Oaxaca, taking on entrenched economic interests and regional political bosses in the process. Ramírez in turn chose a young member of the reformist wing of the PRI in Juchitán as candidate for municipal president there, confirming the regime's commitment to reforming the local party. Political leaders in Juchitán, however, responded by physically threatening the newly appointed candidate and replacing him with their own choice. The business and professional group in Juchitán, which had allied with Ramírez, thereupon formed its own organization (MIPRI), refused to support the official candidate, and campaigned actively for abstention and for annulment of the elections.

Despite recent repression, the COCEI entered the 1986 municipal elections with the same strong support it had maintained since the 1970s and ran a short, orderly campaign. As in elections in 1980 and 1983, the PRI was declared the winner, despite evidence of fraud. In response, the COCEI repeatedly blocked the Pan-American highway, carried out hunger strikes, and staged demonstrations, actions that led to the annulment of elections in several towns surrounding Juchitán and marked the first official acknowledgment of the COCEI's regional strength. In Juchitán the COCEI's pressures coincided with the views of businesspeople and the new governor. Ramírez annulled the elections and named as municipal administrator a Oaxaca-based *juchiteco* sociologist who had written a book about the conflict in Juchitán. After lengthy negotiations, both the PRI and the COCEI agreed to participate in a coalition government under this administrator, with half of the offices in the city government going to each group. This arrangement was a partial victory for both the COCEI and the reformist MIPRI.[1]

In Juchitán in 1986, and at earlier times as well, the allocation of political and economic power related directly to electoral competition. But elections were not necessarily fair, and whether or not they were fair, and whether the results were recognized or were not, depended on processes of pressure and negotiation between local political groups and national authorities. The process of voting was accompanied by nondemocratic candidate selection processes, explicit threats of violence (on the part of the local PRI), direct-action mobilizations, media publicity, and policy decisions on the part of both state and national governments. The 1986 coalition, considered democratic by many voters because its composition represented two of the three mobilized groups in Juchitán, was appointed by the governor.

The coalition government in Juchitán may represent a new political form in the Isthmus region and demonstrate the possibility for gradual transformation of the Mexican regime. It is too soon to know whether or not the COCEI will endure as a regional political force, and in what ways it will or will not continue to represent and define the interests of its constituents, as well as relate to regional elites and state and national authorities. At present it is clear that the COCEI participates in municipal government while continuing to maintain considerable autonomy, develop the social and cultural aspects of its movement, and pressure for economic benefits through direct-action tactics. The coexistence of official party and opposition in Juchitán represents a new form of politics in the Isthmus region and suggests the possibility of new forms of representation and opposition in Mexico.

The formation of the COCEI did not result from the breakdown of corporatist arrangements in the Isthmus, and the new political result in Juchitán cannot be explained simply as a regime response to a powerful grassroots opposition. The history of politics in Juchitán does not fit the image of the Mexican regime as an institutionalized state exercising control through mass organizations, and opposition politics did not begin in the 1970s under Echeverría's democratic opening. Instead, the fierce class conflict of the 1970s and early 1980s in Juchitán, as well as the conflicts and accommodations that occurred after 1984, relate directly to reform movements that developed in response to cacique rule in the 1940s and 1950s, to campaigns for internal primaries and the establishment of a functioning political party in the mid-1960s, and to demands for democracy, administrative reform, and more equitable economic development on the part of middle-class and elite reformers in the late 1960s and early 1970s. The success of MIPRI in the 1986 electoral period represents the partial (and perhaps quite temporary) victory of a set of groups, including some Mexico City officials, who had fought for reform for fifty years in Juchitán and in the state of Oaxaca.

THE REGIONAL HISTORY

In the 1930s, revolutionary General Heliodoro Charis, a *juchiteco*, succeeded in establishing a form of cacique-based regional rule that lasted through the end of the 1950s. In an arrangement common to Mexican politics during the 1920s, as well as during Cárdenas's presidency, Charis offered support for the newly consolidating national system in exchange for regional control and a share in federal development money, in the form of schools, hospitals, and highways. Charis achieved this position, despite state-level support for his opponents in Juchitán, the conservative "rojos," through a combination of brief, armed rebellion and a 1934 political compromise with the governor of Oaxaca, arranged during a visit by Lázaro Cárdenas during his presidential campaign (see Hernández Chávez 1979; Gruening 1928).

Despite Charis's enduring role as regional boss, his political control engendered considerable opposition almost immediately, often in coordination with national leaders seeking to establish what they called a more "modernized" or "reformist" politics in the state of Oaxaca. These terms were used interchangeably by groups within the PRI to refer to a new politics that would in theory have promoted economic investment, urbanization, and uncorrupt government, rather than the maintenance of traditional agriculture, monopoly commerce, and indigenous isolation. Federally promoted reform efforts at the state level overlapped with local efforts in Juchitán to unseat Charis in 1946 and 1950, but both efforts failed as the result of broad coalitions in the state capital that mobilized effectively to oppose political and economic change. In the Isthmus, a regional Front for Democratic Renovation (FRD) gained considerable support in an explicitly anti-Charis and antimachine campaign. The front emphasized the corrupt and uneducated characteristics of Charis's appointees, fighting for the entry into politics and administration of educated businesspeople and professionals.

In the course of challenges to Charis's control on the part of local opponents and state governments, an arrangement of shared municipal councils developed in Juchitán. In the 1950s, these municipal councils included both *charistas* and members of the FRD. The presence of this practice in the 1950s indicates that the phenomenon of political negotiation based on unfair elections and closed candidate selection processes—a form of politics that figures prominently in the interaction between state and popular movements in the 1970s and 1980s—did not originate with changing electoral rules in the post-1968 period but rather began during the earlier years of cacique rule. Furthermore, the competition between Charis and the front demonstrates that electoral politics have been important in Oaxaca throughout the postrevolutionary period, a role for elections not easily compatible with the usual corporatist state analysis, which sees elections only as a means for ratification of decisions made within the state and enforced through co-optation and repression.

When Charis died in the early 1960s, a different sort of political battle took shape, centered on the question of how to create a political party. Under Charis, there had not really been a party in Juchitán; *charistas* had gradually begun to call themselves *priístas*, but in name only. In the 1960s the very establishment of a procedurally and substantively viable system of politics and government took precedence over the conflict between the *políticos*—those who had supported Charis and looked to a leadership role beyond his reign—and the businesspeople and professionals—those who had sought the new style of politics and administration advocated by the FRD.

In Charis's absence, there was no agreed-upon system of candidate selection or municipal administration. Furthermore, the official mass organizations that had served to structure political negotiation in some regions of Mexico had not been formed in Juchitán, though local livestock and communal land associations played active political roles. Neither peasants nor workers were organized in official confederations for two reasons: first, there were no large ejidos or industries—the economic enterprises around which the national peasant and worker confederations initially formed—in the southern part of the Isthmus in the 1930s, when mass organizations were consolidated by Cárdenas; and second, Charis saw no need for such organizations and ignored the directives to form them that arrived periodically from Mexico City.

The political battles of the 1960s and early 1970s demonstrate the strength of the local alliance between elites and peasants that had developed during the Charis period. This alliance could conceivably have been renewed

254 CHALLENGING TRADITIONAL REPRESENTATION

in the 1960s if reform efforts had led to new economic and political arrangements between opposing elite groups, and among elites and peasants and workers. Instead, when President López Mateos acted to turn the communal land of the Isthmus irrigation district into an ejido, an elite-led movement against the president's decree established committees in each Isthmus town, effectively rallying peasants against a change that might in the long run have protected them against land loss and indebtedness. By means of this mass mobilization, a broad coalition of elite leaders pressured President Díaz Ordaz, López Mateos's successor, to cancel the ejido decree and distribute private property titles.

The second instance of an elite-mass alliance grew out of the problem of candidate selection in the 1960s. In the middle of that decade, PRI president Carlos Madrazo tried unsuccessfully to introduce internal primaries in the party as a way of resolving the problem of political succession following the deaths of revolutionary-era political bosses. This national effort was a crucial political moment in Juchitán, referred to repeatedly by both PRI and COCEI leaders in discussions not only of political history but also of electoral politics in the 1980s. As a result of the Madrazo proposals, several candidates competed openly in a primary election for the PRI candidacy in Juchitán in 1965. The losing group, however, burned ballot boxes during the subsequent elections, resulting in the annulment of the elections and the appointment of an administrative council. New elections were held six months later, with PRI authorities this time supporting a more popular candidate. Madrazo was killed in a plane crash, and the experiment with internal primaries was abandoned by national leaders.

The inability of politicians in Juchitán to protect peasant land claims or reform its candidate selection procedures severely limited the ability of the local PRI to develop into a political party that could represent *juchitecos* and govern the city. The failure of reform efforts resulted in new splits within the PRI, with opposition committees challenging both the autocratic selection procedures within the PRI and, more broadly, the inability of the party and of regional agencies and programs to effectively promote and manage economic and social development.

In 1971 an opposition electoral coalition initiated the second large mobilization of the elite-peasant alliance. Official victory for the PRI candidate was followed by protests of fraud on the part of the opposition, the annulment of the elections, and the appointment of a civil administration headed by Tarú, the leader of the opposition (though not its candidate). The charismatic leader's appointment to office was widely seen as a popular victory of enormous symbolic and practical importance—the end of PRI hegemony, a triumph of democracy, and the beginning of competent and efficient municipal government. The 1971 electoral situation demonstrated once again that elections in Juchitán are central to the allocation of office and power—and that support and votes matter in the final outcome—even when they are not democratic. Widespread satisfaction with the results suggested that democracy, for *juchitecos*, might mean that the end result corresponds to what is perceived to be the popular will, rather than that fair electoral procedures are strictly upheld.

The combination of the 1971 elections and the formation of the COCEI in 1973–1974 together set the political parameters for the future. The PRI's refusal to respond to a popular, vote-based challenge by itself becoming a responsive party made it possible for the COCEI to gain substantial local support. The Tarú administration, which did not live up to its promises, was the last chance for reform within the system in Juchitán, reform without the fierce conflict, violence, and far-reaching goals of radical, class-based politics. The challenges to Charis on the part of the Front for Democratic Renovation in the 1940s and 1950s constituted the first such opportunity for change, the primary elections of 1965 the second, and the 1971 elections and Tarú administration the third and last. (Of another sort, the ejido decree of the early 1960s was an effort from the outside that could have produced a significant political reorientation.)

In the early and mid 1960s, the nature of the local PRI was not yet clear. It was in the process of becoming a political party—that is what much of the procedural conflict was about. By 1968 the PRI had largely defined itself as a narrow group of leaders who would oppose democratic selection procedures, refuse entry to reformers whenever possible, and tolerate and even promote the use of municipal funds for private gain. In some ways, this was similar to the cacique model of previous decades, reestablished after a brief period of contestation over new economic and political proposals in the 1960s. The newly defined ruling group, however, would now call itself a political party, follow the official procedures of a party, and integrate itself progressively more closely into the Mexican bureaucratic and political apparatus.

THE DEBATE ABOUT POLITICS

During the tempestuous years of the 1970s, debate about politics flourished in family courtyards, town plazas, fields, and offices of Juchitán. The growing domain of the COCEI constituted one forum for this debate, as increasing numbers of *juchitecos*, especially poor peasants and workers, came to identify themselves as members of the COCEI and to attend its meetings, march in its demonstrations, and risk their lives in its confrontations with local and national authorities.

The local newspaper, *El Satélite*, published in Juchitán on Sundays from 1968 until 1979, provided another active forum for political debate.[2] The articles in *El Satélite* about the character of the PRI, the legitimacy of opposition, the difficulties of economic development, and the value and limits of democracy, radicalism, and violence offer a picture of the ways in which *juchitecos* developed and modified their beliefs about politics and economic development. *El Satélite* began in 1968 and 1969 with a philosophy of development and modernization, a reform agenda emphasizing the need for investment, industrialization, and honest politics. Confronting bad government and corrupt agrarian bureaucracies in these years and in the early 1970s, it repeatedly condemned abuses, investigated fraud, and called for accountability. Between 1971 and 1973, the pages of *El Satélite* presented critiques of the existing system and reform agendas that closely resembled the demands made by the COCEI in subsequent years, and they appealed to enlightened government leaders at the state and national level to set things right. Some writers went so far as to suggest a need for political activity on the part of the poor, observing that peasants needed to organize so they could be represented in the system and that only new unions and wage increases could prevent explosive class conflict in industry and commerce.

After 1973, the activities of the COCEI stimulated passionate discussion, continuing to the present day, about the morality of radical politics and state repression, the nature of the COCEI's tie to the people, the role of elections, and the proper place for the military in civilian affairs. The goals of the COCEI were measured against the contributors' changing vision about the proper and necessary form of politics: should reform be sought through fair elections, dialogue, and the maintenance of civil liberties, or could the people get a better deal, and perhaps oust the rich and powerful, only through turbulent class conflict?

Different, often contradictory conceptions of democracy were central to this debate. *Juchitecos* argued for competitive politics, for accountable government, for parties with deep social roots, for freedom from coercion and violence, and for radical economic change. Those who called for democracy sought at different times a system of strong, competing parties, a better PRI, and a new ruling party. In the 1980s, faced with militant leftist government, moderates in Juchitán emphasized legality, dialogue, and conciliation, as well as hope for change and reform within the PRI. Alliance between these moderates and the state, in turn, has shaped the strategies and capacities of both the COCEI and the right. In the absence of formal rules and amidst violence and threats of violence, accommodations could be reached that were based on the ambiguous ideas about parties, elections, the PRI, dialogue, and reform set out in *El Satélite* in the 1970s.[3] Political activity in Juchitán focused on who got what in this process of negotiation.

THE SIGNIFICANCE OF JUCHITAN

The postrevolutionary history of Juchitán provides convincing evidence that Mexican politics cannot be accurately understood as the establishment and breakdown of an institutionalized one-party regime exercising control through corporatist mass organizations. Although the implicit bargain struck by Cárdenas, the governor of Oaxaca, and General Charis was typical of the arrangements that underlay the early years of the institutionalized state, the dynamics of this arrangement—with its reliance on bargaining and autonomy—are not acknowledged in the usual corporatist picture. The nature of the relationship between the state and the region after 1930 was neither institutionalized nor corporatist nor strong, in the way these terms are commonly used to describe Mexican politics. The regional cacique did not form an effective political party, official mass organizations did not supplant local ones, and the PRI did not function to mediate conflict among elites or between elites and masses.

Quite contrary to the corporatist picture, the relationship between elites and masses in Juchitán had been structured in the nineteenth century by rivalries between Juchitán and the outside, as well as by shared Zapotec identity and practices. The multiclass alliance that resulted from this local history was never fostered by the political practices of the PRI for long, and it broke down partly as a result of the economic projects and political practices of the party and the regime. In other words, the PRI contributed to the dissolution of a functioning alliance that predated the PRI and the state. To the extent that the accommodations of the 1980s may inaugurate a time of multiclass coexistence and genuine political representation, this has been achieved only in the period when the strong, institutionalized state is supposed to have ceased to function effectively.

Events in Juchitán demonstrate that elections are not a new phenomenon but rather have been important throughout the postrevolutionary period, with some of the rules changing under the political reforms of the 1970s and 1980s. Electoral competition was a focal point for reform efforts in the 1940s and 1950s, and in the 1960s the role of voting in the selection of candidates, as well as in the allocation of political power, was a central question in local and national politics. Furthermore, the question of voting related directly to the particular ways in which the PRI was formed and developed as a political party as well.

The history of Juchitán makes it clear that the conflict between the COCEI and the regime was shaped by regional conflicts and accommodations that originated during and even before the 1930s. The forms that conflict assumed in the 1970s, as well as the accommodations of the 1980s, can only be understood in light of this preexisting conflict. Almost as soon as it was established, the postrevolutionary arrangement linking regional caciques to Cárdenas and to the PRI faced reformist challenges. This conflict between cacique-based politics and reform coalitions has characterized regional politics in the Isthmus and in the state of Oaxaca from the 1940s to the 1980s. Its lack of resolution during the life of General Charis, the regional boss, left local elites with no base upon which to establish a political party that could incorporate diverse groups and mediate conflict among them in the 1960s. In this way, the forms of political alliance developed in the 1920s and 1930s— and the way they were defended in the 1940s and 1950s—complicated reform efforts in the 1960s, and structured political negotiation in the 1980s.

The national reforms sponsored by Carlos Madrazo might have provided the means for instituting mechanisms of political competition within the PRI. The rigid and closed political party that evolved in Juchitán, with considerable turbulence, by the end of the 1960s elicited an opposition much like the earlier Front for Democratic Renovation, with a base of support among middle-class and elite businesspeople and professionals. This opposition provided an explicit critique of political and administrative corruption and of economic stagnation and inequality, and it mobilized mass support in elections. Thus, contrary to the corporate state analysis, with its emphasis on mass incorporation, elite quiescence, and insignificant elections, it was a group of middle-class and elite citizens within the PRI that first articulated the very critique that the COCEI would put forth several years later and that first mobilized peasants and workers to vote against the official party.

The persistence and complexity of the debates in *El Satélite* during these years demonstrate that *juchitecos* were well aware of the broad significance of politics. Regional battles over economic development and political rule were also battles over the meaning of politics and the desirability, in theory and practice, of particular political forms. Furthermore, again in contrast to the corporate state model, this debate was carried on outside of and in explicit critique of official national politics. As the above discussion illustrates, many of the participants in the debate held ambiguous and changing ideas about the way particular procedures and institutions fit with their goals, the nature of those goals themselves, and the meaning and importance of democracy. If the accommodations of the 1980s in Juchitán rest partly on electoral competition, they also depend on other forms of political conflict and negotiation that have been present and debated in Juchitán for decades.

The presence of the COCEI provided, among other things, the means for the central government, in alliance with local reformers, to begin to achieve in the 1980s what it had been unable to achieve before—"modern" politics where businesspeople and professionals could "clean up the city" and provide a good investment climate.[4] This arrangement, however, could only be achieved by recognizing some of the claims of a radical popular movement. This provides a new perspective for Echeverría's democratic opening in the early 1970s. In contrast to the corporate state analysis, which views Echeverría's reforms as failures—evidence of political breakdown—the recent accommodations in Juchitán suggest that Echeverría unleashed a process of mobilization that got out of control in the 1970s and that provoked new, unforeseen sorts of conflicts and accommodations in the 1980s, some of which strengthened the regime. In order to understand the origins of the COCEI and the possibilities for reform in Juchitán, it is thus essential to abandon the framework of post-1968 breakdown of the corporatist state and see the mobilizations and radical politics of the COCEI as part of a long history of conflict and debate about regional, state, and national power.

COMPARATIVE CASES

This conclusion applies to other regions of Mexico as well. In Sonora, politics in the 1920s and 1930s involved confrontation and negotiation, often centered on elections, between regional bosses, and between civil and military leaders. Supporters of General Calles generally prevailed, controlling access to power and running the state branch of the national party, until they were ousted by the combined efforts of religious groups, peasants demanding land, and leftist politicians when Cárdenas won out in his national power struggle with Calles. Peasant and worker organizations sought and partially gained influence in state politics in the 1930s and 1940s, culminating in the activities of the General Union of Workers and Peasants of Mexico under Jacinto López. These activities mirror in some ways the challenges of the FRD in Juchitán, though popular movements in Sonora during this time represented an explicit class challenge in a way that the FRD did not. The successful exclusion of these challenges from Sonoran politics in the 1950s was followed by new forms of organization and opposition within the official party after 1958, and by a series of reform movements, similar to those in Juchitán, in the 1960s. When reform negotiations failed, furthermore, broad popular movements mobilized around gubernatorial elections, a phenomenon similar to the mobilizations in support of opposition candidates in municipal elections in Juchitán (see Guadarrama 1987:45–47).

The regime responded to the radical challenge posed by the 1975 land invasions in Sonora with federal intervention and land expropriation. Land recipients went on to form the Coalition of Collective Ejidos of the Yaqui and Mayo Valleys, an enduring rural organization of collective agricultural enterprises that negotiates successfully with state agencies and addresses the economic and social needs of its members. Business groups responded to their weakened position, first by transforming the PAN into a strong opposition in the 1980s, and then in 1985 by conducting preelection negotiations with the PRI candidate for governor and supporting him in the elections (Guadarrama S. 1987:104–105). This pattern of events closely resembles that in Juchitán, with reform movements within the PRI giving way to class-based challenge, regime intervention, and, in the 1980s, the coexistence of an enduring peasant movement and a strengthened position for probusiness reformers within the PRI. As in Juchitán, furthermore, Sonoran politics does not fit the framework of corporatist peace, post-1968 breakdown, or the appearance of new popular movements. Sonoran politics was not strongly corporatist, but rather was characterized by conflicts among regional bosses, on the one hand, and among bosses, popular movements, and reform groups on the other. Politics involved ongoing challenges to regional authorities, both electoral and nonelectoral, with the class-based conflicts of the 1970s and 1980s closely related, as they are in Juchitán, to the conflicts and accommodations of earlier periods.

Analysis of the Chihuahuan town of Namiquipa poses another sort of challenge to the corporatist state framework. The twentieth-century history of the town, which played an active role in the revolution, including support at alternate moments for Mexican and North American troops, cannot be understood in the context of the national events and patterns of incorporation posited by the corporatist state view. Instead, the nature of the town's own "project"—the significant events in local history and the *namiquipenses'* understanding of their identity and political interests in the context of those events—best explains the townsp. ople's political allegiances during the revolution and their role in alternately supporting and opposing the political goals of state officials in the postrevolutionary period (Alonso 1988; Nugent 1989). This suggests, as do events in Juchitán and Sonora, that discussion of national politics must return repeatedly to local histories of debate and conflict, and that neither the revolution, the Cárdenas period, nor 1968 represent clear-cut divisions between past and present.

POPULAR MOVEMENTS IN POSTREVOLUTIONARY MEXICO: AUTONOMY, NEGOTIATION, AND DEMOCRACY

The COCEI and other post-1968 popular movements share a number of characteristics with labor and agrarian movements of earlier periods. Past popular movements, like recent ones, relied on direct-action organizing and local networks of identity and solidarity, had leaders who had been exposed to urban environments and radical ideologies, paid considerable attention to issues of democracy and participation, and joined peasants, workers, and urban dwellers in implicit and explicit alliances. They were wary of ties to outside organizations, participated in elections as one form of political activity, and negotiated with political leaders and state institutions.[5] The decisions about electoral participation, political party affiliation, and involvement in coalition government made by the COCEI in the 1970s and 1980s can be compared to the ways earlier popular movements accepted or rejected national reforms and joined, with varying degrees of willingness and varying results, with national political parties and labor and peasant confederations.[6]

Popular movements of the past twenty years can thus be seen as a continuation, with some important variations, of what have been characteristic forms of political activity in Mexico throughout this century. The contexts in which these oppositions have occurred—and therefore the ways in which they have balanced enduring concerns for negotiation, autonomy, and democracy—have changed repeatedly since 1900, rather than once after the revolution and again after 1968. The history of twentieth-century opposition labor movements illustrates these related points about continuity and change, as does the constant presence of peasant mobilization and protest in the Mexican countryside. Furthermore, both of these histories support the challenge to the corporatist state framework discussed above.

Radical industrial unions with strong anarchist tendencies formed under the Díaz regime, carrying out major strikes in 1906 and 1907, and the anarcho-syndicalist Casa del Obrero Mundial organized Mexico City workers during the revolution. In the 1920s, the anarcho-syndicalist General Confederation of Workers (CGT), with considerable support from railway and textile workers, repeatedly challenged the progovernment Regional Confederation of Mexican Workers (CROM). Industrial unions contested the growing hegemony of antileft and antidemocratic leaders in the CTM in the mid-1930s and mounted significant leftist challenges to the imposition of state-sponsored leaders in the industrial unions, as well as to the one-party regime more generally in the late 1940s. A variety of unions, including railway workers', teachers', and doctors', fought again to reestablish democratic practices in unions in the late 1950s and the 1960s. In the 1970s, insurgent movements took the form of breakaway, independent unions, rather than acting as oppositional groups within official unions.[7] In the 1980s, in the face of strong and often successful state opposition to union militancy, some of the most enduring movements for union democracy, like the democratic teachers' movement, have occurred within official unions.

In the agrarian sector, regional peasant movements became revolutionary armies under Zapata and Villa. Militant movements for land reform in the 1920s and 1930s in Veracruz, Yucatán, and Michoacán were followed by periods of organizational formation within collective ejidos and conflict with state agricultural agencies in the 1930s and 1940s. Renewed forms of militancy, emphasizing autonomy and direct-action mobilizations, were led in the northwest by Jacinto López and the UGOCM in the 1950s, and in several southern states in the 1960s, some of them culminating in guerrilla movements in the south in the 1970s. In the 1970s and 1980s, peasant movements, like labor insurgencies, alternated between independent stances, favored, for example, by most of the members of the National Coordinating Committee "Plan de Ayala," and efforts to mobilize for democracy and economic well-being within the official National Peasant Confederation (CNC) or within other organizations affiliated with state institutions, such as unions of ejidos.

Post-1968 popular movements are not new, in the sense that observers have claimed, because they share important characteristcs with a succession of earlier mobilizations. At the same time, popular movements and the state have both changed, often in interaction with one another, in the years since the revolution, as have national and international economies—so that the goals and strategies emphasized by oppositions, as well as those of the regime, have assumed different forms. Study of twentieth-century Mexican politics should focus not on corporatist peace and subsequent upheaval but rather on the specific ways in which conflict between popular movements and the regime have affected political and economic life in succeeding decades.

POPULAR MOVEMENTS AFTER 1968

One of the most significant differences between earlier and more recent popular movements appears to be the unwillingness on the part of post-1968 popular movements to accept alliance with or incorporation in national and official organizations.[8] Although this commitment to autonomy has remained relatively constant in the past two decades, there has at the same time been a discernable change in the ideology and practice of popular movements between the 1970s and the 1980s, with the balance shifting away from militant rejection of the institutions and practices of the state and capitalism and away from insistence on unifying ideologies and vanguard leadership. Instead, popular movement activity in the 1980s has emphasized, alongside continuing mobilization, a process of negotiation with the state and participation in elections, on the one hand, and diversity and forms of internal democracy within organizations and coalitions of organizations, on the other. It is on the basis of these 1980s characteristics, as well as on the phenomenon of autonomy, that observers have begun to speak of recent popular movements in Mexico as a new form, at times also characterizing them as new social movements.[9]

Willingness to participate in elections and negotiate with the state, however, albeit different from the strategies of many popular movements of the 1970s, suggests continuity with popular movements of preceding decades. Recent strategies in some ways resemble the willingness on the part of many popular movements to cooperate (often under duress) with Cárdenas in the 1930s and with official organizations in the 1940s and 1950s. What is different is the priority placed on continuing autonomy. But it is not yet clear to what extent it will be possible to maintain autonomy and negotiate successfully in the future. Salinas's *concertación social* promises this, but only for groups that have demonstrated enduring strength, and even then it is not clear what sorts of trade-offs will be necessary. In addition, autonomy in the past did not always disappear abruptly but rather in the course of several years or a decade. Popular movements that appear to be autonomous today may gradually lose their distance from the regime—and contribute to changes in the regime—as a result of benefits and repression over a number of years.

Both kinds of popular movements, those maintaining militancy and rejecting negotiation, and those emphasizing diversity, negotiation and electoral participation, have existed both in the 1970s and the 1980s and during earlier periods. In Monterrey, for example, the leaders of Tierra y Libertad, acting upon a Maoist ideology, sponsored land invasions and self-government, explicitly rejecting negotiation over squatters' rights and electoral participation (Garza del Toro and Pérez Güemes 1984). The COCEI's hostility toward leftist political parties in the 1970s and early 1980s represents a similar insistence on local autonomy. In other places, leaders of popular movements have chosen to rely primarily on negotiation rather than militant mobilization. By combining limited mobilization with a more conciliatory stance, popular movements such as the Union of Ejidos Lázaro Cárdenas and the National Union of Regional Peasant Organizations (UNORCA) use ties to regional and national government officials and agencies, as well as to outside advisers, to secure both autonomy and concrete objectives of rural agricultural development (Fox 1989a; Fox and Gordillo 1989).

Movements such as the democratic wing of the Coordinating Committee of Workers in Education (CNTE) act to change official organizations from within, using the rules of the institutions themselves, together with ongoing mobilizations, to bring about internal democratization, at the same time supporting broader movements for radical political change (Cook, this volume). Still other popular organizations, such as the National Coordinating Committee of the Urban Popular Movement (CONAMUP) and some of its member groups, including the Committee for Popular Defense of Durango (CDP), encouraged mobilization and negotiation but explicitly rejected electoral participation in the 1970s and early 1980s, yet supported such activity after 1985 (Hernández S. 1987; Cruz et al. 1986).

Electoral participation, which has been important in popular movement strategies and activities in recent years, has always been part of a broader, largely nonelectoral politics. In addition, elections have been focal points for popular protest throughout the twentieth century. Recent changes in political strategies regarding elections are best seen as part of ongoing, shifting definitions of and opportunities for negotiation, autonomy, and democracy rather than as part of a historic turn to formal democratic procedure. In Juchitán, elections have been a central aspect of popular opposition, though by no means the only one, as Charis attempted to oust the conservative elite after the revolution. Similarly, elections have been important to the COCEI since its formation, although the movement's electoral participation has never been more than one part of its political strategy, and the distribution of political and economic power in Juchitán, as well as the character of Zapotec cultural identity, have been shaped and contested in a variety of political forms and arenas.

While in office during parts of the 1980s, the COCEI continued to defend workers and *campesinos* through nonelectoral means in matters such as working conditions, irrigation rates, and agricultural credit, thus maintaining the strategies of militancy and mobilization it had developed in the 1970s. This might prove a difficult balance to keep up in coming years, particularly as the COCEI enters its second consecutive period in office. The choices faced by the COCEI as it participates in government are similar to those encountered by the leftist movements of the 1920s and 1930s that first defended independence and later joined Cárdenas's national confederations, still seeking to defend their constituents and maintain autonomy.

The COCEI demonstrates the complex nature of what has been characterized as the shift, in the 1980s, away from militant rejection of the institutions and practices of the state and capitalism and toward negotiation, electoral participation, diversity, and internal democracy. In terms of electoral participation, the COCEI's political strategies matched those of other 1980s popular movements, such as the UNORCA and the CDP of Durango. All of these movements began to define autonomy not as the rejection of official institutions but as the successful representation and negotiation of opposition claims within state agencies and official organizations. At the same time, like the COCEI, most other popular movements of the 1980s have combined direct action with participation and accommodation. Rather than representing a definitive shift to participation in elections and engagement with state

institutions, the recent strategies of popular movements demonstrate that
negotiation and participation coexist with mobilization and direct action in
successful grassroots politics. And past patterns of conflict and change in
Mexico suggest that future circumstances—continuing economic deprivation,
Salinas's economic and political "modernization," changing U.S. policies
toward Mexico and Central America—may contribute to a return to more
confrontational, revolutionary stances.

Accepting new forms of participation in official politics, the COCEI has
nevertheless acted to encourage diversity in only very limited ways, and
it has not fostered formal procedures of internal democracy. In these ways,
it remains distinct from organizations like the CNTE, which emphasize
formal democratic procedure in internal organization and decisionmaking,
and the CONAMUP, which seeks to unite a wide range of different
organizations without insisting on uniformity. Although the COCEI has
recently participated with some success in statewide direct-action and
electoral alliances, its coalitions continue to depend more on unified political
strategies and the dominance of COCEI leaders than do the alliances
established by many other popular movements. In addition, the COCEI
continues to favor leadership-based forms of organizing and decisionmaking,
with mass participation focusing on consultation, mobilization, and
neighborhood solidarity rather than on explicit procedures of representation
or collaborative decisionmaking.

POSSIBILITIES FOR FUTURE TRANSFORMATION

If the balance between different kinds of popular movement activity shifts
further toward electoral participation, autonomy, diversity, and internal
democracy—if these become *the* prevailing characteristics of popular
movement activity over the next decades—then there will indeed be a new
form of leftist opposition in Mexico. In this genuinely new scenario, popular
movements favoring militant rejection of the state and capitalism, as well as
vanguard leadership and grassroots uniformity, on the one hand, and those
willing or forced to exchange autonomy for concessions, on the other, will
disappear; popular movements successfully committed to autonomy *and*
negotiation *and* diversity will become the predominant form of leftist
opposition. If fair elections also become an ongoing attribute of the Mexican
regime, then the coincidence of a new form of popular movements and new
regime rules would together transform the Mexican political system, bringing
about formal democratization and perhaps changing political and economic
power relations in Mexican society to favor those who are now excluded.
This is what is envisioned by many who expect that Cuauhtémoc Cárdenas
and the PRD will one day lead a majority electoral coalition.

The points of similarity between popular movements of the earlier and
later parts of this century suggest, however, that this formal democratization
might not happen or that, if it does, it might not include an autonomous role

for popular movements. The ways in which popular movements have defined their objectives and the constraints under which they have chosen from among them have changed in the course of the postrevolutionary period, but there has been no linear path from less to more autonomy or democracy, and there is no reason to suppose that there will be one in the future. There have instead been several cycles of growing popular movement activity in twentieth-century Mexico, as well as several periods of increased regime responsiveness and accountability. The popular movements of the revolution were shaped and constrained under Obregón, in one form by activities like the *zapatistas'* role in agrarian reform, in another by the military campaigns and the control yielded to regional generals in the 1920s, and in yet another by the formation of a national party in 1929. The organizations and mobilizations of the 1920s and 1930s were reshaped during the Cárdenas years through inducements and coercion that fostered, among peasants and workers, a trade of autonomy for land, wages, and the right to form ejidos, peasant federations, and labor unions.

Peasant and worker movements of the 1940s and 1950s mobilized in the context of anticommunist campaigns, the reorganization of the official party, the continuing (though contested) power of regional and sectoral caciques, and the pervasive model of economic growth of the postwar period. Each of these sets of popular mobilizations influenced the structure of the state and the policies employed by the regime to maintain order and promote particular economic, political, and cultural policies.[10] Although further research may well reveal that specific forms of state and popular movement activity predominated in each decade or period, 1968 does not represent a dividing line between successful and failed corporatism, between old and new popular movements, or between rejection and acceptance of formal democracy.

A shift to negotiation, autonomy, and electoral participation on the part of popular movements, together with increasing formal democratization, could lead to a radically new politics. But past politics in Juchitán, the views of *juchitecos* with regard to democracy and political parties, and the cycles of popular movement growth and change that have characterized twentieth-century Mexico all suggest that new kinds of arrangements, rather than formal democratization, will be the more likely result of recent conflict. Both the left and the different groups within the PRI in Juchitán, as elsewhere, have been fighting for a say in bargains over political power, economic development and distribution, and cultural identity. It is possible that some or all groups will at some point agree on the desirability of fair elections; it is more likely, however, that they will continue to develop arrangements that interweave a variety of political mechanisms and goals.

Furthermore, formal democracy would not necessarily transform the entire political system but rather modify the rules by which it functions. If future developments favor forms of incorporation and autonomy for popular movements, perhaps including formal democratization, then the ways in which the COCEI and other popular movements seek to balance militancy and negotiation, direct action and electoral participation, and autonomy and party affiliation will directly affect the course of political representation and democracy in Mexico. Will popular movements participate in a repeat of the Cárdenas-era pattern, involving both persuasion and coercion, of exchanging benefits for incorporation and demobilization, or will they find ways to maintain and expand a new political role for Mexico's peasant and worker majority?

TOWARD A NEW UNDERSTANDING OF MEXICAN POLITICS

Abandoning the framework of corporatist breakdown and new popular movements allows us to pay attention to the nature, location, and substance of political battles in Mexico—what people have fought over historically and how these battles shape recent conflict. The corporatist story drops history out at every turn. Rather than examining the long-term nature of conflict between regime and opposition, it observes only that conditions changed after 1968 and asks whether or not new forms of political control will meet new challenges.

Instead, we need to recognize that national politics has been considerably more complex than the corporate analysis acknowledges, and that the national story is only a partial one that exists alongside of, in tension with, and enmeshed in numerous complex regional histories. If we want to understand present conflicts, we should not force them into a mold of popular movements committed to negotiation, internal democracy, and electoral participation, and a PRI with limited ability to respond to challenges to its hegemony. Rather, we should look at regional politics as continuations of long histories of conflict among popular movements, elites, and party and state actors over who gets what economically, politically, and culturally, as well as on what terms a centralized state is incompletely, ambiguously, and impermanently established.

NOTES

1. The reform proposals of progressive *priístas* in Juchitán do not acknowledge the underlying causes of poverty or challenge the prevailing patterns of economic development. Rather, they focus on administrative efficiency and an end to corruption, much like reform movements that opposed machine politics in U.S. cities.

2. At various times, writers included residents of Juchitán, as well as *juchitecos* living in Mexico City, students and prominent older local leaders, poets, businesspeople, lawyers affiliated with the PRI, and leftist leaders.

3. This is what the current ambiguity in Mexico regarding elections is about, and why it may not be correct to say there is a groundswell for strict procedural democracy in the 1980s. Each of several political actors in Mexico pursues a variety of goals, among which procedural democracy might be one; it has in the past been negotiable for other economic and political benefits, and this might prove to be the case in the future as well.

4. These are the terms in which members of the business and professional group within the PRI (MIPRI) in Juchitán describe their political goals.

5. A number of different cases, such as the peasant league of Veracruz, the agricultural mobilizations in the Comarca Lagunera, and early industrial unions suggest these similarities for the 1920s and 1930s. See Salamini 1978; Carr 1987; Roxborough 1984; Craig 1983 and in this volume. On successful and unsuccessful collective ejido organizations in the 1930s and subsequent decades, see Stavenhagen 1975 and Hellman 1983a. And on railway workers in the 1950s, see Alonso 1972 and Stevens 1974. The Popular party and the UGOCM, founded by Vicente Lombardo Toledano after the 1947 purge of Communists from the CTM and active through the early 1950s, are also important sources for comparison; they are mentioned briefly in Roxborough 1984:22–24.

6. The history of the *zapatistas* suggests that the necessity for constant trade-offs among negotiation, autonomy, and democracy were as central to the strategies of popular movements early in the century as they have been more recently. See Womack 1968, in particular the discussion of the failure of the *zapatistas* to reach an agreement with Carranza's representatives (chap. 7) and the nature and consequences, after Zapata's death, of Magaña's alliance with Obregón (chap. 11 and epilogue). Hamilton (1982) describes the mix of coercion from above and political strategy on the part of opposition movements and parties that led to the incorporation of many labor and peasant movements under Cárdenas.

7. Roxborough (1984:31, 34) summarizes his analysis of labor history, from which these examples are drawn, by emphasizing "the continuing and widespread combativeness of large sections of the industrial labour force," and he concludes that "corporatist control over labour in Mexico is both weaker and more uncertain than the standard account implies."

8. Greater openness to this sort of arrangement in the earlier period resulted both from the state-centered, centralizing ideologies of the left and from the perceived possibility of achieving satisfactory bargains under the Cárdenas administration and, at times, under subsequent administrations as well.

9. That popular movements are new and that they are "new social movements" should be seen as two distinct claims. (I disagree with both of them.) In discussing Mexico, one can reject the new social movement framework, based as it is on the assumption of a postclass, posteconomistic politics, and still argue that popular movements in Mexico, rooted largely though not exclusively in economic and class conflicts, represent a new form of political mobilization. See Habermas 1981 for the new social movement framework, Fals Borda 1986 for an analysis that fits more closely with Latin American societies, and Knight, this volume, for a discussion of Mexico.

10. See Bennett and Rubin 1988 for a comparison of regional popular movements and state responses in Juchitán and Monterrey in the 1970s and 1980s.

5

Conclusion

16

Institutional Context and Popular Strategies

ANN L. CRAIG

Were popular movements in Mexico after 1968 part of a sea change in Mexican politics? The answer to this question is shaped by the assessment of how new these popular movements are and of what the state's responses have been or are likely to be in the future. The question itself raises issues of theoretical and political significance. Theoretically, it requires us to specify the fundamental relationships among social composition, demand, popular strategy, and state initiative and response. Politically, if they are new, recent movements may be a force for change toward more democratic social relations in Mexican civil society and in the Mexican regime. If they are a continuation of past patterns of mobilization and resistance, and if the state's patterns of accommodation and repression are a persistence of old responses, then anticipation of regime change is premature.

It is around the need to justify 1968 as a benchmark that the question of what is new about popular movements first emerges. Most contributors to this book have a preference for 1968 as the watershed year that marks changes in popular strategy and demands and, in smaller measure, in state policies toward popular movements. The state's violent response to the student movement was followed by a strategic shift by many student activists into popular grassroots organizing and toward a more deliberate strategy of horizontal coalitions. For example, Pérez Arce contends that 1968 marked the emergence of a generation of student leaders who have participated "in all of the important popular movements [of the last two decades] and in every attempt to build new parties and other political organizations." Moreover, the state's response to the student movement raised broader questions about the legitimacy of the regime and the fallibility of the state and incumbents.

My own view is that there is both continuity and change in Mexican popular movements, particularly if we extend the time horizon to cover a rough comparison of 1918–1938 with 1968–1989. There are remarkable parallels—but also some sharp contrasts, particularly in the legal and institutional context of popular mobilization. The contextual changes are associated with modified popular demands and strategies. This chapter addresses the debate about the novelty of contemporary popular movements by focusing on composition, demands, popular strategy, and state response to

271

popular movements, comparing the early and late twentieth century.

NUMBERS AND DEMANDS OF POPULAR MOVEMENTS

Are there *more* popular movements within Mexican civil society in the last twenty years than in the past? We are unable to say whether there were more popular movements in 1989, in real or proportional terms, than in earlier periods of Mexican history. As Knight points out, we simply do not have adequate data for making this judgment. We may have the impression that there are *more* but that organized groups continue to represent a distinct minority of the population. Most contributors would agree with Foweraker ("Popular Movements," this volume) that their numbers are less important than their location, practices, and demands in the current political-economic context.

If we define popular movements principally on the basis of their social composition (peasants, workers, low-income urban residents), then there is clear historical continuity in popular political mobilization in Mexico. As Knight points out, Mexico has regional and community traditions of resistance and mobilization. The apparent continuity is sustained if we describe popular demands as multidimensional—principally protests against unequal social and economic conditions, emerging out of class position but always or often with moral, political, and social dimensions (see, for example, Knight and Rubin, this volume).

From this perspective, contemporary popular movements are not very new. Anyone who has undertaken archival research can find in documents of the 1920s and 1930s that popular organizations of peasants, workers, and low-income urban residents made at once economic/material and political demands. Most demands were localized. Some were put in the "sphere of reproduction," although the balance appears to have shifted further in that direction in recent decades in terms of the numbers and scale of movements protesting inadequate housing, high rent rates, cost of living, and so on.

Nonetheless, if we compare the 1920s and 1930s with the 1970s and 1980s, the essays in this volume point to some important differences both in the nature of demands put and in popular expectations from the state. In the 1920s and 1930s, what was at issue were the rights of peasants and workers vis-à-vis landlords and industrial capital (thus class-linked, if not class-"conscious" demands), or they were struggles against gross abuses of power. Activists appealed to the state to guarantee rights in relationships within civil society. The laws to which petitioners typically appealed were the constitution and the emerging state and federal labor and agrarian codes. Throughout this period, the petitions of popular movements treat the state and individual actors within it as the arbiters of social interests, the guarantors of the rights among groups in civil society. Sometimes individual incumbents or caciques are the target of protest, but on balance the incumbents, more than the system of representation or mediation (the cacique, not *caciquismo*), are under fire. The petitions are predominantly for the state or state functionaries to intervene and hear the appeals of popular groups (see Craig, "Legal Constraints," Knight, and Rubin, this volume).

In the 1980s some popular movements continue to make comparable claims and appeals—for example, for land in urban and rural areas, the use of forests, and the opportunity to form unions or recover lost wages. Some continue to seek state intervention for the resolution of conflicts within Mexican civil society. In addition, however, some popular movements not only call upon the state to protect the rights of citizens vis-à-vis other actors or communities, but also for the state *itself* to respect peasants', workers', and citizens' rights. Thus the demands now are not only for protection of rights and the satisfaction of material needs as between groups in society (for example, some of the struggles of the Nineteenth of September Garment Workers Union), but also between groups in society, on the one hand, and the state, on the other. Moreover, some popular movements not only plead for material and political favors, they demand the right of political representation (see Foweraker, "Popular Organization," Harvey, Ramírez Saiz, and Tarrés, this volume).

This shift to demands against the state and for representation are the result of the federal state's expanded presence in geographic and political space over the last sixty years. Federal government functionaries and agencies have penetrated into the hinterland. State agencies have proliferated to include, for example, federal ministries for water resources and urban planning, state banks for agricultural credit and marketing, and institutions that provide public housing and medical care. The control over these agencies and resources has remained highly centralized. This, combined with the arbitrary implementation of the law and service delivery, has turned the state into a direct party to many conflicts. Often now, the popular movements' adversary—employer, property owner, provisioner of services and credits, regulator of prices and wages, abuser of power—is the state itself. Furthermore, changes in the laws or in their interpretation or implementation have brought the state directly into disputes over land reform, labor union recognition, and electoral practices. For this reason, we argue that the demands made by popular movements are best described as the outgrowth of the organizing experience, the consequence of interactions between popular movements and other actors in civil society and the state laws, institutions, and practices (see, for example, Foweraker, "Popular Organization," Craig, "Legal Constraints," Munck, and Tarrés, this volume).

These are subtle but significant changes in the target and nature of demands now being made by popular movements in Mexico. I am hard pressed to described them as a sea change in Mexican politics. The changes have been gradual. There is no sudden moment when the tide turns nationally. Old issues have not been abandoned; new ones have been added. The political consequences of these changes in demands will depend on popular strategy and state response.

STRATEGIES AND PRACTICES

Are popular movements and the state now employing new strategies and practices, different from those they employed in the 1920s and 1930s, or before 1968? Most of the contributors agree that strategic choices, like demands, are "contingent," the result of interaction among state institutions and laws and popular movements. (This insistence on contingency makes causal and comparative analysis particularly complicated.) Because over time laws have changed, state agencies have proliferated, and institutions have been modified, even strategies that *appear* to be similar (electoral competition or the imposition of union leaders, to cite two current examples) are not the same, for the context in which they occur has changed enough to alter their consequences. If strategies are contingent and context is always changing, then no strategy is ever *really* the same. I turn first to a review of popular strategic choices and then to state responses and an examination of the state context for popular strategic choice.

Popular Strategies

Since the revolution, popular movements have exercised a wide range of strategic or tactical options. Demands are typically posed within the law, yet popular movements have not been self-limiting to legal strategies. The preceding chapters describe numerous specific choices: civil strikes, sit-ins in public offices, formal and informal alliances with other popular movements, cultural events and education campaigns, marches (long and short), voter mobilization and electoral participation, hunger and labor strikes, and alliances with political parties and other popular movements, to name a few. Rarely are these employed in isolation. Although some of our contributors have begun this analysis here and elsewhere, we need more research to explain how strategic decisions are taken within popular movements. Moreover, because leadership has been relatively deemphasized in most studies of recent popular movements in Mexico, we know relatively little about differences in strategic preferences between leaders of popular movements and rank-and-file members.

Much of the political debate and the theoretical analysis of popular movements focuses on two key sets of choices: the decision to work with syndical corporations or agencies of the state, and the decision to form strategic alliances (Foweraker, "Popular Organization," this volume). Occasionally the analysis centers on these key choices as if the options were starkly drawn: incorporation and clientelism versus mass mobilization. Yet as Cook, Harvey, and Rubin demonstrate, negotiation and participation coexist with mobilization and direct action in grassroots politics. When the choices are posed in this way, it appears that there is popular strategic continuity from the 1920s to the present.

The previous essays suggest, however, that several practices of contemporary popular movements are new. Through their strategic choices as well as their demands, popular movements are undermining traditional mechanisms of control (*charrismo*, corporatism, *caciquismo*, and clientelism) in favor of autonomous organization (*autogestión*) and local leadership selection. Popular movements treat these state practices as problematic not only because they lead to vertical control and imposition and may be unresponsive to demands, but also because of their arbitrary application of the law (Foweraker, "Popular Movements," this volume). By establishing competing, relatively autonomous organizations, popular movements challenge one of the fundamental precepts of corporatism, that is, monopoly of representation through state-chartered institutions. The demand for representation and the search for horizontal coalitions built from the ground up also weaken the vertical controls and centralized decisionmaking of corporatism (Foweraker, "Popular Movements," and Tarrés, this volume). The internal democratic practices within some popular movements—such as broad participation, rotation of leadership, and collective decisionmaking—further undermine traditional mechanisms for control and establish new practices for self-regulation, new skills, and natural leaders (Carrillo, Harvey, and Logan, this volume). Let us examine the novelty of these practices.

Linkages between popular movements and the state. In the 1920s and 1930s, popular organizations might look to ally with sympathetic figures in the state (a José Guadalupe Zuno, Margarito Ramírez, Alvaro Obregón, Francisco Múgica, Saturnino Cedillo, Lázaro Cárdenas, or Adalberto Tejeda) in order to secure access to the resources of the state and the protection of the law in support of peasant or worker demands. If popular movements chose not to take up arms against the state, the institutional options for making their demands were twofold: They could channel them through newly formed trade unions or peasant leagues or the confederations of each as they emerged. Alternatively, popular movements could act through nascent political parties, most of which had a regional domain.

Both the corporatist and party options tended to drive popular organizations into clientelistic relationships with caudillistic regional politicians. Such relationships held out the promise that groups could benefit from access to agencies of the local or federal state that dispensed resources or guaranteed rights. Both options also tended to shape popular organizations' demands in sectoral, economic terms by channeling them into *campesino* or trade union institutions that defended the rights of each sector specified in the law. There was little legal or political protection for the expression or formation of feminist demands. Nor were there many appropriate venues for channeling demands for representation or participation in decisionmaking.

Similar strategic options exist today: working through corporatist structures and clientelistic affiliation with individuals and political parties. But there are now few caudillos or white knights within the federal or local state to defend the interests of popular groups. Individuals who make promises comparable to those of a Cárdenas or Zuno would be in opposition political party organizations such as the old PMS or the new PRD. A clientelist affiliation with such organizations (which is not what most movements seek) does not imply the same access to resources or protection as it did half a century ago with regional caudillos. Opposition political parties have the *potential* to redirect popular political strategy away from alliances with state functionaries, state-based political leaders, caciques, or corporatist structures and toward political parties in opposition that promise to use state good offices to protect popular interests. So far, however, this option has rarely been taken by popular movements.

Not only do these strategies lack the promise they held in the past, but some popular movements actively reject them as alternatives. Part of what characterizes the demands of many contemporary popular movements is an attack on the perceived practices of the state—on clientelism, *caciquismo*, corporatism, and presidentialism. Whereas in the past the attack may have been on incumbents, today it is on state practices and mechanisms for political control. The most blatant assaults are verbal. But it is also in some quarters a piecemeal attack through the practices of popular movements that gradually erode state control (Ramírez Saiz, this volume) and wear on the regime. Contemporary movements do not militantly reject the entire regime, rather, they insist on their ability to maintain autonomy while negotiating with it. That insistence becomes in practice a rejection of key regime institutions.

The preceding chapters point to several such practices among popular movements—the collective provision of some of their own services and housing, physical planning of their own communities, direct selection of leaders in open competitive elections, discussion and agreement upon agendas and strategies through the participation of an ample portion of movement members, and the formation of national coordinating committees outside sectoral institutions. Together, these activities, although they may not be widespread, challenge the PRI government's hegemony.

Popular movements in the 1920s and 1930s also called for autonomy and local representation in decisionmaking. But their demands for autonomy ("independence") were more commonly made with respect to other actors in civil society, such as *hacendados* in the case of land reform movements. Now the state is the target of the petitions. Demands for autonomy as we have defined it—the right to organize independently and to negotiate movement demands without vertical imposition—appear to be relatively more widespread in the 1980s than in the 1920s and 1930s.

In the 1980s this demand for autonomy most directly affects clientelism and corporatist institutions. Some popular movements may in fact challenge corporativist systems of control, even when these are not their explicit target. One thinks, for example, of the Nineteenth of September Garment Workers Union, which sometimes struggles to organize against company unions (*sindicatos blancos*) affiliated with corporatist unions, although the latter were never the controlling, verticalist institutions of the PRI government that they have been in the case of the SNTE or the CNC (Carrillo, this volume). Nor are they regarded as the principal enemy. In this case, the de facto challenge to corporatism comes in the independent organization life outside the official labor unions and in the struggle within the Labor Conciliation and Arbitration Board.

In the past, some of the early peasant organizations that challenged rural corporatism took shape as a response to ineffective representation by official institutions. The UGOCM and the CCI were established because the CNC simply failed to represent demands for land to the state (Harvey, this volume). For some movements, however, such as the CNTE, autonomy means eventually dismantling corporatism.

Thus, whether by intent or simply as a consequence of what they *do*, contemporary popular movements in Mexico undermine many of the traditional institutions and mechanisms of control that linked civil society and the state. Both the state and popular movements are engaged in reshaping these linkages.

Popular representation and the formation of horizontal alliances. Like their current counterparts, movements in the 1920s and 1930s also posed representational demands. Popular movements sought and won representation on early labor conciliation and arbitration boards for workers, and in state legislatures and municipal councils. Although the representation of independent popular movements in these bodies was a relatively short-lived and regionally isolated experiment that ended by about 1940, popular movements in the 1980s were not the first to realize that state power should be conquered—even locally—in order to address the demands of popular movements. Indeed, as Rubin reminds us, even the *zapatistas* learned this lesson.

National sectoral organizations and loose horizontal coalitions were also formed in the 1920s and 1930s to compete with official unions, such as the CROM, and the emerging official party. In some respects these were dissimilar to the current coordinating committees as they were often associated with regional caudillos' attempts to establish a personal power base, as was the case, for example, of the early National Peasant League (LNC) with Adalberto Tejeda. Nevertheless, like the current coalitions, these were also affiliations sought out by local and regional movements as mechanisms for securing external support, protection, effective interlocutors, and allies who might help them advance toward their goals.

Under Echeverría's reforms, the labor struggle for representation took place largely within—or in parallel—syndical corporations: it was a struggle for voice within corporate institutions as well as an attempt to have those institutions more directly reflect the voice or preference of members in their interactions with the state (Cook, this volume). In the countryside, *campesinos* formed credit and marketing unions outside of the CNC, some of which were regionally successful, though not part of a national confederation (Harvey, this volume).

By the late 1970s the strategic innovation adopted by regional or sectoral popular movements was the establishment of national coordinating committees such as the CONAMUP, CNPA, and CNTE. They involved the exchange of information, some leadership training, and some collaborative strategies such as for mass mobilizations. These horizontal coalitions joined small local struggles and spawned new ones. Some of these opposition fronts were multisectoral, as in Chiapas (see Harvey, this volume). Pérez Arce argues that without these national organizations, struggles would have been confined to regions, perhaps limited to a shorter life, and unable to achieve the same breadth of social groups. But because they were loose, relatively nondirective, and required to respond above all to local struggles, even with a national presence their impacts have been principally regional.

The struggle for representation at this level was designed to assure a *capacidad de gestión* for popular movements with respect to state institutions so that the former could negotiate the adoption of popularly defined solutions to pressing political-economic problems. The coalitions with other popular movements or political parties were designed to achieve that objective.

By the mid- to late 1980s, the alliance strategy shifted toward the intensification of a struggle for representation in the electoral arena—although not, as before, for the official party to be more responsive to representatives of popular groups. Popular groups began to compete directly for positions of state power in Juchitán, Durango, Baja California, and elsewhere (see Rubin and Tamayo, this volume).

In Mexico there has always been a degree of interpenetration between popular movements and political parties, or activists from them, and electoral coalitions have been locally important in different regions since the revolution (see Craig, Knight, and Rubin, this volume). For the most part, however, after Lázaro Cárdenas, popular movements cast their lot with individual candidates of reformist wings of the PRI in hopes of receiving their favors. Now the preferred option may become to compete for public office directly, perhaps in coalition with opposition political parties. Thus, the willingness of popular groups to contemplate electoral strategies and alliances with opposition parties is a shift but not an entirely new phenomenon.

The decision to extend the struggle for representation into the electoral arena has not been a cost-free strategy for popular movements. Leaders of popular organizations took the initiative in turning to progressive political parties in February 1985 to develop pacts for electoral competition. Until 1988 these were not, in general, very successful efforts, in part because the rank-and-file members of movements were not persuaded about the strategy or the candidates. Candidates supported by movements seldom won, but, more significantly, participation in electoral campaigns weakened, divided, and exhausted movements (see Tamayo, this volume).

In 1988, however, the broad membership of many popular movements turned to Cuauhtémoc Cárdenas and urged leaders to support his candidacy. This was not only a horizontal electoral alliance among popular organizations but also a vertical voting coalition that included some dissatisfied nationalist elements of the middle classes (Foweraker, "Popular Movements," and Tamayo, this volume).

State Strategies

This book was conceived as a response to state-centric studies of Mexican politics and regime transition. We have tried to draw attention to initiatives for change from within civil society as they are expressed by popular movements. These essays focus on how the state shapes—without totally determining—the organizational form, discourse, and demands of popular movements. Our goal is to explain processes within popular movements, not within the state. Most of the authors have not taken on the additional task of explaining how state institutions, laws, and practices emerged, what interests they reflect, or how state strategic decisions were taken.

The contributors are convinced that popular movements seek to be active subjects in Mexican politics, not simply passive targets of state policy. Public policy research in Mexico has seldom treated popular movements as active agents for policy change. Although we prefer to study popular movements' impact on the state from the vantage point of civil society, we nonetheless encourage further research by the "statists," beyond what we have presented, which might examine how state policy choices are shaped in response to popular movements.

Key strategic options for popular movements were characterized above as the decision to work with syndical corporations and agencies of the state, and the decision to form alliances. The counterpart options for the state would be the decision to sustain syndical corporations and state agencies, and the decision to cooperate with popular movements. These are often posed as choices between accommodation or control and co-optation. Yet, as in the case of popular movements, a wide array of instruments and practices have been employed, ranging from the violent and repressive through intimidation to negotiation.

The state responses to popular movements described in this volume include electoral fraud in municipal, state, and federal elections but also fraud in union recount elections, nullification of dissident union registration or recognition of compliant unions, withholding permission for public demonstrations and marches, sanctioning strikebreaker unions, political assassination, military occupation of communities, controlling mobilizations with police and army units, selective access to credits and inputs, arrest and harassment of activists, and control over media coverage, among others. We do not have the data to demonstrate whether the balance is shifting nationally among these several practices in a direction that reflects a redefinition of relations between the state and civil society. Several of the essays suggest that the state's margin of choice has been narrowed by economic as well as political crisis. It remains as yet unclear whether narrowed options will lead to a shift toward greater accommodation or toward more exclusionary and violent state responses.

Some essays in this volume contend that clientelist, presidentialist, corporatist state practices are eroding under the pressure of popular movements' practices (see for example, Foweraker, "Popular Organization," Ramírez Saiz, and Tamayo). This challenge limits the effectiveness of practices traditionally employed by the state to control political organization and to mediate its relations with civil society, reducing state options for strategic response to popular pressure.

Other contributors question whether there has been such a dramatic shift (see Knight and Rubin). To be sure, they also describe clientelist or cacical politics, but associated with a PRI that has been less corporatist, less centralized, less hegemonic, and perhaps with a more limited repressive capability than many contend. For them, the key political phenomena is *caciquismo*, and although it has been modified, it is still a continuous and intractable feature of Mexican politics. From this perspective, the possibility of popular movements forcing political change looks much less promising.

Moreover, many social groups (such as people employed in the informal sector and the middle and upper classes employed in private industry or transnational corporations) have no place in the existing corporatist shell (Tarrés, this volume). Whereas between roughly 1918 and 1968, corporatist institutions drew activist groups in toward the PRI government or severely limited their expansion, now large sectors of the population that are becoming restive have little institutional access to or claim on the state.

In my view, the Mexican state has been more porous and less absolutist at the local and regional level over the last sixty years than many critics have claimed. Controls have been more subnational, cacical, and clientelist than state directed. State and party institutions have differentially penetrated regions as a system of controls. Corporatist institutions have been relatively weak in some regions (for example, the CNC in Chiapas) and more permeable in some industries (for example, automobiles; see Roxborough 1984). In others, such as the Laguna and Chiapas, state agencies such as Banrural and the Ministry of Agriculture have been more important than corporatist institutions.

But if effective national corporatism was a "myth," (see Rubin) it kept company with another myth of a strong, directive central state, widely accepted not only by scholars but by average Mexicans as well. The myth drew its strength from the conviction that the system of local control would be externally, vertically sustained by the state, even if incumbents or caciques might be forced to abdicate. The vision of the state was hegemonic and corporatist, even if the vision did not hold up under careful scrutiny. Like cultural myths and children's fairy tales, the vision could be used to secure order, except among the willful or desperate who insist on traveling "where the wild things are."

Where corporatist institutions and state agencies did successfully mediate relations between the state and civil society, the current economic crisis should weaken their effectiveness. For the foreseeable future, the state will have a much diminished resource capacity to finance the services with which popular groups have been incorporated in the past, although, as Knight points out, scarce goods can still be concentrated in critical localities. The existing corporatist shell, as he calls it, risks becoming more fragile or transparent even among those social groups and in those regions where it has been effective in the past. The neoliberal economic project is changing how political institutions in Mexico function.

What are the political consequences of an economic project that may dismantle corporatist institutions? The project itself is not directly a state strategy for dealing with popular movements, but it is changing the institutional, legal, and resource context within which they must act. In the past some popular organizations accepted corporatism for the benefits of the social pact (Foweraker, "Popular Movements," this volume). The neoliberal economic project removes even the sugar coating on the corporatist pill by wearing away at the pact, reducing subsidies to goods of popular consumption, increasing unemployment, changing state services, and privatizing economic relations.

The modernization project makes the problem of assessing the political changes brought about by popular movements more difficult. Not only are corporatism and clientelism challenged from below but the state itself is undermining how these practices work, and President Salinas and other would-be reformers within the political elite actively seek alternatives to them (Cornelius, Gentleman, and Smith 1989; Tamayo, this volume). If the myth evaporates, the corporatist shell collapses, and the hegemonic vision changes, analysts may only be able to demonstrate that popular movements contributed to their demise in concrete instances and specific localities.

The state has shaped—but not dictated—strategic options and popular discourse through institutions, laws, and policies that mediate relations between the state and civil society. The state does not in this way *create* popular movements. Popular movements have been able to develop strategies positively, opportunistically, which take advantage of the laws and divisions within and among state institutions and incumbents to put demands to the state and urge compliance with the law. Yet they have not resisted going outside the law with land invasions and unauthorized demonstrations, for example, when such a choice seemed necessary.

The state has also amended the legal context within which popular mobilization has developed since 1968. Labor law revisions in 1970 opened the door to independent unions (see Pérez Arce and Cook). Changes in agrarian reform laws and policies pressed some peasant organizations into credit and marketing agendas (Harvey, this volume; Fox and Gordillo 1989; Otero 1989). The several "political reforms" provided (limited) incentives for electoral competition to groups in opposition, especially on the left. These latter reforms created opportunities to develop alliances between popular groups and political parties in opposition.

The alliances among popular movements and political parties, and the struggles between the state and popular movements, present an opportunity for change. The Mexican state, the parties, and the movements can together negotiate the construction of new institutions to link the state and civil society. Or the state can resort to the more exclusionary and repressive practices that correspond to the hegemonic and corporatist myth.

IDENTITY AND LEADERSHIP IN POPULAR MOVEMENTS

By limiting this book to popular movements as we have defined them, and to assessing their impacts on state institutions, laws, and practices, we have set to one side changes in Mexican society that may yet be "prepolitical" and more appropriately the province of ethnographers and social historians. Two topics emerge from the essays in this book as bridges between ethnographic and political research on popular movements: identity and leadership. Each begs for further inquiry and research as it relates to processes of popular organization and strategic choice. Each will require in-depth field research grounded in specific case studies.

Identity, political culture, and consciousness appear here and there throughout the book as important variables in explaining the formation of demands (Carrillo, Harvey, Logan, Munck, Rubin, and Tarrés), strategies (Logan), and the discourse and alliances (Carrillo) of popular movements. The most detailed conceptual exposition of identity is offered by Munck, who argues that we cannot understand collective demands or strategies without knowledge of the process of identity formation. Identity, he contends, is not just based on ascriptive criteria such as ethnicity, gender, community, class, or occupation. Identities are not given but are collectively constructed through the interaction between social groups and their environment, particularly political parties and the state. This broad conceptualization recognizes the temporal and situational specificity of identity, and that nonclass identities can be equally important (with class) in shaping popular movements' demands. From this perspective, autonomy becomes the right of members of social movements to determine their own collective or community identity.

Consciousness, conventionally associated with class and defined roughly as the awareness of a class position of exploitation and a disposition to act against it, appears here in conjunction with gender and politics (Carrillo and Logan, this volume). Here female consciousness "arises out of a culturally framed division of labor that assigns to women the responsibility for preserving life" (Logan, this volume, quoting Kaplan, 1982). In this framing of the issue, women's demands in popular movements arise out of gendered power relations within civil society. That these issues become publicly contested is symptomatic of the "changing boundaries of the political" (Munck).

In the past, identity and political culture were treated as attributes of actors that influenced their political behavior. The literature on political culture in particular focused on the relationship between the distribution of political values as cultural givens and the nature of the government, or the relationship between individual citizens and the government (the classic source is Almond and Verba 1963).

In contrast, among the contributors to this book we might find majority agreement that identity or consciousness or political culture are actively constructed, acquired through experiences of struggle and interaction with the environment, including other actors in civil society, political parties, and the state. They are by-products of popular political practices, not simply ascriptive characteristics.

Political culture still tends to be described in terms of distinct attitudes or values or concrete demands, such as for transparent elections and democracy. Current references to political cultural change in Mexico (for example, Bartra 1989; Loaeza 1989; Monsiváis 1987) try to explain collective democratic demands and behavior. Like Munck's, theirs is a more society-focused, less individual- or state-centered approach that emphasizes that political culture is shaped and formed in interaction with the state (for example, Pérez Arce and Tarrés).

These concepts—identity, consciousness, and political culture—have been employed in this book to refer to phenomena that bind people together in popular movements, shaping their demands and discourse and facilitating cooperation with other popular movements. Yet the contributors have not here focused either theoretically (except for Munck) or empirically on these processes.

This analysis confronts a profound methodological dilemma over how to investigate these collective processes. How are we to describe these collective identities and track processes by which they are formed? Can we only know the identity, consciousness, or political culture of a movement from the demands made and the strategies adopted? If we describe identity, consciousness, or political culture on the basis of the formal political demands put forward by popular movements, we may misread them. Most popular organizations conformed to the law. Laws encouraged political practices defining men (usually not women), and communities, in different social and political categories (*acasillados*, *jornaleros*, *obreros*) at distinct moments in time. Similarly, they permitted or discouraged certain patterns of alliance formation. The law therefore, shaped the form of popular demands and the social groups from which they were likely to be expressed. The state could be expected to hear wage and labor disputes but not complaints about social treatment and human dignity. The state established procedures whereby unions could be recognized but not women's organizations. Should we then assume that women or ethnic groups are just now "discovering" their identities simply because popular movements are only now putting forth such demands? It seems that we must recognize that state practices facilitate the expression of some identities and may help to shape the formation of others. But we must also recognize that the legalist interactions between popular movements and the state are probably an imperfect or partial expression of the social identities within Mexican society.

The approach favored by the contributors to this book emphasizes collective processes of struggle and interaction among groups and the state as the most important and immediate sources for popular identities. This suggests another line of ethnographic and political inquiry related to identity and political culture that is not fully developed in this book. Among popular movements, self-conscious attempts by leaders and political parties to shape identity and politic-al culture may take place at cultural events (Harvey), at church gatherings (Tarrés), or at union meetings (Carrillo), much as they did in earlier anarchist and syndicalist movements. Because autonomy and internal democratic practices are so important to popular movements, there has been a marked reluctance to deal with leadership as a variable explaining strategic choice, organizational formation, and recruitment. Only in the cases of the women garment workers, COCEI, and the CNTE do we have references to the nature of movement leadership or to the relations between leaders and the social bases of popular movements.

Yet one of the distinguishing features of popular movements in the last two decades, and one of the arguments for 1968 as a benchmark year, was the emergence of a generation of student leaders who have become "the seeds of a new political culture" and "catalysts of a new political perspective that was national in scope." Elaborating, Pérez Arce (this volume) contends that middle-level cadres of the student movement "filled leadership positions in the insurgent unions, or acted as advisers or simply supporters. Many militants of the working-class insurgency were afterwards party organizers or nonpartisan activists in the urban popular movements. There is continuity. There is diffusion. This is the creation of a new political culture."

There is still ample room for research to document the nature of the influence exercised by the generation of 1968 on popular movements in Mexico. It is unlikely that students *created* those popular movements. It is possible that they became organic leaders of them. It is more likely that they sought out communities with a tradition of protest, that they gravitated to situations and localities where movements were brewing. And that where they did not contribute to open breaches within these movements, they became interlocutors among and between popular movements and political parties and—more infrequently—with the state and its institutions.

Systematic studies of leadership and the formation of political identity, culture, and consciousness should include careful consideration of the internal practices of popular movements. The essays in this book make only passing reference to movement practices for discussing demands, selecting leaders, making strategic choices, and forging alliances. The strategies adopted by popular movements for negotiating with the state shape the possibility of meeting movement objectives and transforming state-society relations in Mexico. The internal practices of the movement have the further potential for modifying relations within Mexican civil society. They may also help to shape the effectiveness of movements in their confrontations with the state.

Bibliography

Abbagnano, Nicola. 1974. *Diccionario de filosofía*. Mexico: Fondo de Cultura Económica.

Aboites, Hugo. 1984. "El salario del educador en México (1925–1982)," *Coyoacán* 16.

Aboites, Hugo. 1986. "Sesenta años del salario del educador (1925–1985)." In *México: los salarios de la crisis*. Cuadernos Obreros del Centro de Documentación y Estudios Sindicales del Trabajo, A.C. Mexico: Centro de Documentación y Estudios Sindicales del Trabajo.

Adams Dennis, Philip. 1976. *Conflictos por tierras en el valle de Oaxaca*. Mexico: Instituto Nacional Indigenista/Secretaría de Educación Pública.

Adler, Judith. 1970. "The Politics of Land Reform in Mexico, With Special Reference to the Comarca Lagunera (1935–1967)." Master's thesis, London School of Economics and Political Science.

Aguilar Solís, Samuel, and Hugo Andrés Araujo. n.d. *Estado y campesinado en la Laguna: la lucha campesina por la tierra y el excedente*. Folleto de Divulgación, vol. 1, no. 5. Saltillo, Coah.. Universidad Autónoma Agraria Antonio Narro.

Alcántara Ferrer, Sergio. 1977. "Collectivist Peasant Organization in La Laguna, Mexico: 1930–1970." Paper presented at the seventh national meeting of the Latin American Studies Association, Houston, Texas, November.

Almond, Gabriel A., and Sidney Verba. 1963. *The Civic Culture: Political Attitudes and Democracy in Five Nations*. Princeton, N.J.: Princeton University Press.

Alonso, A. 1972. *El movimiento ferrocarrilero en México*. Mexico: Era.

Alonso, A. 1988. "U.S. Military Intervention, Revolutionary Mobilization, and Popular Ideology in the Chihuahuan Sierra, 1916–17." In *Rural Revolt in Mexico and U.S. Intervention*, edited by Daniel Nugent. Monograph Series, no. 27. La Jolla: Center for U.S.-Mexican Studies, University of California, San Diego.

Alonso, Jorge. 1985. *La tendencia al enmascaramiento de los movimientos políticos*. Colección Miguel Othón de Mendizabal. Mexico: CIESAS.

Alonso, Jorge. 1988. "La investigación antropológica y los movimientos políticos." In *Teoría e investigación en la antropología social mexicana*. Cuadernos de la Casa Chata, no. 160. Mexico: CIESAS/Universidad Autónoma Metropolitana-Iztapalapa.

Alvarado, Arturo, ed. 1987. *Electoral Patterns and Perspectives in Mexico*. Monograph Series, no. 22. La Jolla: Center for U.S.-Mexican Studies, University of California, San Diego.

Alvarez, Sonia. 1989. "Women's Movements and Gender Politics in the Brazilian Transition." In *The Women's Movement in Latin America*, edited by Jane S. Jaquette. Boston: Unwin Hyman.

Amnesty International. 1986. *Mexico: Human Rights in Rural Areas. Exchange of Documents with the Mexican Government on Human Rights Violations in Oaxaca and Chiapas*. London: Amnesty International.

Anderson, Rodney D. 1974. "Mexican Workers and the Politics of Revolution," *Hispanic American Historical Review* 54:94–113.

Arreola Ayala, Alvaro. 1985. "Atlacomulco: la antesala de poder." In *Municipios en conflicto*, edited by Carlos Martínez Assad. Mexico: Instituto de Investigaciones

Sociales, Universidad Nacional Autónoma de México.

Arreola Ayala, Alvaro. 1988. "Gustavo Baz: del zapatismo a las instituciones." In *Estadistas, Caciques y Caudillos*, coordinated by Carlos Martínez Assad. Mexico: Instituto de Investigaciones Sociales, Universidad Nacional Autónoma de México.

Arriaga, María de la Luz. 1981. "El magisterio en lucha," *Cuadernos Políticos* 27 (January–March):79–101.

Asamblea de los Barrios de la Ciudad de México. 1987. "Vivienda y suelo urbano suficientes," *El Día*, suplemento *Metrópoli*, August 10.

Ashby, Joe. 1967. *Organized Labor and the Mexican Revolution under Cárdenas*. Chapel Hill: University of North Carolina Press.

Azaola Garrido, Elena, and Esteban Krotz. 1974. *Los campesinos de la tierra de Zapata*. 3 vols. Mexico: CISINAH.

Aziz Nassif, Alberto. 1985. "La coyuntura de las elecciones en Chihuahua, 1983." In *Municipios en conflicto*, coordinated by Carlos Martínez Assad. Mexico: Instituto de Investigaciones Sociales, Universidad Nacional Autónoma de México.

Aziz Nassif, Alberto. 1987. "Electoral Practices and Democracy in Chihuahua, 1985." In *Electoral Patterns and Perspectives in Mexico*, edited by Arturo Alvarado. Monograph Series, no. 22. La Jolla: Center for U.S.-Mexican Studies, University of California, San Diego.

Barros, Roberto. 1986. "The Left and Democracy: Recent Debates in Latin America," *Telos* 68 (Summer):49–70.

Bartra, Armando. 1979. "El panorama agrario de los setentas," *Investigación Económica* 150.

Bartra, Armando. 1980. "Crisis agraria y movimiento campesino en los setenta," *Cuadernos Agrarios* 10/11 (December):15–66.

Bartra, Armando. 1985. *Los herederos de Zapata*. Mexico: Era.

Bartra, Elí, et al. 1983. *La revuelta*. Mexico: Martín Casillas.

Bartra, Roger. 1989. "Changes in Political Culture: The Crisis of Nationalism." In *Mexico's Alternative Political Futures*, edited by Wayne A. Cornelius, Judith Gentleman, and Peter H. Smith. Monograph Series, no. 30. La Jolla: Center for U.S.-Mexican Studies, University of California, San Diego.

Bennett, Vivienne. 1989. "Urban Public Services and Social Conflict: Water in Monterrey." In *Housing and Land in Urban Mexico*, edited by Alan Gilbert. Monograph Series, no. 31. La Jolla: Center for U.S.-Mexican Studies, University of California, San Diego.

Bennett, Vivienne, and Jeffrey W. Rubin. 1988. "How Popular Movements Shape the State: Radical Oppositions in Juchitán and Monterrey, Mexico, 1973–1987." Paper presented at the Fourteenth Latin American Studies Association International Congress, New Orleans, March.

Bensusan, Graciela. 1985. "Construcción y desarrollo del derecho laboral en Mexico." In *El derecho laboral*, edited by G. Bensusan et al. El Obrero Mexicano Series, vol. 4. Mexico: Siglo XXI.

Birnbaum, Pierre. 1988. *States and Collective Action: The European Experience*. Cambridge: Cambridge University Press.

Boletín Interno de Organización Revolucionaria Punto Crítico. Guión de la discusión sobre la cuestión electoral, (April 27, 1985).

Borja, Jordi. 1981. "Movimientos urbanos y cambio político," *Revista Mexicana de Sociología* 43:4 (October–December):1341–1369.

Borja, Jordi. 1988. *Estado y ciudad*. Barcelona: Promociones y Publicaciones Universitarias.

Boschi, Renato. 1984. *On Social Movements and Democratization: Theoretical Issues*. Occasional Papers in Latin American Studies, no. 9. Berkeley: Joint Center for Latin American Studies, Stanford University/University of California, Berkeley.

Boschi, Renato. 1987. "Social Movements and the New Political Order in Brazil." In *State and Society in Brazil: Continuity and Change*, edited by John D. Wirth, Edson de Oliveira Nuñes, and Thomas E. Bogenschild. Boulder, Colo.: Westview.

Brading, D. A., ed. 1980. *Caudillo and Peasant in the Mexican Revolution.* Cambridge and New York: Cambridge University Press.

Brandenburg, Frank. 1964. *The Making of Modern Mexico.* Englewood Cliffs, N.J.: Prentice-Hall.

Brooks, David. 1987. "Mexico: Whose Crisis? Whose Future?" *NACLA Report on the Americas* 21:5/6 (September).

Buve, Raymond. 1975. "Peasant Movements, Caudillos, and Land Reform during the Revolution (1910–1917) in Tlaxcala, Mexico," *Boletín de Estudios Latino Americanos y del Caribe* 18:112–152.

Buve, Raymond. 1982. "The Tlaxcala Revolutionary Movement: Its Identity, Struggles for Power, and the Land Issue (1910–1919)." Paper prepared for a Social Science Research Council Conference on Mexican Peasant Movements, New York.

Calderón G., Fernando. 1986*a.* "Los movimientos sociales frente a la crisis." In *Los movimientos sociales ante la crisis,* edited by F. Calderón G. Buenos Aires: CLACSO.

Calderón G., Fernando. 1986*b. Los movimientos sociales ante la crisis.* Buenos Aires: CLACSO.

Calderón G., Fernando, and Elizabeth Jelin. 1987. *Clases y movimientos sociales en América Latina.* Buenos Aires: CEDES.

Camacho, Daniel. 1987. "Movimientos sociales, algunas definiciones conceptuales," *Revista de Ciencias Sociales* 37–38 (September–December) San José, Costa Rica.

Cammack, Paul. 1988. "The 'Brazilianization' of Mexico?" *Government and Opposition* 23:3 (Summer):304–320.

Camp, Roderic Ai, ed. 1986. *Mexico's Political Stability: The Next Five Years.* Boulder, Colo.: Westview.

Campa, Homero. 1988. "Dividida en grupos y corrientes, la disidencia magisterial de Chiapas se destruye en pugnas internas," *Proceso* 586 (January 25):25–27.

Canabal Cristiani, B. 1981. "Política agraria, crisis y campesinado," *Revista Mexicana de Sociología* 43:1 (January–March):274–287.

Cárdenas, Cuauhtémoc. 1988. Speech to the Instituto Politécnico Nacional, March 3, reported in *La Tuerca* 30 (March 1988):2.

Cardoso, Fernando H. 1984*a.* "La sociedad y el Estado," *Pensamiento Iberoamericano* (Madrid) 5a (January–June):25–36.

Cardoso, Fernando H. 1984*b.* "A Democracia na América Latina," *Novos Estudos* CEBRAP 10 (October):45–56.

Cardoso, Ruth. 1983. "Movimentos sociais urbanos: balanço crítico." In *Sociedade e Política no Brasil Pós-64,* edited by Bernardo Sorj and Maria Hermínia Tavares de Almeida. Sao Paulo: Editora Brasiliense.

Carr, Barry. 1981. *El movimiento obrero y la política en México, 1910–1929.* Mexico: Era.

Carr, Barry. 1983*a.* "The Mexican Economic Debacle and the Labor Movement: A New Era or More of the Same?" In *Mexico's Economic Crisis,* edited by Donald Wyman. Monograph Series, no. 12. La Jolla: Center for U.S.-Mexican Studies, University of California, San Diego.

Carr, Barry. 1983*b.* "Marxism and Anarchism in the Formation of the Mexican Communist Party, 1910–19," *Hispanic American Historical Review* 63:2:277–305.

Carr, Barry. 1985. "Mexican Communism 1968–1981: Eurocommunism in the Americas?" *Journal of Latin American Studies* 17 (May):201–228.

Carr, Barry. 1987. "The Mexican Communist Party and Agrarian Mobilization in the Laguna, 1920–1940: A Worker-Peasant Alliance?" *Hispanic American Historical Review* 67:3 (August).

Carr, Barry, and Ricardo Anzaldúa Montoya, eds. 1986. *The Mexican Left, the Popular Movements, and the Politics of Austerity.* Monograph Series, no. 18. La Jolla: Center for U.S.-Mexican Studies, University of California, San Diego.

Carrillo, Teresa. n.d. "Women, Trade Unions, and New Social Movements in

Mexico: The Case of the Nineteenth of September Garment Workers Union."
Ph.D. dissertation, Stanford University, forthcoming.

Castells, Manuel. 1982. "Squatters and Politics in Latin America: A Comparative
Analysis of Urban Society in Chile, Perú and Mexico." In *Toward a Political
Economy of Urbanization in Third World Countries*, edited by Helen Safa. New
Delhi: Oxford University Press.

Castells, Manuel. 1983. *The City and the Grassroots*. London: Edward Arnold.

Castells, Manuel. 1986. *La ciudad y las masas: sociología de los movimientos
urbanos*. Madrid: Alianza Universitaria.

Castillo, Héctor. 1988. "Chiapas: pasado y futuro," *Proceso* 589 (February 15):32–
36.

Castillo, Héctor, Sergio Zermeño, and Alicia Ziccardi. 1988. "La juventud popular en
el D.F." Paper presented to the Federal District Department, November.

Cavarozzi, Marcelo, and Manuel Antonio Garretón, eds. 1989. *Muerte y
resurrección. Los partidos políticos en el autoritarismo y las transiciones en el
Cono Sur*. Santiago: FLACSO.

CNTE. 1980–1981. *El Movimiento Magisterial* (fortnightly reports on the movement
at national and regional levels by the Asesoría de la CNTE), November 1980–
October 1981.

CNTE. 1982. *Primer Balance. Tácticas para la democratización del SNTE.*
Documento de la Asamblea Nacional de Acapulco, January 17.

CNTE. 1984a. "Informe sobre el VIII Congreso de la Sección 7 de Chiapas,"
Educador Socialista 28 (March–April).

CNTE. 1984b. "El viejo y el nuevo sindicalismo. Ayer y hoy del sindicalismo en la
Sección 7 de Chiapas," *Educador Socialista* 27 (February).

CNTE. 1985a. *Respuestas a nuestras demandas en esta etapa de lucha*. CES de la
Sección 7, Subcomisión de Difusión y Propaganda, March.

CNTE. 1985b. Juicio político a "Vanguardia Revolucionaria," CCL del Magisterio de
Guerrero, Oaxaca (January 30).

CNTE. 1986. "Oaxaca y Chiapas: extragos de un informe a la Asamblea Nacional del
FMIN," *Educador Socialista* 38 (May–June).

CNTE. 1987a. *Caminemos* 4 (June):16.

CNTE. 1987b. "Proyecto de balance, análisis y propuestas políticas y organizativas."
Sección 7 del SNTE, Chiapas (June 12).

CNTE. 1987c. *El disidente (que ni come niños ni mata gente)* 19, 20.

CNTE. n.d. "El XIX Consejo Ordinario del SNTE." Informe de la Comisión
Permanente.

Coatsworth, John H. 1988. "Patterns of Rural Rebellion in Latin America: Mexico in
Comparative Perspective." In *Riot, Rebellion and Revolution: Rural Social
Conflict in Mexico*, edited by Friedrich Katz. Princeton, N.J.: Princeton University
Press.

Cohen, Jean L. 1985. "Strategy or Identity: New Theoretical Paradigms and
Contemporary Social Movements," *Social Research* 52:4 (Winter):663–716.

Coleman, Kenneth. 1975. "The Capital City Electorate and Mexico's Acción Nacional:
Some Survey Evidence and Conventional Hypotheses," *Social Science Quarterly*
56:2 (September):502–509.

Coleman, Kenneth, and Charles Davis. 1978. "Civil and Conventional Religion in
Secular Authoritarian Regimes: The Case of Mexico," *Studies in Comparative
International Development* 13 (Summer).

Collier, Ruth Berins, and David Collier. 1979. "Inducements versus Constraints:
Disaggregating 'Corporatism'," *American Political Science Review* 73:967–986.

Comisión Organizadora del Encuentro de Mujeres de los Sectores Populares de
México et al. 1987. *Las mujeres del pueblo avanzan hacia la unidad*. Mexico:
Comisión Organizadora del Encuentro de Mujeres.

CONAMUP. 1983. *Las Mujeres de las Colonias en el Movimiento Urbano Popular*.
Pamphlet of the Women's Section, Durango, November 25–27.

Concha Malo, Miguel. 1986. *La participación de los cristianos en el proceso popular de liberación en México (1968–1983)*. Mexico: Biblioteca México.

Concha Malo, Miguel. 1988. "Las violaciones a los derechos humanos individuales en México (período: 1971–1986)". In *Primer Informe sobre la Democracia: México 1988*, edited by Pablo González Casanova and Jorge Cadena Roa. Mexico: Siglo XXI.

Connolly, William E. 1987. *Politics and Ambiguity*. Madison: University of Wisconsin Press.

Cook, Maria. 1988. "Organizing Dissent: The Politics of Opposition in Mexican Unions." Paper presented at the Fourteenth Latin American Studies Association International Congress, New Orleans, March.

Cook, Maria. 1990. "Organizing Dissent. The Politics of Opposition in the Mexican Teachers' Union." Ph.D. dissertation, University of California, Berkeley.

Córdova, Arnaldo. 1974. *La política de masas del cardenismo*. Mexico: Era.

Cornelius, Wayne A. 1971. "Nation-Building, Participation, and Distribution: The Politics of Social Reform under Cárdenas." In *Developmental Episodes in Comparative Politics: Crisis, Choice, and Change*, edited by Gabriel A. Almond and Scott C. Flanagan. Boston: Little, Brown.

Cornelius, Wayne A. 1972. "A Structural Analysis of Urban Caciquismo in Mexico," *Urban Anthropology* 1:2:234–261.

Cornelius, Wayne A. 1980. *Los inmigrantes pobres en la Ciudad de México y la política*. Mexico: Fondo de Cultura Económica.

Cornelius, Wayne A., Judith Gentleman, and Peter H. Smith, eds. 1989 *Mexico's Alternative Political Futures*. Monograph Series, no. 30. La Jolla: Center for U.S.-Mexican Studies, University of California, San Diego.

Corriente Democrática. 1986. *Documento de trabajo número uno*. Morelia, Michoacán, October 1.

Corriente Democrática. 1987a. *Documento de trabajo número uno*. Chihuahua, Chihuahua, May 3.

Corriente Democrática. 1987b. *Propuesta democrática*. Mexico: September 9.

Cortina, Regina. 1985. *Power, Gender and Education: Unionized Teachers in Mexico City*. Stanford: School of Education, Stanford University.

Cosío Villegas, Daniel. 1972. *El sistema político mexicano*. Mexico: Joaquín Mortiz.

Coulomb, René, and E. Duhault. 1988. *La ciudad y sus actores*. Mexico: UAM–Azcapotzalco/IFAL.

Craig, Ann L. 1983. *The First Agraristas: An Oral History of a Mexican Agrarian Reform Movement*. Berkeley: University of California Press.

Craig, Ann L. 1989. "An Historical Perspective on Popular Movements: Unions, Political Parties, and Strikes in the Laguna, 1918–1936." Paper prepared for the Workshop on Popular Movements and Political Transformation in Mexico, Center for U.S.-Mexican Studies, University of California, San Diego, March 29–31.

CRN (Coordinadora Revolucionaria Nacional). 1985. *A los partidos políticos democráticos y progresistas con registro a las organizaciones populares de todo el país*. Mexico: February 20.

CRN, PSUM, PMT, and PRT. 1985. *Por el impulso y la legitimación de las luchas populares*. Mexico: February 26.

Cruz, Marcos, Gonzalo Yáñez, Elio Villaseñor, and Julio Moguel, eds. 1986. *Llegó la hora de ser gobierno. Durango: testimonios de la lucha del Comité de Defensa Popular General Francisco Villa*. Mexico: Equipo Pueblo.

Davis, Charles, and Kenneth Coleman. 1977. "Discontinuous Educational Experiences and Political and Religious Nonconformity in Authoritarian Regimes: Mexico," *Social Science Quarterly* 58:3 (December).

De la Garza Toledo, Enrique. 1982. "Estructura organizativa y democracia en el SNTE," *Información Obrera* 1 (Summer).

De la Garza Toledo, Enrique. 1988. *Ascenso y crisis del estado social autoritario*. Mexico: El Colegio de México.

De los Reyes, Yolanda. 1986. "Descentralización de la educación." In *Descentralización y democracia en México*, edited by Blanca Torres. Mexico: El Colegio de México.

De Oliveira, Orlandina, coord. 1989. *Trabajo, poder y sexualidad*. Mexico: PIEM, El Colegio de México.

Despertar Lagunero: Libro que relata la lucha y triunfo de la revolución en la comarca lagunera. 1937. Mexico.

Deutsch, Sandra. 1989. "Gender and Sociopolitical Change in 20th Century Latin America." Unpublished paper.

Diamond, Larry, Juan J. Linz, and Seymour Martin Lipset, eds. 1989. *Democracy in Developing Countries*. 4 vols. Boulder, Colo.: Lynne Rienner.

Durand, C. 1988. *Movimientos campesinos en Guerrero y Oaxaca, 1976–1986*. Mexico: Costa–Amic.

Echeverría Alvarez, Luis. 1976. *Sexto Informe de Gobierno*. Mexico: Presidencia de la República.

Eckstein, Susan. 1977. *The Poverty of Revolution: The State and the Urban Poor in Mexico*. Princeton, N.J.: Princeton University Press.

Eckstein, Susan. 1989. "Power and Popular Protest in Latin America." In *Power and Popular Protest: Latin American Social Movements*, edited by S. Eckstein. Berkeley: University of California Press.

El Día. October 3, 1977. "Indígenas de Chiapas denuncian graves agresiones y atropellos."

El Día. October 10, 1977. "Varios ejidos de Chiapas protestan por graves atropellos a campesinos."

Equipo Pueblo. 1984. "Balance de la CNTE 1984," *Pueblo* 6 (Novem-ber–December):118–119.

Equipo Pueblo. 1985. "Organización y democracia sindical," *Pueblo* 2.

Espinosa, Juan Antonio. 1982. "Los maestros de los maestros: las dirigencias sindicales en la historia del SNTE," *Historias* (Instituto Nacional de Antropología e Historia) 1 (July–September).

Esteva, Gustavo. 1987. "Regenerating People's Space," *Alternatives* 12:125–152.

Evers, Tilman. 1985. "Identity: The Hidden Side of New Social Movements in Latin America." In *New Social Movements and the State in Latin America*, edited by David Slater. Amsterdam: CEDLA.

Fagen, Richard R., and William S. Tuohy. 1972. *Politics and Privilege in a Mexican City*. Stanford: Stanford University Press.

Faletto, Enzo, and G. Rama. 1981. "Cambio social en América Latina," *Pensamiento Iberoamericano* 6 (July–December):13–30.

Fals Borda, Orlando. 1986. "El nuevo despertar de los movimientos sociales." Paper presented at the Twelfth Latin American Seminar on Social Movements, Medellín, July.

FDN (Frente Democrático Nacional). 1988. *Plataforma*. Jalapa, Veracruz, January 12.

Filgueira, C., and C. Geneletti. 1981. "Estratificación y movilidad ocupacional en América Latina," *Cuadernos de la CEPAL* (Santiago de Chile) 39.

Finley, M. I. 1985. *Democracy Ancient and Modern*. New Brunswick, N.J.: Rutgers University Press.

Flores Lua, María Graciela. 1984. "La insurgencia obrera, campesina y popular en la década de los setentas y el Frente Nacional de Acción Popular." Bachelor's thesis, Universidad Nacional Autónoma de México.

FMIN (Frente Magisterial Independiente Nacional). 1981. *Chiapas: testimonios de dirigentes del Movimiento Magisterial*. Mexico: FMIN.

FMIN. 1982. "Estatutos y reglamento general de asambleas del SNTE," *Educador Socialista* 22 (November–December).

FMIN. 1983. *La toma de la Sección XI del SNTE*. Folletos de Educación Sindical, no. 13 (October).

FMIN. 1985. "Gobiernismo y disidencia en Oaxaca." Mimeographed. Mexico: FMIN.

Foucault, Michel. 1978. *The History of Sexuality*, vol. 1. New York: Pantheon.

Foucault, Michel. 1982. *Vigilar y castigar*. Madrid: Siglo XXI.

Fourquet, F., and L. Murad. 1978. *Los equipamientos del poder*. Barcelona: Gustavo Gili.

Foweraker, Joe. 1988. "Transformism Transformed: The Nature of Mexico's Political Crisis." Essex Papers in Politics and Government, no. 46. Colchester: Department of Government, University of Essex.

Foweraker, Joe. 1989a. "Popular Movements and the Transformation of the Mexican Political System." In *Mexico's Alternative Political Futures*, edited by Wayne A. Cornelius, Judith Gentleman, and Peter H. Smith. Monograph Series, no. 30. La Jolla: Center for U.S.- Mexican Studies, University of California, San Diego.

Foweraker, Joe. 1989b. *Making Democracy in Spain: Grassroots Struggle in the South, 1955–1975*. New York: Cambridge University Press.

Fox, Jonathan. 1989a. "Offsetting the Iron Law of Oligarchy: The Ebbs and Flows of Leadership Accountability in a Regional Peasant Organization," *Grassroots Development* 13:2.

Fox, Jonathan. 1989b. "Democratization or Concertación Social? Today's Challenge to Mexican Social Movements." Paper presented at the fall meeting of the New England Council of Latin American Studies, Storrs, Conn.

Fox, Jonathan, and Gustavo Gordillo. 1989. "Between State and Market: The Campesinos' Quest for Autonomy." In *Mexico's Alternative Political Futures*, edited by Wayne A. Cornelius, Judith Gentleman, and Peter H. Smith. Monograph Series, no. 30. La Jolla: Center for U.S.-Mexican Studies, University of California, San Diego.

Friedmann, John, and Mauricio Salguero. 1988. "The Barrio Economy—Collective Self-Empowerment in Latin America: A Framework and Agenda for Research." In *Comparative Urban and Community Research*, edited by Michael Peter Smith. New Brunswick, N.J.: Transaction Books.

Friedrich, Paul. 1970. *Agrarian Revolt in a Mexican Village*. Englewood Cliffs, N.J.: Prentice–Hall.

Friedrich, Paul. 1986. *The Princes of Naranja: An Essay in Anthropological Method*. Austin: University of Texas Press.

Fuentes, Manuel, et al. 1987. "Costureras: puntadas que hablan, mujeres que luchan." In *Historias del sindicalismo mexicano*, no. 3. Mexico: Información Obrera.

Fuentes Molinar, Olac. 1983. *Educación y política en México*. Mexico: Nueva Imagen.

Fundación Rosenbleuth. 1989. *Geografía de las elecciones presidenciales de México*. Mexico: Fundación Rosenbleuth.

García de León, Antonio. 1985. *Resistencia y utopia*. 2 vols. Mexico: Era.

García Mundo, Octavio. 1976. *El movimiento inquilinario de Veracruz*. Mexico: SepSetentas.

Garciadiego Dantan, Javier. 1988. "The Universidad Nacional and the Mexican Revolution 1910–1920." Ph.D. dissertation, University of Chicago.

Garretón, Manuel Antonio. 1986. "Transformación social y refundación política en el capitalismo autoritario." In *Los nuevos procesos sociales y la teoría política contemporánea*, edited by Julio Labastida Martín del Campo. Mexico: Universidad Nacional Autónoma de México/Siglo XXI.

Garretón, Manuel Antonio. 1987. *Reconstruir la política. Transición y consolidación democrática en Chile*. Santiago de Chile: Editorial Andante.

Garrido, Luis Javier. 1987. "Un partido sin militantes." In *La vida política mexicana en la crisis*, compiled by Soledad Loaeza and Rafael Segovia. Mexico: Centro de Estudios Internacionales, El Colegio de México.

Garza del Toro, Alma Rosa, and Efraín Pérez Güemes. 1984. "El Movimiento de Posesionarios en Monterrey, 1970–83." Paper presented at the seminar on

Movimientos Sociales en México–Región Nordeste, Universidad Autónoma de Nuevo León, January.

Genovese, Eugene. 1974. *Roll Jordan Roll, The World the Slaves Made*. New York: Pantheon.

Germani, G. 1962. *Política y sociedad en una época de transición*. Buenos Aires: Eudeba.

Gilly, Adolfo. 1987. "La crisis del PRI/IV," *La Jornada*, November 9.

Gilly, Adolfo. 1988. "La Esperanza," *La Jornada*, March 13.

Gómez Guzmán, Moisés. 1984. "Condiciones laborales de la industria del vestido." Bachelor's thesis, Universidad Ibero-Americana, Puebla.

Gómez Tagle, Silvia. 1974. *Organización de las sociedades de crédito ejidal de la Laguna*. Cuadernos del CES, no. 8. Mexico: El Colegio de México.

Góngora, Janette. 1986. *No tembló igual para todos*. Cuadernos de Insurgencia Sindical. Mexico: Información Obrera/Editorial Extemporáneos.

González Casanova, Pablo. 1970. *Democracy in Mexico*. London: Oxford University Press.

González Casanova, Pablo, and Héctor Aguilar Camín, comps. 1985. *México ante la crisis*. 2 vols. Mexico: Siglo XXI.

Gordillo, Gustavo. 1987. "Estado y movimiento campesino en la coyuntura actual." In *Mexico ante la crisis*, vol. 2, edited by Pablo González Casanova and Héctor Aguilar Camín. Mexico: Siglo XXI.

Gramsci, Antonio. 1971. *Selections from the Prison Notebooks of Antonio Gramsci*, edited by Q. Hoare and G. N. Smith. London: Lawrence and Wishart.

Greaves, Patricia. 1980. "Las relaciones SEP-SNTE." In *Simposio sobre el Magisterio Nacional*, vol. 1. Cuadernos de la Casa Chata, no. 29. Mexico: CIESAS.

Grindle, Merilee. 1977. "Policy Change in an Authoritarian Regime: Mexico under Echeverría," *Journal of Interamerican Studies and World Affairs* 19:4 (November).

Gruening, Ernest. 1928. *Mexico and Its Heritage*. New York: Century.

Grupo Parlamentario del PMS. 1987. "Reporte de los asesinatos cometidos en el campo mexicano durante el período enero de 1982–julio de 1987." Mexico: PMS, August 18.

Guadarrama, Rocío. 1981. *Los sindicatos y la política en México: la CROM 1918-1928*. Mexico: Era.

Guadarrama, Rocío. 1987. "Elections in Sonora." In *Electoral Patterns and Perspectives in Mexico*, edited by Arturo Alvarado. Monograph Series, no. 22. La Jolla: Center for U.S.–Mexican Studies, University of California, San Diego.

Guadarrama S., Graciela. 1987. "Entrepreneurs and Politics: Businessmen in Electoral Contests in Sonora and Nuevo León, July 1985." In *Electoral Patterns and Perspectives in Mexico*, edited by Arturo Alvarado. Monograph Series, no. 22. La Jolla, Calif.: Center for U.S.-Mexican Studies, University of California, San Diego.

Guerra, Eduardo. 1957. *Historia de la Laguna: Torreón, su orígen y sus fundadores*. 2d ed. Torreón: Casán.

Guzmán Ortiz, Eduardo, and Joaquín H. Vela Glez. 1989. "Maestros 1989: crisis, democracia y más salario," *El Cotidiano* 30.

Haber, Stephen R. 1989. *Industry and Underdevelopment: The Industrialization of Mexico, 1890–1940*. Stanford: Stanford University Press.

Habermas, Jürgen. 1981. "New Social Movements," *Telos* 49.

Hackett Fischer, David. 1970. *Historians' Fallacies: Towards a Logic of Historical Thought*. New York: Harper and Row.

Hamilton, Nora. 1982. *The Limits of State Autonomy: Post-Revolutionary Mexico*. Princeton, N.J. Princeton University Press.

Hannerz, Ulf. 1986. *Exploración de la ciudad*. Mexico: Fondo de Cultura Económica.

Hansen, Roger D. 1971. *The Politics of Mexican Development*. Baltimore, Md.: Johns

Hopkins University Press.

Hart, John. 1978. *Anarchism and the Mexican Working Class, 1860–1931*. Austin: University of Texas Press.

Harvey, Neil. 1988. "Personal Networks and Strategic Choices in the Formation of an Independent Peasant Organization: The OCEZ of Chiapas, Mexico," *Bulletin of Latin American Research* 7:2:299–312.

Harvey, Neil. 1989. "Corporatist Strategies and Popular Responses in Rural Mexico: State and Opposition in Chiapas, 1970–1988." Ph.D. dissertation, University of Essex.

Hellman, Judith Adler. 1979. "El cultivo del algodón y la reforma agraria en el norte de México." In *La Comarca Lagunera, Parte III. Análisis de su problemática*, by Tomás Martínez, Judith Adler, and Ricardo Estrada. Cuadernos de la Casa Chata, no. 19. Mexico: CISINAH.

Hellman, Judith Adler. 1981. "Capitalist Agriculture and Rural Protest: The Case of the Laguna Region, Mexico," *Labour Capital and Society* 14:2 (November).

Hellman, Judith Adler. 1983a. *Mexico in Crisis*. New York: Holmes and Meier.

Hellman, Judith Adler. 1983b. "The Role of Ideology in Peasant Politics: Peasant Mobilization and Demobilization in the Laguna Region," *Journal of Interamerican Studies and World Affairs* 25:1 (February).

Hellman, Judith Adler. 1989. "New Social Movements and the Question of Autonomy." Paper presented at the Workshop on Popular Movements and Political Transformation in Mexico, Center for U.S.-Mexican Studies, University of California, San Diego, March 29–31.

Hernández, Luis. 1981. "Paciencia y acabamos con el charrismo," *Cambio* 7:25/28.

Hernández, Luis. 1982a. "México: izquierda y clase obrera," *Información Obrera* 0 (Spring).

Hernández, Luis. 1982b. "Sobre el grupo Vanguardia Revolucionaria," *Información Obrera* 1 (Summer).

Hernández, Luis. 1982c. "Las Corrientes Político Sindicales dentro del SNTE," *Información Obrera* 1 (Summer).

Hernández, Luis. 1983a. "La fuerza ambivalente de la CNTE para el Estado," *Punto* 1:41 (August 15-22).

Hernández, Luis. 1983b. "La violencia charra," *Siempre* 1110, suplemento, September 21.

Hernández, Luis. 1985. "Una historia que es no solo para recordar," *Cuadernos Educativos* 1 (October).

Hernández, Luis. 1986. "The SNTE and the Teachers' Movement, 1982–1984." In *The Mexican Left, the Popular Movements, and the Politics of Austerity*, edited by Barry Carr and Ricardo Anzaldúa Montoya. Monograph Series, no. 18. La Jolla: Center for U.S.–Mexican Studies, University of California, San Diego.

Hernández, Luis. 1987. "Los protagonistas del golpe," *Siempre*, suplemento, April 9.

Hernández, Luis. 1988a. "La construcción social de la autonomía: maestros y autogestión." Presentation at the Foro sobre Movimientos Sociales y Autogestión, Oaxtepec, Morelos.

Hernández, Luis. 1988b. "The Popular Urban Movement and the Elections," *The Other Side of Mexico* 5:8–11.

Hernández, Luis. 1989. "Maestros: jaque al rey," *El Cotidiano* 28.

Hernández, Luis, and Francisco Pérez Arce, eds. 1982. *Las luchas magisteriales 1979/1981 Documentos II*. Mexico: Macehual.

Hernández, Manuel. 1982. *Germen* (Organo de Información y Análysis de la Sección 7 del SNTE), no. 3 (June).

Hernández, Porfirio. 1975. *La explotación colectiva en la comarca lagunera es un fracaso?* Mexico: Costa–Amic.

Hernández Chávez, Alicia. 1979. *La mecánica cardenista*. Historia de la Revolución Mexicana, período 1934–40. Mexico: El Colegio de México.

Hernández S., Ricardo. 1987. *La Coordinadora Nacional del Movimiento Urbano*

Popular, CONAMUP: su historia 1980–86. Mexico: Equipo Pueblo.

Huizer, Gerritt. 1982. *La lucha campesina en México*. 3d. ed. Mexico: Centro Nacional de Investigaciones Agrarias.

Hurtado, Javier. 1989. "Elementos del nuevo escenario político mexicano." Guadalajara: Universidad de Guadalajara. Unpublished paper.

Huyssen, Andreas. 1984."Mapping the Post–modern," *New German Critique* 33 (Fall):5–52.

Jacobs, Ian. 1976. "Genaro Vázquez, Lucio Cabañas, and the Rural Guerrilla in Mexico." Unpublished paper.

Jessop, Bob. 1980. "The Political Indeterminacy of Democracy." In *Marxism and Democracy*, edited by Alan Hunt. London: Lawrence and Wishart.

Johnson, James. 1988. "Symbolic Action and the Limits of Strategic Rationality: On the Logic of Working–Class Collective Action." In *Political Power and Social Theory*, vol. 7, edited by Maurice Zeitlin. Greenwich, Conn.: JAI Press.

Joseph, Gilbert M. 1988. *Revolution from Without: Yucatán, Mexico and the United States, 1880–1924*. 2d ed. Durham, N.C.: Duke University Press.

Kaplan, Temma. 1982. "Female Consciousness and Collective Action: The Case of Barcelona, 1910–1918," *Signs* 7:545–566.

Katz, Friedrich. 1988*a*. "Rural Uprisings in Preconquest and Colonial Mexico." In *Riot, Rebellion and Revolution: Rural Social Conflict in Mexico*, edited by F. Katz. Princeton, N.J.: Princeton University Press.

Katz, Friedrich, ed. 1988*b*. *Riot, Rebellion and Revolution: Rural Social Conflict in Mexico*. Princeton, N.J.: Princeton University Press.

Klandermans, Bert, and Sidney Tarrow. 1988. "Mobilization into Social Movements: Synthesizing European and American Approaches," *International Social Movement Research* 1.

Knight, Alan. 1984. "The Working Class and the Mexican Revolution, c.1900–1920," *Journal of Latin American Studies* 16:51–79.

Knight, Alan. 1985. "The Mexican Revolution: Bourgeois? Nationalist? Or Just a 'Great Rebellion'?" *Bulletin of Latin American Studies* 4:2:1–37.

Knight, Alan. 1986. *The Mexican Revolution*. 2 vols. Cambridge: Cambridge University Press.

Kovacs, Karen. 1983. "La planeación educativa en México: la Universidad Pedagógica Nacional (UPN)," *Estudios Sociológicos* 1:2.

Kowarick, Lucio. 1985. "The Pathway to Encounter: Reflections on the Social Struggle in São Paulo." In *New Social Movements and the State in Latin America*, edited by David Slater. Amsterdam: CEDLA.

Krauze, Enrique. 1976. *Caudillos culturales en la Revolución Mexicana*. Mexico: Siglo XXI.

Kroeber, Clifton B. 1983. *Man, Land, and Water: Mexico's Farmlands Irrigation Policies, 1885–1911*. Berkeley: University of California Press.

Laclau, Ernesto. 1977. *Politics and Ideology in Marxist Theory*. London: New Left Books.

Laclau, Ernesto. 1985. "New Social Movements and the Plurality of the Social." In *New Social Movements and the State in Latin America*, edited by David Slater. Amsterdam: CEDLA.

Laclau, Ernesto, and Chantal Mouffe. 1985. *Hegemony and Socialist Strategy: Toward a Radical Democratic Politics*. London: Verso.

Landsberger, Henry, and Bobby M. Gierisch. 1979. "Political and Economic Activism: Peasant Participation in the Ejidos of the Comarca Lagunera of Mexico." In *Politics and the Poor*, edited by Mitchell Seligson and John Booth. *Political Participation in Latin America*, vol. 2. New York: Holmes and Meier.

Landsberger, Henry, and Cynthia Hewitt de Alcántara. 1970. "Peasant Organizations in La Laguna, Mexico. History, Structure, Member Participation and Effectiveness." Research Papers on Land Tenure and Agrarian Reform, no. 17. Washington, D.C.: Inter-American Committee for Agricultural Development

(CIDA).

Lau, Rubén. 1989. "Las elecciones en Chihuahua (1983–1988)," *Cuadernos del Norte*, January.

Lau Jaiven, Ana. 1987. *La nueva ola del feminismo*. Mexico: Planeta.

Lazcano, A. 1989. Review of *Nada, Nadie* by E. Poniatowska, *La Jornada*, February 15.

Leal, Felipe. 1985. *Agrupaciones y burocracias sindicales en México*. Mexico: Terra Nova.

León, Samuel. 1977. "El Comité Nacional de Defensa Proletaria." In *Estudios Regionales*. Mexico: Centro de Estudios Históricos y Sociales del Movimiento Obrero (CEHSMO).

León, Samuel, and Ignacio Marván. 1984. "Los movimientos sociales en México (1968–1983): Panorama general y perspectivas," *Estudios Políticos*, Nueva Epoca 3:2 (April–June).

Lerner, Victoria. 1979. *Historia de la Revolución Mexicana: período 1934–1940: la educación socialista*. Mexico: El Colegio de México.

Levy, Daniel C. 1986. "The Political Consequences of Changing Socialization." In *Mexico's Political Stability: The Next Five Years*, edited by Roderic Ai Camp. Boulder, Colo.: Westview.

Levy, Daniel C. 1989. "Mexico: Sustained Civilian Rule Without Democracy." In *Democracy in Developing Countries*, vol. 4, *Latin America*, edited by Larry Diamond, Juan Linz, and Seymour Martin Lipset. Boulder, Colo.: Lynne Rienner.

Liga de Agrónomos Socialistas. 1940. *El colectivismo agrario en México: la comarca lagunera*. Mexico: Liga de Agrónomos Socialistas.

Linz, Juan. 1964. "An Authoritarian Regime: Spain." In *Cleavages, Ideologies and Party Systems*, edited by E. Allardt and Y. Littunen. New York: Academic Bookstore.

Linz, Juan. 1987. *La quiebra de las democracias*. Madrid: Alianza.

Loaeza, Soledad. 1988. *Clases medias y política en Mexico*. Mexico: Centro de Estudios Internacionales, El Colegio de Mexico.

Loaeza, Soledad. 1989. *El llamado de las urnas*. Mexico: Cal y Arena.

Loaeza, Soledad, and R. Segovia, comps. 1987. *La vida política mexicana en la crisis*. Mexico: Centro de Estudios Internacionales, El Colegio de México.

Logan, Kathleen. 1984. *Haciendo Pueblo: The Development of a Guadalajaran Suburb*. Tuscaloosa: University of Alabama Press.

Logan, Kathleen. 1988. "Women's Political Activity and Empowerment in Latin American Urban Movements." In *Urban Life*, edited by George Gmelch and Walter P. Zenner. Prospect Heights, Ill.: Waveland.

Logan, Kathleen. n.d. "En las Calles—Women's Collective Actions in Mérida, Yucatán, Mexico." Unpublished manuscript.

López Monjardín, Adriana. 1986. *La lucha por los ayuntamientos: una utopia viable*. Mexico: Siglo XXI/Instituto de Investigaciones Sociales, Universidad Nacional Autónoma de México.

Loyo Brambila, Aurora. 1978. *El movimiento magisterial de 1958*. Mexico: Era.

Lozano Pardinas, Dolores, and Cristina Padilla Dieste. 1988. "La participación de la mujer en los movimientos urbano-populares." In *Mujeres y sociedad*, edited by Luisa Gabayet et al. Guadalajara: El Colegio de Jalisco.

Luna Jurado, Rogelio. 1977. "Los maestros y la democracia sindical," *Cuadernos Políticos* 14 (October–December).

Lustig, Nora. 1987. "Economic Crisis and Living Standards in Mexico: 1982–1985." Mexico: El Colegio de México. Unpublished manuscript.

Lustig, Nora. 1988. "La desigualdad económica," *Nexos* 128 (August):8–11.

Macías, Anna. 1982. *Against All Odds: The Feminist Movement in Mexico to 1940*. Westport, Conn.: Greenwood Press.

Maier, Elizabeth. 1989. "La Coordinadora de Mujeres 'Benita Galeana': una experiencia en el desarrollo de la lucha de género/clase en México." Presentation at the Fifteenth International Congress of the Latin American Studies Association, Miami, Florida, December 4–6.

Mainwaring, Scott. 1987. "Urban Popular Movements, Identity, and Democratization in Brazil," *Comparative Political Studies* 20:2 (July):131–159.

Mainwaring, Scott, and Eduardo Viola. 1984. "New Social Movements, Political Culture, and Democracy: Brazil and Argentina in the 1980s," *Telos* 61 (Fall):17–52.

Mann, Michael. 1988. "The Autonomous Power of the State: Its Origins, Mechanisms and Results." In *States, War and Capitalism: Studies in Political Sociology*, edited by M. Mann. New York: Basil Blackwell.

Margolis, Joseph. 1986. *Pragmatism Without Foundations: Reconciling Realism and Relativism*. New York: Basil Blackwell.

Marion S., Marie-Odile. 1984. *El movimiento campesino en Chiapas, 1983*. Mexico: Centro de Estudios Históricos del Agrarismo en México.

Marion S., Marie-Odile. 1987. "Pueblos de Chiapas: una democracia a la defensiva," *Revista Mexicana de Sociología* 49:4 (October).

Márquez, Enrique. 1987. "Political Anachronisms: The *Navista* Movement and Political Processes in San Luis Potosí, 1958–1985." In *Electoral Patterns and Perspectives in Mexico*, edited by Arturo Alvarado. Monograph Series, no. 22. La Jolla: Center for U.S.–Mexican Studies, University of California, San Diego.

Márquez, Enrique. 1988. "Gonzalo N. Santos o la naturaleza del 'tanteómetro político.'" In *Estadistas, Caciques y Caudillos*, coordinated by Carlos Martínez Assad. Mexico: Instituto de Investigaciones Sociales, Universidad Nacional Autónoma de México.

Martínez Assad, Carlos. 1985. "Nava: de la rebelión de los coheteros al juicio político. In *Municipios en conflicto*, coordinated by C. Martínez Assad. Mexico: Instituto de Investigaciones Sociales, Universidad Nacional Autónoma de México.

Martínez Assad, Carlos, and Alicia Ziccardi. 1988. "La descentralización de las políticas públicas en México." Presentation at the Seminar on Descentralización del Estado, Requerimientos y Políticas en la Crisis, Buenos Aires, November 9–11.

Martínez Saldaña, Tomás. 1980. *El costo social de un éxito político: la política expansionista del estado mexicano en el agro lagunero*. Chapingo: El Colegio de Posgraduados.

Martínez Saldaña, Tomás, and Leticia Gándara Mendoza. 1976. *Política y sociedad en México: el caso de los Altos de Jalisco*. Mexico: CISINAH.

Martínez Vázquez, Víctor Raúl, and Anselmo Arellanes M. 1985. "Negociación y conflicto en Oaxaca." In *Municipios en conflicto*, coordinated by Carlos Martínez Assad. Mexico: Instituto de Investigaciones Sociales, Universidad Nacional Autónoma de México.

Marván Laborde, Ignacio. 1988. "Tendencias actuales de los movimientos sociales en México: expresiones nacionales y regionales." Mexico: Instituto de Investigaciones Sociales, Universidad Nacional Autónoma de México.

MAS (Mujeres en Acción Sindical). 1987. *Nosotras: Organo Informativo de Mujeres en Acción Sindical* 1:3. Mexico: MAS.

McAdam, Doug, J. D. McCarthy, and M. N. Zald. 1988. "Social Movements." In *Handbook of Sociology*, edited by Neil Smelser. Beverly Hills, Calif.: Sage.

Melucci, Alberto. 1988. "Getting Involved: Identity and Mobilization in Social Movements," *International Social Movement Research* 1.

Mercado, A. 1986. "Los barrios frente a la ciudad de hoy y mañana," *El Día*, suplemento *Metrópoli*, December 8.

Mesa Redonda. 1986. "Barrios y ciudad," Jornadas Pro-Conservación del Patrimonio Cultural. Mexico: December 4.

Meyer, Jean. 1973–1974. *La Cristiada*. 3 vols. Mexico: Siglo XXI.

Meyer, Jean. 1979. *El sinarquismo: un fascismo mexicano? 1937–1947*. Mexico: Joaquín Mortíz.

Meyer, Lorenzo. 1977. "Historical Roots of the Authoritarian State in Mexico." In *Authoritarianism in Mexico*, edited by J. L. Reyna and R. S. Weinert. Philadelphia: ISHI.

Meyers, William K. 1979. "Politics, Vested Rights, and Economic Growth in Porfirian Mexico: The Company Tlahualilo in the Comarca Lagunera, 1885–1911," *Hispanic American Historical Review* 57:3.

Meyers, William K. 1980. "Interest Group Conflict and Revolutionary Politics: A Social History of the Comarca Lagunera, Mexico, 1880–1911." Ph.D. dissertation, University of Chicago.

Meyers, William K. 1984. "La Comarca Lagunera: Work, Protest and Popular Mobilization in North Central Mexico." In *Other Mexicos. Essays on Regional Mexican History, 1876–1911*, edited by Thomas Benjamin and William McNellie. Norman: University of Oklahoma Press.

Middlebrook, Kevin J. 1986. "Political Liberalization in an Authoritarian Regime: The Case of Mexico." In *Transitions from Authoritarian Rule: Latin America*, edited by Guillermo O'Donnell, Philippe C. Schmitter, and Laurence Whitehead. Baltimore, Md.: Johns Hopkins University Press.

Molyneux, Maxine. 1985. "Mobilisation without Emancipation? Women's Interests, State and Revolution in Nicaragua." In *New Social Movements and the State in Latin America*, edited by David Slater. Amsterdam: CEDLA.

Moncada O., Carlos. 1985. "El escenario político en Sonora." In *Municipios en conflicto*, coordinated by .Carlos Martínez Assad. Mexico: Instituto de Investigaciones Sociales, Universidad Nacional Autónoma de México.

Monsiváis, Carlos. 1987a. *Entrada libre (crónicas de una sociedad que se organiza)*. Mexico: Era.

Monsiváis, Carlos. 1987b. "Los maestros de Chiapas pagan caro el intento de escapar al poder de Jonguitud," *Proceso* 544 (April 6).

Monsiváis, Carlos. n.d. "Cárdenas, memoria histórica, no (todavía) partido."

Montes de Oca, Rosa Elena. 1977. "The State and the Peasants." In *Authoritarianism in Mexico*, edited by J. L. Reyna and R. S. Weinert. Philadelphia: ISHI.

Moore, Barrington, Jr. 1969. *The Social Origins of Dictatorship and Democracy: Lord and Peasant in the Making of the Modern World*. Boston: Beacon.

Moore, Barrington, Jr. 1978. *Injustice: The Social Bases of Obedience and Revolt*. White Plains, N.Y.: M. E. Sharpe.

Munck, Ronaldo. 1984. "Urban Social Movements: Labour in Argentina and Brazil." In *Politics and Dependency in the Third World. The Case of Latin America*, edited by R. Munck. London: Zed Press.

Munck, Ronaldo. 1989. *Latin America. The Transition to Democracy*. London: Zed Press.

Murmis, M., and M. C. Portantiero. 1971. *Estudios sobre los orígenes del peronismo*. Buenos Aires: Siglo XXI.

Navarro, Bernardo. 1986. "Crisis y Movimiento Urbano Popular en el Valle de México." Mimeographed.

Niblo, Stephen. 1988. *The Impact of War: Mexico and World War II*. Occasional Paper, no. 10. Bundoora, Aus.: Institute of Latin American Studies, La Trobe University.

Nivón, E. 1988. "Identidad y barrio en Tepito: expresiones de la cultura urbana," *El Día*, suplemento *Metrópoli*, May 2.

Novelo U., Federico. 1989. "Cambio estructural hacia el retroceso: los años ochenta en la sociedad mexicana." Mexico: Universidad Autónoma Metropolitana-Xochimilco. Mimeographed.

Nugent, Daniel. 1989. "Are We Not [Civilized] Men? The Formation and Devolution of Community in Northern Mexico," *Journal of Historical Sociology*, September.

O'Donnell, Guillermo. 1988a. "Transiçoes, Continuidades e Algumas Paradoxos." In *A Democracia no Brasil: Dilemas e Perspectivas*, edited by Fábio Wanderley Reis and Guillermo O'Donnell. São Paulo: Ediçoes Vértice.

O'Donnell, Guillermo. 1988b. "Hiatos, Instituiçoes a Perspectivas Democráticas." In

A Democracia no Brasil: Dilemas e Perspectivas, edited by Fábio Wanderley Reis and Guillermo O'Donnell. São Paulo: Ediçoes Vértice.

O'Donnell, Guillermo, Philippe Schmitter, and Laurence Whitehead, eds. 1986. *Transitions from Authoritarian Rule: Tentative Conclusions about Uncertain Democracies*. Baltimore, Md.: Johns Hopkins University Press.

Offe, Claus. 1985. "New Social Movements: Challenging the Boundaries of Institutional Politics," *Social Research* 52:4 (Winter):817–868.

Olson, Mancur. 1965. *The Logic of Collective Action*. Cambridge, Mass.: Harvard University Press.

Ortega Aguirre, Alfonso. 1986. "La mujer trabajadora de la industria de la confección de prendas de vestir." Bachelor's thesis, Universidad Nacional Autónoma de México.

Otero, Gerardo. 1989. "The New Agrarian Movement: Self-Managed Democratic Production," *Latin American Perspectives* 63:16:4.

Paige, Jeffery M. 1975. *Agrarian Revolution: Social Movements and Export Agriculture in the Underdeveloped World*. New York: Free Press.

Paré, Luisa. 1977. *El proletariado agrícola en México*. Mexico: Siglo XXI.

Paré, Luisa. 1982. "La política agropecuaria: 1976–1982," *Cuadernos Políticos* 33 (July–September):59–72.

Peláez, Gerardo. 1980. *Insurgencia magisterial*. Mexico: Edisa.

Peláez, Gerardo. 1984. *Historia del Sindicato Nacional de Trabajadores de la Educación*. Mexico: Ediciones de Cultura Popular.

Pellicer de Brody, Olga, and José Luis Reyna. 1981. *Historia de la Revolución Mexicana. 1952–1960: El afianzamiento de la estabilidad política*. Mexico: El Colegio de México.

Pérez Arce, Francisco. 1980. "Los signos de la insurgencia." *Memoria del 2 Congreso de Historia Obrera*. Mexico: CESMO.

Pérez Arce, Francisco. 1982a. "Itinerario de las luchas magisteriales" *Información Obrera* 1 (Summer).

Pérez Arce, Francisco. 1982b. "Los maestros vinieron del sur," *Siempre*, suplemento, December 22.

Pérez Arce, Francisco. 1987a. "Chiapas: 8 años de rebeldía," *Siempre*, suplemento, April 9.

Pérez Arce, Francisco. 1987b. *A muchas voces*. Mexico: Universidad Autónoma de Sinaloa.

Pérez Fernández del Castillo, Germán. 1989. "Clase obrera, sector social y proyecto nacional." In *75 años de sindicalismo mexicano*. Mexico: INEHR.

Perló, Manuel, and Martha Schteingart. 1984. "Movimientos sociales urbanos en México," *Revista Mexicana de Sociología* 44:4.

Pescador, José Angel, and Carlos Alberto Torres. 1985. *Poder político y educación en México*. Mexico: UTEHA.

Piven, Frances Fox, and Richard A. Cloward. 1979. *Poor People's Movements: Why They Succeed, How They Fail*. New York: Vintage Books.

Pizzorno, Alessandro. 1985. "On the Rationality of Democratic Choice," *Telos* 63 (Spring):41-69.

Polanyi, Karl. 1957. *The Great Transformation*. Boston: Beacon.

Pontigo Sánchez, J. L. 1985. "Dinámica social y movimientos campesinos en Simojovel y Huitiupán, Chiapas." Bachelor's thesis, Universidad Autónoma de Chapingo.

Porter, A. 1985. "Latin American Class Structures: Their Composition and Changes during the Last Decades," *Latin American Research Review* 20:3.

Poster, Mark. 1989. *Critical Theory and Poststructuralism*. Ithaca, N.Y.: Cornell University Press.

Pozas Garza, María de los Angeles. 1989. "Land Settlement by the Poor in Monterrey." In *Housing and Land in Urban Mexico*, edited by Alan Gilbert. Monograph Series, no. 31. La Jolla: Center for U.S.-Mexican Studies, University of California, San

Diego.

PPR. 1987. *El Movimiento Obrero y el PPR*, Mimeo.

Prieto, Ana María. 1986. "Mexico's National *Coordinadoras* in a Context of Economic Crisis." In *The Mexican Left, the Popular Movements, and the Politics of Austerity*, edited by Barry Carr and Ricardo Anzaldúa Montoya. Monograph Series, no. 18. La Jolla: Center for U.S.-Mexican Studies, University of California, San Diego.

Proceso. 1985. No. 469 (October 28, 1985): 30.

Przeworski, Adam. 1977. "Proletariat into a Class: The Process of Class Formation from Karl Kautsky's *The Class Struggle* to recent controversies," *Politics and Society* 7:4.

Przeworski, Adam. 1985. *Capitalism and Social Democracy*. New York: Cambridge University Press.

Przeworski, Adam. 1986. "Some Problems in the Study of the Transition to Democracy." In *Transitions from Authoritarian Rule: Comparative Perspectives*, edited by Guillermo O'Donnell, Philippe C. Schmitter, and Laurence Whitehead. Baltimore, Md.: Johns Hopkins University Press.

Punto Crítico. 1981. *Punto Crítico*. No. 115 (February).

Punto Crítico. 1989. *Punto Crítico*. No. 164 (July).

Purcell, Susan Kaufman. 1973. "Decision Making in an Authoritarian Regime: Theoretical Implications from a Mexican Case Study," *World Politics* 26 (October).

Raby, David. 1974. *Educación y revolución social en México, 1921–1940*. Mexico: Secretaría de Educación Pública.

Ramírez López, Heladio. 1981. "La sindicalización de trabajadores agrícolas en México: la experiencia de la Confederación Nacional Campesina (CNC)." Working Papers in U.S.-Mexican Studies, no. 26. La Jolla: Center for U.S.-Mexican Studies, University of California, San Diego.

Ramírez Saiz, Juan Manuel. 1986*a*. *El movimiento urbano popular en México*. Mexico: Siglo XXI.

Ramírez Saiz, Juan Manuel. 1986*b*. "Organizaciones populares y lucha política," *Cuadernos Políticos* 45 (January–March).

Ramírez Saiz, Juan Manuel. 1987*a*. *Política urbana y lucha popular*. Mexico: Universidad Autónoma de México, Xochimilco.

Ramírez Saiz, Juan Manuel. 1987*b*. "El Movimiento Urbano Popular en la administración del Miguel de la Madrid." In *17 Angulos de sexenio*, edited by Germán Pérez and Samuel León. Mexico: Plaza y Valdés.

Ramírez Saiz, Juan Manuel. 1987*c*. "Para comprender el 'Movimiento Urbano Popular'," *Tiempos de Ciencia* (Universidad de Guadalajara) 9 (September–December).

Ramírez Saiz, Juan Manuel. 1988. "Autogestión y Movimiento Popular Urbano." In *Movimientos Sociales y Autogestión*. Mexico: Fundación Friedrich Nauman.

Ramírez Saiz, Juan Manuel. n.d. *Actores sociales y proyecto de ciudad*. Mexico: Plaza y Valdés.

Ramos, Sergio, et al. 1979. *Empresa y conflictos laborales.* Mexico: Instituto de Investigaciones Sociales, Universidad Nacional Autónoma de México.

Ramos Oranday, Rogelio. 1985. "Oposición y abstencionismo en las elecciones presidenciales, 1964–1982." In *Las elecciones en México. Evolución y perspectivas*, coordinated by Pablo González Casanova. Mexico: Siglo XXI/ Instituto de Investigaciones Sociales, Universidad Nacional Autónoma de México.

Reding, Andrew. 1989. "Mexico under Salinas," *World Policy Journal* 6,4, (Fall).

Regalado Santillán, Jorge. 1986. "El movimiento independiente en Guadalajara." In *Perspectivas de los movimientos sociales en la región centro-occidente*, edited by Jaime Tamayo. Mexico: Línea.

Rello, Fernando. 1984. "El Leviatán Lagunero: ensayo sobre una agricultura estatizada." Unpublished monograph.

Renard, M. C. 1985. "Historia de la comunidad de San Bartolemé de los Llanos, Chiapas." Master's thesis, Universidad Nacional Autónoma de México.

Restrepo, Iván, and Salomón Eckstein. 1975. *La agricultura colectiva en México: La experiencia de la Laguna*. Mexico: Siglo XXI.

Reyna, José Luis, and Marcelo 'Miquet. 1976. "Introducción a la historia de las organizaciones obreras en México: 1912–1926." In *Tres estudios sobre el movimiento obrero en México*, edited by José Luis Reyna et al. Mexico: El Colegio de México.

Reyna, José Luis, and Richard S. Weinert, eds. 1977. *Authoritarianism in Mexico*. Philadelphia: ISHI.

Rodríguez, O. 1987. "Partidos políticos en el Distrito Federal." In *Distrito Federal: gobierno y sociedad civil*, edited by J. M. Ramírez Saiz. Mexico: El Caballito.

Rodríguez, Victoria. 1987. "The Politics of Decentralization in Mexico: Divergent Outcomes of Policy Implementation." Ph.D. dissertation, University of California, Berkeley.

Romero, Lauro. 1986. "El movimiento fascista en Guadalajara." In *Perspectivas de los movimientos sociales en la región centro-occidente*, edited by Jaime Tamayo. Mexico: Línea.

Roxborough, Ian. 1981. "The Analysis of Labor Movements in Latin America: Typologies and Theories," *Bulletin of Latin American Research* 1:1 (October).

Roxborough, Ian. 1984. *Unions and Politics in Mexico: The Case of the Automobile Industry*. Cambridge: Cambridge University Press.

Rubin, Jeffrey W. 1987. "State Policies, Leftist Oppositions, and Municipal Elections: The Case of the COCEI in Juchitán." In *Electoral Patterns and Perspectives in Mexico*, edited by Arturo Alvarado. Monograph Series, no. 22. La Jolla: Center for U.S.-Mexican Studies, University of California, San Diego.

Rubio, B. 1987. *Resistencia campesina y explotación rural en México*. Mexico: Era.

Rubio López, Marín. 1985. "Formas de organización campesina y conciencia de clase: el caso de la Unión de Ejidos Quiptic Ta Lecubtesel del municipio de Ocosingo, Chiapas." Bachelor's thesis, Universidad Autónoma de Chapingo.

Salamini, Heather Fowler. 1978. *Agrarian Radicalism in Veracruz, 1920–1938*. Lincoln: University of Nebraska Press.

Salinas Alvarez, Samuel, and Carlos Imaz Gispert. 1984. *Maestros y estado: estudio de las luchas magisteriales 1979 a 1982*. 2 vols. Mexico: Línea.

Samaniego, N. 1986. "Los efectos de la crisis 1982–1986 en las condiciones de vida de la población en México," *CEPAL* (Lima).

San Juan, Carlos. 1984. "El dilema de la historia obrera reciente: revolución pasiva y acumulación de fuerzas en 1970–1982," *Historias* 5.

San Juan, Carlos. 1989. "Tragedias, presagios y esperanzas del movimiento magisterial," *Crítica* (Universidad Autónoma de Puebla) 39 (Summer).

Sanderson, Steven. 1981. *Agrarian Populism and the Mexican State: The Struggle for Land in Sonora*. Berkeley: University of California Press.

Sandoval Flores, Etelvina. 1987. "Los supervisores: una de las formas de la presencia del sindicato en la vida cotidiana del maestro," *Cuadernos Educativos* 3/4 (Spring).

Santos Valdés, José. 1973. *Matamoros: Ciudad Lagunera*. Mexico: Editora y Distribuidora Nacional de Publicaciones.

Schiera, Pierangelo. 1984. In *Diccionario de política, A–J*, edited by Norberto Bobbio and Nicola Matte Ucci. Mexico: Siglo XXI.

Schryer, Frans J. 1980. *The Rancheros of Pisaflores: The History of a Peasant Bourgeoisie in Twentieth-Century Mexico*. Toronto: University of Toronto Press.

Schteingart, Martha. 1987. "Desarrollo urbano y problemática habitacional popular. El sismo y la reconstrucción." In *Participación social, reconstrucción y mujer. El sismo de 1985*, edited by A. Massolo and M. Schteingart. Mexico: El Colegio de México/UNICEF.

Scott, James C. 1976. *The Moral Economy of the Peasant: Rebellion and Subsistence in Southeast Asia*. New Haven, Conn.: Yale University Press.

Scott, Robert E. 1964. *Mexican Government in Transition*. Urbana: University of Illinois Press.

SEDUE (Secretaría de Desarrollo Urbano y Ecología). 1987. *Programa de Vivienda, 1987 (Vivienda en arrendamiento, regeneración urbana y mejoramiento de vivienda y suelo para vivienda)*. Mexico: SEDUE.

Senior, Clarence. 1940. *Democracy Comes to a Cotton Kingdom: The Story of Mexico's La Laguna*. Mexico: Centro de Estudios Pedagógicos e Hispanoamericanos.

Senior, Clarence. 1958. *Land Reform and Democracy*. Gainesville: University of Florida Press.

Slater, David. 1985a. "Social Movements and a Recasting of the Political." In *New Social Movements and the State in Latin America*, edited by D. Slater. Amsterdam: CEDLA.

Slater, David, ed. 1985b. *New Social Movements and the State in Latin America*. Amsterdam: CEDLA.

Smith, Peter. 1986. "Leadership and Change, Intellectuals and Technocrats." In *Mexico's Political Stability: The Next Five Years*, edited by Roderic Ai Camp. Boulder, Colo.: Westview.

SNTE, Sección 7. 1983. "El nuevo sindicalismo y las luchas de la CNTE." Mimeographed. Mexico: SNTE.

Soares, Glaucio Ary Dillon. 1986. "Elections and the Redemocratization of Brazil." In *Elections and Democratization in Latin America, 1980–85*, edited by Paul Drake and Eduardo Silva. La Jolla: CILAS, Center for U.S.–Mexican Studies, IOA, University of California, San Diego.

Solari, A. 1981. "Desigualdad educacional en América Latina." In *Planificación social en América Latina y El Caribe*. Santiago de Chile: ILPES-UMICEF.

Sosa Riddell, Adaljiza. 1986. "The Status of Women in Mexico: The Impact of the 'International Year of the Woman.'" In *Women in the World*, edited Lynne B. Iglitzin and Ruth Ross. Santa Barbara, Calif.: ABC-Clio.

Stavenhagen, Rodolfo. 1975. "Collective Agriculture and Capitalism in Mexico: A Way Out or a Dead End?" *Latin American Perspectives* 2:2 (Summer).

Stepan, Alfred. 1988. *Rethinking Military Politics*. Princeton, N.J.: Princeton University Press.

Stephen, Lynn. 1989. "Not Just One of the Boys: From Female to Feminist in Popular Rural Movements in Mexico." Presentation at the Fifteenth International Congress of The Latin American Studies Association, Miami, Florida, December 4–6.

Stern, Steven J. 1987. *Resistance, Rebellion, and Consciousness in the Andean Peasant World*. Madison: University of Wisconsin Press.

Stevens, Evelyn P. 1974. *Protest and Response in Mexico*. Cambridge, Mass.: MIT Press.

Stinchcombe, Arthur L. 1962. "Agricultural Enterprise and Rural Class Relations," *American Journal of Sociology* 68:165–176.

Street, Susan. 1983. "Burocracia y educación: hacia un análisis político de la desconcentración administrativa en la Secretaría de Educación Pública (SEP)," *Estudios Sociológicos* 1:2 (May–August).

Street, Susan. 1984. "Los distintos proyectos para la transformación del aparato burocrático de la SEP," *Perfiles Educativos* 7 (October–December).

Street, Susan. 1987a. "Vuelven los maestros chiapanecos," *Siempre*, suplemento, March 5.

Street, Susan. 1987b. "Los maestros chiapanecos y la calidad educativa," *Excélsior*, March 25.

Street, Susan. 1987c. "Maestros chiapanecos: la lucha que vendrá," *Excélsior* April 1.

Street, Susan. 1987d. "Defienden los maestros de Chiapas sus ideales y el derecho a la dignidad," *Excélsior*, April 10.

Taller de Investigación Obrera. 1987. "La lucha de las costureras y el sindicato 19 de septiembre," *Cuadernos Obreros* 2.

Tamayo, Jaime, coord. 1986. *Perspectivas de los movimientos sociales en la región centro–occidente*. Mexico: Línea.

Tamayo, Jaime, and Oscar Ladrón de Guevara. 1986. "Los cholos: una respuesta juvenil." In *Perspectivas de los movimientos sociales in la región centro-occidente*, coordinated by J. Tamayo. Mexico: Línea.

Tarrés, María Luisa. 1986. "Del abstencionismo electoral a la oposición política. Clases medias en Cd. Satélite," *Estudios Sociológicos* 4:12 (September–December).

Tarrés, María Luisa. 1987. "Crisis and Political Opposition among Mexican Middle Classes," *International Sociology* 2:2.

Tarrés, María Luisa. 1988. "Campos de acción de las mujeres de clase media." Informe de Investigación. Mexico: PIEM, El Colegio de México.

Tarrés, María Luisa. 1989. "Más allá de lo público y lo privado. Participación social y político de las mujeres de clase media. El caso de Satélite." In *Trabajo, poder y sexualidad*, coordinated by Orlandina de Oliveira. Mexico: PIEM, El Colegio de México.

Tarrow, Sidney. 1988. "National Politics and Collective Action: Recent Theory and Research in Western Europe and the United States," *Annual Review of Sociology* 14:421–440.

Tarrow, Sidney. 1989. *Struggle, Politics, and Reform: Collective Action, Social Movements, and Cycles of Protest*. Western Societies Program Occasional Paper, no. 21. Ithaca, N.Y.: Center for International Studies, Cornell University.

Taylor, William B. 1979. *Drinking, Homicide and Rebellion in Colonial Mexican Villages*. Stanford: Stanford University Press.

Tello, Carlos. 1979. *La política económica en México, 1970–1976*. Mexico: Siglo XXI.

Tello, Carlos. 1985. "La crisis en 1985: saldos y opciones." In *México ante la crisis*, compiled by Pablo González Casanova and Héctor Aguilar Camín. Mexico: Siglo XXI.

Terán, Liberato, and Melchor Inzunza. 1985. "Consideraciones sobre el movimiento estudiantil en Sinaloa." In *Movimientos sociales en el noroeste de México*, edited by Rubén Burgos. Mexico: Universidad Autónoma de Sinaloa.

Thompson, E. P. 1962. *The Making of the English Working Class*. New York: Pantheon.

Tilly, Charles. 1978. *From Mobilization to Revolution*. Reading, Mass.: Addison-Wesley.

Tironi, Eugenio. n.d.*a*. "Para una sociología de la decadencia," *Proposiciones* (Santiago de Chile) 12.

Tironi, Eugenio. n.d.*b*. "Pobladores e integración social," *Proposiciones* (Santiago de Chile) 14.

Torres Mejía, David. 1987. *Política y partidos en las elecciones federales de 1985*. Mexico: Universidad Nacional Autónoma de México.

Torres Mejía, David. 1989. "Movimientos populares y sistema político." Paper presented at the Workshop on Popular Movements and Political Transformation in Mexico, Center for U.S.–Mexican Studies, University of California, San Diego, March 29–31.

Touraine, Alain. 1987. *Actores sociales y sistemas políticos en América Latina*. Santiago de Chile: PREALC/OIT.

Touraine, Alain. 1988*a*. *La Parole et la Sang: Politique et Societé en Amérique Latine*. Paris: Odile Jacob.

Touraine, Alain. 1988*b*. *The Return of the Actor: Social Theory in Postindustrial Society*. Minneapolis: University of Minnesota Press.

Touraine, Alain. n.d. "La centralidad de los marginales," *Proposiciones* (Santiago de Chile) 14.

Treviño Carrillo, Ana Helena. 1984. "El movimiento magisterial en México: el caso de Morelos (1980–81)." Master's thesis, FLACSO, Mexico.

Unger, Roberto M. 1987. *False Necessity: Anti-Necessitarian Social Theory in the Service of Radical Democracy*. Cambridge: Cambridge University Press.
Unión de Uniones. 1983. "Nuestra lucha por la tierra en la selva lacandona," *Textual* 4:13 (September):151–163.
Uno más Uno. June 2, 1980. "Entre cuatro y seis los muertos en Chiapas."
Uno más Uno. April 16, 1981. "La sindicación de 4 millones de jornaleros agrícolas garantizará la paz en el campo," and "Los trabajadores del agro podrían ser engañados por la sindicación estatal."
Uno más Uno. April 22, 1981. "Sin tierra ni protección 58 por ciento de campesinos."
Uno más Uno. February 26, 1982. "'Carcería' contra líderes campesinos en Chiapas."
Uno más Uno. February 27, 1982. "¡Alto a la represión en Chiapas!"
Uno más Uno. October 30, 1982. "Dos indígenas tzotziles, asesinados."
Uno más Uno. November 7, 1982. "Piden castigo en Simojovel a homicidas."
Uno más Uno. April 24, 1989. "Carlos Jonguitud se mantuvo 17 años en el poder mediante la corrupción."
Valdez Vega, María Eugenia. 1986. "Participación de los maestros de primaria del Distrito Federal en la insurgencia magisterial de 1979–1983." Master's thesis, FLACSO, Mexico.
Villavicencio, J. 1988. "El centro de la Ciudad de México: consideraciones preliminares para la definición de su función a nivel metropolitano," *Revista "A"* (Universidad Autónoma Metropolitana, Azcapotzalco), September–December, pp. 109–122.
Viola, Eduardo, and Scott Mainwaring. 1985. "Transitions to Democracy: Brazil and Argentina in the 1980s," *Journal of International Affairs* 38:2 (Winter):193–219.
Weber, Max. 1949. *The Methodology of the Social Sciences*. New York: Free Press.
Weyl, Nathaniel, and Sylvia Weyl. 1939. *The Reconquest of Mexico: The Years of Lázaro Cárdenas*. London and New York: Oxford University Press.
Whitehead, Laurence. 1981. "On 'Governability' in Mexico," *Bulletin of Latin American Research* 1:1 (October).
Wilkie, Raymond. 1971. *San Miguel: A Mexican Collective Ejido*. Stanford: Stanford University Press.
Wolf, Eric. 1973. *Peasant Wars of the Twentieth Century*. New York: Harper and Row.
Womack, John, Jr. 1968. *Zapata and the Mexican Revolution*. New York: Random House.
Womack, John, Jr. 1988. "The Meaning of the Mexican Elections," *Socialist Review*, October–December.
Worsley, Peter. 1985. "Communities and Cities." In *Modern Sociology*, edited by P. Worsley. Harmondsworth: Penguin.
Yescas Martínez, Isidoro, and Gloria Zafra. 1985. *La insurgencia magisterial en Oaxaca, 1980*. Oaxaca: Instituto de Investigaciones Sociológicas, Universidad Autónoma Benito Juárez de Oaxaca.
Zepeda, Jorge. 1986. "No es lo mismo agrario que agrio ni comuneros que comunistas, pero se parecen." In *Perspectivas de los movimientos sociales en la región centro-occidente*, edited by Jaime Tamayo. Mexico: Línea.
Zermeño, Sergio. 1987. "La democracia como identidad restringida," *Revista Mexicana de Sociología* 49:4 (October).

The Contributors

Teresa Carrillo is a Ph.D. candidate in political science at Stanford University, where she is completing her dissertation on "Women, Trade Unions, and New Social Movements: The Case of the Nineteenth of September Garment Workers Union in Mexico."

Maria Lorena Cook is a postdoctoral fellow at the University of California, San Diego. She recently completed a dissertation on "Organizing Dissent: The Politics of Opposition in the Mexican Teachers' Union" for the University of California, Berkeley.

Ann L. Craig is associate professor of political science at the University of California, San Diego. Her publications include *The First Agraristas: An Oral History of a Mexican Agrarian Reform Movement* and "Political Culture in Mexico: Continuities and Revisionist Interpretations" (with Wayne A. Cornelius) in *The Civic Culture Revisited*, edited by Gabriel Almond and Sidney Verba.

Joe Foweraker is senior lecturer in Latin American politics in the Department of Government at the University of Essex. He is the author of *The Struggle for Land in Brazil*, and *Making Democracy in Spain: Grassroots Struggle in the South*.

Neil Harvey is a research fellow at the Institute of Latin American Studies, University of London. His doctoral thesis, "Corporatist Strategies and Popular Responses in Rural Mexico: State and Opposition in Chiapas, 1970–1988," was completed for the Department of Government, University of Essex.

Alan Knight is C. B. Smith Professor of History at the University of Texas at Austin. His many publications include "Peasant and Caudillo in Revolutionary Mexico, 1910–1917," in *Caudillo and Peasant in the Mexican Revolution*, edited by D. A. Brading and the two-volume *The Mexican Revolution*.

Kathleen Logan is professor in the Department of Sociology and Anthropology at Florida International University. Her publications include *Haciendo Pueblo: The Development of a Guadalajaran Suburb* and "Women's Political Activity and Empowerment in Latin American Urban Movements," in *Urban*

Life, edited by George Gmelch and Walter P. Zenner.

Gerardo L. Munck is assistant professor of political science at the University of Illinois. He completed a doctoral dissertation entitled "State Power and Civil Society in the Context of Military Rule: Labor Politics, Peronism, and the Armed Forces in Argentina, 1976–1983," at the University of California, San Diego.

Francisco Pérez Arce is a researcher at the Instituto Nacional de Antropología e Historia in Mexico City. He is the author of *A muchas voces* and coauthor (with Luis Hernández) of *Las luchas magisteriales 1979/1981*.

Juan Manuel Ramírez Saiz teaches at the University of Guadalajara, where he is also affiliated as a researcher with the Centro de Investigaciones Sobre Movimientos Sociales (CISMOS). His publications on urban popular movements include *El movimiento urbano popular en México* and *Política urbana y lucha popular*.

Jeffrey W. Rubin is assistant professor of political science at Amherst College. His analysis of post-1968 politics in Juchitán, Oaxaca, can be found in "State Policies, Leftist Oppositions, and Municipal Elections: The Case of the COCEI in Juchitán," in *Electoral Patterns and Perspectives*, edited by Arturo Alvarado.

Jaime Tamayo is director of the Centro de Investigaciones Sobre Movimientos Sociales (CISMOS) at the University of Guadalajara and researcher in the National Research Program (SNI). His publications on social movements and regional politics include *Perspectivas de los movimientos sociales en la región centro-occidente*, as well as *La conformación del estado moderno y los conflictos políticos, 1917–1929*, and *Los movimientos sociales, 1917–1929*.

María Luisa Tarrés is professor and researcher at the Centro de Estudios Sociológicos and director of teaching in the Programa Interdisciplinario de Estudios de la Mujer (PIEM) at El Colegio de México. Her publications include "Luchas agrarias tradicionales y Estado en Mexico," in *Clases sociales y desarrollo rural* and "Mas allá de lo público y lo privado: Participación social y política de las mujeres de clase media," in *Trabajo, poder y sexualidad*.

Sergio Zermeño is a researcher at the Instituto de Investigaciones Sociales at Mexico's National University. His publications on social movements include *México: una democracia utópica: el movimiento estudiantil de 1968* and *Juchitán: la cólera del régimen*.

Index

ADESE. *See* Democratic Assembly for an Effective Vote
Agrarian sector, 62, 63, 91, 198(n15), 261, 265, 267(n5); legislation, 65–66, 67; de la Madrid's policies, 191–192; organization of, 183–186; strikes, 73–74, 186; unions, 72, 188–190
Agriculture Department, 66
Ajusco Conservation Project, 242
Alliances, 17, 60; formation of, 193, 277–279, 281–285; teachers' movement, 50–51. *See also* COCEI
Almazán, Juan Andreu, 89
Amilpa, 89
ANAGSA. *See* National Agricultural and Livestock Insurance Company
ANCIFEM. *See* National Feminine Civic Association
ANOCP. *See* National Popular Assembly of Workers and Peasants
Argentina, 31, 32, 172
Armies, revolutionary, 261
Atomization, 170–171
Authentic Labor Front (FAT), 223
Autonomy, 101(n14); political, 92, 178; of popular movements, 16, 261–262, 276; of social movements, 26, 27; state, 43–44; teachers' movement, 44–45, 201

Baja California, 86, 105, 176, 278

Baja California Norte, 175
Bajío, 92
Banco Ejidal, 92
Bancrisa, 188
Banditry, 90
Banks, 85, 188
Banrural. *See* National Bank of Rural Credit
Barrios, 88; Mexico City, 240–241, 242
Brazil, 31, 32, 172
Bureaupolitics, 10, 170, 171, 178

Caballero Aburto, Arturo, 89
Cacicazgos, 16, 17, 45, 52
Caciquismo, 8, 14, 101–102(n17), 192, 276; challenges to, 16, 17, 18, 98; continuation of, 99–100; growth of, 96–97
Calles, Plutarco Elías, 70–71, 76, 259
Camacho Solís, Manuel, 244
Campesinos. *See* Peasantry
Capitalism, 92
Cárdenas, Cuauhtémoc, 54, 55, 107, 168, 170, 172, 174; PRD, 212(n4), 264; presidential candidacy, 12, 121, 124, 126, 129, 130–131, 133, 136(n7); support, 6, 76, 113, 175–176, 177, 195, 209–210, 278–279
Cárdenas, Lázaro, 16, 88, 92, 97, 107, 115, 135(n2), 175, 197(n4), 256, 259, 262, 267(n8), 278; labor organizations, 69, 70–71; social justice, 19–20; strikes, 59, 74
Cardenismo, 67, 88, 91, 95, 129–130, 176,

180(nn8, 9); impact of, 131–132, 134, 177–178, 179. *See also* *Neocardenismo*
Cardenista Front for National Reconstruction, 139, 140
Cardenista Peasant Union, 131
Carranza, 191, 192, 196; Casa del Pueblo, 193–194
Carrillo Puerto, Felipe, 97
Casa del Obrero Mundial (COM), 69, 111, 193, 260
Casa del Pueblo, 186, 188, 191, 198(n7); leadership in, 193–194
Castellanos, Andrés, 168
Catholic church, 8, 82, 89; peasant cooperatives, 192–193, 194
Catholicism, 86; social, 88, 89
CCI. *See* Independent Peasant Confederation
CCL. *See* Central Struggle Committee
CDP. *See* Committee for Popular Defense of Durango
CEN. *See* National Executive Committee
Central Coordination of the National Plan of Economically Depressed Regions and Marginalized Groups (COPLAMAR), 189
Central Struggle Committee (CCL), 46, 116
Cerón, Leopoldo, 111
Cervera Pacheco, Víctor, 185
CEU, 130
CGOCM. *See* General Labor

Jeffrey Puryear
Inter-American
Dialogue